Mastering Collateral Management and Documentation

Prentice Hall
FINANCIAL TIMES

In an increasingly competitive world, we believe it's quality of thinking that will give you the edge – an idea that opens new doors, a technique that solves a problem, or an insight that simply helps make sense of it all. The more you know, the smarter and faster you can go.

That's why we work with the best minds in business and finance to bring cutting-edge thinking and best learning practice to a global market.

Under a range of leading imprints, including *Financial Times Prentice Hall*, we create world-class print publications and electronic products bringing our readers knowledge, skills and understanding which can be applied, whether studying or at work.

To find out more about our business publications, or tell us about the books you'd like to find, you can visit us at www.business-minds.com

For other Pearson Education publications, visit www.pearsoned-ema.com

Pearson Education

Mastering Collateral Management and Documentation

A Practical Guide for Negotiators

PAUL C. HARDING
AND
CHRISTIAN A. JOHNSON

FINANCIAL TIMES
Prentice Hall

An imprint of **PEARSON EDUCATION**

London • New York • San Francisco
Toronto • Sydney • Tokyo • Singapore • Hong Kong
Cape Town • Madrid • Amsterdam • Munich • Paris • Milan

PEARSON EDUCATION LIMITED

Edinburgh Gate
Harlow CM20 2JE
Tel: +44 (0)1279 623623
Fax: +44 (0)1279 431059
Website: www.pearsoned.co.uk

First published in Great Britain in 2002

© Pearson Education Limited 2002

The right of Paul C. Harding and Christian A. Johnson to be identified as Authors of this Work
has been asserted by them in accordance with the Copyright, Designs and Patents Act 1988.

ISBN 978-0-273-65924-2

British Library Cataloguing in Publication Data
A CIP catalogue record for this book can be obtained from the British Library.

This publication is designed to provide accurate and authoritative information in regard to the
subject matter covered. It is sold with the understanding that neither the authors nor the publisher
is engaged in rendering legal, investing, or any other professional service. If legal advice or other
expert assistance is required, the service of a competent professional person should be sought.

This publisher and contributors make no representation, express or implied, with regard to the
accuracy of the information contained in this book and cannot accept any responsibility or
liability for any errors or omissions that it may contain.

10 9 8 7 6 5 4

Typeset by Pantek Arts Ltd, Maidstone, Kent.
Printed and bound in Great Britain by Ashford Colour Press Ltd, Gosport, Hampshire
The Publishers' policy is to use paper manufactured from sustainable forests.

CONTENTS

4 Credit issues relating to collateral   61

5 The English Law ISDA Credit Support Annex   79

Contents

ABOUT THE AUTHORS

Paul Harding graduated from London University in 1972 and has worked in several UK and foreign banks in London in credit, marketing and documentation roles. Since 1990, he has been involved with derivatives documentation and was a well known negotiator in the City of London with Barclays Capital Securities Limited and Hill Samuel Bank Limited, where he was Head of Treasury Documentation.

In 1997, he founded Derivatives Documentation Limited, a derivatives consultancy and project management company based in the City of London and providing negotiation, recruitment and in-house training services in derivatives documentation. Its clients include many of the world's leading banks.

In November 2001, he published *Mastering the ISDA Master Agreement*, also in this series.

He brings over ten years' in-depth market experience to the subject of this book.

Christian A. Johnson is an associate law professor at Loyola University Chicago School of Law where he teaches courses on derivatives, banking and taxation. He graduated from Columbia Law School and was the Executive Editor of the Columbia Law Review. He practised law with Milbank Tweed Hadley & McCloy in New York and Mayer Brown Rowe & Maw in Chicago before teaching.

Christian Johnson has published extensively on over-the-counter derivatives and has developed the swaplaw.com website. He also has over ten years of derivatives experience, having represented several international derivative dealers, Federal Home Loan Banks and hedge funds in their derivative documentation negotiations.

DISCLAIMER

This book is intended to provide an informational and illustrative overview of its subject, mainly to non-lawyers, and is not at all intended to provide legal or tax advice in respect of any particular situation, contractual relationship or contemplated transaction. The laws and regulations applicable to over-the-counter derivatives transactions are complex and subject to frequent change. Users of this book should consult their legal and other advisers as they deem appropriate in the preparation and negotiation of over-the-counter derivatives documentation. The authors of this book regard the examples given herein as illustrative only and assume no responsibility for any use to which ISDA standard documentation or any definition or provision set forth in this book may be put.

ACKNOWLEDGEMENTS

Paul Harding

First and foremost I would like to thank my family for their involvement with this book.

I should like to thank my wife Sheila again for all her support in keeping me focused and on track while writing this book. As usual she knew when to urge me to press on and when to give me space. She invariably helped me keep things in perspective, especially when the going got tough. I thank her for all her patience and sacrifices over the past few months.

Our daughter, Mary-Anne, who also works in derivatives documentation, was as usual an invaluable sounding board on what was useful for a novice negotiator to know about collateral documentation. I would like to thank her for many perceptive comments on the manuscript and for some typing.

The brunt of the typing fell on our son Chris and our daughters Abby, Alex and Isabelle who gave up several weekends and parts of their university and school vacations interpreting my writing and typing up the text. Abby also solved various technological problems ably. Their support was invaluable. Chris's fractured knee was a lucky break for me, as it confined him to the keyboard for some weeks. I hope they learned something about collateral during all their work!

I am extremely grateful for the input of various professionals on the book. Richard Holmes and Simon McKernan of the Global Collateral Management Unit of ABN AMRO Bank NV London permitted me to sit on their desk for a day and bombard them with questions which they patiently and good humouredly answered between telephone calls. They also reviewed drafts of Chapter 2 as it evolved.

A big thank you is also due to Evelyn Dewaele of Sentry Financial, a division of Algorithmics who helped develop the screen prints for Chapter 2 and who also reviewed the chapter and made many excellent amendments. Evelyn combines experience as a former collateral manager with knowledge of the functionalities of market leading collateral software. Her approach was always unfailingly practical.

Keith Spiller, Executive Director, Credit Risk Management, UBS Warburg also spent significant time reviewing Chapter 2 and made numerous incisive comments which have been incorporated.

So Chapter 2 was much trawled over and combines the best efforts of us all!

I should like to thank Simon Leifer, a director in Dresdner Kleinwort Wasserstein's Trading and Derivatives Legal Services Department for his useful comments on the English law section of Chapter 3.

Chapter 4 benefited greatly from the input of Paul Berry, Head of Trading Credit Risk Management, ABN AMRO Bank NV, a true credit professional, whose insights on the risks impacting collateral were both valuable and instructive. I thank him very much for his contribution.

I should also like to thank the following professionals who gave freely of their time and read first proofs of the whole book:

David Suetens, ABN AMRO Bank NV.
Keith Spiller, UBS Warburg
Wilfried Schütte, Landesbank Hessen- Thüringen Girozentrale

The thanks of both authors are offered to the International Swaps and Derivatives Association, Inc. for their kind permission to reproduce various ISDA Credit Support Documents in the text and Annexes. Special thanks are due to Kimberly Summe, ISDA's General Counsel.

We should also like to thank the editorial staff at Financial Times-Prentice Hall for all their excellent editing and support. Special thanks are due to Laurie Donaldson, Linda Dhondy, Elizabeth Wilson, Amanda Thompson and Michelle Sinclair.

Last but not least, it was again a real pleasure working with my co-author Christian Johnson who was always positive and practical. Ours is a relationship conducted by e-mail and telephone. I look forward to meeting him one day!

Christian Johnson

I begin by thanking my lovely wife Cori for her patience with me and the late nights as the book progressed and took shape.

I would also like to thank Barry Taylor-Brill and Eileen Effinger of Wachovia Bank for their patience in answering endless questions about the finer points of the collateralisation of over-the-counter derivative transactions. Any errors in the book, however, are all my own.

I extend special thanks to Dean Nina Appel and the faculty of Loyola University Chicago School of Law for providing me with financial and moral support. I also would like to thank my research assistants, Christine Thomson and Andrew White, for able research assistance and help in editing and proofing the manuscript.

Finally, I want to thank Paul Harding for inviting me to work with him on this book. This book is Paul's brainchild and he brought tremendous energy, enthusiasm and work to completing it. He was also tremendously helpful in editing my contributions regarding New York law and the New York Law Credit Support Annex. Paul also has a gift of simplifying and explaining difficult financial and legal concepts, enabling both novice and experienced negotiators to draft derivatives documentation better.

AUTHORS' FOREWORD

As Ogden Nash would have said, had he thought of it:

> "It's only nateral
> To take collateral
> And that's becoz
> It lessens your loss."

Collateral is now very big business, with some US$ 250 billion of it (mostly in cash and government securities) supporting derivatives risk at the start of 2001 (latest ISDA figures). This represents some 20–25% of the global derivatives market on a replacement value basis.

Collateral does not in the authors' view eliminate credit risk entirely. The market value of derivatives positions fluctuates constantly as do collateral values (especially securities), but it certainly supports risk exposure and can reduce it considerably. Obviously, it is most useful in a close-out or insolvency situation which is why collateral takers perform detailed legal analysis to find out what steps may be necessary in each jurisdiction to perfect and perhaps enforce their interests in their collateral. To this end, ISDA has commissioned 30 legal opinions of which 28 have so far been published.

This book has been written for people with 0–3 years' experience in collateral documentation covering risk exposure under derivatives.

It is divided into nine chapters.

Chapter 1 defines terms, outlines the size of the market, explains why collateral is taken and what types are acceptable and which products can be covered. It also describes how collateral documentation, and particularly that issued by ISDA, has evolved over the past 15 years.

Chapter 2 is about collateral management itself. The authors considered that readers should have some knowledge about what happens on a collateral management desk in a bank. We hope this will provide useful background for a study of the collateral documentation itself. The chapter has several examples of screen prints which have been developed with the invaluable assistance of Sentry Financial, a division of Algorithmics.

Chapter 3 outlines the legal issues affecting the taking and enforcement of collateral in Europe and the US. Paul Harding wrote the section on the European law position and Christian Johnson wrote the New York law part of this chapter. In Europe, considerable harmonisation of laws relating to collateral is in prospect following the recent adoption of a Directive on collateral financial arrangements by the European Commission which needs to be implemented in EU states by the end of 2003.

Chapter 4 describes the credit issues surrounding collateral, such as the need to establish detailed policies to cover numerous risks including market risk, liquidity risk and concentration risk among others. It also describes the latest proposals relating to collateral under the Basel II Accord as well as crystal ball gazing on the future of collateral from a risk point of view.

In Chapter 5, we get to the ISDA documentation itself. In this chapter, the ISDA English law Credit Support Annex is fully reviewed on a text with facing page commentary basis which seemed to prove a useful format in *Mastering the ISDA Master Agreement*. The constituents of Paragraph 11 (the Elections and Variables Paragraph) which is similar to an ISDA Master Agreement Schedule are also analysed and examples given of different types of wording seen in the market. Paul Harding wrote Chapter 5.

Chapter 6 was written by Christian Johnson. It analyses the provisions of the ISDA New York Law Credit Support Annex in the same format as Chapter 5. It ends with a comparison and contrast between the two documents.

In both Chapters 5 and 6, the examples in the respective Elections and Variable Paragraphs of wording seen in the market are illustrative only. They are not meant to be imported wholesale, piecemeal or uncritically into these Paragraphs but could be seen as a starting point for developing your own wording for the requirements of your own negotiations.

While these two Credit Support Annexes are used by the market in nearly 90% of cases, there are other ISDA Credit Support Documents, i.e. the English Law Credit Support Deed and the Japanese Law Credit Support Annex, which are also occasionally used. These are summarised in Chapter 7 for the sake of completeness of coverage.

One of the highlights of 2001 for the world of collateral and its documentation was the publication in May 2001 of the *2001 ISDA Margin Provisions* which introduce a new, streamlined regime for taking collateral. Its operationally challenging deadlines have resulted in little take up at the moment, but it is regarded by ISDA as the collateral document of the future. Given its potential importance, it is analysed in Chapter 8 in the text and facing page commentary format.

Chapter 9 discusses recent developments in the collateral documentation market. These are the ISDA Credit Support Protocol (now closed), the ISDA Amendment Agreement for agreeing certain provisions in the *2001 ISDA Margin Provisions* on a bilateral basis for two parties' existing Credit Support Annex with each other and the new ISDA *Collateral Asset Definitions* Project.

The book concludes with the following nine Annexes which are meant to provide useful information in one place. They are:

Annex 1
A facsimile of the ISDA Credit Support Annex (Bilateral Form-Transfer. Subject to English Law) (reproduced with the kind permission of the International Swaps and Derivatives Association, Inc.).

Annex 2
A facsimile of the ISDA Credit Support Annex (Bilateral Form. Subject to New York Law) (reproduced with the kind permission of the International Swaps and Derivatives Association, Inc.).

Annex 3
List of countries where ISDA has obtained collateral legal opinions.

Annex 4
Relevant extracts from the New York Uniform Commercial Code.

Annex 5
Form of Amendment Agreement from Appendix A of the *User's Guide to the ISDA Credit Support Documents under English Law*.

Annex 6
A facsimile of the ISDA Credit Support Deed (Bilateral Form-Security Interest. Subject to English Law) (reproduced with the kind permission of the International Swaps and Derivatives Association, Inc.).

Annex 7
A facsimile of the ISDA Credit Support Annex (Bilateral Form-Loan and Pledge. Subject to Japanese Law) (reproduced with the kind permission of the International Swaps and Derivatives Association, Inc.).

Annex 8
Two Amendment Agreements for agreeing certain provisions in the *2001 ISDA Margin Provisions* on a bilateral basis.

Annex 9
A facsimile of the *2001 ISDA Margin Provisions* (reproduced with the kind permission of the International Swaps and Derivatives Association, Inc.).

What does the book not contain? We have attempted no description of how taxes impact on collateral taken in England and the State of New York, because we believe this is a matter for specialists. Nor have we discussed in any depth, guarantees or letters of credit which are relatively rarely used in the context of collateral for derivatives transactions and which we consider are better treated in more general banking books. The use of equities as collateral is also not much discussed. Otherwise, we hope our coverage of collateral documentation is comprehensive at the time of writing.

Any opinions expressed are those of the authors themselves and do not necessarily reflect those of their employers.

We hope you enjoy this book and find it useful.

Paul Harding
Christian Johnson

Introduction   I

DEFINITION OF TERMS

What is collateral?

In this book it is security for derivatives exposure.

Just as your house is security or collateral for your mortgage, so cash and government bonds can be collateral or security for credit exposure under swaps and other derivatives products.

Some of the dictionary meanings of the word "collateral" are:

- **side by side**
- **parallel**
- **additional but subordinate**
- **contributory**
- **connected with but aside from the main subject.**

All these definitions are interesting, but I think the last one is particularly apt – "connected with but aside from the main subject".

The main subject is counterparty quality or credit risk. Collateral is no substitute for a full risk analysis of your counterparty. For me the message is:

> **By itself, collateral will not turn a poor credit risk into a good credit and it *never* eliminates credit risk. It just improves your rate of recovery.**

Indeed, it could be said in a cross-border situation, that the reduction in credit risk through taking collateral is counterbalanced by an increase in legal, documentation and operational risk. As collateral is transferred across national borders, there have been significant concerns about whether the bankruptcy courts in different jurisidictions will uniformly enforce a bank's interest in its collateral.

Taking collateral is not risk free because a bank can lose money under a fully collateralised transaction. This could happen where a counterparty defaulted at the same time as the collateral value plummeted, perhaps because the bond issuer had defaulted or the currency of the cash collateral is devalued. Money could also be lost if a custodian failed. Furthermore, the bank could have failed to observe the legal requirements necessary to perfect the security interest and to protect its foreclosure rights. As we shall see later, collateral is not just about capture, it's very much about control too.

How could we define collateral? My definition is:

> **Legally watertight, valuable liquid property supporting a risk.**

It has to be legally watertight so you can enforce it; valuable, so as to be worth something; liquid, so you can sell it; property, so you can own it or control it. However, with all these qualities it only supports a risk. It does not eliminate it completely.

In my definition, collateral *is* collateral – side by side with the main risk.

WHY COLLATERAL IS TAKEN

Why do parties take collateral from each other?:

- to reduce but not eliminate credit risk;
- to reduce exposure in order to do more business with each other when credit limits are under pressure;
- because one party may only be able to deal with another on a collateralised basis due to its counterparty credit ratings policy;
- to net exposure to achieve regulatory capital savings by transferring or pledging eligible assets. The latest Basel II proposals allow this if the taking of collateral is backed up by positive legal opinions in the jurisdictions concerned;
- to offer keener pricing of credit risk (credit charges are usually included in derivatives spreads);
- to give improved access to market liquidity by collateralising interbank derivatives exposures.

These motivations are not completely separate and distinct, but interlinked. For if you reduce credit risk by taking collateral, you could reasonably expect to reduce the capital you need to allocate against derivatives risk if you are a financial institution. Lower capital costs should lead to keener pricing of derivatives trades because they are cheaper to conduct. In addition, lower credit risk should encourage more business being transacted, leading to greater liquidity in the market and the possibility of doing riskier or more exotic trades.

However, despite being interlinked, usually one factor will predominate in any given situation. Normally, this will be the desire to reduce credit risk. This is borne out by the *ISDA Margin Survey 2001* where the motivations for taking collateral were listed in the following order:

1 credit risk reduction;

2 regulatory capital savings;

3 increased competitiveness;

4 improved market liquidity;

5 access to more exotic business.

The Russian debt default, the Asian currency crisis and the failure of Long-Term Capital Management, a major hedge fund, all of which occurred in 1997/1998, gave impetus to tighter credit controls and greater interest in credit risk reduction techniques such as taking collateral.

Many banks will not trade with a counterparty until an appropriate collateral agreement has been put into place. This is typically the case with hedge funds and other unrated counterparties.

TYPES OF COLLATERAL

The types of collateral parties take from each other are as follows:

- **cash in currencies where they make markets;**
- **government securities (often direct obligations of G10 countries);**
- **mortgage-backed securities;**
- **corporate bonds;**
- **letters of credit;**
- **equities.**

The G10 countries are Belgium, Canada, France, Germany, Great Britain, Italy, Japan, Netherlands, Sweden, Switzerland and the US.

The last four types are least used as collateral and we shall mostly ignore them for the rest of this introduction. The key concerns for parties receiving collateral is that the collateral be easily transferable and valued. In fact, some parties will only agree to accept cash or US government securities because of these two concerns.

PRODUCT EXPOSURE COVERED

The following products could be covered under collateral agreements, depending upon the needs of the parties:

- **interest rate swaps and options;**
- **cross currency swaps;**
- **forward rate agreements;**
- **commodity derivatives;**
- **equity derivatives;**
- **bond options;**
- **credit derivatives;**
- **foreign exchange;**
- **currency options.**

Only the biggest players currently have the systems to collateralise all these products. Transactions with short-term maturities such as spot foreign exchange trades (where settlement is in two Local Business Days' time) are often not collateralised at all.

However, there is an increasingly strong trend towards cross product collateralisation (e.g. derivatives, repo, forward foreign exchange), which is likely to grow in the future as institutions manage collateral on a fully integrated basis across all these products. This is logical because if a counterparty went bust, it would affect its obligations under all its product agreements and not just under one group of them. It is, therefore, important that as many products as possible are eventually brought under a common collateral management and reporting structure, especially in times of crisis.

Taking security for credit risk has been common practice for centuries in money-lending, pawnbroking and, from the nineteenth century, in housing finance. Collateral is, therefore, not unique to derivatives. Many other commercial and financial transactions are undertaken on a secured basis.

EVOLUTION OF COLLATERAL DOCUMENTATION

The first swap transaction (in the familiar market form) took place in 1981, between IBM and the World Bank, with Salomon Brothers acting as the intermediary.

Taking collateral for derivatives exposure began in the US in the mid 1980s. Major players in the early days were Salomon Brothers and Bankers Trust, among others. There was no standardisation in legal documentation and control was via Excel or earlier spreadsheets. Calculating exposure and collateral took place monthly or weekly at best.

Taking collateral for derivatives exposure in Europe started in the early 1990s and followed the US precedent closely. The process worked, but was highly manual and rather laborious. It is much more automated nowadays as we shall see in Chapter 2.

Cash and government securities with a remaining maturity up to ten years were the most acceptable collateral and parties only gradually ventured outside their domestic currency for each unless they could link in a foreign exchange feed to their spreadsheet.

Each major player had its own legal documentation and preferences. This was largely pledge documentation which usually took a long time to negotiate.

In late 1994, the International Swaps and Derivatives Association, Inc. ("ISDA") tried to bring some standardisation to market documentation by issuing, after extensive consultation, its New York Law Credit Support Annex ("New York Law CSA") which operates as a pledge or security interest. It also permits the collateral taker, referred to as the Secured Party, to use and even sell the collateral, subject to an obligation to return equivalent collateral to the Pledgor in due course. A *User's Guide* focusing on the completion of Paragraph 13 (the Variables Paragraph which is similar to an ISDA Master Agreement Schedule) was published in 1995. The New York Law CSA is reproduced in Annex 2 with the kind permission of the International Swaps and Derivatives Association, Inc.

In late 1995, ISDA published its Credit Support Annex under English Law ("English Law CSA") under which title to, or ownership of the collateral is transferred to the collateral taker who is called the Transferee again with redelivery obligations to the Transferor provided the latter has not defaulted. The English Law CSA is reproduced in Annex 1 with the kind permission of the International Swaps and Derivatives Association, Inc.

At the same time, ISDA also issued its Credit Support Deed under English Law, under which the Secured Party has a security interest in the collateral but cannot reuse it (this is expressly forbidden in Paragraph 6(d) because the Pledgor retains an ownership interest in it).

Also in 1995, ISDA published its Japanese Law Credit Support Annex, a security interest document which works on a lending and/or pledge basis with set-off rights.

The market quickly adopted the ISDA documentation, so much so that the *ISDA Collateral Survey 2000* showed the following usage figures among its respondents:

- **New York Law Credit Support Annex** 61%
- **English Law Credit Support Annex** 27%
- **English Law Credit Support Deed** 1%
- **Japanese Law Credit Support Annex** 1%
- **AFB (French) and its Credit Support Annex** 1%
- **Other** 9%
- **Total** 100%

The category "Other" includes the German Rahmenvertrag and its Credit Support Annex, margined FX Agreements and a corpus of old pledge agreements and local law agreements around the world. ISDA Credit Support Documents were, therefore, used by 90% of the market then and the coverage has probably increased since.

The *ISDA Collateral Survey 2000* also categorised end users as a proportion of all signed agreements as follows:

Signed collateral agreements by counterparty type
TABLE 1.1

Entity type	Percentage share	Estimated monetary equivalent*
Wholesale market counterparties	43%	US$ 86 billion
Hedge funds	26%	US$ 52 billion
Corporates	14%	US$ 28 billion
Other institutional investors	13%	US$ 26 billion
Others	4%	US$ 8 billion
TOTAL	100%	US$ 200 billion

*Based on ISDA's top estimate of c. US$ 200 billion of collateral outstanding in the derivatives market at the start of 2000.

The *ISDA Margin Survey 2001* estimated total market growth of 25% to US$ 250 billion of collateral outstanding in the derivatives market at the start of 2001. However, it did not provide a percentage split by end user type.

Since 1999, ISDA has been working on documentation which simplifies and streamlines collateral processes. This work culminated in the publication of the *2001 ISDA Margin Provisions* in May 2001 and a choice of Credit Support Protocol (now closed) or bilateral amendment documentation in order to update the modus operandi of an existing collateral relationship between two parties.

We shall be examining the ISDA English Law CSA and the New York Law CSA in depth in Chapters 5 and 6 as well as highlighting the differences between them.

The English Law Credit Support Deed and the Japanese Law Credit Support Annex are discussed in summary form in Chapter 7.

Chapter 8 looks at the *2001 ISDA Margin Provisions* and the new ways of documenting a collateralised relationship which ISDA has proposed and which may eventually supplant the current generation of ISDA credit support documentation. The adoption of these new provisions will probably take several years as both dealers and end users require time to understand how these new provisions impact upon their way of doing business and they will also need to enhance their systems in most cases.

While acknowledging their differences, each ISDA Credit Support Document has certain common features:

- **calculation of collateral calls and returns**
- **the mechanics and timing of transfers**
- **method and timing of valuations by whoever is the Valuation Agent**
- **collateral substitutions**
- **dispute resolutions**
- **enforcement on default**
- **representations and warranties**
- **allocation of expenses**
- **reuse of collateral or not**
- **default interest**
- **an Elections and Variables Paragraph or a Margin Supplement to operate the arrangement.**

Collateral is now a big business. With approximately 20–25% of the OTC derivatives market now subject to collateral documentation, it is important that such documentation is robust, legally watertight and effective particularly as the market continues to expand and greater risks are collateralised.

Collateral management from a European perspective

2

Defaults

Branches

External collateral management services

SOME FACTS AND FIGURES

If collateral is king, control of it is key and that is the function of a collateral management unit.

The *ISDA Collateral Survey 2000* and the *ISDA Margin Survey 2001* estimated some interesting figures which have a bearing on the scope of collateral management, viz:

- some 16,000 signed Agreements exist – a 45% increase from the start of 2000 (*2001*);

- firms collateralised between 30% and 88% of their OTC derivatives trading (*2001*);

- at the end of 1999 some 1.3 million trades were outstanding under collateral agreements (*2000*);

- US$ cash and government securities were the most commonly taken collateral, being eligible collateral in over 90% of programmes. Eurozone cash and government securities (including Sterling securities) were acceptable collateral in about 70% of programmes). Cash is being taken more and more for operational convenience and because fewer US government securities are in issue (*2001*);

- about 75% of margin calls were made daily (*2000*);

- initial margin requirements appeared in 20% of agreements (*2000*);

- over 70% of institutions reused the collateral they received mostly to meet outgoing collateral requirements. About 60% of firms repoed securities collateral (*2001*);

- 70% of collateral management units had been established since 1995 (*2000*);

- the proportion of institutions with more than 500 agreements rose from 8% to 21% between the two surveys (*2001*);

- large scale firms on average spent more than US$ 5 million per annum on operating their collateral management function much of which was spent on technology development and systems support (*2001*).

The *ISDA Margin Survey 2001* points out that traditionally collateral management was classified as an operations function. However, some banks now regard it as a credit or derivatives risk management function while others see it as part of their liquidity management or even as a profit centre in its own right. Basel II proposes to move collateral programmes from a "separate" back-office function to one that is integrated closely with credit risk management. Nonetheless, however individual institutions may wish to categorise it, the important thing is that collateral management must be able to perform its functions effectively in normal times and in crises.

WHAT COLLATERAL MANAGEMENT UNITS DO

Collateral management units have much to do, including the following:

- to record details of the collateralised relationship in the collateral management system;

- to monitor customer exposure and collateral received or posted on the agreed mark to market frequency (often daily);

- to call for margin as required on the agreed mark to market frequency (often daily) taking into account collateral already held, Independent Amounts, Thresholds, Minimum Transfer Amounts and rounding (these terms are explained on pp. 15–16);

- to transfer collateral to its counterparty where a valid call has been made. The collateral manager will try to source collateral internally first to do this;

- to review the same matters if a margin call is received from a counterparty;

- to check that collateral to be received from a counterparty is of an eligible type agreed in the collateral documentation;

- where a custodian is involved, i.e. under pledge documentation, to ensure that the collateral is transferred by the counterparty to the custodian within the agreed period. Where a custodian is not used the collateral management unit does this for its own account;

- to deal with any failures to deliver securities collateral and cash margin;

- to call for initial margin where required;

- to apply the agreed "haircuts" to collateral being called or received;

- to reuse collateral where permitted in line with policy guidelines;

- to return surplus collateral when requested in accordance with the documentation's terms;

- to deal with requests for collateral substitutions both ways;

- to pay over coupons on securities promptly after receipt to collateral providers where this does not create or increase a margin call. This function is very often sourced out to the corporate actions or settlements department which already deals with this function for other areas (e.g. repos);

- to pay over interest on cash collateral at agreed intervals and to monitor its receipt;

- to deal with disagreements or disputes over exposure calculations and collateral valuations as they arise in accordance with the collateral documentation and market practice;

- to act as Valuation Agent where agreed in the collateral documentation;

- to reconcile portfolios of Transactions at regular intervals. This happens when a new counterparty is taken on, or when new products are being collateralised and in any case when a dispute over a margin call arises. Many larger organisations are currently working on their reconciliation backlogs. In this case, the work involved at dispute times will focus on reconciling new trades;
- to co-ordinate exposure and collateral valuations of various branches if the collateral management function is centralised;
- to deal with default situations in conjunction with the legal and credit functions and with senior management;
- to become involved as necessary in collateral agreement negotiation;
- to perform special collateral projects.

So a collateral management unit is very busy and we will shortly study most of these elements individually. First, however, I want to underline the importance of having written collateral policies and operating procedures in place because without them collateral management would just be "making it up as it goes along".

THE IMPORTANCE OF POLICIES AND PROCEDURES

Control is key with collateral and a robust control regime is vital in managing collateral (to avoid a false sense of security) and should contain the following elements:

- a well defined and enforceable general collateral policy in writing approved by senior management and understood and widely distributed in the organisation. It should be regularly updated (I would say every six months) and provide built in procedures for departures from it. Such concessions would usually be approved by a credit function. As well as the benefit of not having too many variations of the parameters used in collateral agreements, such a policy would also speed up the negotiation process considerably because the collateral agreement would not always need to be reviewed by credit or legal departments within the bank if some negotiation boundaries are clearly established;
- a set of clear and flexible operating procedures;
- clear communication lines with the counterparty;
- standardised legal documentation where possible;
- as much automation as possible.

In my opinion, time spent in getting these matters right is time well spent. Credit, Legal, Operations and Collateral Management must all be happy with the end result. Collateralisation is very much a team effort in an organisation.

The collateral management functions mentioned above are controlled by a collateral management system. A collateral management system is essentially a series of interlinked automated databases which bring together all the elements agreed in the collateral agreements so that they can be implemented on a day-to-day basis. Essentially, the front-office deal valuation systems feed into the collateral database.

At this stage I should like to acknowledge my gratitude to the Collateral Management Unit of ABN AMRO Bank NV London for its input on the practical aspects of this chapter and also to Sentry Financial, a division of Algorithmics, for their kind permission to illustrate the text with screen print examples and for their input on the practical aspects of collateral management arising from their experience of implementing such systems in numerous institutions of different sizes. The Algo Collateral (Sentry) software is representative of the software available to collateral managers and the screen prints are illustrative of the information they need and use.

SETTING UP THE COLLATERAL RELATIONSHIP

Once all the terms of the collateral agreement are agreed and the documentation completed, it is necessary for the bespoke elements of the collateral arrangements between the parties to be input in the collateral management system. These include:

- the Base Currency;
- whether the collateral arrangements are one-way or two-way (unilateral or bilateral). Unilateral agreements are common with supranational institutions (i.e. one-way to the supranational institution) or with corporates/hedge funds (i.e. one-way to well rated financial institutions who are their counterparties);
- the nature of eligible collateral;
- the level of haircuts applying to the collateral;
- the level of Independent Amounts, Thresholds, Minimum Transfer Amounts and rounding;
- frequency of marking to market and collateral valuation;
- notification times;
- delivery periods (these could be shortened, for example, with hedge funds);
- the type of quotations to be sought for securities collateral in a dispute (e.g. bid or mid market valuations);
- the level of interest to be paid on cash collateral.

It might be useful to explain some of these terms at this point:

Independent Amount

Depending upon the wording you use in the ISDA collateral agreement, this term either means collateral given by your counterparty as initial margin and excluded from the exposure calculation or it is equivalent to maintenance or variation margin (i.e. an amount which is included in the exposure calculations). The *2001 ISDA Margin Provisions* more helpfully differentiate between these types of Independent Amounts by calling them Lock-up Margin and Additional Margin Amount respectively.

Independent Amounts and initial margins can change over the life of a relationship. They are expressed as either fixed sums or percentages of the notional amounts of underlying transactions and are both set by credit departments. They can also be linked to credit ratings. Sometimes they are linked to large individual trades and may need review by the credit function where these trades are highly structured and involve periodic amortisation, for instance. Initial margins are typically applied for trading with hedge funds. In this case, it could happen that the hedge fund has to maintain a certain level of initial margin with the counterparty while at the same time that counterparty is posting variation margin to the hedge fund.

In the English Law CSA Paragraph 10, the net exposure the Transferee has on the Transferor at any one time is called the Credit Support Amount. This is defined as:

- **the Transferee's Exposure, plus**
- **all Independent Amounts applicable to the Transferor, if any, minus**
- **all Independent Amounts applicable to the Transferee, if any, minus**
- **the Transferor's Threshold, if any.**

Example

Party A upon calculating the valuation of the swap transactions he has entered into with Party B, finds that he has a risk exposure of US$ 5 million on Party B. Neither party has any Independent Amounts and Party B's Threshold is US$ 500,000. This means that Party A can make a collateral call on Party B for US$ 4.5 million (assuming that Party B's Minimum Transfer Amount is below this figure, which it probably is).

However, the Credit Support Amount is deemed to be zero where it results in a negative figure.

In the New York Law CSA the Credit Support Amount is calculated in essentially the same way.

Threshold

This is the monetary figure agreed in the collateral agreement below which a call for collateral cannot be made. It represents the unsecured credit risk you are prepared to accept upon your counterparty when added to the Minimum Transfer Amount. The Threshold will vary depending upon the formal credit rating of the collateral giver although fixed amount Thresholds are often used with lower rated or unrated counterparties.

Minimum Transfer Amount

Collateral transfers cost time and money and so it is useful to have a minimum monetary figure, e.g. US$ 50,000 below which a collateral call does not come into effect. This is often called a "nuisance amount" and is usually set at a high enough level to avoid all but significant collateral calls. In the US, Minimum Transfer Amounts can exceed US$ 1 million. Sometimes this is linked to a credit ratings matrix and sometimes it is a fixed amount.

Rounding

A rounding convention is normally used so that the transfer of uneven amounts of collateral, e.g. US$ 78,946.92 are avoided. Typically, such amounts are rounded to the nearest US$ 1,000 or multiples of US$ 10,000.

Set out below are some screen prints which show how these matters could be input in the Algo Collateral (Sentry) collateral management system. For the purposes of this exercise, please assume that our Collateral Management Unit is that of PCH Bank and the counterparty is XYZ Bank plc.

First of all, the basic terms of the Credit Support Document (in this instance an English Law CSA) could be input as in Figure 2.1.

FIG. 2.1

Basic terms of the Credit Support Document

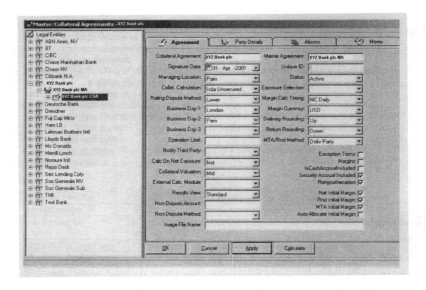

While all these boxes may be specific to the Algo Collateral (Sentry) system, the key matters are that the English Law CSA is active; margin calculations are done daily; if a party has more than one rating from a credit rating agency for its long-term senior unsecured debt, the lower rating will apply; the Base Currency (Margin Currency on the screen) is US Dollars; Delivery Amounts are rounded up and Return Amounts rounded down and collateral can be reused or rehypothecated.

Eligible Credit Support

Figure 2.2 shows that cash in US Dollars and US government securities are Eligible Credit Support under the collateral agreement between PCH Bank and XZY Bank plc. The haircuts (i.e. the agreed discounts to face value) are shown in the third column.

Eligible Credit Support

FIG. 2.2

✲ Principal Eligible		
Collateral ID	Adjust Mthd	Adjust Pct
USD Cash	Multiplier	100.
US RE x<=1	Multiplier	99.5
US RE 1<x<=10	Multiplier	98.
US RE 10<x	Multiplier	95.

This screen shows that PCH Bank (which is called the Principal for this purpose) can receive US$ cash (with no haircut), and US Treasuries with tenors of up to one year (0.5% haircut), between one and five years (2% haircut) and beyond that up to ten years (5% haircut). The third column shows the relevant Valuation Percentages which would appear in the collateral agreement itself.

There would be a separate screen for the collateral which the Counterparty (XYZ Bank plc) could receive and this is likely to be the same as that for PCH Bank, but it could be different.

Threshold, Minimum Transfer Amounts, Independent Amounts and Rounding

These matters are all shown in the example in Figure 2.3 and they are linked to credit ratings from Moody's and Standard & Poor's. In the example, PCH Bank is rated Aa2/AA and XYZ Bank plc is rated A3/A-. They have chosen zero Thresholds (in order to obtain maximum regulatory capital savings from their respective bank regulators), Minimum Transfer Amounts for US$ 100,000 and rounding amounts of US$ 50,000. Because it has a lower credit rating than PCH Bank, XYZ Bank plc also has to place a US$ 2 million Independent Amount with PCH Bank which will be used in the calculation of the Credit Support Amount.

Threshold, Minimum Transfer Amounts, Independent Amounts and Rounding

Master/Collateral Agreements - Thresholds

Moody	S & P	Div Rounding	Threshold	Div MTA	Independent	Independent Amt. Mthd	Rtn Rounding
NR	NR	50,000.	.	100,000.	.	Flat	50,000.
Aaa	AAA	50,000.	.	100,000.	.	Flat	50,000.
Aa1	AA+	50,000.	.	100,000.	.	Flat	50,000.
Aa2	AA	50,000.	.	100,000.	.	Flat	50,000.
Aa3	AA-	50,000.	.	100,000.	.	Flat	50,000.
A1	A+	50,000.	.	100,000.	.	Flat	50,000.
A2	A	50,000.	.	100,000.	.	Flat	50,000.
A3	A-	50,000.	.	100,000.	2,000,000.	Flat	50,000.
Baa1	BBB+	50,000.	.	100,000.	2,000,000.	Flat	50,000.
Baa2	BBB	50,000.	.	100,000.	2,000,000.	Flat	50,000.
Baa3	BBB-	50,000.	.	100,000.	2,000,000.	Flat	50,000.
Ba1	BB+	50,000.	.	100,000.	2.	Pct.Notional	50,000.
Ba2	BB	50,000.	.	100,000.	2.	Pct.Notional	50,000.
Ba3	BB-	50,000.	.	100,000.	2.	Pct.Notional	50,000.
B1	B+	50,000.	.	100,000.	5.	Pct.Notional	50,000.
B2	B	50,000.	.	100,000.	5.	Pct.Notional	50,000.
B3	B-	50,000.	.	100,000.	5.	Pct.Notional	50,000.
Caa	CCC	50,000.	.	100,000.	10.	Pct.Notional	50,000.

Please note that here the Independent Amount from Baa1/BBB+ downwards might be expressed as an escalating percentage (e.g. 5–10% of the notional amount of the collateralised trade(s)). This would also be the case with an unrated counterparty or a hedge fund. Often, fixed amounts are used with corporate counterparties.

Interest Rate and payment frequency

Figure 2.4 shows the agreed Interest Rate or Rates for cash collateral together with the frequency at which Interest will be paid. This will usually be monthly, but can also occur whenever a Return Amount of cash collateral is made by the collateral taker to the collateral giver. Whether this is possible will depend upon the parties' systems.

Interest Rate and payment frequency

FIG. 2.4

Currency	Index	Lag	Bid/Ask	Spread	Basis	Can Be Neg	Cmp Period	Timing	Rnd Places	Rnd Mthd	ResetPrdOn
USD	Fed Funds	1		0	Act/360	☐		ID 2nd	5	Closer	Transit End
EUR	EONIA			0	Act/360	☐		ID 2nd	5	Closer	Transit End

On this screen, cash collateral in US$ and EUR is permitted and interest will be paid respectively at Fed Funds flat and EONIA flat (identified by the 0 spread). Interest will be paid on the second Local Business Day of each calendar month (see the Timing column) and will be rounded to five decimal places. How interest is calculated can often cause disputes between collateral managers because the collateral agreement is not always specific enough. Is interest to be calculated on a calendar day (like most French institutions) or on a business day basis? Or is it to be calculated on a simple or compound basis? The simple basis is the market convention.

EXPOSURE MONITORING AND COLLATERAL VALUATION AND CALLING

This is one of the most important functions of a collateral management unit.

The market value of collateral is comprised of a market price, haircut rate and accrued interest.

Each day the unit will receive an automated list of tasks showing which customers need to be called for collateral or top up margin and which calls the unit can expect from its counterparties in this respect. This is the result of the exposure and collateral held calculations performed by the collateral management system. The collateral manager will call up an individual customer positions report which will show all Transactions and their individual exposures. These will be totalled to show the net mark to market valuation of these Transactions. Under this total the collateral position will be shown. This report can be printed off and sent to the counterparty as necessary. This is usually done in disputes. There is not much standardisation in the market of the elements or presentation of this portfolio information, but Algo Collateral (Sentry) users are formulating a standard in this respect and this also forms part of a project on electronic data interchange recently set in motion by ISDA (see page 438).

A different screen such as the one shown in Figure 2.5 summarises the precise position for an individual customer (in this case XYZ Bank plc).

This report shows details of aggregate trades and their present mark to market value. These items feed in automatically from the trading systems, back-office systems or any other system where the value of the transactions is calculated. The report also shows collateral received or posted, revalued using the latest bond prices for securities balances and interest rates for cash balances with the proper haircut applied.

In this example, PCH Bank is in the money for US$ 6.5 million with XYZ Bank plc or, in other words, it is exposed to XYZ Bank plc for US$ 6.5 million. However,

FIG. 2.5 Report showing a possible collateral call on the counterparty

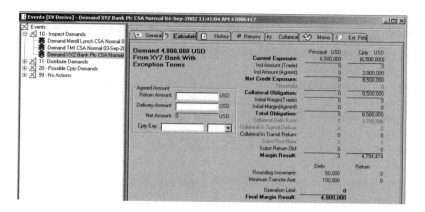

XYZ Bank owes PCH Bank US$ 2 million of Independent Amount due to its lower A3/A- rating and this needs to be taken into account. Therefore, its adjusted exposure on XYZ Bank plc is US$ 8.5 million. There is no Threshold to be applied and so the collateral required is US$ 8.5 million. PCH Bank has already received US$ 3,705,586 in collateral from XYZ Bank plc which means that its net unsecured exposure is US$ 4,794,414. This figure is greater than the Minimum Transfer Amount of US$ 100,000 and a margin call can be made which would be rounded up. The rounding amount is US$ 50,000 and the standard convention is to round up for Delivery Amounts. With a zero Threshold and a Minimum Transfer Amount of US$ 100,000, a collateral call can be made in the sum of US$ 4.8 million if the other party agrees. Sometimes they might only agree to transfer a slightly lower amount.

At this point, assuming they agree the full amount, PCH Bank will send a Collateral Notice to XYZ Bank plc by fax or e-mail. Such a notice might take the form of Figure 2.6.

As mentioned above, the collateral manager will normally fax or e-mail the Collateral Notice to the counterparty and follow this up with a telephone call to see if they agree with the call figure. Differences are inevitable because the exposure may have been calculated by each of them at slightly different times using differently constituted yield curves. Such differences can be large, for instance, with cross currency swaps as these involve FX rates as well as yield curves. Trades may also have been overlooked by one of the parties. Collateral valuation for mainstream government securities should be exactly or almost exactly the same. Some larger players also accept equities as collateral.

In the vast majority of cases, collateral calls are smoothly agreed over the telephone but where this is not the case the parties can invoke a dispute resolution procedure (see pp. 25–26).

Of course, it is possible that XYZ Bank plc could be in a position to make a collateral call on PCH Bank on another Local Business Day. Figure 2.7 shows how PCH Bank would be advised of this from the Algo Collateral (Sentry) system.

Collateral Notice

FIG. 2.6

Collateral Notice

Contact Name: Joe Bloggs, XYZ Bank plc
Contact Phone: 1243678
Contact Fax: 3298572

This fax is confidential. Unauthorised use is forbidden. Please destroy it if you are not the addressee.

Pursuant to the ISDA Credit Support Annex dated as of 1 April 2001 between PCH Bank and XYZ Bank plc.

Variation Margin Details

We hereby give notice of the following Collateral movement as at the close of business on 9 October 2001. Collateral movement is calculated as follows:

		All Figures in US$
Portfolio MTM		**6,500,000**
Total Independent Amount		2,000,000
Net Exposure		**8,500,000**
less Threshold		0
Credit Support Amount (Exposure)		**8,500,000**
less Value of Collateral held		**(3,705,586)**
Value of Collateral Pending		0
Value of Outstanding Substitution Transactions		0
Delivery Amount		**4,794,414**
Minimum Transfer Amount	100,000	
Rounding	50,000	
Total Collateral Call Amount		**4,800,000**

Please confirm your agreement to the amount of the Collateral movement and advise settlement details

....

Authorised Signatory

FIG. 2.7 Report showing a possible collateral call from the counterparty

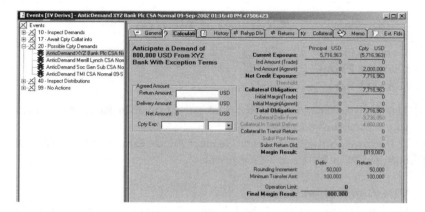

The next day the exposure has gone down from US$ 6.5 million to US$ 5,716,963. The previous posting of US$ 3,705,586 of collateral has been revalued with the latest bond prices and is now worth US$ 3,736,050 in credit support value. Together with the US$ 4.8 million of collateral in transit, PCH Bank is now overcollateralised by US$ 819,087. It is the standard convention to round down Return Amounts and so PCH Bank may expect a collateral call for US$ 800,000 from XYZ Bank plc.

If both parties are acting as their own Valuation Agents, it is possible but unlikely that XYZ Bank plc may not call at all. If it does not, PCH Bank is under no obligation to point out to XYZ Bank plc that it could make a collateral call. Where a third party Valuation Agent is involved, a call would be certain. However, third party Valuation Agents are rare.

Based on the information recorded in the collateral management database a collateral call notice would be generated.

TRANSFERS

Where cash is the only collateral, transfers are relatively easy, involving as they do the electronic transfer of currencies normally on the same or following Local Business Day.

With securities, transfers are more tricky. First of all the collateral manager needs to check, as he would with cash, that the securities he will receive are acceptable under the collateral agreement. He will check this from an agreement database which will form part of his automated collateral management system. If the collateral is not eligible this will be flagged. He will also check if a haircut applies to this security. It is, however, the responsibility of the collateral giver to deliver correctly haircutted collateral amounts. If the securities are lodged with a custodian or central securities depository system like Euroclear or Clearstream, they will either have to be transferred to the collateral manager's custodian or to his institution's account at Euroclear or Clearstream. Transfers to an external custodian can take up to three Local Business Days depending upon the terms of the collateral agreement. However, it is possible to make same day transfers if this is agreed early enough. Internal transfers can take place on the same day within Euroclear or Clearstream if matching instructions for the transfer are received by the cut-off time (e.g. 6.00 p.m. Brussels time for Euroclear Euclid (4.00 p.m for non-Euclid)), or on the next business day if received after that time. Euclid is Euroclear's proprietary communications system. Again, we often see a separation of duties here between the collateral manager who will agree the call and the details of the collateral that will be posted by/to the counterparty, and the settlements department who will take over from there and alert the collateral manager where a failure of receipt or delivery occurs.

Where this is the case, charges for late delivery are likely to be made. Normally, the collateral agreement will not cover interest on late deliveries. Where cash is involved it is just a simple matter of not paying interest on it until it is received. With securities, the default interest provisions of Section 2(e) of the ISDA Master Agreement will apply due to the close links between the two documents.

In making exposure calculations, collateral managers in Europe need to take account of any collateral already called for and in transit.

REUSE OF COLLATERAL

Under the ISDA Credit Support Annexes collateral received is regularly reused by the collateral taker who, as owner, has completely free choice on how he deals with the collateral. He can sell it, hold it or reuse it. Most is used to meet incoming collateral calls. Often it is also reinvested with other desks within a bank, e.g. the repo desk. If the collateral portfolio is well managed, profits could be made. However, whether this is really a task for the collateral department depends upon the policy of the individual institution. This matter is discussed further on pp. 35 and 55 in Chapter 3.

COLLATERAL SUBSTITUTIONS

Sometimes a collateral giver may need his securities collateral back to meet a delivery commitment to another party or a repo or stock loan needs to be unwound.

In some countries like Belgium, the current law and tax practice requires you to substitute the collateral before a coupon payment date as the collateral taker could face tax liabilities if it is holding the bond on the date an interest payment is made.

Where the collateral giver makes a collateral substitution request, it is essential he obtains the consent of the collateral taker under the English Law CSA and advisable under the New York Law CSA especially where an English incorporated collateral giver is involved.

This is because where ownership of the bond has passed to the collateral taker, he has to have a free choice to consent to the substitution, or the arrangement could be legally reclassified as a pledge or security interest which could fail for lack of registration in a liquidation (see p. 36).

Collateral substitution requests are normally made in writing and are followed by a telephone call. Normally, the receiving collateral manager will write "Agreed" on the fax and send it back or will agree it by e-mail.

The collateral manager will consider if the bonds proposed for substitution are acceptable collateral and will consent if they are. Collateral managers would not refuse consent purely because the bonds for substitution had been repoed or had been posted to another counterparty. In these circumstances the collateral manager would have agreed with the repo desk that these bonds would be returnable upon request or the collateral manager will initiate a substitution with the counterparty to whom they have posted the bonds.

Assuming consent is given, the collateral taker will always check that he has received the substitution bonds before he will release the collateral being substituted. If receipt of the substitution collateral can be verified early enough in the day, the retransfer of the original collateral can be made on the same day. Before the collateral taker releases the bonds to be substituted he will, of course, be overcollateralised and the collateral giver will have a double exposure on the collateral taker in case he goes bankrupt before he returns the substituted bonds. So same day retransfer is desirable in these circumstances.

Cash collateral is sometimes substituted where a collateral giver requests this for the purposes of its own funding profile.

Currently, the market seems more interested in cash collateral and, over the past two years, many cash for bond substitutions have taken place largely because cash is regarded as easier to manage. In addition, the growing scarcity of G10 governments securities due to redemptions has increased the cost of obtaining such collateral and has pushed the market towards cash.

DISTRIBUTIONS

Distributions cover payment of interest on cash collateral and coupons on bonds either receivable or payable.

Interest on cash collateral and any interest coupons on securities are always passed on to the collateral giver. This is because market practice is to regard the collateral giver as the owner of the securities *for economic purposes* and, by the collateral taker passing on distributions, to place the collateral giver in the same position he would have been in had he not transferred or pledged the securities collateral over the coupon payment date.

When bond coupons are paid, the collateral value of the bond will reduce because accrued bond interest is included in the bond price. Payment of bond coupons can, therefore, create a margin call and the ISDA collateral agreements allow the collateral taker to hold on to these payments in those circumstances as part of the collateral balance he holds (see commentary on Paragraph 5 of the English Law CSA on p. 99).

Payment of interest on cash collateral is agreed at a benchmark rate (e.g. EONIA or Fed Funds Rate), with or without a spread at an agreed interval (e.g. on the first Local Business Day of a month for the previous calendar month). During negotiation of collateral agreements between significant market players the payment date for interest is often one of the areas requiring compromise due to the particular functionalities of each party's operating systems.

EONIA means European Overnight Index Average and is the interest rate banks will pay for overnight deposits in Euros. Fed Funds Rate is the interest rate at which US banks with surplus reserves lend to other banks which are temporarily short of reserves. It is set by the US Federal Reserve Board. It is worth pointing out that the Fed Funds Rate for the close of business on the previous Local Business Day is not available until New York opening time, so interest calculations for US$ positions have to wait until early afternoon for European collateral managers. It is also common practice to send out detailed interest statements which will list the interest accrued per day.

As regards distributions on securities this is, as usual, slightly more complicated.

Under the English Law CSA the Transferee needs to transfer dividend or coupon payments on the Settlement Day following their payment. The Settlement Day is the first Local Business Day on which a trade in the relevant securities would customarily settle. In practice they will try to do this on the same Local Business Day as they are received.

DISPUTES

Most disagreements are resolved before they reach the stage of a formal dispute.

Collateral disagreements centre on the calculation of exposure for the collateral call or the valuation of the collateral itself. The first of these is by far the more common. Such disputes can arise for three main reasons, viz:

Mark to model differences

This is where the parties calculate exposure as of different times along the zero yield curve. Where the parties operate in different time zones one will close earlier than the other and if close of business prices are used they are bound to be different.

Such differences also arise where an incorrect yield curve or trade details are input in the trading system. This could impact the whole day's trading records. Differences in valuation models also arise when valuing complex and highly structured trades.

Different trade population

This simply means that the parties have overlooked or omitted some trades in their collateralised portfolios. This point is considered further in the section on Reconciliations which follows. Different trade populations are the most common source of exposure disputes.

Aggregating

This is where a mark to model difference affects each trade compounding the difference across the whole portfolio. For example, if your model gives an exposure valuation difference of US$ 10,000 for each trade then if a portfolio has 500 trades the result would be a US$ 5 million difference.

Disputes on the valuation of collateral are rarer and would only usually arise where lower quality or less liquid securities are accepted as collateral and prices are difficult to obtain.

ISDA's Credit Support Documents individually contain a dispute procedure under which undisputed amounts are transferred to the collateral taker and the remaining amount at issue falls under a structured process involving primarily obtaining independent exposure calculations within agreed deadlines. The process is described in detail in the commentary on the relevant sections of the English Law CSA and the New York Law CSA respectively on pp. 95–97 and pp. 215–217.

However, most disputes are resolved informally in one of three ways, viz:

- **a mutually agreed tolerance level is included in the Credit Support Document. The level may be expressed as a percentage or in US$ terms;**

- **each firm will "split the difference" of the disputed amount and will deliver only the undisputed amount as required by the Credit Support Document;**

- **both parties agree to the undisputed amount only and revalue portfolios again the following day for comparison. If an exposure amount differs by a consistent amount, this amount is used to calculate a tolerance level.**

Disputes on collateral values are relatively rare and usually arise with exotic secutities. Normally the difference is simple – a fault in pricing information or the wrong haircut. If it persists, the collateral taker usually requests the collateral giver to substitute the disputed collateral.

RECONCILIATIONS

Reconciliations are important because parties need to know that the same trades are being collateralised and hence the level of collateral is correct. Most differences occur for two reasons, i.e. differences in trade valuation or trade population (especially with structional products).

In its *Collateral Survey 2000*, ISDA reported that only 57% of market players reconciled their portfolios before trading on a collateralised basis. Therefore, alarmingly in my opinion, 43% went in blind on Day 1. Reconciliation of deal portfolios is also an ongoing necessity and, at one point in the discussions which ultimately led to the *2001 ISDA Margin Provisions*, it was proposed to introduce compulsory half yearly portfolio reconciliations with sanctions if they were not performed. This idea was dropped but it remains good practice to perform such reconciliations and this often happens where the parties decide to extend their collateral arrangements to new products. It is also now normal at the start of the collateralised relationship in order to reduce the risk of a dispute at that time.

Reconciliations are one of the regular and most time consuming features of a collateral manager's work and most frequently arise with mark to market exposure differences. For this purpose an automated reconciliation programme can be used which will initially record matched trades on a permanent basis. When a periodic reconciliation is done, if one of these trades is not shown this will be flagged by the system and can be investigated.

However, the most common problem is that parties' trade portfolios are not in one common standard format, and so collateral managers reconciling such portfolios can spend much time reconfiguring the counterparty's trade information so that it can be compared to its own. This may have acted as a deterrent for entering into the *2001 ISDA Margin Provisions* where strict deadlines apply to the reconciliation of portfolio information to resolve disputes.

I believe Algo Collateral (Sentry) pioneered an initiative with its own clients to compose a common market standard and recently ISDA has taken up the baton on this for the market as a whole.

DEFAULTS

What every collateral manager dreads is the non-delivery of collateral leading to a default situation under which all transactions are closed out under the ISDA Master Agreement. Conversely, where there is an unremedied Event of Default under an ISDA Master Agreement, this will also trigger the collateral agreement's termination provisions.

Either of these circumstances entails a lot of urgent work involving the collateral management unit, the dealer concerned, the legal department (who will send out the necessary notices), credit officers and the back office. The impact of the default upon the bank's profit and loss account will be calculated by the Financial Control function and progress will be reported to senior management. Defaults of this nature are extremely rare.

FIG. 2.8 # Timescale for liquidating collateral

Activity	Time	Day
Collateral Valuation	Close of Business	Monday 1
Collateral Call	By 1.00 p.m.	Tuesday 1
Counterparty to reply	By 5.00 p.m	Wednesday 1
If agreed; ok. If not, dispute procedure applies. Dispute now assumed. Undisputed amount transferred and market quotations for exposure called for.	By 5.00 p.m.	Thursday 1
Agreement	By 1.00 p.m.	Friday 1
Settlement T+2	By close of business	Tuesday 2
Settlement fails. Event of Default notice issued.	N/A	Wednesday 2
Three Local Business Days' grace allowed for settlement under Section 5(a)(i) of the Master Agreement.	By close of business	Monday 3

Collateral management units factor in up to a 14-day period for the liquidation of their collateral. This is calculated as shown in Figure 2.8.

A shorter period would apply to payments of cash collateral because there is no need for a two Local Business Day settlement period as for securities.

Valuation Agent

The Valuation Agent is specified in the Credit Support Document. In a collateral agreement between banks, the Valuation Agent will be the party calling for either a delivery or return of collateral. However, where a large bank has a collateral arrangement with a small corporate it will invariably want to be the Valuation Agent for all purposes if it is the only party with the necessary systems to calculate exposure. It must act in good faith and in a commercially reasonable manner in this role. A Valuation Agent calculates exposure and makes collateral calls for both parties. However, where this arrangement does not apply, if a collateral giver could claim return of collateral but does not do so, the collateral taker is under no obligation to return it. However, where one party acts as Valuation Agent for both it is under an obligation to make such a collateral return. Sometimes a Valuation Agent's role can be split with a third party. For instance, the Valuation Agent will value the trade portfolio and the third party will value the collateral.

BRANCHES

Where a bank regularly takes collateral from customers in various financial centres around the world, each may have its own collateral management function operating under the global collateral policies of the central collateral management unit (probably located at the bank's head office) with permitted necessary local variations.

Monitoring of collateral on a global basis is not a perfect science. Take, for example, a bank which has three collateralised branches, e.g. Singapore, New York and London.

In all cases, the mark to market valuation of trades will not be available until reports are compiled a few hours after each branch closes.

The London and New York branch reports with close of business figures of previous Local Business Days are unlikely to be available to the Singapore branch if it has to make its collateral calls for local Asian counterparties early. In this case its total exposure may be based on Singapore mark to market figures as at close of business yesterday, but London and New York mark to market figures as at close of business two Local Business Days before.

As a result a collateral management unit in any of these locations might report different exposure on the same counterparty on the same day. Because no intra-day calling takes place and because counterparties are normally allocated to collateralised branches on a geographical basis and only one collateral management unit will call them, this is not a major problem.

However, it is fair to say that the global picture only stands still at weekends and on 1 January.

So where a customer is multibranch, each of the bank's branches, perhaps in different time zones, will be checking their exposure on local customers and the collateral held on a daily basis and calling for collateral, returning collateral or doing nothing as appropriate.

However, some major banks, with the necessary systems, would make one global collateral call.

For this reason consistent internal risk management reporting is vital.

EXTERNAL COLLATERAL MANAGEMENT SERVICES

Where a corporate or a small bank lacks the internal resources or volume to establish its own collateral management unit, it can still engage in collateralised business using a third party service.

Euroclear Bank N.V./S.A. offers one through its Integrated Collateral Management Service and Clearstream through its Tripartite Credit Support Agency Service.

The use of a third party collateral management service provider is likely to be where both parties are small, because otherwise a large counterparty with its own collateral management system will just propose that it be Valuation Agent under the Credit Support Document.

Assuming both parties are small and that they want to use an external collateral management service, they still enter into an ISDA Master Agreement and an ISDA Credit Support Document with each other in the normal way. They also enter into a triparty agreement with the external collateral management service provider which covers operating arrangements with all counterparties in its securities clearing system.

The external collateral management service provider will do the following:

- **receive net exposure figures from either or both counterparties;**

- **seek to resolve any disputes about these;**

- **value collateral and check adequacy of cover;**

- **check eligibility of proposed collateral assets;**

- **transfer collateral assets according to the Credit Support Document terms and the predefined preferences of both counterparties;**

- **accept same day delivery of assets from outside its clearing system and make intra-account transfers as appropriate within it;**

- **process substitutions;**

- **route coupon payments to the holder of securities;**

- **hold collateral assets in its own custody system;**

- **identify best available reuse of collateral opportunities;**

- **produce comprehensive daily valuation reports.**

Such a service saves on infrastructure, technology and administrative costs for each party (although they still each have to value the exposure) but it does come at a price and will probably only be used as a precursor to each party establishing its own collateral management unit.

In the US, such a service is provided by The Bank of New York, JP Morgan Chase Bank and Citibank among others.

Legal issues relating to collateral from the European and US perspectives

3

Paul Harding

Christian Johnson

US perspective

EUROPEAN PERSPECTIVE BY PAUL HARDING

INTRODUCTION

Laws relating to collateral are in flux. In December 1999, ISDA's Collateral Law Reform Group reported that despite legislative improvements in recent years it remained the case that:

> ...**current laws and rules throughout the European Union relating to the use of collateral are in many instances complex, inconsistent, impractical and/or out of date.**

This undesirable state of affairs can result in uncertainty about the effectiveness of collateral arrangements and lead to inefficiency, higher costs and increased risk. For the past two years the Group has been seeking wide ranging law reform and I shall revert to this later in this chapter in connection with the forthcoming European Directive on collateral financial arrangements.

Clearly their concern was legal risk – the risk that the collateral taker's rights would not be recognised in line with contract terms.

For the moment let us examine the usual legal factors that need to be considered when completing collateral documentation. These are:

- **your laws;**
- **your counterparty's laws;**
- **the laws applying to the collateral arrangement;**
- **the laws applying to the collateral assets;**
- **the laws applying to the location of the collateral assets (the "lex situs" as it is called in common law countries or the "lex re sitae" in civil code countries).**

The ultimate goal is to create a perfected interest in the collateral. However, the possible interplay of five different legal regimes and their conflict of laws rules can produce a complex pattern requiring detailed legal analysis. Take the following example for instance:

Example

> Party A agrees to act as giver under a collateral arrangement with Party B (the taker). The agreement between Party A and Party B is expressed to be governed by the laws of jurisdiction C. Party A provides bonds as collateral. The bonds are issued by a bank organised in jurisdiction D through its branch located in jurisdiction E and the bonds are expressed to be governed by the laws of jurisdiction F. They are held in a settlement and clearing system in jurisdiction G.

In order to ensure that it has perfected its collateral with Party A, Party B (the taker) will need to consider the impact of the laws of each of jurisdictions A to F (if only to discount them from its analysis). Moreover, it will need to analyse the conflict of laws rules in each of the jurisdictions relevant to the collateral arrangements to ensure that they recognise and apply the laws of the other jurisdictions, so that Party B can achieve its goal of perfecting its collateral arrangement.

GENERAL ISSUES

Because most collateral agreements are two-way or bilateral, the two parties to the collateral agreement (which we will assume is one of the ISDA Credit Support Documents) need to answer two basic questions first of all, viz:

1 **Do they each have the capacity to enter into derivatives transactions and provide collateral? This is to confirm they are not acting ultra vires.**

2 **Is close-out netting fully enforceable in their respective jurisdictions and if the underlying ISDA Master Agreement is multibranch and collateral is to be given or received, is close-out netting effective in those branches' jurisdictions?**

In connection with the first point where an English company is concerned, Section 35 of the 1985 Companies Act will generally protect third parties against ultra vires acts of their counterparties but this is not so in many other jurisdictions.

Close-out netting is very important, because it is against the closed-out net exposure that the collateral is applied in a default situation. So close-out netting needs to be robust if collateral is to be enforced successfully.

The market has focused on two approaches to taking collateral – security interest and title transfer.

Of these two approaches, the traditional one has been the creation of a security interest or pledge.

Security interest

Here the party giving the collateral is called the pledgor and the party receiving the collateral is called the pledgee. It is important to remember that the pledgor retains an ownership interest in the collateral assets pledged to the pledgee. This interest is subject to the pledgee's right to sell the securities or take the cash if the pledgor defaults.

Collateral perfection requirements take various forms in different countries including the execution of the pledge documentation itself, the filing or registration of the pledge, the use of a segregated account to hold securities and/or the delivery of notices to third parties. With securities, precise perfection requirements depend upon whether they are debt or equity; bearer or registered; in physical or book entry form; or held with a single custodian or through a chain of them. For many reasons, including uncertainty as to which rules apply (and when) and the difficulty of complying with these requirements in fast-moving securities markets or in relation to book entry securities held through a chain of custodians, these rules can often impede or delay perfection of pledge collateral arrangements.

However, failure to comply with them could result in the invalidity or unenforceability of the collateral under the pledge.

All European jurisdictions appear to require at least notice to a third party custodian holding pledged assets that these assets are subject to a security interest. These notice requirements vary in their degree of formality and inconvenience. Several require either an acknowledgement by the custodian of the security interest or an annotation by the custodian on the account of the existence of the security interest, namely in Denmark, Finland, France, Italy, Luxembourg, Netherlands, Portugal and Spain.

Most financial institutions holding securities as collateral want to deal freely with them until they are required to re-deliver equivalent securities under the collateral arrangement. This includes freedom to sell, lend or repo the securities or to repledge, i.e. rehypothecate them to a third party subject always to the return of equivalent fungible securities (i.e. of the same issue and issuer) to the collateral giver provided it performs its obligations in full. By dealing freely with the securities the pledgee can use them efficiently and lower its costs.

However, under pledge arrangements in England and Wales the pledgee cannot use the collateral as he only has a partial interest in it and not outright ownership. Therefore, any use of the collateral risks destroying the security interest because the pledgee's rights are based upon the pledger retaining its ownership interest. The position is different under a New York Law CSA as we shall see. However, in both jurisdictions a pledgee generally has fiduciary obligations for the safe custody of collateral.

England, France, Greece, Ireland, Netherlands, Portugal and Spain have potentially onerous formal requirements for the creation of a pledge or other security interest, particularly in relation to securities. Because of this some people prefer to use title transfer collateral. Implementation of the European Directive on collateral financial arrangements will ease these problems relating to security interests.

Title transfer

The title transfer approach is based on netting and set off and was developed as an alternative to the cumbersome rules for the creation and perfection of pledge collateral and the restrictions on its use. Under title transfer collateral arrangements, the collateral giver is usually called the transferor and the collateral taker is called the transferee. Because the transferee of title transfer collateral in the form of securities is the legal owner of those securities, it can do what it likes with them, subject only to a contractual obligation to return equivalent fungible securities to the transferor. Because it is the owner, it is also free of fiduciary obligations to the transferor for the safe custody of the collateral. So the transferor transfers full title in the securities or cash to the transferee and gives him the right to set off or net his credit exposure on the transferor under the Master Agreement if the transferor defaults. However, if the transferor performs its obligations in full, it is entitled to the return of fungible securities from the transferee or repayment of cash in the same currency.

It is important to note that the transferor only has a contractual claim against the transferee in relation to title transfer collateral and therefore would be an unsecured creditor for the value of the collateral if the transferee became insolvent. Under a pledge, as we know, a pledgee only has a partial interest in pledge collateral and the pledgor remains its owner. Therefore, in the insolvency of the pledgee, the pledgor will generally be able to redeem the collateral out of the pledgee's bankruptcy estate on the basis of its continuing ownership interest in the collateral which is, therefore, not available to the pledgee's general creditors. A transferor cannot do this with his transferee.

While title transfer collateral works well with modern methods of trading, holding and transferring securities, in some jurisdictions there is thought to be a significant risk that it could be recharacterised as pledge collateral or a security interest.

RECHARACTERISATION

Recharacterisation arises from a court decision that the nature of a transaction is different from the way it is presented in the documentation covering it. Recharacterisation undermines legal certainty.

An action for recharacterisation could be brought, for instance, by a liquidator of an insolvent collateral giver.

Under English law recharacterisation of title transfer collateral may have the following drawbacks:

- title transfer collateral recharacterised as a security interest could be invalidated in a liquidation because it was not registered at Companies House pursuant to s 395 of the 1985 Companies Act within 21 days of creation;
- if the collateral giver goes into administration there is an automatic freeze on the enforcement of security interests granted by it. Title transfer collateral is not caught by the asset freeze under sections 10 and 11 of the Insolvency Act (1986);
- it is just possible that a collateral giver might have had the capacity under its constituting documents to enter into title transfer arrangements but not security interest arrangements before it became insolvent. This is, however, unlikely;
- the title transfer documentation would be defective as it would need different provisions to be a security interest;
- recharacterisation as a security interest would run foul of third parties receiving a negative pledge (a general undertaking not to provide security or collateral to any other party) from the insolvent collateral giver.

Recharacterisation would, of course, defeat the purpose of entering into a title transfer collateral arrangement to avoid cumbersome pledge formalities and restrictions on use. Probably speaking, the recharacterised arrangement would not satisfy the necessary formalities and restrictions for security interests and could therefore be void or unenforceable.

It is also possible for a security interest to be recharacterised as a floating charge. If this happens the floating charge would rank lower in the liquidation pecking order behind both fixed charges (i.e. security interests) and preferential creditors (e.g. the Inland Revenue). It might also not be recognised in some jurisdictions.

In some jurisdictions, including England, recharacterisation risk in relation to title transfer collateral is avoided. This is because despite the arrangement's purpose being essentially the same as a pledge, the insolvency risk taken by the transferor on the transferee means that there is a major difference between pledge collateral and title transfer collateral. On that basis, the choice of the title transfer approach is not a sham but genuine and legitimate. This is because the transferor accepts the risk of the transferee becoming insolvent and unable to return equivalent securities and, therefore, ranking as an unsecured creditor in the transferee's insolvency.

Other jurisdictions lay more stress on the arrangement's intended purpose and might, therefore, recharacterise notwithstanding the differences between the approaches. Moreover, since title transfer collateral arrangements are ultimately based on set-off or netting, they are vulnerable if there are restrictions on insolvency set-off in the parties' home jurisdictions or if the relevant netting legislation in those jurisdictions is not broad enough to cover title transfer collateral.

ISDA's Collateral Law Reform Group reported that jurisdictions appearing to have significant risk of recharacterisation of title transfer collateral arrangements are Denmark, Finland, Greece, Italy, Netherlands and Spain.

Again the European Directive on collateral financial arrangements should improve this situation.

CONFLICT OF LAWS RULES

Conflict of laws (also known as private international law) concern the discordance between the laws of one country and another applied to the same subject matter.

One of the most difficult areas for global financial institutions operating across borders is determining which jurisdiction's laws apply to which part of a collateral arrangement. This includes the creation/perfection of collateral, priority between claimants in an insolvency and enforceability of the collateral arrangement. Not only are the choice of law rules potentially difficult to apply within a single jurisdiction, but your counterparty's jurisdiction might choose to interpret them differently, meaning that the same question (for example, whose law governs perfection in a particular case?) could be answered differently by courts in various jurisdictions.

In addition, the law applying to collateral assets may not necessarily be the same law as the lex situs governing the place where the assets are located. Since securities and cash are most commonly taken as collateral, it is not unknown for these assets to be subject to a different governing law to that of their lex situs. Indeed with some assets (e.g. bearer bonds in a definitive form), the lex situs may change during the life of the collateral arrangement as ownership changes. Finally, not all jurisdictions' conflict of laws rules necessarily apply the concept of lex situs when determining which governing law applies to assets.

So it's all a bit of a minefield.

Conflict of laws rules are rather old fashioned in this context. Where they apply to securities, they are generally based on the assumption that the security exists as a certificate in the hands of the collateral giver. They deal inadequately with securities held in dematerialised form in modern clearing systems and/or through a chain of custodians.

A single stock could, for instance, be deemed to be located where its issuer has its head office or where the share register is kept or where the share itself is kept.

In the US, this conflict of laws situation has been simplified by the adoption of revised Article 8 of the Uniform Commercial Code which provides that the location of a party's interest in securities held through a custodian is the place where the custodian holds the account of such party.

THE PRIMA RULE

In Europe, the situation has been somewhat eased by Article 9(2) of the 1998 European Union Settlement Finality Directive where the approach adopted is the PRIMA, i.e. the place of the relevant intermediary approach. This is where the collateral is deemed to be legally located.

Not only is PRIMA practically desirable, but it also has a sound technical basis. The lex situs principle was developed to determine the law governing the perfection of interests in real property and other tangible assets by looking to the law of the place where the assets are physically located. However, interests in securities held in clearing systems are evidenced by book entries and are intangible, which means, by definition, they are not located anywhere. As far as most clearing systems are concerned the only place at which there exists any evidence of the collateral taker's interest is on the books of its immediate intermediary or custodian. Further up the chain, the interests of the collateral taker's custodian and that custodian's sub-custodian are reflected in book entries, but the collateral taker itself is not recorded at all. So, when trying to determine the lex situs of the collateral taker's interest in the securities, it makes sense to look to the location of its immediate intermediary or custodian.

The certainty of PRIMA has been adopted by statute in Belgium, Luxembourg and the US.

On 19 May 1998, the European Parliament and Council adopted the Directive which had to be implemented in all European Member States by 11 December 1999.

Article 9(2) closely follows the PRIMA principle. However, the scope of the provision is qualified by the definition of collateral security in Article 2(m) which led to two views:

Under one view – the narrow view – Article 9(2) would only eliminate this aspect of legal risk for certain collateral takers, viz:

- **central banks of Member States;**
- **the European Central Bank; and**
- **liquidity providers to an EU payment or securities settlement system to which the Finality Directive applies (for example, clearing houses or investment exchanges).**

Under the other view – the broad view – Article 9(2) would eliminate this aspect of legal risk for all participants in an EU settlement system. Article 9, therefore, establishes a conflicts of laws rule for EU Member States as to the location of securities held indirectly.

Opinions of the Member States have varied, but the broad view has gained most ground.

OTHER LEGAL ISSUES

Governing law

You may wish for practical reasons to use a Credit Support Document governed by a different law than the related ISDA Master Agreement. It is possible and regularly seen in the market to have the Credit Support Document under a different governing law to the ISDA Master Agreement, especially between English law and New York law documents, but you should take specific legal advice on this if you want other laws to apply.

Set-off

In nearly all jurisdictions, on insolvency, set-off is restricted to mutual debts owed between the insolvent party and its creditor. Generally speaking, the same mutuality requirement applies to netting of claims owed between them. For title transfer arrangements this means the collateral giver must be contractually liable for the obligations which are collateralised and fully entitled to return of equivalent collateral under the arrangement.

If a third party is able to intervene and claim the collateral back from the collateral taker in priority to the collateral giver, then the mutuality requirement has been disrupted and the set-off or netting upon which the arrangement is based will probably fail. Typical third parties which could disrupt the mutuality in this way would include a third party to whom the collateral giver had assigned its right to return of the collateral or a third party creditor seeking to attach the collateral giver's contractual right to return of the collateral for a debt owed to it. This sort of disruption could occur because of default or negligence by the collateral giver or perhaps by operation of law.

The main jurisdiction where this risk is thought by the ISDA Collateral Law Reform Group to arise is Spain although there is considered to be some risk, or at least uncertainty, on this point in Finland, France, Germany, Greece, Italy and Portugal.

Preference rules

Under the preference rules of some jurisdictions, deliveries of top-up collateral made by a party because of margin calls during a specific period before insolvency (called the suspect or preference period) may be invalidated by a liquidator. If successful, this would require the collateral taker to return the top-up collateral without deduction or set-off against its exposure on the insolvent collateral giver.

In addition, under "zero hour" rules of some jurisdictions, formal insolvency proceedings are deemed to commence at midnight immediately before the time that the formal insolvency proceedings were actually started (for example, by a creditor petition or court order). This can mean that transfers of collateral occurring before proceedings actually commenced could also be attacked by an insolvency official. So if a collateral transfer was made at 9.00 a.m. and a court approved insolvency proceedings at 10.00 a.m. in a "zero-hour jurisdiction" the court approval would be backdated to midnight and the collateral transfer could be deemed void.

Moreover, when daily collateral movements have occurred over say, a six-month suspect period, a large portion of the collateral held by the collateral taker could be subject to avoidance in this way, with potentially serious consequences for the collateral taker (and possibly for its own creditors).

Where the collateral arrangement is not itself a preference, it should not make deliveries of top-up collateral voidable as a preference during a suspect period.

The risk also arises where parties propose to collateralise pre-existing Transactions under an ISDA Master Agreement which already exists.

The ISDA Collateral Law Reform Group considered there to be a material risk that top-up collateral deliveries might be vulnerable as a preference during the relevant suspect period in each of Denmark, France, Greece, Italy and Spain. Again the European Directive on collateral financial arrangements should help here.

Given all the problems it is no wonder that the ISDA Collateral Law Reform Group lobbied for change with the following objectives:

- rules and procedures for implementing and maintaining a collateral arrangement to be simple, clear and cost-effective;

- cumbersome formalities such as registration, notification, filing and similar requirements to be abolished;

- a collateral taker to be free to deal with the collateral until it needs to return it. Third parties receiving such collateral from the collateral taker should receive clean title to the collateral whether or not they have notice of the collateral giver's original interest.

- a giver of pledge collateral (a pledgor) to be protected from the insolvency of the taker of that collateral (the pledgee);
- the law governing the creation and priority of the collateral arrangement to be the law chosen by the parties;
- where no law has been chosen by the parties, the governing law to be the law of the place where the collateral is held, collateral held through a custodian being deemed held where the custodian maintains the account, register or other official record for such collateral;
- the legal nature of a party's holding of securities in a clearing system to be clarified;
- collateral arrangements to be protected from the challenges of third parties;
- top-up deliveries of collateral under mark to market collateral arrangements to be protected from avoidance under preference and similar insolvency rules.

The European Commission and the European Central Bank both supported a more harmonised collateral regime for Europe and collateral featured as a high priority point in the Action Plan agreed by EU Finance Ministers in May 1999. In September 1999, the EU established a consultative Forum Group to study the issue further. In March 2001, a draft European Directive on Collateral was published and this is reviewed on pp, 44–45.

ISDA COLLATERAL LEGAL OPINIONS

ISDA has commissioned legal opinions on the enforceability of close-out netting from lawyers in 37 countries and opinions on collateral issues from lawyers in 30 countries, of which 28 have been completed. The current position with completed ISDA collateral opinions is shown in Annex 3.

When relying on a netting or collateral opinion from ISDA, you should ensure that your counterparty is a type of entity covered by the opinion. While these opinions typically cover corporates and banks, they do not always cover more specialised entities such as insurance companies, partnerships and government entities which may well be subject to separate insolvency regimes in the country concerned. You also need to check product coverage and if there are major assumptions or qualifications which would significantly affect the opinion's scope.

It is vitally important to understand and apply the findings of the ISDA legal opinions in such areas as the creation and perfection of security rights, asset ownership rights, law governing the collateral, registration, enforceability, insolvency netting, set-off, choice of law issues and the use of third party custodians/sub custodians.

LEGAL ISSUES RELATING TO INTERNATIONAL SECURITIES CLEARING SYSTEMS

Introduction

Where securities are held in an international securities clearing system like Euroclear in Belgium, or Clearstream in Luxembourg, care needs to be taken in establishing a collateral arrangement appropriate for the very specific rights participants have in those clearing systems.

Securities held in both Euroclear and Clearstream are "fungible" – that is, they are interchangeable with and indistinguishable from other securities of the same type and terms.

Euroclear and Clearstream participants do not possess individual physical securities which are credited to their securities clearance account but rather have a pro rated proprietary claim for a share in a pool of equivalent securities in common with other participants. These are called "co-ownership rights". These rights are established in Belgium for Euroclear by Royal Decree No. 62 of 1967, and in Luxembourg for Clearstream by the Grand Ducal Decree of 1971. Under Belgian and Luxembourg law, the location or situs of these rights is Belgium and Luxembourg respectively.

To avoid an overlong analysis, the following discussion will focus mainly on Euroclear, although many of the same issues apply to Clearstream.

The two most appropriate collateral arrangements in respect of co-ownership rights are a pledge or title transfer document. In other words, the usual routes.

Pledge

Pledges of securities held by Euroclear participants are explicitly regulated by Royal Decree 62. All that is required under this Decree to create a valid and enforceable pledge over such securities in addition to a valid pledge document, is to credit them to a securities account with Euroclear Bank NV/SA. This account will be specially designated as a "Pledged Account".

The pledge documentation itself can take the form of a New York Law CSA or an English Law ISDA Credit Suppport Deed. Provided that market prices for the pledged collateral are easily obtainable, if the pledgor defaults, the pledgee can realise the value of the pledged collateral immediately after sending a default notice to the pledgor. There is no need to seek prior authorisation from a Belgian court.

Any reuse of collateral under a New York Law CSA would have to comply with the Belgian Law requirements for an onward pledge in order to be enforceable under Belgian law.

Title transfer

By statute, Belgian law fully recognises the enforceability of title transfer in collateral transactions under the law of 15 July 1998.

This law removed uncertainties under Belgian law by ensuring that certain provisions governing the creation and enforceability of pledges did not apply to title transfer collateral. By doing this it prevented recharacterisation of such transfers into an invalid pledge or security interest.

It also provided that such title transfers are valid and enforceable when insolvency proceedings started against one of the parties to the transaction. A transaction cannot be invalidated under Belgian law even if insolvency proceedings are commenced later against the transferor or transferee of the collateral.

Finally the law of 15 July 1998 excludes the application of Article 17 of the Belgian Bankruptcy Code to collateral transactions. This prevents them being regarded as suspect period transactions.

The law of 15 July 1998, therefore, provides a safe harbour against recharacterisation for most transactions entered into between market professionals provided they comply with the following conditions:

- the transferred assets must be cash, securities or other financial instruments credited to an account;
- the purpose of the transfer must be the collateralisation of certain obligations owed by the transferor to the transferee;
- the transferor must be a bank or one of a list of specified financial or other institutions; and
- the transfer of title arrangement must contain a contractual obligation from the transferee of the collateral to transfer the cash or securities back to the transferor upon complete fulfilment by the transferor of its obligations.

If these very normal conditions are complied with, the protection against recharacterisation applies not only to the initial transfer of collateral but also extends to later such transfers and to substitutions of the original collateral assets by new securities or cash.

Clearly, the scope of protection introduced by this law is very broad and useful, and basically only excludes transactions collateralised by debtors who are individuals or small enterprises.

It was also influential in framing the new European Directive on collateral financial arrangements, the main work on which was done during Belgium's EU presidency in the second half of 2001.

THE EUROPEAN DIRECTIVE ON COLLATERAL FINANCIAL ARRANGEMENTS

This Directive, which was published in draft form at the end of March 2001, is part of the EU's Financial Services Action Plan. It also builds upon the 1998 Settlement Finality Directive and seeks to provide a uniform legal framework across the EU for taking collateral. This is part of a master plan to integrate the European financial markets in a cost effective manner and ensure the smooth functioning of the Euro in opted in EU states.

The Directive's main objectives are:

- to ensure simple, effective regimes for creating title transfer or pledge collateral;
- to provide limited but useful protection from insolvency laws where these are hostile to effective realisation of collateral, close-out netting, top-up margining and collateral substitution;
- to extend PRIMA across the EU;
- to reduce administrative burdens in creating, using or enforcing collateral;
- to permit reuse of pledge collateral;
- to prohibit title transfer arrangements being recharacterised as pledges.
- to protect top-up margin from insolvency suspect period rules. The Directive does not disapply preference or fraudulent conveyance laws.

The draft is divided into 13 Articles and has been positively greeted by the market, tackling as it does many of the ISDA Collateral Law Reform Group's main concerns. It will also clear up current uncertainty over the effectiveness of cross-border transactions by harmonising the legal regimes in the 15 EU Member States.

However, it had been criticised in three main ways, viz:

- as originally drafted, it only applied to public authorities, central banks, regulated financial institutions and persons other than natural persons with a capital base exceeding Euro 100 million or gross assets exceeding Euro 1 billion. These tests limited the Directive to wholesale market players and excluded all but the largest corporates. Following objections from ISDA and others, corporates are included and are not subjected to the above financial limits. However, an EU Member State can decide to exclude them, in which case it must inform the European Commission (Articles 1.2(e) and 1.3). Moreover, the corporate must have a public authority or a qualifying financial institution as its counterparty under the collateral agreement (Article 1.2.(e));
- in many European legal systems collateral top-ups and substitutions are vulnerable to insolvency suspect periods because they are treated as new transactions. Provided that the original collateral agreement is not a preference itself, the Directive protects top-ups and substitutions during an insolvency hardening period. However, the Directive only protects top-up

collateral where it is taken following normal marking to market and margin call arrangements and not where linked to credit rating downgrade provisions or when caught by the onset of insolvency. ISDA and others wanted all forms of top-up collateral to be protected but this has not happened;

● another problem area is the appropriation of assets by the collateral taker (upon the liquidation of collateral) which is only possible if stipulated in the collateral agreement and provided that the parties have agreed on the valuation of the assets in it (Article 4.2). Again, EU Member States may opt out of this provision provided that they inform the European Commission about it.

However, the problem with opt-outs is that they could render the legislation ineffective in some EU jurisdictions and jeopardise banks in those Member States benefiting from regulatory capital savings. However, it is thought that few, if any, EU states will opt out of these provisions.

On 15 May 2002 the European Commission adopted the Directive.

The EU Commission will require it to be implemented by Member States by late 2003 (18 months after its publication in the Official Journal of the European Union).

Member States are obliged to bring in basic minimum standards.

DRAFT HAGUE CONVENTION ON INDIRECTLY HELD SECURITIES

The Hague Conference on International Private Law is also working on collateral but in a global context. Its main aims are to adopt a future Convention on the law for proprietary or ownership rights in securities held in clearing systems and to harmonise laws around the world where the perfection or completion of security interest or title transfer collateral involves a number of jurisdictions. In short, it aims to globalise the conflict of laws issues of Article 9 of the EU Collateral Directive.

In January 2001, a group of collateral experts met and produced a draft Convention text on which comments were invited by 1 October 2001. A revised text was then produced for a meeting of the Hague Conference's Special Committee in January 2002. From that meeting a further draft Convention was produced. Further drafting sessions continue with the view of producing a final version of a Convention for a special Diplomatic Session of the Hague Conference in December 2002.

The text's authors strongly recommend PRIMA because of its simplicity and certainty as far as book entry securities held by central securities depositories are concerned. There is still debate on who can be regulated as an intermediary and which is the relevant jurisdiction where the relationship spans several countries.

It is hoped that the Convention will be adopted by Hague Member States (of which there are currently 61) by 2004.

US PERSPECTIVE BY CHRISTIAN JOHNSON

INTRODUCTION

In contrast to Europe, US laws governing the pledging of collateral have been historically stable and generally uniform across the various states. The State of New York, in particular, has developed a sophisticated set of statutory and judicial rules that govern the pledging of collateral. These rules provide a predictable and stable legal environment that enforce the rights of parties under security agreements, such as the ISDA Credit Support Annex, that are governed by New York law.

Even given this stability however, parties should be aware that in the US, the pledging of collateral and the enforcement of a party's rights under a security agreement are governed by statute and are, therefore, strictly enforced and construed. Failure to follow the statutory requirements can render a secured party's rights in collateral unenforceable. This discussion only outlines the general concepts that a party should understand before entering into a security agreement. Parties should consult US legal counsel as they enter into security agreements governed by US law.

This part of Chapter 3 discusses the legal issues (and any uncertainties) affecting the pledging of collateral to secure obligations under the ISDA Master Agreement and the New York Law CSA in the US. We will assume that both the ISDA Master Agreement and the New York Law CSA are governed by the laws of the State of New York.

In this discussion, the party giving the collateral is called the pledgor and the party receiving the collateral is called the secured party (as such terms are used in the New York Law CSA). We will further assume that the pledgor is always a US party and that only US dollar cash collateral or US government treasury securities are being pledged and that all collateral is held in the State of New York.

Much of the early documentation for pledging collateral to secure obligations under the ISDA Master Agreement was drafted using New York law. In addition, the collateral pledged was typically US dollar cash collateral or US government treasury securities, both of which were generally held in New York. Both US and foreign parties have become comfortable pledging collateral in the US. Many dealers such as Salomon Brothers Holding Company have been entering into security agreements with US and foreign counterparties on a regular basis since the early 1990s.

The early security agreements governing the pledging of collateral to secure obligations under ISDA Master Agreements were non-standard agreements that were developed by each dealer. This often led to serious and extended negotiations as parties attempted to reconcile the differences between their security agreement's respective terms. In late 1994, ISDA introduced the New York Law CSA which has done much to standardise the documentation process. Today, virtually all parties doing business in the US use the New York Law CSA to pledge collateral to secure obligations under an ISDA Master Agreement.

Although ISDA is continuing to develop new forms of collateral documentation such as under the *2001 ISDA Margin Provisions*, the legal issues discussed here will also apply to any future standardised agreements developed by ISDA. Although new standardised documentation may be stylised quite differently from the current New York Law CSA, the legal issues should remain constant.

There are several legal factors that need to be considered when completing collateral documentation in the US. These are:

- **the enforcement of the choice of New York law;**
- **the creation and perfection of a security interest under New York law;**
- **the enforcement of a secured party's rights under the collateral agreement;**
- **other issues involved in pledging collateral under New York law.**

ENFORCEMENT OF NEW YORK CHOICE OF LAW

When entering into a New York Law CSA, both the US and non-US parties anticipate that a New York court would enforce the selection of New York law, regardless of whether either party is organised in New York.

New York statutory law is unusual in that it expressly provides that the choice of New York law in a contract will be enforced. The only caveat is that the aggregate amount of obligations arising out of the contract is not less than US$ 250,000 (NY General Obligation Law, Paragraph 5-1401(1)). It is generally assumed that it would be sufficient that the notional amount of any transaction entered into must exceed US$ 250,000 as opposed to the net mark to market value.

New York law also expressly agrees to enforce New York as the forum for litigation "for which a choice of New York has been made" (NY General Obligation Law, Paragraph 5-1402(1)).

However, it must involve an obligation arising out of a transaction covering not less than US$ 1 million. Again, it is generally assumed that it would be sufficient for the notional amount of any transactions entered into to exceed US$ 1 million as opposed to the net mark to market value.

SECURITY INTEREST CREATION AND PERFECTION

In the US, OTC derivative market participants almost always take collateral by taking a security interest as opposed to title transfer. As with many jurisdictions, in order for a secured party to enforce its rights with respect to a security interest under New York law, the security interest must first attach and then be perfected.

In the US, generally every state, including New York, has adopted a version of the Uniform Commercial Code (relevant extracts of which may be found in Annex 4) that governs the attachment and perfection of a security interest in collateral. Article 9 governs how a secured party first attaches and perfects a security interest in collateral, and second, how it can exercise its rights with respect to the collateral (see NYUCC, Article 9).

As parties begin to hold and transfer securities held by large multi-tiered financial intermediaries by book entry, New York law has recognised that older rules based on certificated securities held and transferred directly by the parties have become outmoded. Now, for example, a party may own a US Treasury Security that is held in book entry form on the account of the party's bank in the Federal Reserve System. When a party pledges that security to another, the pledgor will instruct its bank to transfer the security to the secured party. The pledgor's bank will then notify the Federal Reserve to move the security from its account at the Federal Reserve to the Federal Reserve account of the secured party's bank.

New York law has been amended to recognise that such transfers by the parties through various financial intermediaries have the same effect as if the parties had transferred certificated securities between themselves. (See NYUCC, Article 8.) For example, New York law recognises that a party giving instructions to its financial intermediary (generally referred to as a securities intermediary) to transfer the treasury security is sufficient to constitute a transfer to that person for purposes of creating a security interest.

Attachment and perfection

Under New York law, for a security interest to attach, there generally must be (1) a security agreement in writing, (2) the pledgor must have rights in the collateral pledged, and (3) the secured party must give the pledgor value. Once the security interest has attached to the collateral, then the secured party may exercise its rights against the pledgor with respect to the collateral.

For a party to exercise its rights against third parties, however, the security interest must also be perfected. This typically requires the secured party either expressly or indirectly to give third parties notice that the security interest has attached. With respect to collateral such as cash and securities, New York law requires the secured party to have possession of the collateral (either directly or through an intermediary).

These general rules, however, are pre-empted by Federal law with respect to the attachment and perfection of security interests in US government treasury securities. These rules are set forth in Federal regulations, commonly referred to as the "Trades Regulations" (13 Code of Federal Regulations (CFR) Part 357). The attachment and perfection of similar types of book entry collateral such as securities issued by the Federal National Mortgage Association ("Fannie Mae") or the Federal Home Loan Mortgage Corporation ("Freddie Mac") are also governed by Federal rules.

The Trades Regulations, however, do not create a new method for attaching and perfecting a security interest in US government treasury securities. Instead they specify that the attachment and perfection are governed by the securities intermediary's jurisdiction. In the case of the New York Law CSA, this jurisdiction will generally be New York because the parties almost always require that collateral be held in New York.

A securities intermediary is an entity that, in the ordinary course of business, maintains securities accounts for others. For example, a large financial institution such as The Bank of New York, maintains a securities account at the Federal Reserve Bank of New York. In that account, The Bank of New York acts as a securities intermediary as it holds book entry US treasury securities on behalf of literally thousands of different parties.

Once the parties have entered into the New York Law CSA and the pledgor has pledged collateral to the secured party by transferring US government treasury securities to the secured party through a securities intermediary, the secured party will have an attached and perfected security interest in the collateral.

Perfection of cash deposits is discussed on pp. 57–58.

Under New York law, fluctuations in the amount to be secured under the New York Law CSA should not affect the validity of the secured party's security interest in the collateral. New York law provides that collateral may secure future obligations and that fluctuations in the amount owing will not affect the security interest.

Federal Deposit Insurance Act requirements

In dealing with US parties that are subject to the Federal Deposit Insurance Act (such as banks that hold insured deposits), foreign counterparties should be aware that there are certain additional requirements that must be met.

Generally, to establish a security interest that would be enforceable against the Federal Deposit Insurance Corporation (the "FDIC") after it had taken over an insolvent financial institution, the security interest must be (i) in writing, (ii) executed contemporaneously with the transaction, (iii) approved by the bank's board of directors, and (iv) an official record of the bank (12 US Code (USC), Section 1823(e)).

It would appear easy to fail any of these requirements in considering how OTC derivative documentation is often negotiated. However, the FDIC has provided several safe harbours for OTC derivative documentation to meet these requirements. For example, a Confirmation will generally be considered to meet the writing requirement. In addition, a party may rely on corporate resolutions provided by the bank to meet the board of directors' approval requirement. Finally, the non-bank party may meet the official record requirement by providing copies of its own records documenting the transactions (FDIC, Statement of Policy on Qualified Financial Contracts, 1989).

In another policy statement, the FDIC has stated that it will not seek to void an otherwise enforceable security interest based on the "contemporaneous" requirement (FDIC, Statement of Policy Regarding Treatment of Security Interests After Appointment of the FDIC as Conservator or Receiver, 1993).

ENFORCING RIGHTS UNDER THE COLLATERAL AGREEMENT

New York and US bankruptcy law provide strong statutory protections that permit a secured party to dispose of or liquidate collateral pledged to it upon the occurrence of an event of default under the security agreement. There are additional issues, however, that a secured party needs to take into account depending upon whether the pledgor is solvent or insolvent.

Solvent pledgors

The most straightforward (but probably most uncommon) situation involves a solvent pledgor who defaults under the terms of the ISDA Master Agreement (and/or the corresponding credit support document). New York law permits the secured party to dispose of the collateral to satisfy the pledgor's obligations to it under the ISDA Master Agreement (NYUCC, Section 9-504(1) (2001)). The only requirement on the secured party is that the disposition or liquidation of the collateral must be done in a commercially reasonable manner. (NYUCC, Section 9-504(3) (2001).)

Assuming that the collateral comprises such items as US treasury securities or similar types of collateral that are traded on a recognised market, the secured party does not even need to notify the pledgor of the disposition. However, the secured party has a duty to return any proceeds to the pledgor that are in excess of the amount owed to it. (NYUCC, Section 9-504(2) (2001).) The secured party may even retain the collateral provided that it complies with certain procedural safeguards set forth in the statute. (NYUCC, Section 9-505(2) (2001).)

The secured party should always be aware, however, that the pledgor has the right to redeem the collateral by meeting in full its obligations to the secured party before the secured party has disposed of or liquidated the collateral. (NYUCC, Section 9-506 (2001).)

Insolvent pledgors

Historically, there has been great concern about the secured party's rights under New York and US bankruptcy law to exercise its rights under a security agreement with an insolvent pledgor. Fortunately, these concerns have largely been eliminated in the US by statutory changes to the US Bankruptcy Code and banking insolvency law.

Resolution of these issues, however, was complicated by the number of different bankruptcy and insolvency law regimes in the US. Most insolvent or bankrupt corporations in the US are governed by the US Bankruptcy Code. The US Bankruptcy Code is Federal law and governs those bankrupt corporations subject to it regardless of where they are located. If the pledgor is a financial institution with federally insured deposits, the insolvent institution will likely be governed by the Federal Deposit Insurance Act ("FDIA"), as amended by the Financial Institutions Reform, Recovery and Enforcement Act of 1989 ("FIRREA").

Although most counterparties will be governed by the US Bankruptcy Code or the FDIA, broker dealers, insurance companies, and quasi-government agencies such as the Federal National Mortgage Association or the Federal Home Loan Banks all have their own statutory insolvency regimes and regulators. This discussion, however, will only focus on those pledgors that are subject to either the US Bankruptcy Code or banking insolvency law.

Prior to the statutory changes discussed above, parties were concerned about several issues. Secured parties were concerned that a court would not permit a party to terminate the ISDA Master Agreement upon the occurrence of the insolvency or enforce the close out and other netting provisions of the Agreement. They were also worried that they would be subject to the automatic stay under the US Bankruptcy Code and its statutory equivalents under the banking insolvency law and thus be unable to realise the collateral. Such restrictions would delay the ability of the secured party to exercise self-help remedies such as set-off and the liquidation of collateral pledged to secure the now insolvent party's obligations.

To fully understand a secured party's rights, it is necessary to discuss and compare how a secured party's rights differ depending upon whether the pledgor is subject to the US Bankruptcy Code or banking insolvency law.

The US Bankruptcy Code has special rules dealing with a bankrupt pledgor that has entered into a "swap agreement" with a "swap participant". The US Bankruptcy Code defines a swap participant as "an entity that, at the time before the filing of the petition, has an outstanding swap agreement with the debtor" (11 USC, Section 101(53C)). A swap agreement is broadly defined to include the majority of OTC derivative transactions and any master agreement governing those transactions (11 USC, Section 101(53B)).

Although both the definitions of a swap participant and a swap agreement are very broad, there is still some concern that certain types of transactions may not be included in the definition, thus depriving a party of the protections of these special rules governing swap agreements. Specifically, some concern has been raised as to whether the definition of a swap agreement under the US Bankruptcy Code would include equity derivatives and credit derivatives. Even given these concerns, the general market considers that these transactions should be included in the definition of a swap agreement. In addition, there is currently legislation in front of the US Congress to further broaden the definition of a swap agreement to eliminate these ambiguities.

Upon the filing of a bankruptcy petition, the automatic stay under Section 362 of the US Bankruptcy Code generally prevents the secured party of a bankrupt pledgor from exercising the legal rights and remedies in its collateral agreement. The automatic stay ordinarily remains in effect until the case is dismissed, completed or the judge grants relief. Because of the automatic stay, a swap participant would normally be automatically prevented from exercising any of the self-help remedies found in the collateral agreement, such as foreclosing on collateral without the court's permission.

The US Bankruptcy Code, however, provides a specific exemption from the automatic stay for swap agreements (11 USC, Section 362(b)(17)). This exemption also permits a swap participant to liquidate any collateral or margin held to secure the bankrupt pledgor's obligations under a swap agreement just as the secured party could have done had the pledgor been solvent. The exemption permits a swap participant to set-off any amounts that the bankrupt pledgor owes to it against any amounts that the swap participant owes to the bankrupt pledgor under the ISDA Master Agreement.

There was also concern that a secured party could not terminate the ISDA Master Agreement without the bankruptcy court's permission even though the Agreement provides that a party may terminate it upon the bankruptcy or insolvency of its counterparty. The US Bankruptcy Code, however, now permits a swap participant to exercise its rights under the ISDA Master Agreement to terminate it and any underlying Transactions upon the bankruptcy of its counterparty (11 USC, Section 560).

Secured parties were concerned about limitations upon their close-out netting rights under the ISDA Master Agreement resulting in the possibility of a bankruptcy trustee "cherry picking" among the various derivative transactions between the secured party and its bankrupt pledgor. Cherrypicking occurs when a bankruptcy trustee can terminate individual transactions for which the bankrupt pledgor was out-of-the-money (i.e. had payment obligations to the secured party) and keep those transactions for which the bankrupt pledgor was in-the-money (i.e. was entitled to payments from the secured party).

Congress resolved the cherrypicking concern by first permitting the secured party to terminate the ISDA Master Agreement and all of the underlying Transactions upon the bankruptcy of the pledgor. Section 560 of the US Bankruptcy Code also allows close-out netting. Close-out netting permits the secured party to net together any amounts payable under all of the Transactions to be terminated under the ISDA Master Agreement.

Debtors subject to banking insolvency laws

Debtors which are financial institutions that take federally insured deposits such as banks and savings institutions are not subject to the insolvency rules in the US Bankruptcy Code. Instead, they are subject to insolvency rules found in the Federal

Deposit Insurance Act ("FDIA"), as amended by the Financial Institutions Reform, Recovery and Enforcement Act of 1989 ("FIRREA").

Many of the same concerns that worried secured parties dealing with pledgors subject to the US Bankruptcy Code were still a concern in dealing with pledgors that are subject to the FDIA and FIRREA. Similar to the changes made to the US Bankruptcy Code, Congress has now resolved concerns around the rights of a secured party to exercise its rights under a security agreement with an insolvent financial institution subject to FDIA.

FDIA, as amended by FIRREA, now provides similar protections for secured parties that have entered into a "swap agreement" with the pledgor. "Swap agreement" is defined in a manner similar to the US Bankruptcy Code definition and is broadly defined to include the majority of typical OTC derivatives and any master agreement governing these transactions (12 USC, Section 1821(e)(8)(D)(iv)).

Under the FDIA, the secured party will generally have the right to terminate the ISDA Master Agreement upon the appointment of a receiver (and under certain circumstances upon the appointment of a conservator). Upon a permitted termination of the ISDA Master Agreement, the secured party can exercise its rights under the New York Law CSA with respect to such termination including its close-out netting rights (12 USC, Section 1821(e)(8)(a)).

Under the FDIA's general rules, a creditor of an insolvent financial institution is generally precluded from terminating the ISDA Master Agreement and underlying transactions solely because of the financial institution's insolvency. The FDIA, however, provides that a swap agreement can be terminated under certain circumstances depending upon whether the Federal Deposit Insurance Corporation ("FDIC") is appointed as a receiver or a conservator of the insolvent financial institution.

The secured party of an insolvent financial institution can terminate the swap agreement upon the appointment of the FDIC as a receiver one day after such appointment (12 USC, Section 1821(e)(8)(D)(vii)). As a receiver, the FDIC has the power to liquidate (but not operate) the financial institution and wind up its affairs.

In contrast, if the FDIC is appointed as conservator of the insolvent financial institution, the secured party will not have the right to terminate the ISDA Master Agreement because of the insolvency of the financial institution. The FDIC, as conservator, has the right to operate the financial institution as a going concern. The FDIC essentially steps into the shoes of the now insolvent pledgor. To terminate the ISDA Master Agreement upon appointment of the FDIC as a conservator, an Event of Default (other than an insolvency) or a Termination Event would have to occur.

Upon a permitted termination of the ISDA Master Agreement, the FDIC must recognise the close-out netting rights under the Agreement. This permits the secured party to net any amounts that it owes the pledgor under the Agreement with any amounts owing to the secured party (12 USC, Section 1821(e)(8)(A)(iii)).

Under general insolvency rules, the FDIC has the right to repudiate the contracts of an insolvent financial institution. This could result in the FDIC cherrypicking by selectively terminating or transferring the disadvantageous contracts and maintaining the advantageous ones. The FDIA, however, provides that if the FDIC is going to transfer any swap agreements, it must transfer all the swap agreements of a creditor to the same party if it is going to transfer any (12 USC, Section 1821(e)(3)(C)). The FDIC also may not selectively repudiate or terminate any individual transaction or contract under an ISDA Master Agreement that the insolvent financial institution had with its counterparty; rather it must terminate the Agreement and any underlying transactions all at once if it intends to terminate any individual transaction (12 USC, Section 1821(e)(8)(D)(vii)).

Secured parties have also worried in the past that the FDIC may try to avoid certain payments made before the insolvency of the financial institution as a preferential payment. Such payments, however, may not be avoided unless "the transferee had actual intent to hinder, delay, or defraud such institution" (12 USC, Section 1821(e)(8)(c)). This should protect the vast majority of payments made in the normal course of business under the ISDA Master Agreement.

It is possible that the New York Banking Law may apply to the insolvency of a pledgor. These rules generally parallel those described above under FDIA. Generally, however, an insolvency that would involve the New York Banking Law would also involve FDIC and the rules discussed above with respect to the FDIA. Although it is possible that the New York Banking Law may apply alone, it is more likely that this would occur with a New York branch of a non-US bank that does not have deposits insured by the FDIC, a situation beyond the scope of this discussion.

FDICIA

In addition to the statutory provisions favouring secured parties under both FDIA and the US Bankruptcy Code, the US Congress has enacted additional statutory provisions as part of the Federal Deposit Insurance Corporation Improvement Act of 1991 ("FDICIA") to enforce close-out netting. Under FDICIA, netting rights are enforced regardless of whether they would be enforced under the US Bankruptcy Code or the FDIA provided that both parties are "financial institutions" as defined in FDICIA. In addition, under current law, the ISDA Master Agreement would have to be governed by Federal law or by state law (such as the laws of the State of New York). There is also pending legislation before Congress that will strengthen and broaden the FDICIA provisions.

The definition of financial institution includes not only financial institutions that accept federally insured deposits, but also "a broker or dealer, a depository financial institution, a futures commission merchant, or any other financial institution as determined by the Board of Governors of the Federal Reserve System" (12 USC, Section 4402(9)). Under Federal Reserve Board regulations, a financial institution also includes large parties that meet quantitative and qualitative tests that generally describe the characteristics of a dealer in the derivatives area. The financial institution, however, does not need to be chartered or organised under US Federal or state law in order to benefit from FDICIA.

The qualitative test requires that a party "engage in financial contracts as a counterparty on both sides in one or more financial markets". The quantitative test measures the volume of a party's activity in the derivatives markets. If a party has entered into financial contracts totalling at least $1 billion in outstanding notional principal amount, it will meet the quantitative test. It will also satisfy the test if it can demonstrate that it has financial contracts with gross mark to market positions of at least $100 million. Financial contracts include securities contracts, commodity contracts, forward contracts, repurchase agreements, swap agreements and any similar agreement as defined in the FDIA (12 USC, Section 1821(e)(8)(D)(i)).

OTHER ISSUES

Substitution

Frequently, a pledgor will discover that it has pledged collateral that it now requires for other uses and wants to substitute that collateral with different collateral. Secured parties have been concerned that providing for such substitution may affect the attachment and perfection of their security interests. However, the official comments to New York's UCC indicate that such substitution should not affect the secured party's rights in the collateral. (See Official Comment 7 to UCC, Section 8-106.)

Care of collateral

A secured party under New York law generally has a duty of reasonable care with respect to the collateral that it holds from the pledgor (NYUCC, Section 9-207). Generally, such a duty would require that the secured party keep the collateral identifiable which would restrict the secured party from commingling it with other collateral or property. However, if the collateral is considered to be "fungible collateral" there is no such duty. The market generally considers cash and US treasury securities to be fungible collateral.

Rehypothecation

As explained above, Paragraph 6(c) of the NY CSA permits what is commonly referred to as rehypothecation or "use rights". This permits a dealer to rehypothecate or "use" for its own purposes the posted collateral, subject to the obligation to return the collateral once the pledgor has satisfied all its obligations under the ISDA Master Agreement. Dealers will repo this collateral or may even repledge it as security for their own obligations.

There are two issues with respect to rehypothecation. The first is whether a secured party risks losing its security interest if it rehypothecates the collateral. The second is whether the pledgor faces any risk in permitting the secured party to rehypothecate the collateral that it has pledged.

There is some concern that a secured party may be required actually to maintain possession or control of collateral pledged to it at all times. By rehypothecating the collateral through a repurchase transaction, there may be an argument that the secured party no longer controls that collateral. It is generally believed, however, that the New York statutes do not require such continuous control in order for the secured party to maintain its security interest, only that the secured party was in possession of the pledged collateral when the collateral was initially pledged.

There has also been some concern that rehypothecation potentially represents a new risk for a pledgor. By agreeing to rehypothecation, there is the possibility that the secured party could become insolvent and, therefore, be unable to return the posted collateral after the pledgor has met its payment obligations. The pledgor could possibly end up having met its contractual payment obligations under a transaction yet not have the collateral returned to it because it was no longer in the secured party's possession. This is because a pledgor only has a contractual right to the return of the collateral if it agrees to rehypothecation.

The pledgor, however, is probably protected against this possibility by its set off rights. If the secured party became insolvent, the pledgor would set off the amount that it owes the secured party against the collateral held by the secured party. Both the Schedule to the ISDA Master Agreement and the New York Law CSA generally give the pledgor such a set off right. This contractual right of set off should be recognised under applicable US state, banking and bankruptcy law. The pledgor also has a set off right under the New York set off statute (NY Debt & Cred. Law, Section 151) or under common law.

The set off right, however, would not fully protect the pledgor in the event that it had overcollateralised its obligation to the secured party. The set off would only protect it up to the amount owing to the secured party. The pledgor would probably be a general creditor with respect to any excess collateral.

Capacity to pledge collateral

As with European documentation, it is important that the US party has the capacity to enter into derivative transactions and provide collateral. Where a US entity is concerned, however, there is no precedent under New York law where a party has been found to lack the capacity to enter into derivatives and provide collateral.

Unfortunately, there are no statutory protections against ultra vires actions in this area as are found in English law as discussed above. In contrast to England, US parties generally have not suggested or pushed for such legislation in the US.

Generally, US dealers (whether they are a bank or non-bank entity) take the position that such capacity is understood and such powers are part of its business as a dealer. A foreign party can generally eliminate such concerns, however, by requesting that the US party deliver a secretary's certificate that certifies that its board of directors has approved such actions.

A foreign party may want to be more vigilant, however, when dealing with non-dealers such as government entities, pension plans and similar entities that are governed by special statutory rules and regulations. For example, it was suggested by some in the Orange County repo litigation that the Orange County government might have lacked authority to engage in such transactions.

Cash collateral pledged and held outside of the State of New York

There has been much confusion outside of the US with respect to pledging collateral to US counterparties that are located in a state other than the State of New York. Because most over-the-counter derivative activity has been centred in New York, non-US parties have become comfortable posting collateral to New York counterparties who hold it in New York. There are, however, several large dealers whose home offices are not located in New York and who insist on holding cash collateral outside of New York.

Most US counterparties located outside of New York will generally agree to hold collateral in the form of securities in New York. However, these same dealers generally insist on holding cash at their home offices located outside of New York. This issue typically arises with dealers located in the State of Illinois or the State of North Carolina.

Security interests in pledged collateral under laws of the State of New York, the State of Illinois and the State of North Carolina are governed by the 1999 revised version of the Uniform Commercial Code (the "UCC"). This version of the UCC has been adopted and is effective in New York, Illinois and North Carolina. The 1999 revised versions of the UCC adopted by New York, Illinois and North Carolina are essentially identical, except with respect to minor differences that are not relevant to this discussion.

As discussed above, to obtain and exercise rights with respect to a security interest in collateral, the UCC provides that a security interest must first "attach" and then be "perfected". Once the security interest has attached to the collateral, then the secured party may exercise its rights against the pledgor with respect to the collateral. For a party to exercise its rights against third parties, however, the security interest must also be perfected. This typically requires the secured party either expressly or indirectly to give third parties notice that the security interest has attached.

Under each of the New York, the Illinois and North Carolina UCC, the secured party perfects its security interest in Cash by taking possession (UCC, Section 9-313(a)). Prior to the 1999 revisions, courts had held that a party could not take a security interest in a deposit under the UCC; instead it could be taken under common law. The 1999 revisions, however, now provide that a secured party may expressly take a security interest in a deposit account. The New York Law CSA presumes that possession of Cash will occur through deposit accounts controlled by the secured party. For example, the New York Law CSA provides in its Paragraph 13 that Transfers of Cash will be made by wire transfers and held in deposit accounts.

Under the UCC, secured parties prove their possession of Cash and perfect their security interest therein by taking a security interest in the deposit account that holds the pledged Cash. The ISDA US Collateral opinion given by Cravath, Swaine and Moore follows this same line of analysis. Under the New York, Illinois and North Carolina UCC, a "deposit account" is defined in the UCC as "a demand, time, savings, passbook, or similar account maintained with a bank" (UCC, Section 9-102(29)).

The New York Law CSA is not a freestanding agreement, but rather supplements and forms a part of the ISDA Master Agreement. Accordingly, the New York Law CSA is governed by the law designated by the parties to govern the ISDA Master Agreement. This is almost always New York law if the New York Law CSA is chosen.

Section 5-1401 of the New York General Obligation Law provides that the parties may choose New York law to govern an agreement, regardless of "whether or not such contract, agreement or undertaking bears a reasonable relation to [New York State]". Therefore, the ISDA Master Agreement and the New York Law CSA will be governed by New York law. However, Section 5-1401 provides that "This section shall not apply to any contract, agreement or undertaking . . . to the extent provided to the contrary in subsection two of section 1-105 of the uniform commercial code".

NY UCC, Section 1-105 provides that the parties generally can designate that the New York UCC will govern their rights and duties with respect to pledged collateral. However, Section 1-105 provides that the conflict of law rules found in NY UCC, Section 9-304 will govern the perfection and priority of a security interest in a deposit account, regardless of the agreement of the parties.

NY UCC, Section 9-304 provides that "the local law of a bank's jurisdiction governs perfection, the effect of perfection or nonperfection, and the priority of a security interest in a deposit account maintained with that bank". Because the bank holding the pledged deposit account is often located in either Illinois or North Carolina, Illinois or North Carolina law will, therefore, govern the perfection and priority of the security interest in the deposit account holding the Cash pledged by the non-US pledgor.

Both the Illinois and North Carolina UCC, Section 9-312(b) provide that a security interest in a deposit account is perfected by taking control of the deposit account as described in UCC, Section 9-314. Control of a deposit account under UCC, Section 9-314 is taken as set forth in UCC, Section 9-104. Under UCC, Section 9-104(a)(1), a bank has taken control of a deposit account if "the secured party is the bank with which the deposit account is maintained". Under either Illinois or North Carolina law, the US secured party should have a perfected security interest in any deposit account that it maintains for the purpose of holding Cash pledged to it.

It is important to remember that the perfection provisions under the NY UCC are identical with those of the Illinois UCC or North Carolina UCC.

Even if the New York, Illinois and North Carolina UCC were not identical, this should not generally concern a foreign pledgor. First, the principal risk of holding collateral still rests with the secured party not the foreign pledgor that is pledging it. It is up to the US secured party holding the collateral to determine how to attach and perfect its interests in the posted collateral. The worst that can happen is that the US secured party fails to perfect its interest in the posted collateral and is, therefore, unable to exercise its rights under the New York Law CSA. The non-US pledgor presumably would hold collateral pledged to it by the US party in New York.

Some non-US parties have suggested that obligations that are collateralised outside of New York should be "ringfenced" because there is no ISDA legal opinion governing the enforceability of security interests in states other than the State of New York. Although there is no non-New York US legal opinion, the author has never encountered a situation where there was concern that a security interest attached and perfected in a state other than New York could not be enforced. In addition, the risk of the security interest being unenforceable would still rest with the US secured party that chooses to hold the collateral outside of New York and not with the foreign pledgor.

OTHER ENFORCEMENT CONCERNS

Non-US parties are often concerned about dealing with the non-New York head office of a US counterparty. There are several large US dealers with their head offices located outside of New York and there are even a few large foreign banks with US branch offices located outside of New York. Non-US parties are concerned about whether the close-out netting provisions found in the ISDA Master Agreement will be enforced in the event of an insolvency of these US dealers.

Initially, non-US parties should remember that FDICIA (as discussed above) will always enforce close-out netting between "financial institutions" under the ISDA Master Agreement, provided that the Agreement is governed by US Federal or state law. Even if the ISDA Master Agreement is not governed by US Federal or state law, there is legislation before Congress that would broaden FDICIA to include Agreements governed by non-US law such as English law. In addition, as discussed above, the financial institutions themselves do not need to be chartered under US Federal or state law to qualify as a financial institution; they only need to meet the definition in order to benefit from FDICIA.

There should be little concern about a US dealer that is a national bank, even if its home office is outside of New York. A national bank is organised under the laws of the US and is regulated by the Office of the Comptroller of the Currency. The netting protections found in FIRREA will ensure that close-out netting provisions (as discussed above) will be enforced.

There should also be little concern about a US dealer that is a state chartered bank or an insured depository institution (i.e. the bank accepts deposits insured by the Federal Deposit Insurance Corporation). The netting protections found in FIRREA (as discussed above) will ensure that close-out netting provisions will be enforced for an insured depository institution.

There are two situations that may be more problematic. The first is a state chartered bank that is not an insured depository institution or that is not chartered under New York state law. The second is a foreign bank that has a US branch located outside of New York. The first concern is that such institutions would not be subject to the netting protection provisions of either FIRREA or the US Bankruptcy Code. Most state banking laws (other than those of New York) do not have express provisions that protect netting for a state chartered bank or for a US branch of a foreign bank. Because of this, there may be some concern that a state banking authority may engage in ringfencing in the event that the bank or branch became insolvent.

This may be less problematic than it appears, however. First, assuming that both parties are financial institutions and the ISDA is governed by New York law, they would still be subject to the netting protection provisions of FDICIA. As explained above, even if the ISDA Master Agreement is not governed by US Federal or state law, there is currently legislation pending before Congress that will expand FDICIA's reach by including ISDA Master Agreements governed by non-US law.

Second, there is no authority that a state banking authority would engage in ringfencing in the event of such an insolvency. This is still an issue that many state banking authorities (unlike New York's) have never had to addresss.

Finally, the author is unaware of any OTC derivatives dealer that is a state chartered bank that is not an insured depository or is not chartered under New York state law. There are also few if any US branches of foreign banks that are not licensed in New York and many of these probably have some kind of an office or branch in New York that they could utilise for these particular trading relationships.

Credit issues relating to collateral

4

Hedge funds

Other duties

Risks

The Basel II Capital Accord

The future

Collateral is primarily a credit risk mitigation technique. It alleviates a party's concerns about its counterparty's creditworthiness, essentially by substituting the credit risk of the collateral issuer.

Other credit risk reduction techniques are netting, guarantees, letters of credit, credit derivatives, close-out netting, break clauses or not trading with the counterparty at all.

In this chapter credit risk is the probability of a counterparty defaulting on its future payment obligations.

As stated in Chapter 1, taking collateral is no substitute for a full credit analysis of your counterparty and it does not eliminate credit risk. It just improves your rate of recovery in the event of your counterparty's default or bankruptcy, sometimes substantially. However, as we also pointed out this improvement in counterparty credit risk could be offset by possible legal, documentation and operational risks. In addition, collateral has no bearing on your counterparty's default probability or credit rating.

Collateral offsets credit exposure because it can be claimed upon if the counterparty defaults on its obligations during the Transaction's life. Collateral is also convenient. It is not as capital intensive as a Triple A special purpose vehicle; it does not involve the cumbersome procedures of early termination provisions; or involve third parties with guarantees.

As far as collateral management is concerned, a credit department is likely to concern itself with the following matters:

- **establishment of collateral management risk guidelines;**
- **establishment of parameters for Independent Amount, Threshold and Minimum Transfer Amounts often using formal credit ratings to formulate an appropriate matrix;**
- **scope of products to be collateralised and location of branches;**
- **establishment of a haircut methodology;**
- **establishing choice of eligible collateral for the institution;**
- **establishing collateral parameters for certain categories of counterparties;**
- **processing of collateralised trading line applications where special considerations apply (e.g. hedge funds);**
- **considering policy exceptions requested by counterparties;**
- **considering the impact of the following risks:**
  - **Issuer or Position Risk;**
  - **Delivery Risk;**
  - **Custodian Risk;**
  - **Legal Risk;**
  - **Market Risk;**

- Concentration Risk;
- Correlation Risk;
- Liquidity Risk;
- Liquidation Risk;
- Operational Risk;
- FX Risk.

ESTABLISHMENT OF COLLATERAL MANAGEMENT RISK GUIDELINES

When it is proposed to establish a collateral management unit and periodically thereafter, the credit function will be involved in formulating risk guidelines for the institution's collateralised derivatives business and for reviewing and updating them. This is best achieved through discussions with the collateral management unit who would usually propose what they want, taking into account the day-to-day practicalities of collateral management itself.

First and foremost, the credit function will be concerned with the frequency of marking the derivatives exposure to market and valuing any collateral already held. Ideally the credit function would want this done on a daily basis (this is favoured by regulators), so that any collateral shortfall can be called for and transferred either on the same day (e.g. for cash), or within two to three Local Business Days for securities. This limits the time during which the institution's risk exposure is uncovered to a one to three Local Business Day timescale. It also avoids the danger of "stale prices" where illiquid collateral is taken and up to date prices are in short supply. Collateralisation, therefore, takes into account not only current exposure but also potential future credit exposure between mark to market and collateral transfer dates.

Second, the credit function will want to determine the likely timescale for realising its collateral upon a counterparty's default or insolvency. In Figure 2.8 in Chapter 2, we saw that it was possible for a 14 day period to elapse before securities collateral could be realised. Please note that this did include a period where a dispute had arisen.

Credit officers are, therefore, interested both in volatility of exposure and volatility of collateral valuations. They seek to protect against these through the respective use of initial margin and haircuts.

INITIAL MARGIN

Initial margin is collateral which may be offered up front by one or both parties to the collateral agreement. Normally initial margin may be required from the weaker of the two parties. A well rated bank is very unlikely to put up initial margin for its own liabilities. Occasionally, a letter of credit or guarantee is offered to cover the initial margin requirement but more normally cash collateral is taken. This could be a fixed sum such as US$ 5 million or a small percentage of the notional amount of individual transactions based upon their maturity plus an add on for volatility.

As mentioned in Chapter 2, the *ISDA Collateral Survey 2000* estimated that initial margin applied in 20% of collateral agreements. Initial margin is held separately throughout the collateral arrangement's life and is not used in exposure calculations. It serves as a buffer or comfort. ISDA covers initial margin under the term Independent Amount. Confusingly, this term also covers amounts which are paid over later by a collateral giver and which *are* included in the exposure calculations. The situation is much clearer in the *2001 ISDA Margin Provisions* where initial margin is called Lock-Up Margin and the other sort of margin is called Additional Margin Amount.

Independent Amounts are used as add-ons to Exposure to reflect the possible increase in Exposure that may occur between Valuation Dates due to volatility in mark to market values or between the time collateral is called for and actually delivered.

HAIRCUTS

While initial margin tries to deal with the volatility of exposure, "haircuts" deal with the volatility of collateral price movements between the time of the margin call and receipt of the collateral as well as covering the likely costs of liquidating assets (e.g. securities selling commissions).

Collateral is normally valued using bid prices from a major automated price information service like Reuters, Telerate or Bloomberg.

A haircut is a discount applied to the value of your collateral to cover the worst expected price movements over the mark to market frequency period and a holding period if collateral needs to be liquidated because of a default. It provides a cushion of additional value to the collateral taker. Typical haircuts are 0% for cash and between 1% and 5% for government securities up to ten years' remaining maturity. Corporate bonds often attract a 5–10% haircut depending upon tenor; equities up to 40%. Haircuts can, in disaster scenarios, be very inaccurate. Witness the 1998 Russian debt crisis where the value of Russian GKOs fell 80% in value in a short time. No institution had a haircut of that level for them.

A haircut being a discount on your security value, means that more collateral has to be given to cover the exposure. This is why some people talk about "overcollateralisation", e.g. with a 5% haircut, 105% of the security value needs to be given to cover the net exposure. The longer the maturity or the more volatile the collateral price movements, the higher the haircut should be. Some banks apply a 10% haircut to government securities whose residual maturity exceeds ten years. Tenors should be measured in residual maturities and not original maturities because prices are based upon an instrument's residual maturity. Institutions should review their haircut percentages every six to twelve months to assess whether they are still reasonable.

Haircuts provide an extra cushion to protect collateral value between Valuation Dates or during a liquidation period. They are highly correlated to the tenor and price volatility of the collateral.

Haircuts should not be adjusted for counterparty risk. By margining you automatically reduce counterparty credit risk but it is not a substitute for a full credit analysis. To believe it may result in a haircut becoming a close shave!

THRESHOLDS

A Threshold is the unsecured exposure you are prepared to allow your counterparty or receive from him before any collateral becomes callable. This could be a fixed sum of money or it may be linked to a credit ratings matrix. Thresholds are an important factor in operating a collateral policy.

The credit function will also decide an appropriate level for Threshold either on a credit ratings basis or individually in certain cases. Figure 2.3 in Chapter 2 gives an example of the former.

If you are concerned about the counterparty's credit quality you would probably want to apply a low or zero Threshold to them.

Some institutions are more interested in the regulatory capital savings possibilities of collateral. To maximise these they propose a zero Threshold each way. This is unlikely to be acceptable to counterparties which cannot obtain such savings, e.g. corporates.

MINIMUM TRANSFER AMOUNTS

The credit function is likely to be only marginally involved in setting Minimum Transfer Amounts to avoid costly transfers of small amounts of collateral. At least initially Operations or Collateral Management will set appropriate levels for this. Minimum Transfer Amounts vary from US$ 50,000 to US$ 1 million. However, a credit function will be involved initially if it is decided to link Minimum Transfer Amounts to formal credit ratings as in Figure 2.3 in Chapter 2. Otherwise the credit function is only likely to be interested where the Minimum Transfer Amount is the control mechanism for the level of unsecured exposure (i.e. where there is a zero Threshold). In these circumstances, the credit function would, therefore, focus on the combined level of the Threshold and Minimum Transfer Amount.

For example, assume that the Threshold is US$ 10 million and the Minimum Transfer Amount is US$ 1 million. Your counterparty effectively does not need to transfer collateral until your exposure level on them reaches US$ 11 million.

ELIGIBLE COLLATERAL

When you think about it, collateral is in great demand. Apart from collateralising derivatives it is needed in the following circumstances:

- **for repos and securities lending;**
- **in Euroclear it is normal for all credit lines to be secured;**
- **the Target Euro payments system uses high quality collateral to secure all intra day payments.**

This means that collateral could become a scarce resource. A highly restrictive collateral policy (cash and G7 government securities only) may be good for gaining regulatory capital benefits, but could be bad for diversification, client relationships and business facilitation and might push up collateral prices if everyone is chasing the same collateral types. In addition, with G7 government debt levels falling especially in the US, this also is creating a scarcity of such paper.

For this reason some of the larger banks have expanded their eligible collateral to the following:

- **cash in currencies where they make markets;**
- **government securities (often direct obligations of G10 countries);**
- **US government agency securities such as Fannie Mae or Freddie Mac debt securities;**
- **mortgage backed securities;**
- **corporate bonds/commercial paper;**
- **bank Letters of Credit and guarantees;**
- **equities.**

Of course, each of these will be subject to various haircuts (cash, though, invariably has a 0% haircut). The credit function will decide on these. A typical example which might appear in Paragraph 11 of an English Law CSA is set out in Figure 4.1. Many smaller banks and institutions new to collateralisation will only offer cash as collateral in the first instance because it is easiest to value and transfer. However, where they do expand the range of their eligible collateral they will need to have good collateral management systems and understand the collateral types well in order to avoid substituting or adding collateral risk for or to credit risk.

In all cases collateral should only be accepted where there is a high degree of legal certainty about the collateral taker's ability to enforce the collateral agreement and realise the collateral if a counterparty defaults or becomes insolvent.

Example of eligible collateral from the English Law CSA   FIG.

	Party A	Party B	Valuation Percentage
(A) cash in an Eligible Currency	X	X	100%
(B) negotiable debt obligations issued by the Government of the United States of America, the United Kingdom or Germany having a remaining maturity of not more than one year	X	X	98%
(C) negotiable debt obligations issued by the Government of the United States of America, the United Kingdom or Germany having a remaining maturity of more than one year but not more than ten years	X	X	95%
(D) negotiable debt obligations issued by the Government of the United States of America, the United Kingdom or Germany having a remaining maturity of more than ten years	X	X	90%

SCOPE OF COLLATERALISATION

As taking collateral has become a more established credit risk mitigation technique, credit functions are keen to extend the range of derivatives exposure they want covered by eligible collateral. They also want to cover all branches through which they can value collateral and exposure through automatic feeds.

The scope for doing this will depend upon the sophistication of their counterparties' systems. Products typically proposed for collateralisation are:

- interest rate swaps and options;
- cross currency swaps;
- forward rate agreements;
- commodity derivatives;
- equity derivatives;
- bond options;

- credit derivatives;
- foreign exchange;
- currency options.

If you are entering a collateralised relationship with a counterparty, it is better to go the whole hog. Excluding some transactions from the collateral arrangements leaves unsecured credit risk exposure and in a close-out situation it may be difficult to co-ordinate partial collateralisation with close-out netting for all transactions. In the past, separate ISDA Master Agreements for collateralised and uncollateralised transactions were the only solution but now parties often prefer to amend the definition of Exposure in its fourth line by replacing the word "Transactions" by the term Collateralised Transactions (which is also defined) and with its scope usually set out in an Appendix. There is an example of this on pp. 185–187. The result is that only agreed Transactions are collateralised.

ESTABLISHING A POLICY FOR ELIGIBLE COLLATERAL

The credit function will liaise closely with the Collateral Management Unit on this and, in the early days of its involvement with collateral, may limit eligible collateral to Euro, US Dollar or Sterling cash and G10 government securities rated AA or above. It will also set the haircuts for these. Eventually these requirements may be relaxed and different kinds of collateral accepted if the business case for doing so is very convincing and to do otherwise would result in the loss of lucrative and safe business.

SPECIAL COUNTERPARTIES

Credit functions often have to consider what special provisions might need to apply to certain counterparties. Typically these are:

- sovereigns
- supranational entities
- hedge funds.

SOVEREIGNS

Generally speaking a sovereign entity especially in Europe may well insist upon the following:

- a Threshold of Infinity for itself where it has a Triple A rating. All the G7 countries have such ratings;

- one-way collateralisation from their counterparty. This is achieved through their Threshold of Infinity or a simple statement that the collateral agreement is one-way;

- Specified Conditions (see pp. 227 and 262–263 for an explanation of this term) if an ISDA English Law Credit Support Deed or New York Law CSA is used for the non-sovereign counterparty.

SUPRANATIONAL ENTITIES

Supranational entities include such bodies as the European Bank for Reconstruction and Development, the European Central Bank and the World Bank.

Again, if these are Triple A rated they may require the same Threshold of Infinity and one-way collateral in their favour. Alternatively, if they accepted two-way collateralisation they might propose a very high Threshold for themselves, e.g. US$ 150 million, making it unlikely that they would ever have to put up collateral.

HEDGE FUNDS

Hedge funds are at the other end of the credit spectrum. There are numerous types of hedge funds which reflect different investment styles, product lines and geographic regions. They use complex computer investment programmes and strategies to enhance returns on their investments. They make frequent use of leverage, are usually unrated, offshore and lightly regulated. Consequently, banks will normally only deal with them on a collateralised basis.

Credit officers are concerned about the management and performance of the hedge fund and will usually require Additional Termination Events in the ISDA Master Agreement in respect of:

- a Minimum Net Asset Value to be maintained at all times; or

- maximum permitted declines in Net Asset Values measured over agreed periods of time; and

- resignation of key investment managers.

ISDA Master Agreement Schedules and Credit Support Annexes involving hedge funds are often intensively negotiated by both parties. Hedge funds are usually very sophisticated and thorough negotiators.

Credit functions would typically want to apply initial margin requirements and low Thresholds to them. They will also usually require external legal opinions on a hedge fund's capacity to enter into derivatives transactions which are collateralised and, as with many other counterparty types will also want to ensure that close-out netting and collateral realisation are easily enforceable in the hedge fund's jurisdiction of incorporation.

The largest hedge funds may well refuse to pay for legal opinions on their own capacity to transact and collateralise and the bank may well need to pay for these itself.

OTHER DUTIES

As well as setting policy, credit units process applications for dealing lines as well as evaluating concessions sought by counterparties from the collateral documentation negotiation policy they have issued. Typically these concessions relate to the level of initial margin and Threshold, nature of acceptable collateral and the frequency of marking to market.

RISKS

It is, of course, a credit issue whether or not collateral is taken. However, badly chosen collateral gives rise to unacceptable levels of price risk, liquidity risk, operational risk and legal uncertainty.

Taking collateral is, therefore, not risk free and credit units will typically be aware of the following risks for any particular counterparty:

Issuer or position risk

This is the risk that the issuer of the bond or equity used as collateral will seriously default or go bust during the life of the collateral arrangement. The credit function will evaluate the likelihood of this happening and apply a haircut which it considers appropriate. This will increase recovery at least in part because the exposure will be overcollateralised. However, in an insolvency, bond prices, for instance, will probably plummet and full recovery may well not be possible. This risk can sometimes be mitigated by "the right of substitution" which may be negotiated. It can be agreed that if a security falls below a certain pre-determined credit rating or if more than a certain percentage of an issue is held as collateral, then the affected collateral will be substituted for collateral meeting the required conditions.

Delivery risk

This is simply the risk that the cash or securities collateral is not delivered within the agreed deadline following a collateral call. This could lead to an Event of Default and close-out of all Transactions under the ISDA Master Agreement.

Custodian risk

If securities collateral is taken under an ISDA English Law Credit Support Deed or a New York Law CSA it might be placed with a custodian for safekeeping. In the respective Paragraphs 13 of those two collateral agreements, parties can include certain criteria which the custodian has to fulfil before securities collateral can be placed with it. These criteria typically include:

- minimum credit rating or level of assets held;
- minimum level of share capital and reserves;
- limitations on jurisdictions where collateral may be held;
- the custodian (if one of the parties to the collateral agreement) is not a Defaulting Party nor subject to an unsecured Specified Condition.

Custodian risk typically takes four forms, viz:

(a) the custodian becomes insolvent. To mitigate this risk, apart from pre-vetting the custodian, it is also important to know if the custodian commingles securities with those of its other custody clients. If so, (see (d) below) it may prove difficult to reclaim collateral held in the event of the custodian's insolvency because the collateral itself may be difficult to identify. The preference should be for collateral to be held in segregated accounts which, in theory at least, should make it easier to identify the collateral and therefore to reclaim it;

(b) the custodian deposits the securities collateral with another (probably foreign) sub-custodian and that sub-custodian becomes insolvent. The custodian might do this, for example, if it is a custodian in Country A and it is holding bonds issued in Country B which it considers could be administered more effectively if sub-deposited with a custodian in Country B;

(c) a party agrees that instead of pledging or transferring collateral to it, its counterparty can hold the collateral on its behalf in a segregated account. It might do this if it was new to collateralisation and had made no arrangements to hold collateral either in-house or with an external custodian. In other words, it allows its counterparty to hold its collateral in its custody. Despite the level of trust it may have for its counterparty this is rarely a good idea because, despite a promise to hold the collateral in a segregated account, the counterparty could withdraw it, pledge it elsewhere and then go bust. In that case the original party would rank as a general, unsecured creditor;

(d) even if its custodian does not become insolvent, the danger of commingling its collateral with other collateral of the same type and class might render identification difficult if the original party was dealing with a small custodian with imperfect records. This risk represents inadequate performance by the custodian.

Legal risk

Legal risk typically arises where legal due diligence both with respect to the counterparty's capacity to enter into derivatives transactions and the collateral agreement's enforceability has not been completed properly. This is a serious risk and can invalidate the whole collateral arrangement.

First of all, it is important to verify that the ISDA Master Agreement is legally enforceable in the counterparty's jurisdiction of incorporation and that its close-out netting mechanism is positively recognised there.

Second, any ISDA opinion on the enforceability of collateral in that country should also be carefully studied and the effect of any limitations, reservations or exceptions on the type of collateral which can be taken should be evaluated by the Legal Department and reported to the credit function where significant. For instance, if bonds issued by a particular government can only be accepted as collateral if held offshore, this should be advised to the credit unit.

These ISDA opinions do not cover all types of entities and if the counterparty falls into an uncovered category the credit function will probably request that an external legal opinion is commissioned which would be paid for by the trading desk (if they agree). The details in such an opinion would need to be closely followed.

Legal risk also arises if collateral perfection formalities are not performed promptly and in the form required. The penalties can be severe and could include invalidation of the collateral arrangement. If that happened when the counterparty became insolvent it would have serious consequences on collateral realisation.

Market risk

Market risk is also called price risk and rate risk and affects both risk exposure and collateral value calculations. A movement in market rates could cause a temporary or permanent loss in value in a Transaction which is why collateral is taken. In turn the market or price risk of the collateral is primarily controlled by the haircuts applied to the collateral type, normally calculated based on historic volatility plus an add-on to cover unforeseen circumstances and coupled with the frequency of the valuation periods (daily marking to market preferred).

Concentration risk

Concentration risk arises where significant amounts of the same bond or equity issue are taken as collateral by an institution from a number of its counterparties with the unintended effect that the institution finds itself relying upon that collateral too much. Much depends on the size of an issue, but some institutions apply a single issue concentration limit of 5–10% of the total issue size or of the issuer's market capitalisation. Clearly, if these instruments are highly volatile, low maximum concentration limits and high haircuts are advisable.

These limits are meant to protect against the effects of a collapse in the instrument's price and avoid a prolonged sale of the collateral.

Concentration risk can also arise with sectors, currencies, maturities and even with custodians (if too much collateral is being held in one location).

Correlation risk

There is also the question of correlation (something corresponding to something else). Collateral correlates to its issuer.

In the case of collateral management the primary correlation concern is any direct or indirect link between the collateral's value and the creditworthiness of the counterparty itself. Clearly the higher the correlation between the two, the less value that can be ascribed to the collateral offered. In extreme cases this could totally negate the value of the collateral.

Any collateral whose value is highly or perfectly correlated to the credit worthiness of the counterparty should not be accepted or, if taken, be subject to low maximum concentration limits and high haircuts. In particular, securities issued by your counterparty itself are not acceptable collateral because this supports credit risk with the same credit risk. Caution should be exercised in accepting securities collateral in markets where the counterparty is known to be heavily exposed as a downturn in that market could well adversely affect the counterparty too.

So collateral which is highly positively correlated to the fortunes of the counterparty should not be accepted. Neither should collateral which is negatively correlated to their exposure be accepted. Negative correlation occurs where the collateral value decreases as the exposure increases usually in the same market. This can arise from a high degree of correlation between Treasury rates that might apply to the collateral and market interest rates that would apply to the exposure. A general increase in rates could cause the exposure to rise rapidly while the collateral value falls.

No correlation between the collateral and the underlying exposure is best of all. Weak correlation is next best.

Liquidity risk

This is connected with market risk and is specifically the risk that collateral realisations will be reduced and a loss made because of prevailing bid-offer spreads in the market especially where this is due to a lot of collateral being sold in a short time. This risk is increased if illiquid collateral or very large tranches of even a well rated issue or conversely "odd lots" (i.e. usually small, non-standard, amounts) are taken.

Liquidation risk

This is the risk that collateral realisations may be delayed by events in the market and an opportune selling window may be missed. Banks take account of this risk in the period they estimate for collateral realisations which underpins their collateral credit policy (see Figure 2.8 in Chapter 2 on p. 28).

Operational risk

ISDA usefully defines operational risk as "the risk of direct or indirect loss resulting from inadequate or failed internal processes, people and systems and from external events". This clearly would embrace missed collateral calls, failed deliveries, computer breakdown, human error or fraud and impractical and prejudicial provisions in collateral documentation.

Foreign exchange risk

For a small bank or company new to collateralisation of its derivatives exposure, it is best to take collateral (whether cash or securities) in the same currency as the exposure in order to avoid foreign exchange risk or mismatch risk. Where the two parties to the collateral agreement are in the same country or in the Eurozone this should be possible. Otherwise, it is likely that at least one party will need to bear this risk. Large banks with global portfolios of collateralised exposure habitually accept this risk.

The above risks highlight the need to have a well diversified, liquid collateral portfolio. This is happening as more market players become familiar with collateral types and the haircuts to apply to them. Of course, a well diversified portfolio is better protected against the effects of economic downturns.

THE BASEL II CAPITAL ACCORD

Although the Basel Committee has announced that the implementation of its revised Capital Accord has been postponed until 2005, work is still continuing on the recognition of credit risk mitigation techniques such as taking collateral. The treatment of collateral for capital allocation purposes for underlying risks falls under Pillar 1 – Minimum Capital Requirement.

The eligibility of collateral for regulatory capital relief depends upon banks fulfilling certain minimum requirements:

- the collateral taker must have clear legal rights over the collateral and be able to liquidate it following the collateral giver's default or insolvency;
- the collateral taker must have taken all steps to perfect its legal rights over the collateral;
- positive legal opinions on the collateral enforceability must have been obtained from the relevant jurisdiction. These must be updated at least annually;
- the collateral arrangements must be properly documented with a clear procedure laid down for liquidation;

- there must be a low correlation between the collateral giver's credit quality and the value of the collateral;
- robust risk management and collateral management systems must be in place;
- frequent revaluation of collateral (ideally daily) required;
- there must be disclosure on how collateral is reused.

The Basel II Accord proposes two standardised treatments of collateralised transactions, viz:

- the simple approach; or
- the comprehensive approach.

The simple approach is likely to be used by banks with relatively few collateralised transactions. As with the substitution approach of the current Accord, it will substitute the collateral issuer's risk weighting for that of the collateral giver subject to a floor of 20% (which may be reduced to 10% if certain other conditions are fulfilled).

Partial collateralisation will also be recognised in the simple approach. It will, however, entail higher capital requirements for collateralised transactions than the more sophisticated comprehensive approach. Under the simple approach the collateral must be available for the whole life of the exposure and be revalued with a minimum frequency of six months.

Under the comprehensive approach, haircuts are applied to the collateral value to protect against price volatility. After that the residual risks of the collateralised position are given a further haircut to cover the volatility of the underlying derivatives exposure and any foreign exchange conversion risk. Against this, some recognition is given for diversification achieved in a bank's collateral portfolio.

Partial collateralisation will also be recognised in this approach.

Banks must choose one approach to cover all their collateralised transactions.

Under the standardised treatment eligible collateral may include:

- cash;
- gold bullion;
- sovereign debt rated above BB-;
- corporate debt rated above BBB-;
- equities comprised in major stock indices;
- equities traded on major exchanges;
- certain collective investment scheme assets.

Supervisors may permit banks to estimate their own haircuts, but this will be limited to those banks which received supervisory approval for using their own internal market risk valuation models under the current Accord's 1996 Market Risk

Amendment. A ten business day holding period is the benchmark for haircuts in the internal estimates approach.

There is also a table of standard haircuts which is based upon this ten business day holding period, daily marking to market and collateral calls. Its current composition is set out in Figure 4.2.

Basel Committee proposals for standardised supervisory haircuts (December 2001)

FIG. 4.2

Type	Up to I year	I–5 years	Over 5 years
Sovereigns			
AAA/AA	0.5%	2%	4%
A/BBB	1%	3%	6%
BB	20%	20%	20%
Banks/Corporates			
AAA/AA	1%	4%	8%
A/BBB	2%	6%	12%
BB	N/A	N/A	N/A
Other Assets			
Cash	0%		
Main equity index shares	20%		
Other quoted shares	30%		
Gold	15%		
FX	8%		

A contingent credit risk factor is included to cover correlation risk where there is a risk of joint default under both the collateral and the underlying derivatives transaction(s).

Consideration is also being given to the treatment of maturity mismatches.

It should be borne in mind that all these elements remain proposals at this stage although clearly the Accord's treatment of collateral for capital relief purposes is taking shape.

THE FUTURE

There is a growing trend among institutions towards considering the integration of their collateral and credit risk management systems.

In a book like this, it is easy to see collateral management as the centre of the universe. In fact if you view it in the context of global credit risk platforms, netting engines and data warehouses, it becomes a small but, nonetheless, important part of an institution's overall risk and information systems.

Historically, within banks, products like repo, foreign exchange, swaps, commodities trading and options have been developed by individual (or independent!) specialists or fiefdoms. Sometimes the credit risk management system has not been well integrated with the collateral management system in relation to the product base with the result that trading lines might have been recorded as fully utilised when in fact they are wholly or partly collateralised and there was headroom for further trading both in individual countries and globally.

This situation arose because banks developed systems for these various products over time so that each tended to operate in semi-isolation from the others. It has, of course, been a challenge to integrate product trade data into a collateral management system but now some banks are looking to extend collateralisation across more products and to bolster their risk management systems in the process.

It is not too difficult to imagine that eventually banks will need to merge their various departments and desks where product collateralisation is taking place into one global margining centre. This will particularly help in identifying areas where collateral is required and the preferred types needed and areas where surplus assets are available for reuse. Automated systems can be designed to pair off likely matches and optimise the use of surplus cash or securities where they are most needed.

However, even in that brave new world, risk could still be lurking. For instance, there may be occasions where it would be better to close out deals rather than take ever increasing amounts of collateral. Moreover, a collateral manager might create unwanted concentrations of securities collateral while channeling such assets where they are most needed – an example of efficiency actually increasing risk in a collateralised portfolio.

At present no firm can net and collateralise globally in this way.

Nevertheless the collateral juggernaut is rolling along the highways of more sophisticated settlement netting and cross product collateralisation. Such a journey will both reduce risks and spawn new ones.

The English Law ISDA Credit Support Annex

5

Paragraph by paragraph analysis

Glossary of terms in Paragraph 10

Examples of Paragraph 11 provisions

This chapter sets out a paragraph by paragraph interpretation of the English Law CSA. Where greater detail is required on a particular point, reference should be made to the *User's Guide to the ISDA Credit Support Documents under English Law*.

After Paragraph 11 (the Variables Paragraph), the remainder of the chapter focuses on common and rare amendments seen in the market. Chapter 6 written by Christian Johnson on the New York Law CSA takes a similar approach.

(Bilateral Form – Transfer)[1] (ISDA Agreements subject to English Law)[2]

1 This document is not intended to create a charge or other security interest over the assets transferred under its terms. Persons intending to establish a collateral arrangement based on the creation of a charge or other security interest should consider using the ISDA Credit Support Deed (English law) or the ISDA Credit Support Annex (New York law), as appropriate.

2 This Credit Support Annex has been prepared for use with ISDA Master Agreements subject to English law. Users should consult their legal advisers as to the proper use and effect of this form and the arrangements it contemplates. In particular, users should consult their legal advisers if they wish to have the Credit Support Annex made subject to a governing law other than English law or to have the Credit Support Annex subject to a different governing law than that governing the rest of the ISDA Master Agreement (e.g., English law for the Credit Support Annex and New York law for the rest of the ISDA Master Agreement).

PARAGRAPH BY PARAGRAPH ANALYSIS

Headings

1 The English Law CSA, in its standard form, is a bilateral title transfer document meaning that collateral given under it passes fully into the ownership of the collateral taker. Footnote 1 stresses that it is not a pledge or a security interest document and if parties want to achieve that position they must use either the ISDA Credit Support Deed (English law) or the New York Law CSA.

2 This document is an English Law CSA and it is recommended that specific legal advice is necessary if it is to be subject to any other governing law. Indeed this extends in Footnote 2 to governing law mixing arrangements, e.g. English law for the Credit Support Annex and New York law for the rest of the ISDA Master Agreement. However, in practice, such a combination of these particular governing laws in these documents has not proved a problem.

ISDA®

International Swaps and Derivatives Association, Inc.

CREDIT SUPPORT ANNEX

to the Schedule to the

ISDA Master Agreement

dated as of [   ]

between

XYZ Bank plc and Counterparty

("Party A") ("Party B")

Dating and nomenclature

The English Law CSA will be dated as of the same date as the ISDA Master Agreement. It is normal to date the Agreement as of the date of the first trade between the parties, even if it is not signed until several months later. This is based on US practice where the words "as of" mean "with effect from" a specified date. Since the Annex forms part of the Agreement Schedule (see commentary on preamble below) it is dated as of the same date as the Agreement.

The parties next enter their full legal names in the spaces provided.

This Annex supplements, forms part of, and is subject to, the ISDA Master Agreement referred to above and is part of its Schedule. For the purposes of this Agreement, including, without limitation, Sections 1(c), 2(a), 5 and 6, the credit support arrangements set out in this Annex constitute a Transaction (for which this Annex constitutes the Confirmation).

Preamble

Much is going on in these five lines of text.

Technically, the Annex is described as part of the ISDA Master Agreement Schedule and, like its supplements, forms part of and is subject to the Master Agreement itself. It is not a standalone document like the ISDA Credit Support Deed (English law).

By reference the single agreement concept of Section 1(c) of the Agreement is reinforced here. This concept prevents a liquidator cherrypicking (i.e. making payments under those Transactions favourable to his insolvent client and refusing to pay on those unprofitable to it). Section 6(e) of the Agreement prevents this by effectively collapsing all the Transactions into a single net termination payment due to one party or the other.

What happens in the Annex is that eventually (in Paragraph 6) the collateral held under it is transformed into an additional Transaction which can be netted off against the net termination payment calculated by closing out all the derivatives Transactions under the Agreement itself. Technically this would be treated as if it were an Unpaid Amount (see commentary on Paragraph 6 (p. 103)).

In essence then, the most important thing about the English Law CSA is that collateral balances held by either party may be included in the close-out netting calculations under Section 6(e) of the related ISDA Master Agreement.

Therefore, the Annex relies on the close-out netting provisions of Section 6(e) of the Agreement unlike the ISDA Credit Support Deed (English law) where proprietary rights are enforced under the security interest.

The Annex is stated to be the Confirmation for the putative Transaction which is technically correct but no actual Confirmation is sent out. It is just a mechanism for legitimising the offsetting of the collateral held under the CSA against the net termination payment in a close-out situation under the ISDA Master Agreement.

The references to the Sections of the Agreement are as follows:

- Section 1(c) **Single Agreement;**
- Section 2(a) **Payments in the normal course and when an event intervenes leading to close-out;**
- Section 5 **The Agreement's Events of Default and Termination Events;**
- Section 6 **The close-out netting modus operandi.**

Paragraph 1. Interpretation

Capitalised terms not otherwise defined in this Annex or elsewhere in this Agreement have the meanings specified pursuant to Paragraph 10, and all references in this Annex to Paragraphs are to Paragraphs of this Annex. In the event of any inconsistency between this Annex and the other provisions of this Schedule, this Annex will prevail, and in the event of any inconsistency between Paragraph 11 and the other provisions of this Annex, Paragraph 11 will prevail. For the avoidance of doubt, references to "transfer" in this Annex mean, in relation to cash, payment and, in relation to other assets, delivery.

Paragraph 1. Interpretation

Paragraph 1 states that if there is any inconsistency between the Annex and the other provisions of the ISDA Schedule the Annex will prevail. However, Paragraph 11 (the Elections and Variables Paragraph) will prevail if it clashes with the other provisions of the Annex.

Paragraph 1 also clarifies certain basic matters, e.g. that the term "transfer" embraces the payment of cash and the delivery of securities and other assets as appropriate.

Paragraph 2. Credit Support Obligations

(a) *Delivery Amount*. Subject to Paragraphs 3 and 4, upon a demand made by the Transferee on or promptly following a Valuation Date, if the Delivery Amount for that Valuation Date equals or exceeds the Transferor's Minimum Transfer Amount, then the Transferor will transfer to the Transferee Eligible Credit Support having a Value as of the date of transfer at least equal to the applicable Delivery Amount (rounded pursuant to Paragraph 11(b)(iii)(D)). Unless otherwise specified in Paragraph 11(b), the "Delivery Amount" applicable to the Transferor for any Valuation Date will equal the amount by which:

(i) the Credit Support Amount

exceeds

(ii) the Value as of that Valuation Date of the Transferor's Credit Support Balance (adjusted to include any prior Delivery Amount and to exclude any prior Return Amount, the transfer of which, in either case, has not yet been completed and for which the relevant Settlement Day falls on or after such Valuation Date).

(b) *Return Amount*. Subject to Paragraphs 3 and 4, upon a demand made by the Transferor on or promptly following a Valuation Date, if the Return Amount for that Valuation Date equals or exceeds the Transferee's Minimum Transfer Amount, then the Transferee will transfer to the Transferor Equivalent Credit Support specified by the Transferor in that demand having a Value as of the date of transfer as close as practicable to the applicable Return Amount (rounded pursuant to Paragraph 11(b)(iii)(D)) and the Credit Support Balance will, upon such transfer, be reduced accordingly. Unless otherwise specified in Paragraph 11(b), the "Return Amount" applicable to the Transferee for any Valuation Date will equal the amount by which:

(i) the Value as of that Valuation Date of the Transferor's Credit Support Balance (adjusted to include any prior Delivery Amount and to exclude any prior Return Amount, the transfer of which, in either case, has not yet been completed and for which the relevant Settlement Day falls on or after such Valuation Date)

exceeds

(ii) the Credit Support Amount.

Paragraph 2. Credit Support Obligations

Essentially this Paragraph concerns collateral calls and returns and how they are calculated.

Basically, the Transferee compares his exposure to the collateral he holds and calls for more, returns any excess or does nothing depending upon the calculations after taking into account Independent Amounts, Thresholds and/or Minimum Transfer Amounts.

In Paragraph 2(a) the collateral taker (the Transferee) can call for collateral from the collateral giver (the Transferor) where his derivatives risk exposure on the Transferor is greater that the Minimum Transfer Amount applicable to the Transferor and the exposure amount exceeds the Transferor's Threshold.

The calculation of exposure of the Credit Support Amount will take into account:

- **the net mark to market valuation of all Transactions under the Agreements plus or minus;**
- **the net Independent Amounts between the parties (please see p. 15 for an explanation of this term); and**
- **any Threshold (see p. 15 for an explanation of this term) applicable to the Transferor.**

When called upon, and assuming there is no dispute, the Transferor will transfer the requested amount of collateral (the "Delivery Amount") to the Transferee. Any transfers already in transit in respect of previous collateral calls or returns are also taken into account in the calculation of the Delivery Amount.

So a Delivery Amount arises where the Transferee's risk exposure on the Transferor exceeds the level of the collateral he holds from the Transferor after taking into account Threshold, Independent Amounts and Minimum Transfer Amount and any rounding of collateral amounts transferred.

Paragraph 2(b) covers the position where the Transferee holds surplus collateral which it must return to the Transferor if it is above the Transferee's Minimum Transfer Amount *and* the Transferor calls for the return of the collateral. Please note that if the Transferor fails to make a call, the Transferee is not obliged to transfer the collateral or point this out to the Transferor. However, if a third party Valuation Agent is involved this, of course, will not arise assuming that the Valuation Agent is managing the relationship properly.

A Return Amount arises where the value of the collateral held by the Transferee exceeds its risk exposure on the Transferor and is above the Transferee's agreed Minimum Transfer Amount and Threshold.

Again with a Return Amount any collateral already in transit will be taken into account in calculating the collateral amount to be returned.

Of course, where the Transferee's exposure reduces to zero (assuming no Independent Amount applies), the Transferee will be obliged to return all collateral he holds to the Transferor.

Paragraph 3. Transfers, Calculations and Exchanges

(a) *Transfers*. All transfers under this Annex of any Eligible Credit Support, Equivalent Credit Support, Interest Amount or Equivalent Distributions shall be made in accordance with the instructions of the Transferee or Transferor, as applicable, and shall be made:

(i)   in the case of cash, by transfer into one or more bank accounts specified by the recipient;

(ii) in the case of certificated securities which cannot or which the parties have agreed will not be delivered by book-entry, by delivery in appropriate physical form to the recipient or its account accompanied by any duly executed instruments of transfer, transfer tax stamps and any other documents necessary to constitute a legally valid transfer of the transferring party's legal and beneficial title to the recipient; and

(iii) in the case of securities which the parties have agreed will be delivered by book-entry, by the giving of written instructions (including, for the avoidance of doubt, instructions given by telex, facsimile transmission or electronic messaging system) to the relevant depository institution or other entity specified by the recipient, together with a written copy of the instructions to the recipient, sufficient, if complied with, to result in a legally effective transfer of the transferring party's legal and beneficial title to the recipient.

Subject to Paragraph 4 and unless otherwise specified, if a demand for the transfer of Eligible Credit Support or Equivalent Credit Support is received by the Notification Time, then the relevant transfer will be made not later than the close of business on the Settlement Day relating to the date such demand is received; if a demand is received after the Notification Time, then the relevant transfer will be made not later than the close of business on the Settlement Day relating to the day after the date such demand is received.

(b) *Calculations*. All calculations of Value and Exposure for purposes of Paragraphs 2 and 4(a) will be made by the relevant Valuation Agent as of the relevant Valuation Time. The Valuation Agent will notify each party (or the other party, if the Valuation Agent is a party) of its calculations not later than the Notification Time on the Local Business Day following the applicable Valuation Date (or, in the case of Paragraph 4(a), following the date of calculation).

Paragraph 3. Transfers, Calculations and Exchanges

3(a) All transfers of collateral, interest on cash or coupons on securities are to be made in accordance with the instructions of the Transferor or Transferee, as appropriate:

(i)   with cash this is by transfer to the recipient's nominated bank account(s);

(ii)   with securities certificates this will involve physical delivery to the recipient or its account together with all necessary transfer documentation which will vest legal ownership of the securities in the recipient with full title guarantee;

(iii) with book entry or dematerialised securities this entails the transferring party giving written instructions in a choice of media to the recipient's central securities depository system (e.g. Euroclear or Clearstream) where he holds his account. A copy of such instructions (which must be sufficient to transfer legal ownership of the securities with full title guarantee) must be sent to the recipient.

In the normal course (i.e. no dispute is in progress), if a collateral call notice is received for a Delivery Amount or a Return Amount before the deadline (Notification Time) agreed in Paragraph 11(c)(iv), then with securities the transfer must be made no later than the close of business on the first trade settlement day thereafter in the relevant market. If the deadline is missed, transfer will occur on the next following trade settlement day in that market.

This provision was drafted to be sufficiently flexible to cover various settlement periods for different types of securities in different international domestic markets and securities settlement systems.

The Paragraph 10 definition of Settlement Day states that cash will be transferred on the next Local Business Day.

3(b) Paragraph 3(b) provides for the calculation of exposure and the value of collateral held to be made by the relevant Valuation Agent specified in Paragraph 11 for the purposes of calculating Delivery Amounts and Return Amounts both in the normal course and in disputes. The Valuation Agent will notify its calculations to the other party (or to both parties if it is a third party) by the deadline (Notification Time) on the Local Business Day after it makes its calculations.

(c) *Exchanges.*

(i) Unless otherwise specified in Paragraph 11, the Transferor may on any Local Business Day by notice inform the Transferee that it wishes to transfer to the Transferee Eligible Credit Support specified in that notice (the "New Credit Support") in exchange for certain Eligible Credit Support (the "Original Credit Support") specified in that notice comprised in the Transferor's Credit Support Balance.

(ii) If the Transferee notifies the Transferor that it has consented to the proposed exchange, (A) the Transferor will be obliged to transfer the New Credit Support to the Transferee on the first Settlement Day following the date on which it receives notice (which may be oral telephonic notice) from the Transferee of its consent and (B) the Transferee will be obliged to transfer to the Transferor Equivalent Credit Support in respect of the Original Credit Support not later than the Settlement Day following the date on which the Transferee receives the New Credit Support, unless otherwise specified in Paragraph 11(d) (the "Exchange Date"); *provided* that the Transferee will only be obliged to transfer Equivalent Credit Support with a Value as of the date of transfer as close as practicable to, but in any event not more than, the Value of the New Credit Support as of that date.

Paragraph 3(c)

Paragraph 3(c) is about substitutions of collateral.

(i) Unless prohibited in Paragraph 11, the collateral giver may request by notice to the collateral taker a substitution of part or all of the collateral it has already transferred to the collateral taker in exchange for new collateral acceptable to the collateral taker.

(ii) If the collateral taker consents to this by written or oral notice to the collateral giver, then the latter must transfer the new collateral to the collateral taker on the first trade settlement date thereafter. After it has received the new collateral, the collateral taker must return the original collateral which has been substituted no later than the trade settlement date after he has received the new collateral from the collateral giver. This will usually be the following Local Business Day. In any case, on the transfer date the collateral must be worth the same or nearly the same and in no circumstances is he obliged to retransfer original collateral worth more than the new collateral. The consent point is important at least under English law because if the Transferee were not completely free to consent or not he could be deemed not to be the true owner of the collateral and this could lead to the title transfer nature of the English Law CSA being recharacterised as a security interest or pledge which would fail for lack of registration in a liquidation situation (please refer to the discussion of this point in Chapter 3, pp. 36–37).

There is, of course, a risk for the Transferor that the Transferee could go bust just after receiving the New Credit Support and before transferring back the Equivalent Credit Support. However, this is a risk the market accepts.

Please note that technically under the English Law CSA an exchange is a sale of New Credit Support to the Transferee coupled with a sale of Equivalent Credit Support (i.e. the Original Credit Support) back to the Transferor. As both legs of the exchange are a "sale" this precludes any recharacterisation challenge.

Paragraph 4. Dispute Resolution

(a) *Disputed Calculations or Valuations.* If a party (a "Disputing Party") reasonably disputes (I) the Valuation Agent's calculation of a Delivery Amount or a Return Amount or (II) the Value of any transfer of Eligible Credit Support or Equivalent Credit Support, then:

(1) the Disputing Party will notify the other party and the Valuation Agent (if the Valuation Agent is not the other party) not later than the close of business on the Local Business Day following, in the case of (I) above, the date that the demand is received under Paragraph 2 or, in the case of (II) above, the date of transfer;

(2) in the case of (I) above, the appropriate party will transfer the undisputed amount to the other party not later than the close of business on the Settlement Day following the date that the demand is received under Paragraph 2;

(3) the parties will consult with each other in an attempt to resolve the dispute; and

(4) if they fail to resolve the dispute by the Resolution Time, then:

(i) in the case of a dispute involving a Delivery Amount or Return Amount, unless otherwise specified in Paragraph 11(e), the Valuation Agent will recalculate the Exposure and the Value as of the Recalculation Date by:

(A) utilising any calculations of that part of the Exposure attributable to the Transactions that the parties have agreed are not in dispute;

(B) calculating that part of the Exposure attributable to the Transactions in dispute by seeking four actual quotations at mid-market from Reference Market-makers for purposes of calculating Market Quotation, and taking the arithmetic average of those obtained; *provided* that if four quotations are not available for a particular Transaction, then fewer than four quotations may be used for that Transaction, and if no quotations are available for a particular Transaction, then the Valuation Agent's original calculations will be used for the Transaction; and

Paragraph 4. Dispute Resolution

(a)   If a party disputes the Valuation Agent's calculation of exposure or the value of collateral held, Paragraph 4 provides a framework for resolving the dispute if it cannot be settled informally.

Collateral disputes *always* relate to these two matters and the calculation of exposure is the most common kind of dispute. Disputes may also arise over the valuation of collateral if illiquid securities are being transferred.

Please note in Paragraph 4(a) the Disputing Party has to observe a standard of reasonableness in initiating a dispute with its counterparty.

The steps are outlined in Paragraph 4(a)(1)–(4) and involve:

(1)   a requirement for the Disputing Party to notify its counterparty or the third party Valuation Agent that it wishes to dispute the exposure calculation or collateral valuation no later than the close of business on the Local Business Day after either the date the collateral call notice is received or the date the collateral transfer has been made;

(2)   in the case of disputes over exposure calculation for collateral calls, the Disputing Party agrees to transfer the undisputed amount to the other party no later than the close of business on the trade settlement date following the date he receives the collateral call notice from the collateral giver;

(3)   the parties will attempt to resolve the dispute by the deadline nominated in Paragraph 11(e)(i) – the Resolution Time;

(4)   if they fail then:

(i)   (A)   if the dispute involves the amount of collateral called for, the Valuation Agent will recalculate his figures for exposure and collateral value (including any haircut) by reusing any calculation of the undisputed part of the exposure;

(B)   it will then approach four Reference Market-makers for mid market quotations (i.e. the average of the bid and offer prices of the Transactions concerned) for the part of the exposure calculation which is in dispute. Provided four quotations are received the arithmetic mean of these quotations is used. To this is added the exposure calculation which is not in dispute. However, fewer than four quotations may be used in the recalculation of exposure but if no quotations are available for a particular Transaction then the Valuation Agent's original calculation will be used for that Transaction because it is the only reasonable thing to do in the circumstances;

(C) utilising the procedures specified in Paragraph 11(e) (ii) for calculating the Value, if disputed, of the outstanding Credit Support Balance;

(ii) in the case of a dispute involving the Value of any transfer of Eligible Credit Support or Equivalent Credit Support, the Valuation Agent will recalculate the Value as of the date of transfer pursuant to Paragraph 11(e)(ii).

Following a recalculation pursuant to this Paragraph, the Valuation Agent will notify each party (or the other party, if the Valuation Agent is a party) as soon as possible but in any event not later than the Notification Time on the Local Business Day following the Resolution Time. The appropriate party will, upon demand following such notice given by the Valuation Agent or a resolution pursuant to (3) above and subject to Paragraph 3(a), make the appropriate transfer.

(b) *No Event of Default.* The failure by a party to make a transfer of any amount which is the subject of a dispute to which Paragraph 4(a) applies will not constitute an Event of Default for as long as the procedures set out in this Paragraph 4 are being carried out. For the avoidance of doubt, upon completion of those procedures, Section 5(a)(i) of this Agreement will apply to any failure by a party to make a transfer required under the final sentence of Paragraph 4(a) on the relevant due date.

(C) the Valuation Agent will also follow the method specified in Paragraph 11(e)(ii) for calculating the value of collateral held. This method has to be specified in Paragraph 11(e) or the dispute resolution provisions become inoperative. There is no fallback.

(ii) The Valuation Agent will directly home in on Paragraph 11(e)(ii) where the dispute solely involves the value of collateral held.

When all the recalculations have been done, the Valuation Agent will notify each party (if it is a third party) and the other party (if it is not) of the revised figures not later than the deadline (Notification Time) on the Local Business Day after the Resolution Time (i.e. the dispute resolution deadline agreed in the English Law CSA).

Once all is agreed a revised collateral call notice is re-sent and the necessary collateral transfer is made.

(b) Paragraph 4(b) clarifies that failure to transfer a disputed amount does not constitute an Event of Default under Paragraph 6 while the above process is being carried out. However, when the process is ended and the transfer is still not made then Section 5(a)(i) of the Master Agreement – Failure to Pay or Deliver – comes into play and an Event of Default will be called if the transfer is not made within three Local Business Days following notice to the party who has failed to transfer the collateral.

Paragraph 5. Transfer of Title, No Security Interest, Distributions and Interest Amount

(a) *Transfer of Title.* Each party agrees that all right, title and interest in and to any Eligible Credit Support, Equivalent Credit Support, Equivalent Distributions or Interest Amount which it transfers to the other party under the terms of this Annex shall vest in the recipient free and clear of any liens, claims, charges or encumbrances or any other interest of the transferring party or of any third person (other than a lien routinely imposed on all securities in a relevant clearance system).

(b) *No Security Interest.* Nothing in this Annex is intended to create or does create in favour of either party any mortgage, charge, lien, pledge, encumbrance or other security interest in any cash or other property transferred by one party to the other party under the terms of this Annex.

(c) *Distributions and Interest Amount.*

(i) *Distributions.* The Transferee will transfer to the Transferor not later than the Settlement Day following each Distributions Date cash, securities or other property of the same type, nominal value, description and amount as the relevant Distributions ("Equivalent Distributions") to the extent that a Delivery Amount would not be created or increased by the transfer, as calculated by the Valuation Agent (and the date of calculation will be deemed a Valuation Date for this purpose).

Paragraph 5. Transfer of Title, No Security Interest, Distributions and Interest Amount

(a) Paragraph 5(a) clearly states that each party, when making transfers of various sorts under the English Law CSA, thereby transfers outright ownership to the collateral concerned or any distributions or interest on it to the other party completely free of all encumbrances except for liens (i.e. charges) routinely imposed on all securities by clearance systems.

(b) This subparagraph categorically states that no security interest of any kind is created over collateral transferred between the parties under the English Law CSA.

(c) (i) A guiding principle of collateral arrangements is that the collateral giver should not be disadvantaged by them. While ownership of the collateral clearly passes to the collateral taker it is anticipated that at some point the collateral taker will be obliged to return the collateral to the collateral giver, e.g. when exposure moves in favour of the collateral giver or when the Transactions covered by the collateral terminate.

During this period, coupons will be paid on bonds or dividends on equity securities to the collateral taker because he will be registered as owner in the books of the issuer of the shares or bonds.

However, it is considered fair that when such a coupon or dividend is paid or if further shares are issued under what is called a scrip dividend that these are passed on 100% to the collateral giver. This is what is stipulated in Paragraph 5(c). In the world of repos this is called a "manufactured dividend", i.e. the Buyer who is the income receiver manufactures or makes a payment to the Seller because he is holding the securities over a coupon date and has received a payment from the issuer.

Where, for tax purposes, a collateral taker is reluctant or concerned about doing this, parties provide for this in Paragraph 11(h) and arrange a substitution before the coupon payment date.

Please note that when collateral transfers or income flows from the collateral taker to the collateral giver, it is preceded by the word "Equivalent" as here in "Equivalent Distributions".

However, such payments are not made if they give rise to creating or increasing a collateral call. In these circumstances, they will remain part of the collateral balance held by the collateral taker.

(ii) *Interest Amount.* Unless otherwise specified in Paragraph 11(f)(iii), the Transferee will transfer to the Transferor at the times specified in Paragraph 11(f)(ii) the relevant Interest Amount to the extent that a Delivery Amount would not be created or increased by the transfer, as calculated by the Valuation Agent (and the date of calculation will be deemed a Valuation Date for this purpose).

(ii) Interest Amount is the interest payable by the collateral taker on cash deposits he holds as collateral from the collateral giver. The frequency at which cash interest is paid over to the collateral giver is stated in Paragraph 11(f)(ii). It is usually monthly. Again it will not be paid over if it creates or increases a collateral call and will continue to be held as part of the collateral taker's balance in those circumstances. Typically such interest is paid in arrears on the first, second or third Local Business Day of the following month depending upon a party's operational capability.

Paragraph 6. Default

If an Early Termination Date is designated or deemed to occur as a result of an Event of Default in relation to a party, an amount equal to the Value of the Credit Support Balance, determined as though the Early Termination Date were a Valuation Date, will be deemed to be an Unpaid Amount due to the Transferor (which may or may not be the Defaulting Party) for purposes of Section 6(e). For the avoidance of doubt, if Market Quotation is the applicable payment measure for purposes of Section 6(e), then the Market Quotation determined under Section 6(e) in relation to the Transaction constituted by this Annex will be deemed to be zero, and, if Loss is the applicable payment measure for purposes of Section 6(e), then the Loss determined under Section 6(e) in relation to the Transaction will be limited to the Unpaid Amount representing the Value of the Credit Support Balance.

Paragraph 6. Default

Much is also going on in these few lines.

This is a technical Paragraph, but very important. First of all in a close-out situation under the Master Agreement the date on which termination calculations are made (the Early Termination Date) will be treated as if it were an exposure calculation date. The collateral previously transferred by the collateral giver to the collateral taker becomes an Unpaid Amount under the early termination provisions of Section 6 of the Master Agreement.

Close-out involves the netting off of the termination values of all Transactions under the Master Agreement and bringing Unpaid Amounts into the close-out calculations.

You will recall from the preamble to the English Law CSA that the collateral arrangements under it constitute a Transaction. This is why.

The collateral balance held by the collateral taker is deemed to be an Unpaid Amount owing to the collateral giver (who could be but need not be the Defaulting Party).

In Part 1(f) of the Master Agreement Schedule the payment measure for calculating termination payments is chosen. Market Quotation involves obtaining close-out quotations for Transactions from four leading dealers and averaging them out after discarding the highest and lowest. Loss is a more subjective measure and is the Non-defaulting Party's good faith determination of its losses and costs minus its gains. A more detailed description of the mechanics of the close-out calculations under the ISDA Master Agreement may be found on pages 77–99 of my book, *Mastering the ISDA Master Agreement* ((2002) Financial Times-Prentice Hall) in this series.

Here there is no need to obtain four quotations on the likely value of the collateral and so Market Quotation is discarded as inappropriate. It will be considered to be zero which is no help at all in calculating a "Transaction'[s]" value. Loss is used here either in its own right or as a fallback to value the Unpaid Amount requested by the Non-defaulting Party. However, Loss is limited to 100% of the collateral's value on the basis of the common law principle that in a liquidation or close-out you cannot recover more than 100% of the amount owed to you.

It should be noted that Paragraph 6 only applies to Events of Default and not Termination Events. By a Paragraph 11 amendment you can extend this to Termination Events but only those where all Transactions can potentially be closed out.

Paragraph 7. Representation

Each party represents to the other party (which representation will be deemed to be repeated as of each date on which it transfers Eligible Credit Support, Equivalent Credit Support or Equivalent Distributions) that it is the sole owner of or otherwise has the right to transfer all Eligible Credit Support, Equivalent Credit Support or Equivalent Distributions it transfers to the other party under this Annex, free and clear of any security interest, lien, encumbrance or other restriction (other than a lien routinely imposed on all securities in a relevant clearance system).

Paragraph 7. Representation

This is a representation that each transferring party confirms to the other (on each date it needs to make a transfer of various sorts) that it is the sole owner or has the sole right to transfer the collateral or any income payments it receives. It repeats that such transfers are free of all encumbrances in a similar manner as in Paragraph 5(a).

Paragraph 8. Expenses

Each party will pay its own costs and expenses (including any stamp, transfer or similar transaction tax or duty payable on any transfer it is required to make under this Annex) in connection with performing its obligations under this Annex, and neither party will be liable for any such costs and expenses incurred by the other party.

Paragraph 8. Expenses

This is a simple statement that each party will pay its own expenses (including any stamp or transfer taxes) relating to its performance obligations under the English Law CSA and will not be liable for any costs or expenses incurred by its counterparty.

Paragraph 9. Miscellaneous

(a) *Default Interest.* Other than in the case of an amount which is the subject of a dispute under Paragraph 4(a), if a Transferee fails to make, when due, any transfer of Equivalent Credit Support, Equivalent Distributions or the Interest Amount, it will be obliged to pay the Transferor (to the extent permitted under applicable law) an amount equal to interest at the Default Rate multiplied by the Value on the relevant Valuation Date of the items of property that were required to be transferred, from (and including) the date that the Equivalent Credit Support, Equivalent Distributions or Interest Amount were required to be transferred to (but excluding) the date of transfer of the Equivalent Credit Support, Equivalent Distributions or Interest Amount. This interest will be calculated on the basis of daily compounding and the actual number of days elapsed.

(b) *Good Faith and Commercially Reasonable Manner.* Performance of all obligations under this Annex, including, but not limited to, all calculations, valuations and determinations made by either party, will be made in good faith and in a commercially reasonable manner.

(c) *Demands and Notices.* All demands and notices given by a party under this Annex will be given as specified in Section 12 of this Agreement.

(d) *Specifications of Certain Matters.* Anything referred to in this Annex as being specified in Paragraph 11 also may be specified in one or more Confirmations or other documents and this Annex will be construed accordingly.

Paragraph 9. Miscellaneous

This Paragraph contains a number of protective boilerplate provisions.

(a) This sub-paragraph states that the collateral taker will pay interest at the Default Rate (i.e. 1% over the collateral giver's cost of funds to paraphrase the Master Agreement's definition of this term) on any overdue return of collateral or payment of interest on cash collateral or distributions on securities. The default interest period includes the date on which such return or payment was due to but excluding the date on which it is actually made (in accordance with the normal practice in the derivatives markets). It will also be subject to daily compounding.

(b) Each party must perform all its obligations under the English Law CSA in good faith and in a commercially reasonable manner. This level of care is also set for a Calculation Agent under the various sets of ISDA general and product Definitions.

(c) All demands and notices under the English Law CSA will be given in one of the traditional or electronic means stated in Section 12 of the Master Agreement.

(d) This tucked away provision enables any matters referred to in a Confirmation or other document which could alternatively be specified in the English Law CSA's Elections and Variables Paragraph (Paragraph 11), to be interpreted as being a provision of the English Law CSA itself. If any such use of a Confirmation is made it should state that the provision will survive the maturity of the Transaction which is the subject of the Confirmation.

Paragraph 10. Definitions
As used in this Annex:

"Base Currency" means the currency specified as such in Paragraph 11(a)(i).

"Base Currency Equivalent" means, with respect to an amount on a Valuation Date, in the case of an amount denominated in the Base Currency, such Base Currency amount and, in the case of an amount denominated in a currency other than the Base Currency (the "Other Currency"), the amount of Base Currency required to purchase such amount of the Other Currency at the spot exchange rate determined by the Valuation Agent for value on such Valuation Date.

"Credit Support Amount" means, with respect to a Transferor on a Valuation Date, (i) the Transferee's Exposure plus (ii) all Independent Amounts applicable to the Transferor, if any, minus (iii) all Independent Amounts applicable to the Transferee, if any, minus (iv) the Transferor's Threshold; *provided, however,* that the Credit Support Amount will be deemed to be zero whenever the calculation of Credit Support Amount yields a number less than zero.

"Credit Support Balance" means, with respect to a Transferor on a Valuation Date, the aggregate of all Eligible Credit Support that has been transferred to or received by the Transferee under this Annex, together with any Distributions and all proceeds of any such Eligible Credit Support or Distributions, as reduced pursuant to Paragraph 2(b), 3(c)(ii) or 6. Any Equivalent Distributions or Interest Amount (or portion of either) not transferred pursuant to Paragraph 5(c)(i) or (ii) will form part of the Credit Support Balance.

"Delivery Amount" has the meaning specified in Paragraph 2(a).

"Disputing Party" has the meaning specified in Paragraph 4.

"Distributions" means, with respect to any Eligible Credit Support comprised in the Credit Support Balance consisting of securities, all principal, interest and other payments and distributions of cash or other property to which a holder of securities of the same type, nominal value, description and amount as such Eligible Credit Support would be entitled from time to time.

"Distributions Date" means, with respect to any Eligible Credit Support comprised in the Credit Support Balance other than cash, each date on which a holder of such Eligible Credit Support is entitled to receive Distributions or, if that date is not a Local Business Day, the next following Local Business Day.

Paragraph 10. Definitions

With, no doubt, a big government health warning from lawyers, I set out below a simplified glossary of all terms in a bilateral English Law CSA.

GLOSSARY OF TERMS IN PARAGRAPH 10

Base Currency	The currency into which exposure and collateral is converted to calculate if a collateral call needs to be made.
Base Currency Equivalent	If collateral is denominated in another currency, the amount in the Base Currency needed to buy the other currency at the spot rate of exchange so as to convert it into the Base Currency.
Credit Support Amount	The net risk exposure the collateral taker has on the collateral giver and which needs to be collateralised.
Credit Support Balance	The actual amount of collateral held at any one time by the collateral taker.
Delivery Amount	The amount of collateral the collateral giver needs to deliver if he agrees with a collateral call from the collateral taker.
Disputing Party	A party who disputes the other party's calculation of Transaction values in determining risk exposure and/or the value of any collateral held or to be returned.
Distributions	Periodic payments of interest or dividends on bonds or shares by issuers of the same to their holders.
Distributions Date	The date upon which holders of bonds or shares are entitled to receive interest or dividends from their issuers.

"Eligible Credit Support" means, with respect to a party, the items, if any, specified as such for that party in Paragraph 11(b)(ii) including, in relation to any securities, if applicable, the proceeds of any redemption in whole or in part of such securities by the relevant issuer.

"Eligible Currency" means each currency specified as such in Paragraph 11(a)(ii), if such currency is freely available.

"Equivalent Credit Support" means, in relation to any Eligible Credit Support comprised in the Credit Support Balance, Eligible Credit Support of the same type, nominal value, description and amount as that Eligible Credit Support.

"Equivalent Distributions" has the meaning specified in Paragraph 5(c)(i).

"Exchange Date" has the meaning specified in Paragraph 11(d).

"Exposure" means, with respect to a party on a Valuation Date and subject to Paragraph 4 in the case of a dispute, the amount, if any, that would be payable to that party by the other party (expressed as a positive number) or by that party to the other party (expressed as a negative number) pursuant to Section 6(e)(ii)(1) of this Agreement if all Transactions (other than the Transaction constituted by this Annex) were being terminated as of the relevant Valuation Time, on the basis that (i) that party is not the Affected Party and (ii) the Base Currency is the Termination Currency; *provided* that Market Quotations will be determined by the Valuation Agent on behalf of that party using its estimates at mid-market of the amounts that would be paid for Replacement Transactions (as that term is defined in the definition of "Market Quotation").

"Independent Amount" means, with respect to a party, the Base Currency Equivalent of the amount specified as such for that party in Paragraph 11(b)(iii)(A); if no amount is specified, zero.

"Interest Amount" means, with respect to an Interest Period, the aggregate sum of the Base Currency Equivalents of the amounts of interest determined for each relevant currency and calculated for each day in that Interest Period on the principal amount of the portion of the Credit Support Balance comprised of cash in such currency, determined by the Valuation Agent for each such day as follows:

(x) the amount of cash in such currency on that day; multiplied by

(y) the relevant Interest Rate in effect for that day; divided by

(z) 360 (or, in the case of pounds sterling, 365).

Eligible Credit Support	The collateral types and maturities agreed by the parties which can be transferred under the English Law CSA.
Eligible Currency	The agreed currency or currencies for cash collateral transferred under the English Law CSA.
Equivalent Credit Support	The collateral the collateral taker is obliged to return to the collateral giver when its risk exposure on the collateral giver reduces or when the collateral taker agrees a substitution. The returned collateral must be of the same issuer, class, type and issue but need not be the identically numbered bonds or shares.
Equivalent Distributions	The payment or manufactured dividend the collateral taker makes to the collateral giver of 100% of the interest or dividend he has received from the issuer.
Exchange Date	The deadline for the collateral taker to return designated previously delivered collateral to the collateral giver following an agreed substitution.
Exposure	The estimated replacement value of all Transactions (using mid market quotations from dealers) so as to calculate risk exposure. The calculation is made as if the Transactions were being closed out on the basis described in the definition.
Independent Amount	A confusing term meaning either initial margin taken at the start of a collateral relationship and not counted in risk exposure calculations, or a sum taken later in the relationship and which is counted in the risk exposure calculations.
Interest Amount	The aggregate sum of interest due on cash collateral including its conversion into the Base Currency Equivalent where interest is due on cash collateral in various currencies.

"Interest Period" means the period from (and including) the last Local Business Day on which an Interest Amount was transferred (or, if no Interest Amount has yet been transferred, the Local Business Day on which Eligible Credit Support or Equivalent Credit Support in the form of cash was transferred to or received by the Transferee) to (but excluding) the Local Business Day on which the current Interest Amount is transferred.

"Interest Rate" means, with respect to an Eligible Currency, the rate specified in Paragraph 11(f)(i) for that currency.

"Local Business Day", unless otherwise specified in Paragraph 11(h), means:

   (i)   in relation to a transfer of cash or other property (other than securities) under this Annex, a day on which commercial banks are open for business (including dealings in foreign exchange and foreign currency deposits) in the place where the relevant account is located and, if different, in the principal financial centre, if any, of the currency of such payment;

   (ii) in relation to a transfer of securities under this Annex, a day on which the clearance system agreed between the parties for delivery of the securities is open for the acceptance and execution of settlement instructions or, if delivery of the securities is contemplated by other means, a day on which commercial banks are open for business (including dealings in foreign exchange and foreign currency deposits) in the place(s) agreed between the parties for this purpose;

   (iii) in relation to a valuation under this Annex, a day on which commercial banks are open for business (including dealings in foreign exchange and foreign currency deposits) in the place of location of the Valuation Agent and in the place(s) agreed between the parties for this purpose; and

   (iv) in relation to any notice or other communication under this Annex, a day on which commercial banks are open for business (including dealings in foreign exchange and foreign currency deposits) in the place specified in the address for notice most recently provided by the recipient.

"Minimum Transfer Amount" means, with respect to a party, the amount specified as such for that party in Paragraph 11(b)(iii)(C); if no amount is specified, zero.

"New Credit Support" has the meaning specified in Paragraph 3(c)(i).

"Notification Time" has the meaning specified in Paragraph 11(c)(iv).

Interest Period	The period from the date when interest was last paid on cash collateral to the date on which it is next due to be paid.
Interest Rate	The particular benchmark interest rate (e.g. EONIA, Fed Funds) which the parties agree shall be paid on cash deposited as collateral. It may include a spread.
Local Business Day	A normal business day for commercial banks in the location required for the valuation of Transactions and collateral under the English Law CSA. With securities transfers it is a normal business day for securities clearance systems.
Minimum Transfer Amount	The agreed minimum level that the Credit Support Amount must reach after taking account of any Threshold before a party is obliged to deliver or return collateral.
New Credit Support	Where agreed by the collateral taker, collateral transferred by the collateral giver in substitution for other collateral already held by the collateral taker.
Notification Time	The agreed deadline for making a collateral call.

"Recalculation Date" means the Valuation Date that gives rise to the dispute under Paragraph 4; *provided, however*, that if a subsequent Valuation Date occurs under Paragraph 2 prior to the resolution of the dispute, then the *"Recalculation Date"* means the most recent Valuation Date under Paragraph 2.

"Resolution Time" has the meaning specified in Paragraph 11(e)(i).

"Return Amount" has the meaning specified in Paragraph 2(b).

"Settlement Day" means, in relation to a date, (i) with respect to a transfer of cash or other property (other than securities), the next Local Business Day and (ii) with respect to a transfer of securities, the first Local Business Day after such date on which settlement of a trade in the relevant securities, if effected on such date, would have been settled in accordance with customary practice when settling through the clearance system agreed between the parties for delivery of such securities or, otherwise, on the market in which such securities are principally traded (or, in either case, if there is no such customary practice, on the first Local Business Day after such date on which it is reasonably practicable to deliver such securities).

"Threshold" means, with respect to a party, the Base Currency Equivalent of the amount specified as such for that party in Paragraph 11(b)(iii)(B); if no amount is specified, zero.

"Transferee" means, in relation to each Valuation Date, the party in respect of which Exposure is a positive number and, in relation to a Credit Support Balance, the party which, subject to this Annex, owes such Credit Support Balance or, as the case may be, the Value of such Credit Support Balance to the other party.

"Transferor" means, in relation to a Transferee, the other party.

"Valuation Agent" has the meaning specified in Paragraph 11(c)(i).

"Valuation Date" means each date specified in or otherwise determined pursuant to Paragraph 11(c)(ii).

"Valuation Percentage" means, for any item of Eligible Credit Support, the percentage specified in Paragraph 11(b)(ii).

Recalculation Date	In a dispute the date or dates upon which recalculation of Transaction and collateral values are made.
Resolution Time	The agreed deadline for resolving disputes.
Return Amount	The collateral amount to be returned by the collateral taker to the collateral giver because it is surplus to the collateral taker's risk exposure on the collateral giver.
Settlement Day	For cash collateral transfers, the following Local Business Day. For securities collateral, the next Local Business Day when transfer of such securities can be completed in the normal course.
Threshold	The unsecured risk exposure each party allows the other. Collateral may only be called or returned where the risk exposure exceeds the relevant party's Threshold and Minimum Transfer Amount.
Transferee	The collateral taker.
Transferor	The collateral giver.
Valuation Agent	Either each party to the English Law CSA performing their own valuations of Transactions and collateral and making calls as appropriate, or a third party doing this for them both.
Valuation Date	The Local Business Day upon which risk exposure calculations and collateral valuations are made to determine if a collateral call is needed.
Valuation Percentage	The remaining value of collateral expressed in percentage terms after the agreed haircut has been deducted.

"Valuation Time" has the meaning specified in Paragraph 11(c)(iii).

"Value" means, for any Valuation Date or other date for which Value is calculated, and subject to Paragraph 4 in the case of a dispute, with respect to:

(i) Eligible Credit Support comprised in a Credit Support Balance that is:

    (A) an amount of cash, the Base Currency Equivalent of such amount multiplied by the applicable Valuation Percentage, if any; and

    (B) a security, the Base Currency Equivalent of the bid price obtained by the Valuation Agent multiplied by the applicable Valuation Percentage, if any; and

(ii) items that are comprised in a Credit Support Balance and are not Eligible Credit Support, zero.

Valuation Time	The reference time as at which calculations for collateral calls are made. They are often based on prices at the close of business on the Local Business Day before the Valuation Date.
Value	The agreed valuation bases in Paragraph 11(e) of the English Law CSA for cash and securities collateral required to value collateral in a dispute.

Paragraph 11. Elections and Variables

(a) *Base Currency and Eligible Currency.*

   (i) *"Base Currency"* means United States Dollars unless otherwise specified here.

   (ii) *"Eligible Currency"* means the Base Currency and each other currency specified here: ....

(b) *Credit Support Obligations.*

   (i) *Delivery Amount, Return Amount and Credit Support Amount.*

      (A) *"Delivery Amount"* has the meaning specified in Paragraph 2(a), unless otherwise specified here: ....

      (B) *"Return Amount"* has the meaning specified in Paragraph 2(b), unless otherwise specified here: ....

      (C) *"Credit Support Amount"* has the meaning specified in Paragraph 10, unless otherwise specified here: ....

   (ii) *Eligible Credit Support.* The following items will qualify as *"Eligible Credit Support"* for the party specified:

	Party A	Party B	Valuation Percentage
(A) cash in an Eligible Currency	[ ]	[ ]	[ ]%
(B) negotiable debt obligations issued by the Government of [ ] having an original maturity at issuance of not more than one year	[ ]	[ ]	[ ]%
(C) negotiable debt obligations issued by the Government of [ ] having an original maturity at issuance of more than one year but not more than 10 years	[ ]	[ ]	[ ]%
(D) negotiable debt obligations issued by the Government of [ ] having an original maturity at issuance of more than 10 years	[ ]	[ ]	[ ]%
(E) other	[ ]	[ ]	[ ]%

Paragraph 11. Elections and Variables

This is the Elections and Variables Paragraph where the parties choose the specific provisions for operating the collateralised relationship between them. Paragraph 11 is the equivalent of the ISDA Master Agreement Schedule.

For the purpose of illustrating market practice on various choices made in Paragraph 11, I have reviewed some 35 versions of Paragraph 11 to the English Law CSA used by various dealers and sophisticated end users which I consider to be a reasonable cross-section of the documentation seen in the market. An explanation of the Paragraph 11 provisions and variant wording seen in the market follows.

(iii) *Thresholds.*

    (A) *"Independent Amount"* means with respect to Party A: ......

       "Independent Amount" means with respect to Party B: ......

    (B) *"Threshold"* means with respect to Party A: ....

       "Threshold" means with respect to Party B: ....

    (C) *"Minimum Transfer Amount"* means with respect to Party A: ....

       "Minimum Transfer Amount" means with respect to Party B: ....

    (D) *"Rounding".* The Delivery Amount will be rounded up and the Return Amount will be rounded [down to the nearest integral multiple of ..../up and down to the nearest integral multiple of .... respectively].

(c) *Valuation and Timing.*

  (i) *"Valuation Agent"* means, for the purposes of Paragraphs 2 and 4, the party making the demand under Paragraph 2, and for the purposes of Paragraph 5(c) the Transferee, as applicable, unless otherwise specified here: ....

  (ii) *"Valuation Date"* means: ....

  (iii) *"Valuation Time"* means:

    [ ] the close of business in the place of location of the Valuation Agent on the Valuation Date or date of calculation, as applicable;

    [ ] the close of business on the Local Business Day immediately preceding the Valuation Date or date of calculation, as applicable;

    provided that the calculations of Value and Exposure will, as far as practicable, be made as of approximately the same time on the same date.

  (iv) *"Notification Time"* means 1:00 p.m., London time, on a Local Business Day, unless otherwise specified here: ....

(d) *Exchange Date.* *"Exchange Date"* has the meaning specified in Paragraph 3(c)(ii), unless otherwise specified here: ....

(e) **Dispute Resolution.**

(i) **"Resolution Time"** means 1:00 p.m., London time, on the Local Business Day following the date on which the notice is given that gives rise to a dispute under Paragraph 4, unless otherwise specified here: ....

(ii) **Value.** For the purpose of Paragraphs 4(a)(4)(i)(C) and 4(a)(4)(ii), the Value of the outstanding Credit Support Balance or of any transfer of Eligible Credit Support or Equivalent Credit Support, as the case may be, will be calculated as follows: ....

(iii) **Alternative.** The provisions of Paragraph 4 will apply, unless an alternative dispute resolution procedure is specified here: ....

(f) **Distributions and Interest Amount.**

(i) **Interest Rate.** The "Interest Rate" in relation to each Eligible Currency specified below will be:

Eligible Currency	Interest Rate
....	....
....	....
....	....

(ii) **Transfer of Interest Amount.** The transfer of the Interest Amount will be made on the last Local Business Day of each calendar month and on any Local Business Day that a Return Amount consisting wholly or partly of cash is transferred to the Transferor pursuant to Paragraph 2(b), unless otherwise specified here: ....

(iii) **Alternative to Interest Amount.** The provisions of Paragraph 5(c)(ii) will apply, unless otherwise specified here: ....

(g) **Addresses for Transfers.**

Party A: ....

Party B: ....

(h) Other Provisions.

(a) *Base Currency and Eligible Currency.*

    (i) *"Base Currency"* means United States Dollars unless otherwise specified here.

    (ii) *"Eligible Currency"* means the Base Currency and each other currency specified here: ....

EXAMPLES OF PARAGRAPH II PROVISIONS

(a) Base Currency and Eligible Currency

Euro and United States Dollars are the most common currencies specified as the Base Currency. I have also seen Sterling and even Japanese Yen. The Base Currency is the currency into which the collateral and the exposure are converted in order to determine if a collateral call is needed. If the underlying exposure is in Euro, then the Euro should be the Base Currency.

Eligible Currency is the currency or currencies the parties agree are acceptable for cash collateral transferred under the English Law CSA.

The Eligible Currency is sometimes just limited to cash collateral denominated in the Base Currency. The Base Currency is *always* included to which may be added one or two other mainstream currencies depending upon the scope of collateral which a party to an English Law CSA will accept.

(b) **Credit Support Obligations.**

   (i) **Delivery Amount, Return Amount and Credit Support Amount.**

      (A) *"Delivery Amount"* has the meaning specified in Paragraph 2(a), unless otherwise specified here: ....

      (B) *"Return Amount"* has the meaning specified in Paragraph 2(b), unless otherwise specified here: ....

      (C) *"Credit Support Amount"* has the meaning specified in Paragraph 10, unless otherwise specified here: ....

(b) (i) Credit Support Obligations

Most often (A), (B) and (C) remain unaltered, but should you make any changes to (A) Delivery Amount, it is important to make corresponding changes to (B) Return Amount.

(C) is sometimes amended in respect of hedge funds where the following wording may occur:

(C) **"Credit Support Amount"** means, for any Valuation Date (i) the Transferee's Exposure for that Valuation Date plus (ii) the aggregate of all Independent Amounts applicable to the Transferor, if any, minus (iii) the Transferor's Threshold; provided, however, that (x) in the case where the sum of the Independent Amounts applicable to the Transferor exceeds zero, the Credit Support Amount will not be less than the sum of all Independent Amounts applicable to the Transferor and (y) in all other cases, the Credit Support Amount will be deemed to be zero whenever the calculation of Credit Support Amount yields an amount less than zero.

The purpose of this amendment is to eliminate the subtraction of Independent Amounts applicable to the Transferee from the calculation of Credit Support Amount. Many parties view Independent Amount as akin to the margin required to be posted by futures exchanges. Even though a party's positions may be "in the money" it is still required to maintain initial margin with the futures exchange. The example in (C) above would leave the calculation of Credit Support Amount to the following:

The Transferee's Exposure

plus

all Independent Amounts applicable to the Transferor

minus

the Transferor's Threshold.

This could result in both parties holding Eligible Credit Support. The Transferor will hold collateral taken for the Transferee's Independent Amount while the Transferee will hold collateral from the Transferor following a Delivery Amount under a collateral call. Both sides are, therefore, fully collateralised.

A further amendment is usually made in the Other Provisions section of Paragraph 11, viz:

Additions to Paragraph 2. The following subparagraph (c) is hereby added to Paragraph 2 of this Annex:

(c)   *No offset.* On any Valuation Date, if either (i) each party is required to make a transfer under Paragraph 2(a) or (ii) each party is required to make a transfer under Paragraph 2(b), then the amounts of those obligations will not offset each other.

This prohibition on offset clarifies the position that collateral held by the Transferee is not to be offset against collateral it gives to a Transferor as support for its Independent Amount.

Appendix B to the *User's Guide to the ISDA Credit Support Documents under English Law* gives a useful worked example of why this is important. Its example is based upon the ISDA English law Credit Support Deed, but it can be paraphrased for the English Law CSA as follows:

On a Valuation Date, Party A makes a collateral call on Party B who transfers EUR 50 as a Delivery Amount to cover Party A's risk exposure on Party B. On the same Valuation Date Party A transfers EUR 10 to Party B in connection with an Independent Amount applying to it under the English Law CSA.

On a later Valuation Date:

The value of the collateral held by Party B for Party A's Independent Amount has reduced to EUR 9, while the risk of exposure of Party A on Party B has increased to EUR 70.

If these obligations were offset, Party B would transfer EUR 19 to Party A, which would leave each party under collateralised by EUR 1, i.e. Party A would have total collateral of EUR 69 (50+19) against a risk exposure of EUR 70 on Party B. Party B would still have collateral of EUR 9 in respect of collateral for Party A's Independent Amount.

If these obligations cannot be offset as per the prohibition above, Party A would transfer EUR 1 to Party B and Party B would transfer EUR 20 to Party A. Both would be fully collateralised.

This is particularly important where dealing with hedge funds, as no bank would want to be undercollateralised in those circumstances.

(ii) *Eligible Credit Support.* The following items will qualify as *"Eligible Credit Support"* for the party specified:

		Party A	Party B	Valuation Percentage
(A)	cash in an Eligible Currency	[ ]	[ ]	[ ]%
(B)	negotiable debt obligations issued by the Government of [ ] having an original maturity at issuance of not more than one year	[ ]	[ ]	[ ]%
(C)	negotiable debt obligations issued by the Government of [ ] having an original maturity at issuance of more than one year but not more than 10 years	[ ]	[ ]	[ ]%
(D)	negotiable debt obligations issued by the Government of [ ] having an original maturity at issuance of more than 10 years	[ ]	[ ]	[ ]%
(E)	other	[ ]	[ ]	[ ]%

(b) (ii) Eligible Credit Support

If only cash is taken as Eligible Credit Support it alone will be shown in the table. However, it is more normal to include securities as well and I reproduce the sample table shown in Figure 4.1 from the previous chapter as Figure 5.1.

		Party A	Party B	Valuation Percentage	
(A)	cash in an Eligible Currency	X	X	100%	**FIG. 5.1**
(B)	negotiable debt obligations issued by the Government of the United States of America, the United Kingdom or Germany having a remaining maturity of not more than one year	X	X	98%	
(C)	negotiable debt obligations issued by the Government of the United States of America, the United Kingdom or Germany having a remaining maturity of more than one year but not more than ten years	X	X	95%	
(D)	negotiable debt obligations issued by the Government of the United States of America, the United Kingdom or Germany having a remaining maturity of more than ten years	X	X	90%	

Here the Eligible Credit Support includes securities issued by the governments of the US, the UK and Germany. Clearly, other countries are possible such as Austria, Belgium, Canada, France, Italy, Japan and the Netherlands. This list is not exhaustive. In other jurisdictions, e.g. Spain, Portugal or South Africa, you would need to obtain or review the ISDA collateral legal opinion for the relevant country to check how robust their legal regime is in respect of taking and enforcing collateral and whether securities collateral has to be held offshore or with a particular depository.

In contrast to other countries, a wide range of securities issued by US government agencies could be taken as Eligible Credit Support. These could be:

Debt obligations of agencies and instrumentalities of the United States Government which are completely and unconditionally guaranteed by the full faith and credit of the United States as to timely payment of principal and interest; and	95%
Certificates, notes and bonds issued or directly and fully guaranteed by the Student Loan Marketing Association, Government National Mortgage Association, Federal National Mortgage Association or Federal Home Loan Mortgage Corporation.	95%

Finally, you occasionally see general wording for other Eligible Credit Support, e.g.

Such other Eligible Credit Support as the parties may from time to time agree in writing as being acceptable	To be agreed by the parties on a case by case basis.

In a bilateral English Law CSA both boxes (for Party A and Party B) would be checked and the appropriate Valuation Percentage, determined by the credit function, entered alongside.

No haircut is normally applied to Cash and so its Valuation Percentage is usually 100%.

Reviewing a cross-section of English Law CSAs, the Valuation Percentages of G7 government securities were in the range shown in Figure 5.2.

FIG. 5.2

Residual term	Valuation Percentage range
Up to one year	98% – 100%
Over one year but less than five years	95% – 97%
Over five years but less than ten years	94% – 95%
Over ten years	90%

Some market players put an upward limit on the last residual term of 20 or 30 years.

The most aggressive Valuation Percentages I saw are shown in Figure 5.3.

FIG. 5.3

Residual term	Valuation Percentage
Up to one year	100%
Over one year but less than ten years	98%
Over ten years	97%

The normal Valuation Percentage for guaranteed US agencies was 95% as shown above.

Some parties will exclude certain types of US Treasury Securities, especially inflation linked ones (see p. 437 for reasons). You might, therefore, see the following wording at the end of the Eligible Credit Support table:

> **Provided, however, that any debt obligations issued by the US Treasury Department which has a coupon or a redemption amount which is determined by reference to an inflation index shall not qualify as Eligible Credit Support. For the avoidance of doubt, Treasury Inflation Protected Securities shall not qualify as Eligible Credit Support.**

Sometimes at the end of the Eligible Credit Support table the following wording will be added:

> **Notwithstanding the foregoing, the Valuation Percentage with respect to all Eligible Credit Support shall be deemed to be 100% with respect to a Valuation Date which is an Early Termination Date designated or deemed to have occurred as a result of an Event of Default.**

The purpose of this is to limit the recovery of a Non-defaulting Party to 100% of what he is owed. Variations of this wording may be found on pp. 184–185.

(iii) *Thresholds.*

(A) "*Independent Amount*" means with respect to Party A: ....

"*Independent Amount*" means with respect to Party B: ....

(iii) Thresholds

(A) Independent Amount

As mentioned previously, Independent Amounts can be an initial amount deposited by a less creditworthy party with its counterparty before any trading takes place. In this case it is excluded from the Exposure calculations upon which any collateral call is based. Alternatively, it can be a sum which is callable after trading has occurred and may affect either party, possibly as a result of a credit ratings downgrade. This type of Independent Amount will be included in the calculation of Exposure for collateral call purposes.

An Independent Amount may be a fixed monetary sum or a percentage of the notional amount of an individual Transaction or Transactions. This is usually graduated according to the maturity of the individual Transaction. It aims to protect against mark to market volatility of Transaction values between Valuation Dates. Independent Amounts are typically lower for Transactions involving fixed income derivatives than those for equity or credit derivatives.

The effect of an Independent Amount is to increase the Credit Support Amount due by a Transferor and to reduce the Credit Support Amount due by a Transferee.

Independent Amount may not apply to either party in which case it is stated as follows:

(A) *"Independent Amount"* means with respect to Party A: Zero
"Independent Amount" means with respect to Party B: Zero

Alternatively, where it is ratings linked you may see a provision like the following:

(A) *"Independent Amount"* means with respect to Party A.: US$ 10 million if the Rating assigned to such party by S&P is BB+ or lower or by Moody's Ba1 or lower, and otherwise zero.

"Independent Amount" means with respect to Party B: US$ 10 million if the Rating assigned to such party by S&P is BB+ or lower or by Moody's Ba1 or lower, and otherwise zero.

Where the parties wish to refer to Independent Amounts in Confirmations linked to individual Transactions you might see the following wording:

(A) *"Independent Amount"* means with respect to Party B only: the aggregate sum of each of the amounts specified in any Confirmation governed by the Agreement as an "Independent Amount" (for the purpose of this definition, each an "Individual Independent Amount"), provided that, in respect of the Individual Independent Amount set out in the Confirmation relating to any given Transaction, such Individual Independent Amount shall not be taken into account in calculating the Independent Amount after such Transaction has expired.

Sometimes in hedge fund Credit Support Annexes you find Independent Amounts linked to falls in Net Asset Value rather than credit ratings as in the following example:

(A) *"Independent Amount"* for Party B means, with respect to each Transaction the greater of (i) zero, (ii) any amount specified in a Confirmation for a Transaction; and (iii) if the Net Asset Value ("NAV") (as defined in the Schedule to the Master Agreement dated as of the date hereof between Party A and Party B) of Party B declines by more than [ ]% from the NAV at a time 12 months prior to the date of any such determination, an amount equal to [ ]% of the Notional Amount.

The credit function will decide on the appropriate level of Net Asset Value decline and percentage of the Notional Amount.

With collateralisation of equity derivative transactions in respect of a less credit-worthy counterparty, I have seen the following wording for Independent Amount:

"Independent Amount" means with respect to Party B: the aggregate of (i) 50,000 GBP and (ii) 10% of the amount produced by multiplying the Number of Shares by the Initial Price for each Transaction entered into between parties.

Finally, with corporate counterparties, the term Independent Amount is sometimes abandoned in favour of Initial Margin and in one example this was defined as follows:

Calculation of Initial Margin

Initial Margin for any Valuation Date means, the aggregate of (1) with respect to interest rate swap Transactions only, the estimated Value at Risk (as specified below) of all outstanding interest rate swap Transactions as of that Valuation Date, and (2) with respect to all other Collateralised Transactions, the percentage of the notional that is specified by Party A in the relevant Confirmation to that Collateralised Transaction.

The estimated Value at Risk shall be calculated by Party A, (in accordance with its standard practices for making such a calculation) for a two week time period within a 95% confidence level.

Such wording, however, is rare.

If an Independent Amount is not specified it is deemed to be zero.

(B)   *"Threshold"* means with respect to Party A: ....
      "Threshold" means with respect to Party B: ....

(B) Threshold

The Threshold is the level of unsecured exposure each party is content to allow the other before any collateral is called. This unsecured exposure will be increased by any Minimum Transfer Amount applying to the parties.

Generally speaking Thresholds are recorded either as a monetary amount (or zero) or in the form of a credit ratings matrix. An example of the first is:

> (B) *"Threshold"* means with respect to Party A: US$ 10 million
> *"Threshold"* means with respect to Party B: US$ 5 million

An example of the second kind is:

> (B) *"Threshold"* means the amounts determined on the basis of the lower ratings assigned by either Standard & Poor's Ratings Group ("S&P"), a division of McGraw-Hill, Inc. or Moody's Investor Services, Inc. ("Moody's") to the long term, unsecured and unsubordinated debt of Party B; provided that if (x) Party B has no such ratings or (y) an Event of Default has occurred and is continuing, the Threshold with respect to the relevant party shall be zero:

S&P Rating	Moody's Rating	Threshold (US$ million)
AAA	Aaa	
AA+	Aa1	
AA	Aa2	
AA-	Aa3	
A+	A1	
A	A2	
A-	A3	
BBB+	Baa1	
BBB	Baa2	
BBB-	Baa3	
BB+	Ba1	
BB	Ba2	
BB- and below	Ba3 and below	

Again the credit function would supply the necessary figures.

From previous discussion (see p. 69), the English Law CSA can be made unilateral by assigning a Threshold of Infinity to one of the parties. Where the credit quality differential between the parties is broad, this can look quite stark:

> (B) *"Threshold"* means with respect to Party A: Infinity
> *"Threshold"* means with respect to Party B: Zero

You will also recall (see p. 66) that a zero Threshold is not only used where a counterparty is considered a weak credit but also to maximise regulatory capital savings because collateral is callable all the sooner where there is a zero Threshold. In fact, the lower the Threshold and Minimum Transfer Amount, the lower the capital that needs to be set aside by financial institutions to cover trading book risk. This in turn could have a beneficial effect on the pricing of Transactions.

If a Threshold is not specified it is deemed to be zero.

(C) *"Minimum Transfer Amount"* means with respect to Party A: ....

"Minimum Transfer Amount" means with respect to Party B: ....

(C) Minimum Transfer Amount

Minimum Transfer Amounts are designed to prevent costly transfers of low or "nuisance" amounts of collateral. Occasionally you see a Minimum Transfer Amount of zero which if combined with a zero Threshold means that you do not wish to take any unsecured risk on your counterparty.

Normally, the Minimum Transfer Amount is expressed in a fixed monetary sum, e.g. US$ 50,000 or linked to a credit ratings matrix as in the following example:

> **"Minimum Transfer Amount"** means with respect to Party A and Party B, the amount determined on the basis of the lower of the Long Term Debt Ratings in the table set forth below; provided however that if (i) a party has no Long Term Debt Ratings or (ii) an Event of Default has occurred and is continuing with respect to such party, such party's Minimum Transfer Amount shall be zero.

S&P Rating	Moody's Rating	Minimum Transfer Amount
AAA to A-	Aaa to A3	US$ 500,000
BBB+ to BB	Baa1 to Ba2	US$ 100,000
BB- and below	Ba3 and below	US$ 50,000

From my experience, Minimum Transfer Amounts tend to be larger in the US than in Europe.

A common amendment is to include a zero Minimum Transfer Amount if a party suffers an Event of Default:

> (C) **"Minimum Transfer Amount"** means, with respect to a party, US$ 100,000; provided, that if an Event of Default has occurred and is continuing, the Minimum Transfer Amount with respect to such party shall be zero.

With equity derivatives, the calculation can be a little more complicated, viz:

> **"Minimum Transfer Amount"** means with respect to Party B: the lower of (i) 10,000 GBP and (ii) on any day an amount equal to 10% of the amount produced by multiplying the Number of Shares by the Initial Price in respect of all Transactions entered into between the parties on such day.

Sometimes the Minimum Transfer Amount can shift with a decline in formal credit ratings, e.g.

> **"Minimum Transfer Amount"** means with respect to Party A: US$ 100,000 unless the Rating assigned to such party by S&P is BB+ or lower or by Moody's is Ba1 or lower, in which case the Minimum Transfer Amount means US$ 10,000.

A common amendment relates to the situation where a party's risk exposure on the other party is, or is deemed to be, zero in which case it is often stated that the Minimum Transfer Amount will also be zero:

(C) *"Minimum Transfer Amount"* means, with respect to each party, US$ 1 million; provided that (i) if an Event of Default has occurred and is continuing with respect to a party, or (ii) for the purpose of the calculation of the Return Amount where a party's Credit Support Amount is, or is deemed to be, zero, the Minimum Transfer Amount with respect to that party shall be zero and Rounding shall not apply.

OR

Notwithstanding the provisions of Paragraph 11(iii)(C), when the Credit Support Amount with respect to a party on a Valuation Date is zero, the Minimum Transfer Amount with respect to both parties shall be zero.

OR

Notwithstanding the provisions of Paragraph 11(iii)(C), when the Credit Support Amount with respect to a Transferor on a Valuation Date is zero, then for the purposes of any Return Amount due to such Transferor the Minimum Transfer Amount with respect to the Transferee shall be zero.

Where the Minimum Transfer Amount is not specified it is deemed to be zero.

You often see credit rating matrices covering Independent Amount, Thresholds and Minimum Transfer. Such matrices normally define the ratings as a new sub-paragraph (E) along the following lines:

(E) *"Rating"* means the rating issued by either Moody's Investor Services (Moody's) or Standard and Poor's Rating Group, a division of McGraw-Hill, Inc. (S&P) in respect of either party's long-term, unsecured and unsubordinated debt securities.

Because the Minimum Transfer Amount only establishes a floor for transfers it does not avoid transfers of uneven amounts of collateral. Applying a rounding convention overcomes this.

(D) *"Rounding"*. The Delivery Amount will be rounded up and the Return Amount will be rounded [down to the nearest integral multiple of ..../up and down to the nearest integral multiple of .... respectively].

(D) Rounding

One of the following options is usually selected:

- **round the Delivery and Return Amount down to the nearest integral multiple specified; or**
- **round the Delivery Amount up and the Return Amount down to the nearest integral multiple specified. (This is the most common choice.)**

If no rounding convention is specified, then the Delivery Amount and the Return Amount will not be rounded.

You would not normally specify that both Delivery and Return Amounts are to be rounded up as this could leave a Transferee undercollateralised after transferring a Return Amount.

A rounding convention can be used as an alternative to specifying a Minimum Transfer Amount. Appendix B of *The User's Guide to the ISDA Credit Support Documents under English Law* (page 70) gives an example of this.

A typical example of a rounding provision is:

(D) *Rounding*. The Delivery Amount and the Return Amount will be rounded up and down respectively to the nearest integral multiple of US$ 10,000.

(c) *Valuation and Timing.*

   (i)   *"Valuation Agent"* means, for the purposes of Paragraphs 2 and 4, the party making the demand under Paragraph 2, and for the purposes of Paragraph 5(c) the Transferee, as applicable, unless otherwise specified here: ....

(c) Valuation and Timing

(i) Valuation Agent

The Valuation Agent calculates the Delivery Amount and the Return Amount and reports these calculations to the Transferor and Transferee so that they can fulfil their obligations under Paragraph 2 of the English Law CSA.

It does this by calculating:

- the Exposure;
- the value of posted collateral;
- the Credit Support Amount; and
- the Delivery or Return Amounts

all as of the Valuation Time (see below).

The parties may specify one of themselves or a third party as the Valuation Agent. If no Valuation Agent is specified here, then the party calling for the collateral (the Transferee) under Paragraph 2(a) is the Valuation Agent. The Transferee is also the Valuation Agent for transferring Distributions or Interest Amounts under Paragraph 5(c). The Transferor would be the Valuation Agent if it were calling for a Return Amount under Paragraph 2(b).

The standard wording is most commonly used.

However, sometimes alternative provision is made where the Valuation Agent suffers an Event of Default:

(i) *"Valuation Agent"* means, for purposes of Paragraphs 2 and 4, the party making demand under Paragraph 2, and, for purposes of Paragraph 5(c), the Transferee, as applicable, unless there has occurred and is continuing any Event of Default or Potential Event of Default with respect to a party, in which case the other party shall be the Valuation Agent.

A variation on this theme allows the appointment of a third party Valuation Agent instead of the other party:

(i) *"Valuation Agent"* means, for purposes of Paragraphs 2 and 4, the party making the demand under Paragraph 2, and for purposes of Exchanges and Distributions under Paragraph 3(c) and Paragraph 5(c) respectively, the Transferee, as applicable, *unless* an Event of Default or Potential Event of Default has occurred and is continuing with respect to such party, or an Early Termination Date has been designated in connection with any such event with respect to such party. In any such event the other party shall be the Valuation Agent or may appoint a third party selected by it as Valuation Agent.

Occasionally, a large bank will insist when dealing with a much weaker counterparty that it alone should be the Valuation Agent. Then you would see the following wording:

"Valuation Agent" means, for the purposes of Paragraphs 2 and 4, Party A.

Where the counterparty has a little more bargaining power you might see:

(i) *"Valuation Agent"* means Party A and any Value shall be subject to the agreement of both parties.

Occasionally, the determination of Valuation Agent will take into account Termination Events as well as Events of Default:

(i) *"Valuation Agent"* means, for purposes of Paragraphs 2 and 4, the party making the demand under Paragraph 2, and, for purposes of Paragraph 5(c), the Transferee, as applicable, provided that in the case of an Event of Default or Termination Event the Non-Defaulting Party or, as the case may be, if there is one Affected Party, then the party which is not the Affected Party, shall be the Valuation Agent. If there are two Affected Parties, then both parties shall be Joint Valuation Agent.

(ii) *"Valuation Date"* means: ....

(ii) Valuation Date

This item must be completed as there is no ISDA fallback position here.

Valuation Date states the frequency at which exposure and collateral are revalued under the ISDA Master Agreement and English Law CSA. On each Valuation Date, the Valuation Agent must calculate the following and advise the other party/parties:

- **the Exposure;**
- **the Value of the Transferor's Credit Support Balance (if any);**
- **the Credit Support Amount;**
- **the Delivery Amount (if any); and**
- **the Return Amount (if any)**

all as at the Valuation Time (see below).

A number of frequencies are, of course, possible, e.g. daily, weekly, monthly or on a particular day of each week or month.

The most common is:

(ii) *"Valuation Date"* means any Local Business Day.

This allows for daily exposure and collateral valuation and is favoured by regulators. Sometimes parties like to specify cities too, e.g.

(ii) *"Valuation Date"* means: Each Local Business Day in Frankfurt am Main and London.

In this case, this would be where each party is located.

This arrangement can, on occasion, become quite complicated:

(ii) *"Valuation Date"* means: the first London, Frankfurt and Amsterdam Business Day on or immediately following each 15th of the month, and any other London, Frankfurt and Amsterdam Business Day designated as an additional Valuation Date by Party A or Party B **provided** that any Delivery Amount or Return Amount, as the case may be, calculated on such additional Valuation Date shall be in excess of 10 million Euro.

A somewhat too flexible arrangement could be:

(ii) *"Valuation Date"* means any Local Business Day selected by a Party.

This is only acceptable if both parties can react operationally within the same timescale.

In a unilateral Agreement the Transferee may insist on something similar as follows:

(ii) *"Valuation Date"* means any day which the Transferee elects shall be designated a Valuation Date (which designation shall be effected by the making of an applicable demand under Paragraph 2(a)).

Looking at less frequent Valuation Dates I have come across the following:

(ii) *"Valuation Date"* means each Wednesday following the Trade Date and in the case of the Termination Date or such earlier date as may be agreed that same day if that is a Wednesday or otherwise the next following Wednesday.

AND

(ii) *"Valuation Date"* means the third Local Business Day or if such day is not a Local Business Day the next following Local Business Day of each calendar week or such other Local Business Day as Party A or Party B may select.

AND

(ii) *"Valuation Date"* means the first Local Business Day of each calendar month and any other Local Business Day selected by a Party, provided, that for the avoidance of doubt, Party A and Party B agree that the same modus operandi will apply to such other Valuation Date as would apply to a Valuation Date on the first Local Business Day of each calendar month.

AND

(ii) *"Valuation Date"* means any Local Business Day in relation to which either party has designated a Valuation Date by giving the other party at least one Local Business Day's prior notice.

AND the *pièce de résistance*:

(ii) *"Valuation Date"* means (a) the Trade Date of each Transaction, if either party has an Independent Amount greater than zero for that Transaction, (b) a day not more than once per calendar week or if such day is not a Local Business Day then the immediately preceding Local Business Day and (c) any other Local Business Day designated as a "Valuation Date" by notice given by one party to the other no later than the Notification Time on the Local Business Day before the Valuation Date so designated.

So a great deal of flexibility is possible here provided it suits both parties.

(iii) *"Valuation Time"* means:

[ ] the close of business in the place of location of the Valuation Agent on the Valuation Date or date of calculation, as applicable;

[ ] the close of business on the Local Business Day immediately preceding the Valuation Date or date of calculation, as applicable;

provided that the calculations of Value and Exposure will, as far as practicable, be made as of approximately the same time on the same date.

(iii) Valuation Time

The Valuation Time is the time at which the Valuation Agent calculates Exposure and the value of collateral held to determine if a Delivery Amount or Return Amount call is needed. The Valuation Agent will also factor in any Distributions or Interest Amounts due to the Transferor at the Valuation Time.

The parties have two main choices, viz:

- **as at the close of business on the Valuation Date or the date of calculation for Paragraph 5(c) payments to the Transferor; or**

- **as at the close of business on the Local Business Day immediately before the Valuation Date or the date of calculation for Paragraph 5(c) payments to the Transferor.**

They can, of course, choose another means for deciding the Valuation Time by amending this sub-paragraph.

Once they have made their choice, the Annex stipulates that the calculation of risk exposure and collateral values has to be made as of approximately at the same time on the selected date. This is to avoid discrepancies in the calculations.

A Valuation Time as at the close of business on the Local Business Day immediately preceding the Valuation Date is the most common choice because collateral management units are then working from reports of exposure and collateral values as at the close of the previous business day.

(iv) *"Notification Time"* means 1:00 p.m., London time, on a Local Business Day, unless otherwise specified here: ....

(iv) Notification Time

This is the time by which, among other things, (1) the Valuation Agent must notify the parties of its calculations under Paragraph 3(b) on the Local Business Day following a Valuation Date and (2) a party must make a demand for a transfer of collateral so that the other party makes the appropriate transfer not later than the close of business on the next Local Business Day. If a demand for a transfer is made after the Notification Time, then the transfer does not have to be made until the close of business on the second Local Business Day following the day on which the demand was made. Such transfers are subject to the absence of a dispute and no condition precedent being unfulfilled in Section 2(a)(iii) of the ISDA Master Agreement.

The Notification Time is specified to mean 1.00 p.m. London time on the appropriate Local Business Day unless the parties agree otherwise. Sometimes parties arrange for the Notification Time for the Valuation Agent's exposure calculations to be earlier than the Notification Time for collateral calls (at least where a third party acts as the Valuation Agent). In these circumstances, a party receiving notice of the Valuation Agent's calculations will be able to make a collateral call on the same day for a transfer to be made on the next Local Business Day.

The latest Notification Time I have seen is 3.00 p.m. London Time.

The one exception to a collateral transfer on the following Local Business Day is with US$ cash where I have seen the following language:

> (iv) *"Notification Time"* means 9:00 a.m. New York time on the Valuation Date provided, however, that, notwithstanding Paragraph 3(a), (x) with regard to Transfers of Eligible Credit Support in the form of US$ cash, if a request for delivery or return is made by the Notification Time, then the relevant Transfer shall be made not later than the close of business on the day on which such a request is received, or if such day is not a Local Business Day or if such request is made after the Notification Time, not later than the close of business on the next Local Business Day and (y) with regard to Transfers of other forms of Eligible Credit Support or posted credit support, the relevant Transfer shall be made in accordance with Paragraph 3(a).

(d) **_Exchange Date._** _"Exchange Date"_ has the meaning specified in Paragraph 3(c)(ii), unless otherwise specified here: ....

(d) Exchange Date

In Paragraph 3(c) the Transferor can notify the Transferee that it wishes to substitute New Credit Support for specified collateral (Original Credit Support) which it previously transferred to the Transferee.

It is advisable for the Transferee to consent to the substitution to avoid any recharacterisation risk as explained on page 93. Assuming that consent is forthcoming the Transferor must then transfer the New Credit Support on the first Settlement Day after the Transferee's consent.

When received, the Transferee must retransfer the Original Credit Support to the Transferor no later than the Settlement Day after the Local Business Day he received the New Credit Support.

However, parties can agree to vary this timescale where the securities have a longer settlement cycle.

Sometimes an Exchange Notification Time is included as follows:

(d) ***Exchanges***

(i) For the purposes of Paragraph 3(c) notice must be given by the ***"Exchange Notification Time"*** which will be 1:00 p.m. London time, on a Local Business Day failing which the relevant notice will be deemed to have been received on the following Local Business Day.

(ii) ***"Exchange Date"*** has the meaning specified in Paragraph 3(c)(ii)."

In unilateral agreements where only cash is Eligible Credit Support or only one type of securities collateral is acceptable you might see a ban on substitutions as follows:

(d) ***Exchanges:*** Paragraph 3(c) shall not apply.

However, this is rare.

Sometimes counterparties are concerned about withholding tax risks if they hold securities collateral over a Distributions Date and so seek to substitute their Original Credit Support with New Credit Support where a coupon or dividend is not due imminently.

It is important at least under English law that they do not have an automatic right to do this but must obtain the Transferee's consent in order to avoid recharacterisation risk.

An example of such wording is the following:

(iv) Paragraph 3(c) is amended by adding the following as Paragraph 3(c)(iii):

(iii) (1) Unless otherwise specified in Paragraph 11, the Transferee, may, on any Local Business Day, by notice, request the Transferor, to transfer to the Transferee by the Exchange Notification Time,

certain New Credit Support, specified in the notice in exchange for certain Original Credit Support specified in that notice comprised in the Transferor's Credit Support Balance. If the Transferor consents to the Transferee's request (such consent not to be unreasonably withheld) the Transferor will be obliged to transfer to the Transferee the New Credit Support by the Exchange Notification Time on the date and having such Value and in the manner specified in the notice to the Transferor and the Transferee will be obliged to transfer to the Transferor Equivalent Credit Support in respect of the Original Credit Support promptly upon receiving such New Credit Support, but in any event not later than the close of business on the next Local Business Day thereafter; provided that the Transferee will only be obliged to transfer Equivalent Credit Support with a Value as at the date of transfer as close as practicable to, but in any event not more than, the Value of the New Credit Support as of that date.

For the purposes of this subparagraph (c)(iii)(1), the definitions of New Credit Support and Original Credit Support are amended accordingly to refer to the Eligible Credit Support specified in the Transferee's notice described above.

(2) Any New Credit Support specified in the Transferee's notice shall have a Distributions Date of not less than thirty (30) days after the date upon which it is delivered to the Transferee; and

(3) All calculations of Value will be made by the Valuation Agent as of the relevant Valuation Time.

This type of provision is likely to be placed in the Other Provisions section of Paragraph 11, i.e. Paragraph 11(h).

(e) **Dispute Resolution.**

(i) *"Resolution Time"* means 1:00 p.m., London time, on the Local Business Day following the date on which the notice is given that gives rise to a dispute under Paragraph 4, unless otherwise specified here: ....

(e) Dispute Resolution

(i) Resolution Time

The Resolution Time is the deadline for the parties to resolve their dispute under Paragraph 4. If they fail, the Valuation Agent makes certain recalculations under Paragraph 4(a)(4)(i).

The fallback dispute Resolution Time is 1.00 p.m. London time on the Local Business Day after the date notice is given that gives rise to a dispute under Paragraph 4 although this wording is sometimes changed to "the date on which notice of dispute is given under Paragraph 4", to avoid confusion with the Valuation Agent's notice of Exposure or collateral valuation.

The latest Resolution Time I have seen is 3.00 p.m. London time.

It is interesting that some market players are importing the dispute resolution procedures of Section 1.6 of Part 1 of the 2001 ISDA Margin Provisions into the Other Provisions of their Paragraph 11s.

(ii) *Value.* For the purpose of Paragraphs 4(a)(4)(i)(C) and 4(a)(4)(ii), the Value of the outstanding Credit Support Balance or of any transfer of Eligible Credit Support or Equivalent Credit Support, as the case may be, will be calculated as follows: ....

(ii) Value

This provision must be completed because there is no ISDA fallback and, without it, the Valuation Agent cannot resolve the dispute because he will be unable to value the outstanding collateral or the transfer in dispute.

The most simple Value provision where only cash collateral is involved is:

> (ii) **The Value of Cash will be the face value thereof multiplied by the applicable Valuation Percentage.**

Where there is a unilateral agreement, you might see:

> (ii) *Value.* **For the purpose of Paragraphs 4(a)(4)(i)(C) and 4(a)(4)(ii), the Value of the outstanding Credit Support Balance or of any transfer of Eligible Credit Support or Equivalent Credit Support, as the case may be, will be calculated by the Valuation Agent.**

I have also seen "by the Transferee".

The most common method for valuing securities collateral is to obtain three bid quotations from leading dealers, e.g.:

> (ii) *Value.* **For the purpose of Paragraphs 4(a)(4)(i)(C) and 4(a)(4)(ii), the Value of the outstanding Credit Support Balance or of any transfer of Eligible Credit Support or Equivalent Credit Support, as the case may be, will be calculated as follows: disputes over value will be resolved by the Valuation Agent seeking three bid quotations as of the relevant Valuation Date or date of transfer from parties that regularly act as dealers in the securities or other property in question. The value will be the arithmetic mean of the quotations received by the Valuation Agent multiplied by the applicable Valuation Percentage.**

If such quotations are not available you sometimes see reference back to the previous Local Business Day when such quotations were available, viz:

> **The mean of the bid prices quoted on such date by any three principal market makers in the securities or property in question, or if three quotations are not available, the mean of three such prices as of the immediate preceding day on which such quotations were available, multiplied by the applicable Valuation Percentage, if any.**

A variation on this takes account of accrued interest too, e.g.:

> **a security, (i) either (x) the Base Currency Equivalent of the arithmetic mean of the closing bid prices quoted on the relevant date of three nationally recognised principal market makers (which may include an Affiliate of Party A) for such security chosen by the Valuation Agent or (y) if no quotations are available from such principal market makers on the relevant date, the Base Currency Equivalent of the arithmetic mean of the closing bid prices on the next preceding date, plus (ii) the Base Currency Equivalent of the accrued**

interest on such security (except to the extent transferred to a party pursuant to any applicable provision of this Agreement or included in the applicable price referred to in (i) of this provision).

Sometimes parties select mid-market quotations:

(ii) **Value.** For the purpose of Paragraphs 4(a)(4)(i)(C) and 4(a)(4)(ii), the Value of the outstanding Credit Support Balance or of any transfer of Eligible Credit Support or Equivalent Credit Support, as the case may be, will be calculated as follows: Disputes over Value will be resolved by the Valuation Agent seeking three mid-market quotations as of the relevant Valuation Date or date of Transfer from parties that regularly act as dealers in the securities or other property in question. The Value will be the arithmetic mean of the quotations received by the Valuation Agent.

However, most market players prefer bid quotations because these are a dealer's buying prices.

Things can sometimes get rather pernickety:

Each party shall name a market maker that regularly acts as dealer in the securities. If the party which is not the Valuation Agent does not name a market maker within 30 minutes of such a request from the Valuation Agent, the Valuation Agent shall choose a second market maker and will ask each market maker for a bid quotation as of the relevant Valuation Date or date of transfer and shall calculate the Value according to the procedures set out in section (B) of the Definition of Value in Paragraph 10 using instead the arithmetic average of the bid quotations obtained from each market maker.

Or just plain comprehensive:

the Value for negotiable debt obligations and treasuries,

(x) the closing bid prices quoted on the relevant date (plus accrued interest if not reflected in such closing bid prices) which appears on the display of Bloomberg Financial Markets Commodities News (or its successor) published by Bloomberg L.P. or such other financial information provider reasonably chosen by the Valuation Agent multiplied by the applicable Valuation Percentage, or

(y) if no quotations are available pursuant to (x) above, the arithmetic mean of the closing bid prices quoted on the relevant date of three recognised principal market makers for such security chosen by the Valuation Agent (plus accrued interest if not reflected in such closing bid prices) multiplied by the applicable Valuation Percentage; or

(z) if no quotations are available from such principal market makers on the relevant date, the arithmetic mean of the closing bid prices on the next preceding date (plus accrued interest if not reflected in such closing bid prices) multiplied by the applicable Valuation Percentage.

(iii) *Alternative.* The provisions of Paragraph 4 will apply, unless an alternative dispute resolution procedure is specified here: ....

(iii) Alternative

This provision enables the parties to adopt a different dispute resolution procedure to that contained in Paragraph 4. Normally parties adopt Paragraph 4.

Where Alternative is involved it can be just to clarify matters:

> (iii) *Alternative.* The provisions of Paragraph 4 will apply, unless an alternative dispute resolution procedure is specified here: The provisions of Paragraph 4 will apply, except to the following extent: (A) pending the resolution of a dispute, Transfer of the undisputed Value of Eligible Credit Support involved in the relevant demand will be due as provided in Paragraph 4 if the demand is given by the Notification Time, but will be due on the second Local Business Day after the demand if the demand is given after the Notification Time; and (B) the Disputing Party need not comply with the provisions of Paragraph 4(a)(2) if the amount to be Transferred does not exceed the Disputing Party's Minimum Transfer Amount.

Sometimes parties seek to resolve disputes by the use of a tolerance amount as in the following example:

> (iii) *Alternative.* The provisions of Paragraph 4 will apply provided that in the case of (I) therein, (A) if the difference between (i) the Delivery Amount or a Return Amount calculated by the Valuation Agent and (ii) the Delivery Amount or Return Amount calculated by the Disputing Party (the "Difference") is Euro 5,000,000 or less, the appropriate party will transfer the undisputed amount plus one half of the Difference to the other party – in full settlement of the dispute – not later than the close of business on the Settlement Day following the date the demand is received under Paragraph 2 (and the parties waive any further recourse to the rights enumerated in Paragraph 4 with respect to such dispute); or (B) if the Difference is greater than Euro 5,000,000, the appropriate party will transfer the undisputed to the other party not later than the close of business on the Settlement Day following the date the demand is received under Paragraph 2 and the parties will seek a resolution of the dispute in accordance with the remaining provisions of Paragraph 4.

Another variation concerns the failure of a Valuation Agent to notify its recalculations to a Disputing Party which can lead to the following circumstances:

> Paragraph 4(a) of this Credit Support Annex shall be amended by the insertion of the following additional paragraph after the last paragraph thereof:
>
> > "If the Valuation Agent fails to notify the Disputing Party of its recalculation pursuant to this Paragraph by the Notification Time on the Local Business Day following the Resolution Time, then the Disputing Party may:

(i)   notify the other party and the Valuation Agent (if the Valuation Agent is not the other party) of the failure (and of the appointment of a Replacement Valuation Agent, where the Disputing Party makes an appointment in accordance with (iv) below) not later than the Notification Time on the second Local Business Day following the Resolution Time; and/or

(ii)   in the case of a dispute involving a Delivery Amount or Return Amount, unless otherwise specified in Paragraph 11(e), recalculate the Exposure and the Value as of the Recalculation Date in accordance with Paragraph 4(a)(4)(i)(A)-(C); and/or

(iii)   in the case of a dispute involving the Value of any transfer of Eligible Credit Support or Equivalent Credit Support, recalculate the Value as of the date of transfer pursuant to Paragraph 11(e)(ii); and/or

(iv)   appoint a replacement Valuation Agent (the "Replacement Valuation Agent") to perform (ii) and (iii) above.

Following a recalculation, the Disputing Party or the Replacement Valuation Agent will notify each party (or the other party, if the Valuation Agent is a party) of the recalculation as soon as possible, but in any event not later than the third Local Business Day following the Resolution Time. The appropriate party will upon demand following such notice, make the appropriate transfer."

Paragraph 4(b) of this Credit Support Annex shall be amended by the replacement of the final sentence thereof with the following:

For the avoidance of doubt, upon completion of those procedures, Section 5(a)(i) of this Agreement will apply to any failure by a party to make a transfer required under either the sub-paragraph in Paragraph 4(a) that commences with "Following a recalculation pursuant to this Paragraph", or the penultimate sentence of Paragraph (4) (as applicable) on the relevant due date.

(f) *Distributions and Interest Amount.*

(i) *Interest Rate.* The "Interest Rate" in relation to each Eligible Currency specified below will be:

Eligible Currency	*Interest Rate*
....	....
....	....
....	....

(f) Distributions and Interest Amount

(i) Interest Rate

The Interest Rate is the interest which will be paid by the Transferee on the cash collateral received from the Transferor plus or minus a spread. It will reflect the frequency of the Valuation Dates. If these are daily, EONIA (Euro Overnight Index Average) could be used; if weekly or monthly EURIBOR might be an option.

This section must be completed as there is no ISDA fallback.

If parties are concerned about potential withholding tax liabilities, they might apply a zero interest rate if this affected them both. This is rare, however, and may be done for other reasons.

Unlike the New York Law CSA where only US$ cash collateral is involved, the English Law CSA caters for EU and non-EU currencies and provides for interest in different currencies to be converted into the Base Currency. Interest is calculated on an Actual/360 or Actual/365 basis depending upon the convention for the particular currency.

A typical example is:

(i) **Interest Rate.** The "Interest Rate" in relation to each Eligible Currency specified below will be:

Eligible Currency	Interest Rate
EUR	EONIA as defined below
US$	US$-Federal Funds-H.15 as defined below
GPB	SONIA as defined below

(i) EONIA: "EONIA" for any day in the Interest Period means the reference rate equal to the overnight rate as calculated by the European Central Bank and fixed between 6:45 and 7 p.m. (CET) as appearing on Telerate Page 247 or as published by Bloomberg on the first TARGET Settlement Day following that day (or if Page 247 ceases to exist, another equivalent page or reference; or if no such rate is set forth for such day as reported on Telerate or Bloomberg, the rate set forth for the next preceding day for which such a rate is set forth therein).

(ii) US$-Federal Funds-H.15 for any day in the Interest Period means the reference rate set forth in H.15(519) for that day opposite the caption "Federal Funds (Effective)", as such rate is displayed on Telerate Page 120 (or if Page 120 ceases to exist or is not yet published in H.15(519), the rate for that day will be the rate set forth in H.15 Daily Update or such other recognised electronic source used for the purpose of displaying such rate for that day opposite the caption "Federal Funds (Effective)". For the avoidance of doubt, the Interest Amount will be calculated on a daily, non-compounded basis.

The last sentence is useful as disagreements have occurred over whether interest is compounded or not.

(iii) the overnight rate as calculated by the Wholesale Market Brokers Association as reported on Telerate Page 3937 under the heading "Sterling Overnight Index" ("SONIA") as of 9:00 a.m. London Time, on such day if it is a London Banking Day, otherwise on the London Banking Day immediately preceding such day in respect of the Eligible Currency being Pounds Sterling.

Interest Rates, as mentioned above can sometimes be quoted minus a spread as in the following example:

Eligible Currency	Interest Rate	Spread basis points	Designated maturity
US$	US$-LIBOR-BBA	minus 12.5	1 week
EURO	EURO-LIBOR-BBA	minus 12.5	1 week

Sometimes, the Interest Rate can be split for cash collateral deposited for the whole of an Interest Period:

(i) *Interest Rate.* The "Interest Rate" in relation to each Eligible Currency specified below will be determined on the following basis:

Eligible Currency	Rate Source	Spread
EURO	EONIA	Zero

Provided, however, any amount of Eligible Currency that constitutes part of the Credit Support Balance for the entire Interest Period, "Interest Rate" in relation to each such Eligible Currency in the type specified below will be determined on the following basis:

Eligible Currency	Rate Source	Spread
EURO	EURIBOR	−.25

Sometimes parties prefer not to have interest amounts in different currencies converted into the Base Currency but for them to be paid separately in their respective currencies. The English Law CSA can be amended to cater for this in Paragraph 11(h) using wording along the following lines:

(a) The definition of *"Interest Amount"* shall be deleted and replaced with the following:

"Interest Amount" means, with respect to an Interest Period and each portion of the Credit Support Balance comprised of cash in an Eligible Currency, the sum of the amounts of interest determined for each day in that Interest Period by the Valuation Agent as follows:

(x)   the amount of such currency comprised in the Credit Support Balance at the close of business for general dealings in the relevant currency on such day (or, if such day is not a Local Business Day, on the immediately preceding Local Business Day); multiplied by

(y)   the relevant Interest Rate; divided by

(z)   360 (or in the case of Pounds Sterling, 365).

OR more plainly:

The definition of *"Interest Rate"* is amended by deletion of the words "the aggregate sum of the Base Currency Equivalents of" with the intention that the amount of interest payable on the principal amount of the portion of the Credit Support Balance comprised of cash will be payable in the currency in which such cash is denominated and not in the Base Currency.

It might be useful to mention here the question of default interest where a Transferee fails to pay Distributions of Interest Amounts or Return Amounts on time. Essentially, what happens here is that default interest under Paragraph 9(a) of the Annex is calculated using the Default Rate (i.e. 1% over the payee's cost of funds) of Section 2(e) of the ISDA Master Agreement on an Actual/Actual day count fraction basis.

(ii) *Transfer of Interest Amount.* The transfer of the Interest Amount will be made on the last Local Business Day of each calendar month and on any Local Business Day that a Return Amount consisting wholly or partly of cash is transferred to the Transferor pursuant to Paragraph 2(b), unless otherwise specified here: ....

(ii) Transfer of Interest Amount

As long as the Transferee does not become undersecured by transferring an Interest Amount, Paragraph 11(f)(ii) proposes that interest on cash collateral is transferred to the Transferee on the last Local Business Day of each month and on any Local Business Day when a cash Return Amount is due to the Transferor.

Whether this payment structure is acceptable will depend upon the parties' operational systems. Many parties prefer such interest transfers to take place on the second Local Business Day of the succeeding calendar month because they can spend the first Local Business Day of that month checking calculations and preparing the necessary electronic transfers.

There are not a large number of variations on this theme but sometimes you see that the interest transfer date must be a Local Business Day in the cities where both parties are located.

With collateralised equity derivatives you might see the following provision:

(ii) *Transfer of Interest Amount/Eligible Credit Support/Equivalent Credit Support.* The transfer on the Interest Amount/Eligible Credit Support/ Equivalent Credit Support will be made on each Equity Payment Date.

Finally, some parties propose that the Interest Amount be added to the Credit Support Balance and not paid over. Where this is agreed you might see the following wording:

(ii) *Transfer of Interest Amount.* The Interest Amount in relation to each currency comprised in the Credit Support Balance for each Interest Period will be credited to the Credit Support Balance on the second Local Business Day following the end of each calendar month.

As regards payments of securities interest or dividends to the Transferor this is dealt with under Paragraph 5(c)(i) of the Annex (see p. 99).

(iii) *Alternative to Interest Amount.* The provisions of Paragraph 5(c)(ii) will apply, unless otherwise specified here: ....

(iii) Alternative to Interest Amount

This provision affords the Transferee, with the Transferor's agreement, the opportunity to invest part of the cash collateral in other instruments, rather than just paying over an agreed interest return. It is rarely used. Some parties amend the provision to clarify that interest is to be compounded where this is required, e.g:

> (iii) **For the avoidance of doubt the Interest Amount will be computed for each Interest Period on a compounded basis.**

OR

> (iii) ***Alternative to Interest Amount.*** **The provisions of Paragraph 5(c)(ii) will apply, provided however, that the Interest Amount will compound on each TARGET Settlement Day. i.e. for Euro cash collateral.**

(g) *Addresses for Transfers.*

Party A: ....

Party B: ....

(h) **Other Provisions.**

(g) Addresses for Transfers

This must be completed if collateral transfers and interest payments and Distributions are to be correctly routed to the recipient. Sometimes these details are spelt out by currency for cash and securities and sometimes a general statement is made as follows:

> *Addresses for Transfers.*
> **Party A: As set forth in notices to Party B pursuant to Paragraph 3(b).**
> **Party B: As set forth in notices to Party A pursuant to Paragraph 3(b).**

Parties often issue separate payment instructions to each other in this respect.

(h) Other provisions

Paragraph 11(h) is similar to Part 5 of the ISDA Master Agreement Schedule – a place where other provisions may be inserted. Virtually anything could potentially be included here, but my review of English Law CSAs has found that the following provisions feature quite regularly:

- **One way agreements**
- **Valuation Percentage at close-out**
- **Exposure and Collateralised Transactions**
- **Exchanges (substitutions)**
- **Notices**
- **Miscellaneous.**

(i) One way agreements

Apart from a Threshold of Infinity for one party, the standard bilateral English Law CSA can be amended to make it unilateral by using the following wording or similar:

> **For the purposes of this Annex Party A is the Transferee and Party B the Transferor.**

OR

> **One-Way Collateral Agreement. Notwithstanding anything in this Agreement to the contrary, Transferee shall mean Party B and Transferor shall mean Party A in all circumstances in this Annex. This Annex provides for one-way transfer of Credit Support from Party A to Party B.**

OR

> ***Agreement as to Single Transferee and Transferor.*** **Party A and Party B agree that, notwithstanding anything to the contrary in the recital to this Annex, Paragraph 2 or the definitions in Paragraph 10, (a) the term *"Transferee"* as used in this Annex means only Party A, (b) the term *"Transferor"* as used in this Annex means only Party B, (c) only Party B makes the representation in**

Paragraph 7 and (d) only Party B will be required to make Transfers of Eligible Credit Support hereunder.

OR

Party A and Party B agree that notwithstanding anything to the contrary set out within this Annex, Party A is under no obligation to make any transfer under this Annex in support of any Transactions under the ISDA Master Agreement. Party B will make any and all transfers required under this Annex in support of any Transactions undertaken under the ISDA Master Agreement. All references in this Annex to the "Transferor" will be to Party B and all corresponding references to the "Transferee" will be to Party A.

Party A will not at any time be expected to make any transfers to Party B save where Party A is under an obligation to Party B to deliver a Return Amount or make an exchange of Original Credit Support in respect of New Credit Support transferred by Party B.

(It is not advisable to make Minimum Transfer Amounts infinite.)

(ii) Valuation Percentage at close-out

As we know, during the collateralised relationship, securities collateral is subject to a haircut or a discount to its face value. However, it would be unfair for this to apply in a close-out situation. Parties, therefore, regularly amend the Annex to provide for realisation of securities collateral at 100% of face value. This is based on the common law principle that a creditor is not entitled to receive more than 100% of what he is owed from the security he holds and must account to the debtor for any surplus.

The amendment can be made in the following or similar wording:

Paragraph 6 is amended by inserting the following at the end thereof:

"Notwithstanding anything to the contrary provided in Paragraph 11(b)(ii) or elsewhere in this Annex, the applicable Valuation Percentage for the purpose of determining the Value of Eligible Credit Support included within the Credit Support Balance shall, for the purpose of this Paragraph 6, be 100%."

OR

The definition of *"Valuation Percentage"* in Paragraph 10 is amended by the addition of the following at the end of the definition:

"except that, for the purposes of Paragraph 6, Valuation Percentage for each item of Eligible Credit Support is 100%."

OR

(i) *Paragraph 6. Default.*

For the purposes of determining the Credit Support Balance pursuant to Paragraph 6 the definition of Value in Paragraph 10 shall be amended by deleting the words "...multiplied by the applicable Valuation Percentage, if any..." from subsections (i)(A) and (B).

OR

"Paragraph 6"
Add at the end of the definition of Value in Paragraph 10 the following:

> provided that for a Valuation Date which is an Early Termination Date designated or deemed to have occurred as a result of an Event of Default, the Valuation Percentage shall be deemed to be 100%.

OR

Amendment to Paragraph 10. The definition of "Value" in Paragraph 10 is amended by adding at the end thereof the following:

> "provided that, for a Valuation Date that is an Early Termination Date designated or deemed to have occurred as a result of an Event of Default or a Termination Event in respect of which all Transactions are Affected Transactions, the Valuation Percentage for all Eligible Credit Support comprised in the Credit Support Balance shall be 100%."

(iii) Exposure and Collateralised Transactions

Exposure is the estimated value of all Transactions (using mid market quotations from dealers) in calculating risk exposure. The calculation is made as if the Transactions were being closed out.

While because of the single agreement concept of the ISDA Master Agreement you cannot include collateralised and uncollateralised Transactions under the same Agreement in a close-out situation, it is possible to apply collateralisation to particular Transactions in such circumstances.

This can be achieved by amending the term "Exposure" to refer only to "Collateralised Transactions" so that the Credit Support Amount only represents net exposure of the Transferee in relation to such Collateralised Transactions. In this way, the single agreement concept is not vitiated.

Relevant wording for this could be:

Definitions. The following amendments shall be made to Paragraph 10.

> (a) The following definition shall be added:
>
> ***"Collateralised Transation"*** means any Transaction designated as such in a relevant Confirmation or specified in the Appendix to this Annex. For the avoidance of doubt, the Transaction constituted by this Annex is not a Collateralised Transaction.
>
> (b) The definition of ***"Exposure"*** shall be amended to replace the words "Transactions (other than the Transaction constituted by this Annex)" in the fourth line with the words "Collateralised Transactions".

A common way to specify Collateralised Transactions is to list them as products in an Appendix sometimes with the relevant Offices of each party through which they can be traded. Whether this is possible will depend upon the valuation feeds and systems of the two parties.

An example of such an Appendix is as follows:

APPENDIX

COLLATERALISED TRANSACTIONS

Each type of Transaction nominated in sub-clauses (1), (2) and (3) below, in relation to which the parties are acting through relevant Offices (as listed in the relevant sub-clause) and each Transaction specified in sub-clause (4) below is a Collateralised Transaction:

(1) Any Transaction which is a:

interest rate swap transaction

currency swap transaction

cross-currency interest rate swap transaction

interest rate cap, collar or floor transaction

swaption transaction

forward rate transaction (FRA)

bond option transaction

equity derivative transaction

credit derivative transaction

For the purposes of this sub-clause (1) the relevant Office(s) of Party A is (are):

For the purposes of this sub-clause (1) the relevant Office(s) of Party B is (are):

(2) Any forward foreign exchange transaction (whether deliverable or non-deliverable) in relation to which each party is acting through one of its Offices specified below:

For the purpose of this sub-clause (2) the relevant Office(s) of Party A is (are):

For the purposes of this sub-clause (2) the relevant Office(s) of Party B is (are):

(3) For the purpose of this sub-clause (3) any currency option transaction in relation to which each party is acting through one of its Offices specified below:

For the purpose of this sub-clause (3) the relevant Office(s) of Party A is (are):

For the purposes of this sub-clause (3) the relevant Office(s) of Party B is (are):

For the avoidance of doubt: with respect to sub-clauses (1), (2) and (3) of this Appendix, the following types of Transactions are not Collateralised Transactions:

Spot foreign exchange transactions
Commodity derivative transactions
Any other type of transaction not listed above.

With very risky counterparties you might seek to include spot foreign exchange transactions but as they are very short-dated, i.e. settlement after two Local Business Days it is often not considered worth it.

Sometimes Offices are not specified but only products as in the following example:

Transactions

The definition of "Exposure" in Paragraph 10 shall be amended by adding the following sentence at the end thereof:

"For purpose of this definition, the term "Transaction" will only cover the following transactions: any rate swap transaction, basis swap, forward rate transaction, bond option, interest rate option, cap transaction, floor transaction, collar transaction, cross-currency rate swap transaction (including any option with respect to any of these transactions), Equity Swap Transactions, Index Transactions, Share Transactions, Index Basket Transactions, Share Basket Transactions, Basket Option Transactions, and any Option Transaction as defined in the 1996 Equity Derivatives Definitions."

This is, of course, subject to operational capability and confirmation that your collateral legal opinion covers all these products in the jurisdiction(s) concerned.

Where there is an imbalance in parties' systems to collateralise a product, I have seen the following example relating to currency options where they are excluded until the other party catches up:

The definition of "Exposure" contained in Paragraph 10 of this Annex is hereby amended by the addition of the following after "Market Quotation" on the last line thereof:

"; and provided further that, during such time as either Party A or Party B is unable for operational reasons to automatically integrate exposures resulting from foreign exchange option transactions with exposures resulting from other Transactions, the Market Quotation or Loss with respect to all Transactions which constitute foreign exchange option transactions shall be deemed to be zero for the purposes of the determination of "Exposure"."

Sometimes parties like to clarify that uncollateralised Transactions shall not form part of the Credit Support Amount for close-out purposes, e.g.:

Insert the following sentence at the end of this definition: [i.e. "Exposure"]

> "For the avoidance of doubt, solely for the purposes of the calculation of Exposure hereunder, the amount payable pursuant to Section 6(e)(ii)(1) in respect of Transactions which are not Collateralised Transactions shall be deemed to be zero (but without prejudice to payment or delivery obligations under the Transaction constituted by this Annex)."

There are also a couple of amendments which I have seen relating to the proviso at the end of the Exposure definition. In a very one-way Annex I have seen:

> The definition of "Exposure", shall be amended by deleting the proviso at the end.

In another a more reasonable provision, viz:

> The definition of "Exposure" in Paragraph 10 shall be amended by adding the words "in accordance with generally accepted industry standard" on line 7 after the words "the Valuation Agent on behalf of that party".

(iv) Exchanges (substitutions)

As mentioned previously in order to be on the safe side and to avoid recharacterisation risk it is best to avoid any amendments which give the Transferor an automatic right of substitution without consent.

One relatively common amendment requires the Transferee to use its best endeavours to return the equivalent of the Original Credit Support on the same Local Business Day as it receives the New Credit Support:

> ***Exchanges:***
>
> Paragraph 3(c)(ii) will be amended by inserting the following after the words "Original Credit Support" in line five "...promptly upon receipt of the New Credit Support (and if practicable on the day of such receipt) and in any case not later...".

Where Original Credit Support becomes downgraded, a Transferee may well wish to have the right to request the Transferor to substitute New Credit Support of the requisite rating to restore the status quo as in the following examples:

> ***Exchange of Eligible Credit Support in the event that the issuer of the Government debt obligations is downgraded.*** If the rating assigned by S&P or Moody's to the negotiable debt obligations held as Eligible Credit Support falls below the minimum rating requirements imposed under the definition of Eligible Credit Support (the Affected Credit Support), then the Party that holds the Affected Credit Support shall be entitled to demand by written notice the further transfer to it of substitute Eligible Credit Support (of equal value) in exchange for the Affected Credit Support. The party obligated to provide such substitute Credit Support shall make such transfer on the first Local Business Day following the date

on which it receives such notice. The other party will only be obligated to return the Affected Credit Support after receiving the substitute Eligible Credit Support.

OR

If at any time the Ratings assigned by S&P and Moody's to any Eligible Credit Support comprising the Credit Support Balance fall below AAA- or Aa3, respectively, (the "Downgraded Credit Support"), the Transferee may by notice in writing to the Transferor require the Transferor to provide a request to exchange the Downgraded Credit Support for New Credit Support (such New Credit Support having a Rating assigned by S&P and/or Moody's of at least AAA- or Aaa3, respectively), in accordance with the provisions of Paragraph 3(c)(i) of the Credit Support Annex, within five Local Business Days of receipt of such notice.

A similar situation might arise if a change in tax regulations occurs:

Taxes. If at any time there occurs a change in taxation in relation to any Eligible Credit Support which has a negative impact on the Transferor or Transferee, the Transferee shall have the right (i) to refuse to accept a transfer of any securities by the Transferor and/or (ii) to insist on the immediate substitution of any securities already held by the Transferee as Eligible Credit Support.

Exchanges or substitutions of cash in different currencies are rare.

(v) Notices

Paragraph 11(h) often starts with a section where the parties provide details of where any notices or demands between them should be sent.

Other notice type provisions include the following:

(ii) *Notices.* Notwithstanding Section 12 of the Agreement, any communication by a party ("X") to the other party ("Y") requesting Eligible Credit Support to be transferred pursuant to Paragraph 3 of this Annex may be given via facsimile at the times specified in this Agreement and during normal business hours in the city in which Y is located on any Local Business Day. Any such facsimile will be deemed received and effective when actually received.

(iii) *Sharing of Information.* The parties hereto agree that a party shall prepare written statements identifying the Transactions included in the calculation of Exposure hereunder (1) at the Notification Time upon making a demand under Paragraph 2, or (2) immediately upon reasonable request by the other party. These statements shall list the Transactions according to their types, their currency and their maturity date.

(iv) *Confidentiality.* Any statement required to be delivered by a party pursuant to Paragraph 11(h)(iii) above may contain information which the party receiving such statements shall use on a confidential basis.

(vi) Other

Among the interesting provisions I have seen are the following:

Other Eligible Credit Support and Other Equivalent Credit Support (Letters of Credit)

(A) **Transfers of Letters of Credit.** All transfers under this Annex of Letters of Credit shall be made, in the case of, (a) a Transferor, by the Transferor giving written instructions (including, for the avoidance of doubt, instructions given by telex, facsimile transmission or electronic messaging system) to an Issuer of a Letter of Credit, (i) to issue a Letter of Credit to the Transferee and such Issuer issuing the requested Letter of Credit to the Transferee or (ii) to increase the amount of an outstanding Letter of Credit such Issuer increasing the outstanding amount of the relevant Letter of Credit accordingly; and (b) in the case of a Transferee, by the Transferee delivering its original copy of the Letter of Credit to the Transferor and any other documents necessary to constitute a legally valid surrender of the Letter of Credit in accordance with applicable law such that the Transferee's rights under the Letter of Credit are effectively terminated.

(B) **Letter of Credit Default.** Upon the occurrence of a Letter of Credit Default, the Transferee shall transfer the Letter of Credit in respect of which a letter of Credit Default has occurred to the Transferor promptly following the Valuation Date immediately following notification of the Letter of Credit Default to both parties.

(C) **Definitions.** Paragraph 10 is hereby amended by:

inserting the following wording as a new subparagraph (v) at the end of the definition of "Local Business Day":

"(*) in relation to a transfer of a Letter of Credit, a day on which commercial banks are open for business (including dealings in foreign exchange and foreign currency deposits) in London and New York.";
(*) by inserting the following wording as a new subsection (iii) at the end of the definition of "Settlement Day":
"and (*) with respect to delivery of Letters of Credit, the Second Local Business Day".
(*) by inserting the following wording as a new subparagraph (iii) at the end of the definition of "Value":
"(*) items that are comprised in the Credit Support Balance that are Letters of Credit, the Base Currency Equivalent of the stated amount under the Letter of Credit multiplied by the applicable Valuation Percentage, if any"; and
(*) adding, in their alphabetic order, the following:

"Credit Rating" means with respect to an entity, on any date of determination, the respective ratings then assigned to such entity's unsecured, senior long-term debt or deposit obligations (not supported by third party credit enhancement) by S&P, Moody's or the other specified rating agency or agencies.

"Issuer" means a major United Kingdom commercial bank or foreign bank which is (a) not the Transferor or an Affiliate of the Transferor, (b) has a branch office in the United Kingdom and (c) has a Credit Rating of at least "A" by S&P or "A2" by Moody's which issues a Letter of Credit.

"Letter of Credit" means an irrevocable, standby letter of credit or bank guarantee, issued by an Issuer in respect of this Agreement utilizing, as appropriate, the form set forth in Exhibit *, with such changes to the terms in that form as that Issuer may require and as may be acceptable to the Transferee.

"Letter of Credit Default" means in respect of a Letter of Credit, the occurrence at any time with respect to the Letter of Credit of any of the following events:

(a) the Issuer fails to maintain a Credit Rating of at least "A" by S&P or "A2" by Moody's;
(b) the Issuer fails to comply with or perform its obligations under such Letter of Credit and such failure continues after the lapse of any applicable grace period;
(c) the Issuer disaffirms, disclaims, repudiates or rejects, in whole or in part, or challenges the validity of such Letter of Credit;
(d) any event analogous to an event specified in Section 5(a)(vii) of the Agreement occurs with respect to the Issuer;
(e) the Letter of Credit fails or ceases to be in full force and effect; or
(f) the Letter of Credit expires or terminates in accordance with its terms within the next twenty [(20)] Local Business Days.

Transfer Timing
An extension of the delivery period for a Delivery or a Return Amount:

Transfer Timing. The final paragraph of Paragraph 3(a) shall be deleted and replaced with the following:

"Subject to Paragraph 4 and unless otherwise specified, if a demand for the transfer of Eligible Credit Support or Equivalent Credit Support is received by the Notification Time, then the relevant transfer will be made not later than the close of business on the second Local Business Day relating to the date such demand is received; if a demand is received after the Notification Time, then the relevant transfer will be made not later than the close of business on the third Local Business Day relating to the day after the date such demand is received."

This should only be granted where the securities collateral concerned has a longer settlement cycle. However, as drafted, it would allow either party two to three Local Business Days to transfer cash collateral!

Interest Amount and withholding tax

A provision relating to withholding tax may be included:

> For the avoidance of doubt, where any Distribution or Interest Amount occurs, the interest and other payments and distributions of cash or other property that the holder of the same type, nominal value, description and amount of such Eligible Credit Support is entitled to, shall be deemed to be such amount free and clear of any deduction or withholding for or on account of any Tax.

With Italian counterparties the following acknowledgement is sometimes made:

> Party A and Party B acknowledge that any transfer of Eligible Credit Support pursuant to this Annex would constitute a *pegno irregolare* if this Annex was governed by Italian law.

This is because in Italy a *pegno irregolare* (irregular pledge) is classified as a type of security interest under Article 1851 of the Italian Civil Code although it essentially acts as a transfer of title document.

In connection with Hong Kong, the definition of Local Business Day is modified to take into account, inter alia, some stormy weather. **The "." at the end of sub-clause (iv) of the definition of "Local Business Day" in Paragraph 10 is hereby deleted, and the following proviso is hereby inserted at the end of the definition of "Local Business Day" as aforesaid (and applying in respect of all sub-clauses thereof):**

> provided that where Hong Kong is the or a relevant location for the purposes of the definition of "Local Business Day", none of the following shall be deemed to be a Local Business Day in Hong Kong:
>
> (a) Any Saturday; and/or
>
> (b) Any day upon which any Adverse Weather Condition is issued or raised (as appropriate), on or before 11:00 a.m. and (a) not lowered or withdrawn at or before 12:00 noon or (b) if so lowered or withdrawn subsequently issued or raised before 2:30 p.m. on that day.
>
> For purposes hereof, "Adverse Weather Condition" means a black rainstorm warning and/or No. 8 or greater typhoon signal in Hong Kong.

A potential example of real life impacting upon the markets!

Finally with unsophisticated counterparties no detail is too small to check in operating the collateral arrangement:

All payments to be made under this Agreement shall be effected through the CHAPS settlement system and unless expressly agreed in writing by both parties, payment by cheque shall not constitute a valid payment.

Figure 5.4 summarises the ISDA fallbacks for Paragraph 11 and the provisions which must be completed for the English Law CSA to be operative.

ISDA fallbacks in the English law CSA

FIG. 5.4

If no choice is made the following apply by default:

Provision	Fallback
Base Currency	US Dollars
Eligible Currency	Base Currency
Independent Amount	Zero
Threshold	Zero
Minimum Transfer Amount	Zero
Rounding	No rounding
Valuation Agent	The party making demand under Paragraph 3 and the Transferee for Paragraph 5 payments
Exchange Date	The Settlement Date following the Transferee's receipt of New Credit Support
Resolution Time	1.00 p.m. London time on the Local Business Day after the day the dispute notice was issued
Alternative	Paragraph 4 dispute resolution procedures apply
Transfer of Interest Amount	Last Local Business Day of a calendar month and any Local Business Day when a cash Return Amount is due to the Transferor
Alternative to Interest Amount	Paragraph 5(c)(ii) and Paragraph 10 definition of Interest Amount applies

Provisions which must be completed as there is no fallback are as follows:

- Eligible Credit Support
- Valuation Date
- Valuation Time
- Notification Time
- Value
- Interest Rate
- Addresses for Transfers.

Amendment Agreements

In many instances, parties may have entered into an ISDA Master Agreement several years before they decide to collateralise their respective trading portfolios by entering into an English Law CSA.

To facilitate this they can either just enter into such an English Law CSA or do so via an Amendment Agreement which adds the Annex to the Schedule of the ISDA Master Agreement.

An example of such an Amendment Agreement may be found in Appendix A of the *User's Guide to the ISDA Credit Support Documents under English Law* which is reproduced in Annex 5 of this book (pages 495–496) by the kind permission of the International Swaps and Derivatives Association, Inc.

The New York Law ISDA Credit Support Annex

6

Paragraph by paragraph analysis

Glossary of terms in Paragraph 12

Examples of Paragraph 13 provisions

Comparison of New York Law CSA with the English Law CSA

This chapter provides a paragraph by paragraph interpretation of the New York Law CSA, including its Paragraph 13 (the Elections and Variables Paragraph) that is individually negotiated by the parties. Terms capitalised in this chapter have the same meaning as used in the New York Law CSA and the ISDA Master Agreement. The discussion of Paragraph 13 also provides common and rare amendments seen in the market. Chapter 5 written by Paul Harding on the English Law CSA takes a similar approach.

(Bilateral Form)   (ISDA Agreements Subject to New York Law Only)

PARAGRAPH BY PARAGRAPH ANALYSIS

Headings

The New York Law CSA, in its standard form, is a bilateral pledge agreement. In contrast to the English Law CSA, the Pledgor grants a security interest in the pledged collateral to the Secured Party as opposed to an actual transfer in ownership.

This document was drafted to be governed by New York law and it is recommended that specific legal advice be taken if it is to be subject to any other governing law.

ISDA®

International Swaps and Derivatives Association, Inc.

CREDIT SUPPORT ANNEX

to the Schedule to the

....

dated as of ....

between

.... and ....

("Party A")   ("Party B")

Dating and Nomenclature

The New York Law CSA will be dated as of the same date as the ISDA Master Agreement. It is normal to date the Agreement as of the date of the first trade between the parties even if it is not signed until several months later. This is based on US practice where the words "as of" mean "with effect from" a specified date. Since the New York Law CSA forms part of the Agreement Schedule (see commentary on preamble below) it is dated as of the same date as the Agreement.

The parties enter their full legal names in the spaces provided.

This Annex supplements, forms part of, and is subject to, the above-referenced Agreement, is part of its Schedule and is a Credit Support Document under this Agreement with respect to each party.

Preamble

Technically, the New York Law CSA is described as part of the ISDA Master Agreement Schedule and like it, supplements, forms part of, and is subject to the Master Agreement itself. It is not a standalone document like the ISDA Credit Support Deed (English law), but it is a Credit Support Document under the ISDA Master Agreement and in this sense is somewhat hybrid in nature.

By reference, the single agreement concept of Section 1(c) of the Agreement is reinforced here. This concept prevents a bankruptcy court or receiver from cherry-picking (i.e. making payments under those Transactions favourable to his insolvent client and refusing to pay on those unprofitable to it). Section 6(e) of the Agreement prevents this by effectively collapsing all the Transactions into a single net termination payment due to one party or the other.

Accordingly, the parties agree as follows:

Paragraph 1. Interpretation

(a) **_Definitions and Inconsistency._** Capitalized terms not otherwise defined herein or elsewhere in this Agreement have the meanings specified pursuant to Paragraph 12, and all references in this Annex to Paragraphs are to Paragraphs of this Annex. In the event of any inconsistency between this Annex and the other provisions of this Schedule, this Annex will prevail, and in the event of any inconsistency between Paragraph 13 and the other provisions of this Annex, Paragraph 13 will prevail.

(b) **_Secured Party and Pledgor._** All references in this Annex to the "Secured Party" will be to either party when acting in that capacity and all corresponding references to the "Pledgor" will be to the other party when acting in that capacity; provided, however, that if Other Posted Support is held by a party to this Annex, all references herein to that party as the Secured Party with respect to that Other Posted Support will be to that party as the beneficiary thereof and will not subject that support or that party as the beneficiary thereof to provisions of law generally relating to security interests and secured parties.

Paragraph 1. Interpretation

(a) Definitions and Inconsistency. It states that if there is any inconsistency between the Annex and the other provisions of the ISDA Schedule, the New York Law CSA will prevail. However, Paragraph 13 (the Elections and Variables Paragraph) will prevail if it is inconsistent with the other provisions of the New York Law CSA.

(b) Under the New York Law CSA, either party may at times be the Secured Party or the Pledgor. A party pledging collateral (or receiving collateral that is being returned) is referred to as the Pledgor. A party receiving pledged collateral (or holding or returning collateral to the Pledgor) is referred to as the Secured Party. In respect of Other Posted Support, the Secured Party will be considered to hold it as a beneficiary as would be the case with a letter of credit or a surety bond rather than as a pledgee.

Paragraph 2. Security Interest

Each party, as the Pledgor, hereby pledges to the other party, as the Secured Party, as security for its Obligations, and grants to the Secured Party a first priority continuing security interest in, lien on and right of Set-off against all Posted Collateral Transferred to or received by the Secured Party hereunder. Upon the Transfer by the Secured Party to the Pledgor of Posted Collateral, the security interest and lien granted hereunder on that Posted Collateral will be released immediately and, to the extent possible, without any further action by either party.

Paragraph 2. Security Interest

Paragraph 2, governed by the New York Uniform Commercial Code (the "UCC"), is typically referred to as the granting clause. Here the Pledgor grants a security interest in (and a lien on) the property that is pledged to the Secured Party. Here, the Pledgor is obligated to grant "a first priority continuing security interest" to the Secured Party. Under the New York UCC, this means that the Secured Party generally has a claim to the pledged collateral superior to any other creditor provided that the Secured Party perfects its rights in the pledge. Assuming that the Pledgor is pledging Cash or US Treasury securities, the security interest in the pledged collateral is perfected by the Secured Party taking possession (although not ownership) of the pledged collateral. Please see Chapter 3 (pp. 48–49) for a complete description of the attachment and perfection of a security interest in Posted Collateral under the UCC.

The Secured Party also agrees in the Paragraph that in the event the Secured Party returns the Posted Collateral to the Pledgor, its security interest in the collateral is automatically released. Because attachment and perfection of Posted Collateral such as Cash and securities is normally done by possession, surrender of such possession will also normally release the Secured Party's lien on the surrendered collateral under the UCC.

Paragraph 3. Credit Support Obligations

(a) *Delivery Amount.* Subject to Paragraphs 4 and 5, upon a demand made by the Secured Party on or promptly following a Valuation Date, if the Delivery Amount for that Valuation Date equals or exceeds the Pledgor's Minimum Transfer Amount, then the Pledgor will Transfer to the Secured Party Eligible Credit Support having a Value as of the date of Transfer at least equal to the applicable Delivery Amount (rounded pursuant to Paragraph 13). Unless otherwise specified in Paragraph 13, the *"Delivery Amount"* applicable to the Pledgor for any Valuation Date will equal the amount by which:

(i) the Credit Support Amount

exceeds

(ii) the Value as of that Valuation Date of all Posted Credit Support held by the Secured Party.

(b) *Return Amount.* Subject to Paragraphs 4 and 5, upon a demand made by the Pledgor on or promptly following a Valuation Date, if the Return Amount for that Valuation Date equals or exceeds the Secured Party's Minimum Transfer Amount, then the Secured Party will Transfer to the Pledgor Posted Credit Support specified by the Pledgor in that demand having a Value as of the date of Transfer as close as practicable to the applicable Return Amount (rounded pursuant to Paragraph 13). Unless otherwise specified in Paragraph 13, the *"Return Amount"* applicable to the Secured Party for any Valuation Date will equal the amount by which:

(i) the Value as of that Valuation Date of all Posted Credit Support held by the Secured Party

exceeds

(ii) the Credit Support Amount.

"Credit Support Amount" means, unless otherwise specified in Paragraph 13, for any Valuation Date (i) the Secured Party's Exposure for that Valuation Date plus (ii) the aggregate of all Independent Amounts applicable to the Pledgor, if any, minus (iii) all Independent Amounts applicable to the Secured Party, if any, minus (iv) the Pledgor's Threshold; provided, however, that the Credit Support Amount will be deemed to be zero whenever the calculation of Credit Support Amount yields a number less than zero.

Paragraph 3. Credit Support Obligations

This Paragraph concerns collateral calls and returns and how they are calculated.

Basically, the Secured Party compares his exposure to the collateral he holds and calls for more, returns any excess or does nothing depending upon the calculations after taking into account Independent Amounts, Thresholds and/or Minimum Transfer Amounts.

In Paragraph 3(a), the Secured Party can call for collateral when the Credit Support Amount exceeds the value of any Posted Collateral (i.e. pledged collateral). This is referred to as the Delivery Amount. When called upon and assuming there is no dispute, the Pledgor will transfer the requested Delivery Amount of collateral to the Secured Party. However, the amount of the call must still be greater than the Pledgor's Minimum Transfer Amount (see p. 16 for an explanation of this term).

In Paragraph 3(b), the Pledgor can request that collateral be returned in an amount equal to the value of any Posted Collateral less the Credit Support Amount. Again, the amount of collateral requested to be returned must be greater than the Pledgor's Threshold and Minimum Transfer Amount. Please note that if the Pledgor fails to make a call, the Secured Party is not obliged to transfer the collateral or point this out to the Pledgor. However, if a third party Valuation Agent is involved, this should not arise if the Valuation Agent is properly managing the relationship.

The Credit Support Amount is determined by first calculating the Secured Party's Exposure as of the Valuation Date. The Secured Party's Exposure is equal to the amount that would be owed to the Secured Party if the Agreement were terminated on the Valuation Date, using a mid-market calculation. The Independent Amount (see p. 15 for an explanation of this term) for the Pledgor is added to the amount of Exposure and the Independent Amount for the Secured Party is subtracted. Finally, the Pledgor's Threshold is subtracted.

Paragraph 4. Conditions Precedent, Transfer Timing, Calculations and Substitutions

(a) *Conditions Precedent.* Each Transfer obligation of the Pledgor under Paragraphs 3 and 5 and of the Secured Party under Paragraphs 3, 4(d)(ii), 5 and 6(d) is subject to the conditions precedent that:

(i) no Event of Default, Potential Event of Default or Specified Condition has occurred and is continuing with respect to the other party; and

(ii) no Early Termination Date for which any unsatisfied payment obligations exist has occurred or been designated as the result of an Event of Default or Specified Condition with respect to the other party.

(b) *Transfer Timing.* Subject to Paragraphs 4(a) and 5 and unless otherwise specified, if a demand for the Transfer of Eligible Credit Support or Posted Credit Support is made by the Notification Time, then the relevant Transfer will be made not later than the close of business on the next Local Business Day; if a demand is made after the Notification Time, then the relevant Transfer will be made not later than the close of business on the second Local Business Day thereafter.

Paragraph 4. Conditions Precedent, Transfer Timing, Calculations and Substitutions

Under Paragraph 4(a)(i), a party is not obligated to transfer collateral that it would otherwise be required to transfer under the New York Law CSA if:

- **an Event of Default,**
- **Potential Event of Default or**
- **a Specified Condition**

has occurred with respect to the other party. This protects a party from having to transfer collateral to a counterparty that is in difficulty. This provision may have the effect of one of the two parties being either under- or over-collateralised. (See p. 227 and pp. 262–263 for a discussion of Specified Conditions.)

Paragraph 4(a)(ii) provides that neither party is obligated to transfer collateral after the designation of an Early Termination Date, regardless of who designated the Early Termination Date, why it was designated or when the termination payment is due. Presumably, this is because the parties will soon be making the early termination payment. If a party is concerned about being exposed during that period, the Early Termination Date should occur as soon as possible after the party gives notice of one.

Under the general rule of Paragraph 4(b), a party is required to deliver collateral by the close of business on the next Local Business Day if it receives notice by the Notification Time. If it receives a call for collateral after the Notification Time, it is required to deliver collateral by the close of business on the second Local Business Day.

It is unclear in the New York Law CSA what is meant by "close of business". Presumably, this would be close of business for banks and other financial institutions in the jurisdiction of the party calling for the collateral transfer.

Some parties amend this provision either to speed up or slow down the transfer of collateral after a call depending upon the sophistication of the parties involved or the type of collateral transferred.

(c) **_Calculations._** All calculations of Value and Exposure for purposes of Paragraphs 3 and 6(d) will be made by the Valuation Agent as of the Valuation Time. The Valuation Agent will notify each party (or the other party, if the Valuation Agent is a party) of its calculations not later than the Notification Time on the Local Business Day following the applicable Valuation Date (or in the case of Paragraph 6(d), following the date of calculation).

(d) **_Substitutions._**

   (i) Unless otherwise specified in Paragraph 13, upon notice to the Secured Party specifying the items of Posted Credit Support to be exchanged, the Pledgor may, on any Local Business Day, Transfer to the Secured Party substitute Eligible Credit Support (the "Substitute Credit Support"); and

   (ii) subject to Paragraph 4(a), the Secured Party will Transfer to the Pledgor the items of Posted Credit Support specified by the Pledgor in its notice not later than the Local Business Day following the date on which the Secured Party receives the Substitute Credit Support, unless otherwise specified in Paragraph 13 (the "Substitution Date"); provided that the Secured Party will only be obligated to Transfer Posted Credit Support with a Value as of the date of Transfer of that Posted Credit Support equal to the Value as of that date of the Substitute Credit Support.

Paragraph 4(c), (d)

Paragraph 4(c) requires the Valuation Agent to make the calculations of Value and Exposure as of the Valuation Time (typically the close of business on the Local Business Day preceding the Valuation Date). It is generally easier to make the required calculations if they are based on previously published quotations of the Value of collateral. The Valuation Agent will notify the other party of its calculations not later than the Notification Time on the Local Business Day following the Valuation Date or in respect of payments of interest on bonds or cash on the date of calculation itself.

Paragraph 4(d) provides the Pledgor with the opportunity to substitute Eligible Collateral for collateral that it had previously posted to the Secured Party. A Pledgor may want to substitute collateral in the event that the previously pledged collateral is needed for a new purpose by the Pledgor.

The Secured Party must agree to such a substitution unless Paragraph 13 requires the Pledgor to obtain the Secured Party's consent for the substitution. A Secured Party may require consent in order to avoid situations where the Pledgor becomes a nuisance by making too many substitutions of Eligible Collateral. Although the Secured Party is not in a weaker position after a substitution, frequent substitutions of collateral by the Pledgor can prove to be a time consuming nuisance for the Secured Party's back office and will involve transfer costs.

The Secured Party is not required to transfer the previously Posted Collateral to the Pledgor until it has received the substitute collateral. The Secured Party is obligated to transfer the previously Posted Collateral on the Local Business Day following receipt of the substitute collateral and then only in an amount that does not exceed the Value of the Substitute Credit Support.

Paragraph 5. Dispute Resolution

If a party (a "Disputing Party") disputes (I) the Valuation Agent's calculation of a Delivery Amount or a Return Amount or (II) the Value of any Transfer of Eligible Credit Support or Posted Credit Support, then (I) the Disputing Party will notify the other party and the Valuation Agent (if the Valuation Agent is not the other party) not later than the close of business on the Local Business Day following (X) the date that the demand is made under Paragraph 3 in the case of (I) above or (Y) the date of Transfer in the case of (II) above, (2) subject to Paragraph 4(a), the appropriate party will Transfer the undisputed amount to the other party not later than the close of business on the Local Business Day following (X) the date that the demand is made under Paragraph 3 in the case of (I) above or (Y) the date of Transfer in the case of (II) above, (3) the parties will consult with each other in an attempt to resolve the dispute and (4) if they fail to resolve the dispute by the Resolution Time, then:

(i) In the case of a dispute involving a Delivery Amount or Return Amount, unless otherwise specified in Paragraph 13, the Valuation Agent will recalculate the Exposure and the Value as of the Recalculation Date by:

    (A) utilizing any calculations of Exposure for the Transactions (or Swap Transactions) that the parties have agreed are not in dispute;

    (B) calculating the Exposure for the Transactions (or Swap Transactions) in dispute by seeking four actual quotations at mid-market from Reference Market-makers for purposes of calculating Market Quotation, and taking the arithmetic average of those obtained; provided that if four quotations are not available for a particular Transaction (or Swap Transaction), then fewer than four quotations may be used for that Transaction (or Swap Transaction); and if no quotations are available for a particular Transaction (or Swap Transaction), then the Valuation Agent's original calculations will be used for that Transaction (or Swap Transaction); and

    (C) utilizing the procedures specified in Paragraph 13 for calculating the Value, if disputed, of Posted Credit Support.

(ii) In the case of a dispute involving the Value of any Transfer of Eligible Credit Support or Posted Credit Support, the Valuation Agent will recalculate the Value as of the date of Transfer pursuant to Paragraph 13.

Following a recalculation pursuant to this Paragraph, the Valuation Agent will notify each party (or the other party, if the Valuation Agent is a party) not later than the Notification Time on the Local Business Day following the Resolution Time. The appropriate party will, upon demand following that notice by the Valuation Agent or a resolution pursuant to (3) above and subject to Paragraphs 4(a) and 4(b), make the appropriate Transfer.

Paragraph 5. Dispute Resolution

If a party disputes the Valuation Agent's calculation of Exposure or the Value of the Posted Collateral, Paragraph 5 provides a framework for resolving the dispute if it cannot be settled informally.

Collateral disputes always relate to these two matters and the calculation of Exposure is the most common kind of dispute. Parties often disagree on the calculation of Exposure if the underlying Transactions are illiquid and difficult to value.

Disputes may also arise over the valuation of collateral if illiquid securities that are difficult to value are being pledged.

The steps are outlined in Paragraph 5(i) and (ii) and involve:

(1)   A requirement for the Disputing Party, (i) if it wishes to dispute the calculation of exposure, to notify its counterparty or the third party Valuation Agent (if any) by the close of business on the Local Business Day after the date the collateral call notice is received or (ii) if it wishes to dispute the calculation of the value of the collateral transferred, to notify the third party Valuation Agent on the date that the collateral transfer has been made.

(2)   The Disputing Party agrees to transfer the undisputed amount to the other party no later than (i) in the case of disputes over exposure, by the close of business on the Local Business Day after the collateral call is made or (ii) in the case of disputes over the valuation of collateral, the date the collateral is transferred.

(3)   The parties will attempt to resolve the dispute by the deadline nominated in Paragraph 13(f)(i) – the Resolution Time.

(4)   If they fail then:

   (i)   (A)   If the dispute involves the amount of collateral called for, the Valuation Agent will recalculate his figures by reusing any calculation of the amount of Exposure not in dispute.

         (B)   It will then approach four Reference Market-makers for mid-market quotations (i.e. the average of the bid and offer prices of the Transactions concerned). Provided four quotations are received the arithmetic average of these quotations is used. To this is added the Exposure calculation which is not in dispute. However, fewer than four quotations may be used in the recalculation of Exposure if four quotations are not available to calculate the amount for a particular Transaction. If no quotations are available, then the Valuation Agent's original calculation will be used for that Transaction. Because this Exposure calculation is important only for purposes of collateral transfer and not for early termination, this

should be a reasonable approach although it could lead to under- or over-collateralisation.

(C) The Valuation Agent will also follow the method specified in Paragraph 13(f)(ii) for calculating the value of collateral held. A method has to be specified in Paragraph 13 or the dispute resolution provisions with respect to the calculations of Value become inoperative. There is no fallback.

(ii) The Valuation Agent will directly focus on Paragraph 13(f)(ii) where the dispute solely involves the Value of collateral held.

When all the recalculations have been done, the Valuation Agent will notify each party (if it is a third party) and the other party (if it is not) of the revised figures not later than the deadline (Notification Time) on the Local Business Day after the Resolution Time (i.e. the dispute resolution deadline agreed in the New York Law CSA).

Once the amount of Exposure and the Value of collateral have been agreed, a revised collateral call notice is sent and the necessary collateral transfer is made.

Paragraph 6. Holding and Using Posted Collateral

(a) *Care of Posted Collateral.* Without limiting the Secured Party's rights under Paragraph 6(c), the Secured Party will exercise reasonable care to assure the safe custody of all Posted Collateral to the extent required by applicable law, and in any event the Secured Party will be deemed to have exercised reasonable care if it exercises at least the same degree of care as it would exercise with respect to its own property. Except as specified in the preceding sentence, the Secured Party will have no duty with respect to Posted Collateral, including, without limitation, any duty to collect any Distributions, or enforce or preserve any rights pertaining thereto.

(b) *Eligibility to Hold Posted Collateral; Custodians.*

(i) *General.* Subject to the satisfaction of any conditions specified in Paragraph 13 for holding Posted Collateral, the Secured Party will be entitled to hold Posted Collateral or to appoint an agent (a "Custodian") to hold Posted Collateral for the Secured Party. Upon notice by the Secured Party to the Pledgor of the appointment of a Custodian, the Pledgor's obligations to make any Transfer will be discharged by making the Transfer to that Custodian. The holding of Posted Collateral by a Custodian will be deemed to be the holding of that Posted Collateral by the Secured Party for which the Custodian is acting.

(ii) *Failure to Satisfy Conditions.* If the Secured Party or its Custodian fails to satisfy any conditions for holding Posted Collateral, then upon a demand made by the Pledgor, the Secured Party will, not later than five Local Business Days after the demand, Transfer or cause its Custodian to Transfer all Posted Collateral held by it to a Custodian that satisfies those conditions or to the Secured Party if it satisfies those conditions.

Paragraph 6. Holding and Using Posted Collateral

Paragraph 6(a) generally imposes the same duty of care on the Secured Party with respect to holding the pledged collateral as is imposed through the New York UCC, Section 9-207. The Secured Party will be deemed to have met that duty if it uses the same care that it would have used in holding its own property. It is also important to note that Secured Party has no duty to collect distributions or to enforce or preserve any rights that the Pledgor has in the Posted Collateral.

Paragraph 6(b)(i) provides that a Secured Party may hold the Posted Collateral itself provided that it meets any eligibility conditions specified in Paragraph 13(g) designated by the parties. The Secured Party may also designate an agent to hold the Posted Collateral. Although the agent is defined in paragraph 6(b) as a "Custodian", it is important to understand that the Custodian is acting as an agent and at the direction of the Secured Party. It is not acting as an escrow agent on behalf of the two parties nor would it have any fiduciary duties to the Pledgor. If the Pledgor desired to create such a relationship, the parties would need to create some kind of custodial agreement similar to the triparty custodial agreements sometimes used with repos.

It is stressed that the holding of Posted Collateral by a Custodian is considered equivalent to the Secured Party holding it himself.

If the Custodian ceases to meet the eligibility conditions, Paragraph 6(b)(ii) provides a Pledgor with an opportunity to require the Secured Party to transfer the Posted Collateral (within five Local Business Days of a demand by the Pledgor) to a custodian which meets the eligibility tests of Paragraph 13(g)(i) or to the Secured Party (if it meets those tests) if no qualifying alternative custodian can be found.

(iii) *Liability.* The Secured Party will be liable for the acts or omissions of its Custodian to the same extent that the Secured Party would be liable hereunder for its own acts or omissions.

(c) *Use of Posted Collateral.* Unless otherwise specified in Paragraph 13 and without limiting the rights and obligations of the parties under Paragraphs 3, 4(d)(ii), 5, 6(d) and 8, if the Secured Party is not a Defaulting Party or an Affected Party with respect to a Specified Condition and no Early Termination Date has occurred or been designated as the result of an Event of Default or Specified Condition with respect to the Secured Party, then the Secured Party will, notwithstanding Section 9-207 of the New York Uniform Commercial Code, have the right to:

(i) sell, pledge, rehypothecate, assign, invest, use, commingle or otherwise dispose of, or otherwise use in its business any Posted Collateral it holds, free from any claim or right of any nature whatsoever of the Pledgor, including any equity or right of redemption by the Pledgor; and

(ii) register any Posted Collateral in the name of the Secured Party, its Custodian or a nominee for either.

For purposes of the obligation to Transfer Eligible Credit Support or Posted Credit Support pursuant to Paragraphs 3 and 5 and any rights or remedies authorized under this Agreement, the Secured Party will be deemed to continue to hold all Posted Collateral and to receive Distributions made thereon, regardless of whether the Secured Party has exercised any rights with respect to any Posted Collateral pursuant to (i) or (ii) above.

Paragraph 6(b)(iii) and (c)

Paragraph 6(b)(iii) is merely a reflection of agency law that requires a party to be liable for the actions of its agent. This also provides some comfort to the Pledgor in that it will always have recourse against the Secured Party regardless of whether it was the Secured Party or the Custodian that breached its duties of care with respect to holding the Posted Collateral.

Paragraph 6(c) grants to the Secured Party what is commonly referred to as "use" or "rehypothecation" rights to the Posted Collateral. To restrict these rights, the parties would need to specify in Paragraph 13 that Paragraph 6(c) did not apply. In addition, these rights do not apply if an Event of Default or Specified Condition had occurred with respect to the Secured Party. For a discussion of the legal effects of rehypothecation, see Chapter 3, at pp. 55–56.

Although it may have reused the Posted Collateral, this sub-paragraph makes it clear that the Secured Party is still regarded as the holder of the Posted Collateral and the recipient of Distributions even if it has used its sale and rehypothecation rights under this sub-paragraph.

(d) *Distributions and Interest Amount.*

    (i) *Distributions.* Subject to Paragraph 4(a), if the Secured Party receives or is deemed to receive Distributions on a Local Business Day, it will Transfer to the Pledgor not later than the following Local Business Day any Distributions it receives or is deemed to receive to the extent that a Delivery Amount would not be created or increased by that Transfer, as calculated by the Valuation Agent (and the date of calculation will be deemed to be a Valuation Date for this purpose).

    (ii) *Interest Amount.* Unless otherwise specified in Paragraph 13 and subject to Paragraph 4(a), in lieu of any interest, dividends or other amounts paid or deemed to have been paid with respect to Posted Collateral in the form of Cash (all of which may be retained by the Secured Party), the Secured Party will Transfer to the Pledgor at the times specified in Paragraph 13 the Interest Amount to the extent that a Delivery Amount would not be created or increased by that Transfer, as calculated by the Valuation Agent (and the date of calculation will be deemed to be a Valuation Date for this purpose). The Interest Amount or portion thereof not Transferred pursuant to this Paragraph will constitute Posted Collateral in the form of Cash and will be subject to the security interest granted under Paragraph 2.

Paragraph 6(d). Distributions and Interest Amount

The general rule under Paragraph 6(d) is that Distributions (such as principal or interest payments on Posted Collateral) are to be passed through to the Pledgor. This rule would generally preserve the rights of the Pledgor, as the owner of the Posted Collateral, to any Distributions made with respect to such Posted Collateral. Such transfer of a Distribution is not required to be passed through to the Pledgor if it would create a Delivery Amount (i.e. a collateral call), because the value of the Posted Collateral held by the Secured Party would decrease due to the transfer of the Distribution to the Pledgor. In this case the amount of the Distribution is retained and forms part of the Posted Collateral.

Paragraph 6(d)(ii) sets forth whether and how the Secured Party will pay interest on Cash that is Posted Collateral. The assumption behind the paragraph is that the Secured Party will, at the minimum, invest the Cash in federal funds or a similar investment during the period that it holds the Cash. In lieu of paying over the actual interest earned, this section provides that the Secured Party will pay the Pledgor a fixed amount based upon an interest rate formula set out by the parties in Paragraph 13.

Where a Delivery Amount would arise from the transfer of the Interest Amount to the Pledgor, the Secured Party is entitled to retain the Interest Amount as part of the Posted Collateral which will also be subject to the New York Law CSA's security interest.

Paragraph 7. Events of Default

For purposes of Section 5(a)(iii)(1) of this Agreement, an Event of Default will exist with respect to a party if:

(i)   that party fails (or fails to cause its Custodian) to make, when due, any Transfer of Eligible Collateral, Posted Collateral or the Interest Amount, as applicable, required to be made by it and that failure continues for two Local Business Days after notice of that failure is given to that party;

(ii)   that party fails to comply with any restriction or prohibition specified in this Annex with respect to any of the rights specified in Paragraph 6(c) and that failure continues for five Local Business Days after notice of that failure is given to that party; or

(iii) that party fails to comply with or perform any agreement or obligation other than those specified in Paragraphs 7(i) and 7(ii) and that failure continues for 30 days after notice of that failure is given to that party.

Paragraph 7. Events of Default

Under Section 5(a)(iii)(1) of the ISDA Master Agreement, it is an Event of Default if there is an event of default under a Credit Support Document. Paragraph 7 sets forth what constitutes an Event of Default under the New York Law CSA for purposes of Section 5(a)(iii)(1).

In particular, it is an Event of Default under the ISDA Master Agreement if a party fails to make a required Transfer of collateral or interest on cash collateral and such failure continues for two Local Business Days after notice. Many parties are now requesting that the cure period for the failure to make a Transfer be reduced to one Local Business Day.

The other Events of Default relate to a party's failure to comply with any restrictions on reuse of collateral five Local Business Days after notice of such failure and its failure to perform any other obligation under the ISDA Master Agreement and the New York Law CSA which remains unremedied 30 days after notice.

Paragraph 8. Certain Rights and Remedies

(a) *Secured Party's Rights and Remedies.* If at any time (1) an Event of Default or Specified Condition with respect to the Pledgor has occurred and is continuing or (2) an Early Termination Date has occurred or been designated as the result of an Event of Default or Specified Condition with respect to the Pledgor, then, unless the Pledgor has paid in full all of its Obligations that are then due, the Secured Party may exercise one or more of the following rights and remedies:

(i) all rights and remedies available to a secured party under applicable law with respect to Posted Collateral held by the Secured Party;

(ii) any other rights and remedies available to the Secured Party under the terms of Other Posted Support, if any;

(iii) the right to Set-off any amounts payable by the Pledgor with respect to any Obligations against any Posted Collateral or the Cash equivalent of any Posted Collateral held by the Secured Party (or any obligation of the Secured Party to Transfer that Posted Collateral); and

(iv) the right to liquidate any Posted Collateral held by the Secured Party through one or more public or private sales or other dispositions with such notice, if any, as may be required under applicable law, free from any claim or right of any nature whatsoever of the Pledgor, including any equity or right of redemption by the Pledgor (with the Secured Party having the right to purchase any or all of the Posted Collateral to be sold) and to apply the proceeds (or the Cash equivalent thereof) from the liquidation of the Posted Collateral to any amounts payable by the Pledgor with respect to any Obligations in that order as the Secured Party may elect.

Each party acknowledges and agrees that Posted Collateral in the form of securities may decline speedily in value and is of a type customarily sold on a recognized market, and, accordingly, the Pledgor is not entitled to prior notice of any sale of that Posted Collateral by the Secured Party, except any notice that is required under applicable law and cannot be waived.

Paragraph 8. Certain Rights and Remedies

Paragraph 8(a) provides important rights and remedies to the Secured Party. It is first important to note that the Secured Party has the right to exercise its rights and remedies under the New York Law CSA (and under applicable law) upon the occurrence of an Event of Default or a Specified Condition (certain Termination Events designated in Paragraph 13), regardless of whether an Early Termination Date has occurred. It is important to note also that the occurrence of a Termination Event or the designation of an Early Termination Date under the ISDA Master Agreement because of a Termination Event will not provide a right or remedy under the New York Law CSA unless it was designated as a Specified Condition.

The term Specified Condition is not specifically defined in Paragraph 12 of the New York Law CSA. Its terms of reference are instead specified in Paragraph 13(d). This is usually a selection of the Termination Events or Additional Termination Events which appear in the ISDA Master Agreement Schedule. If a Specified Condition applies to a party, he cannot call for collateral, substitute it or receive Distributions or interest on collateral posted by it. There is also no reason why the parties could not agree to add additional Specified Conditions beyond those generally designated.

The rights and remedies under Paragraph 8(a) for the Secured Party are:

- **any rights or remedies it has under applicable law, maximising the possibilities for action for the Secured Party;**
- **any rights and remedies under the terms of Other Posted Support such as a letter of credit or surety bond (relatively uncommon types of Eligible Collateral);**
- **the right to set off any amounts payable by the Pledgor under the ISDA Master Agreement against any Posted Collateral held by the Secured Party; and**
- **the right to liquidate Posted Collateral, for example through public or private sales or a sale to himself free from any claim from the Pledgor and without any claim unless required by law.**

The proceeds of the liquidation of Posted Collateral will be applied by the Secured Party in any order it sees fit against the Pledgor's Obligations to it.

In the final paragraph it is acknowledged that time is of the essence in liquidating securities collateral and therefore the Pledger is not entitled to notice of such a sale by the Secured Party unless the law requires this.

(b) **Pledgor's Rights and Remedies.** If at any time an Early Termination Date has occurred or been designated as the result of an Event of Default or Specified Condition with respect to the Secured Party, then (except in the case of an Early Termination Date relating to less than all Transactions (or Swap Transactions) where the Secured Party has paid in full all of its obligations that are then due under Section 6(e) of this Agreement):

(i) the Pledgor may exercise all rights and remedies available to a pledgor under applicable law with respect to Posted Collateral held by the Secured Party;

(ii) the Pledgor may exercise any other rights and remedies available to the Pledgor under the terms of Other Posted Support, if any;

(iii) the Secured Party will be obligated immediately to Transfer all Posted Collateral and the Interest Amount to the Pledgor; and

(iv) to the extent that Posted Collateral or the Interest Amount is not so Transferred pursuant to (iii) above, the Pledgor may:

(A) Set-off any amounts payable by the Pledgor with respect to any Obligations against any Posted Collateral or the Cash equivalent of any Posted Collateral held by the Secured Party (or any obligation of the Secured Party to Transfer that Posted Collateral); and

(B) to the extent that the Pledgor does not Set-off under (iv)(A) above, withhold payment of any remaining amounts payable by the Pledgor with respect to any Obligations, up to the Value of any remaining Posted Collateral held by the Secured Party, until that Posted Collateral is Transferred to the Pledgor.

(c) **Deficiencies and Excess Proceeds.** The Secured Party will Transfer to the Pledgor any proceeds and Posted Credit Support remaining after liquidation, Set-off and/or application under Paragraphs 8(a) and 8(b) after satisfaction in full of all amounts payable by the Pledgor with respect to any Obligations; the Pledgor in all events will remain liable for any amounts remaining unpaid after any liquidation, Set-off and/or application under Paragraphs 8(a) and 8(b).

(d) **Final Returns.** When no amounts are or thereafter may become payable by the Pledgor with respect to any Obligations (except for any potential liability under Section 2(d) of this Agreement), the Secured Party will Transfer to the Pledgor all Posted Credit Support and the Interest Amount, if any.

Paragraph 8(b)–(d)

Paragraph 8(b) is important to the Pledgor, who although "out of the money" with respect to its Transactions with the Secured Party, may still be the Non-defaulting Party or non-Affected Party. In contrast with Paragraph 8(a), the Pledgor cannot exercise its rights and remedies at all until after an Early Termination Date has been designated.

The rights and remedies under Paragraph 8(b) for the Pledgor are:

- any rights or remedies it has under applicable law;
- any rights and remedies under the terms of Other Posted Support such as a letter of credit or surety bond (relatively uncommon types of Eligible Collateral);
- the right to the return of all Posted Collateral and interest on cash collateral from the Secured Party (this may be unrealistic to rely upon, however, if the Secured Party is in trouble financially);
- to the extent that the Posted Collateral is not returned, the right to set off any amounts payable by the Pledgor under the ISDA Master Agreement against any Posted Collateral held by the Secured Party; and
- to the extent that the Pledgor does not exercise its set off rights, the right to withhold residual early termination payments until the Posted Collateral is returned.

Because the Pledgor does not have a "lien" on the Posted Collateral that it has pledged to the Secured Party, the Pledgor would be only an unsecured creditor with respect to its right to the return of any Posted Collateral upon the insolvency of a Secured Party. It will generally be easier to exercise its set off rights, rather than petition the bankruptcy court for the return of its Posted Collateral.

Paragraph 8(c) generally restates a Pledgor's rights under the UCC to any surplus Posted Credit Support after the Secured Party has received its full early termination payment. It also restates a Secured Party's right to further pursue the Pledgor for payment in the event that the Posted Collateral is insufficient to satisfy the Pledgor's Obligations to the Secured Party.

In Paragraph 8(d), the Pledgor is entitled to the return of any Posted Collateral and any interest payable on cash collateral upon the Pledgor's satisfaction of all of its payment obligations to the Secured Party. Any potential liability to withholding tax is ignored in these circumstances.

Paragraph 9. Representations

Each party represents to the other party (which representations will be deemed to be repeated as of each date on which it, as the Pledgor, Transfers Eligible Collateral) that:

(i)   it has the power to grant a security interest in and lien on any Eligible Collateral it Transfers as the Pledgor and has taken all necessary actions to authorize the granting of that security interest and lien;

(ii) it is the sole owner of or otherwise has the right to Transfer all Eligible Collateral it Transfers to the Secured Party hereunder, free and clear of any security interest, lien, encumbrance or other restrictions other than the security interest and lien granted under Paragraph 2;

(iii) upon the Transfer of any Eligible Collateral to the Secured Party under the terms of this Annex, the Secured Party will have a valid and perfected first priority security interest therein (assuming that any central clearing corporation or any third-party financial intermediary or other entity not within the control of the Pledgor involved in the Transfer of that Eligible Collateral gives the notices and takes the action required of it under applicable law for perfection of that interest); and

(iv) the performance by it of its obligations under this Annex will not result in the creation of any security interest, lien or other encumbrance on any Posted Collateral other than the security interest and lien granted under Paragraph 2.

Paragraph 9. Representations

These representations serve the same purpose (and are deemed repeated each time Eligible Collateral is Transferred) as the representations made in Section 3 of the ISDA Master Agreement. A breach of any of the representations set forth in Paragraph 9 would constitute a misrepresentation and thus an Event of Default under Section 5(a)(iv) of the ISDA Master Agreement, permitting the Secured Party to terminate all Transactions under it. These representations are relatively straightforward and are rarely, if ever, amended by the parties.

Paragraph 10. Expenses

(a) *General.* Except as otherwise provided in Paragraphs 10(b) and 10(c), each party will pay its own costs and expenses in connection with performing its obligations under this Annex and neither party will be liable for any costs and expenses incurred by the other party in connection herewith.

(b) *Posted Credit Support.* The Pledgor will promptly pay when due all taxes, assessments or charges of any nature that are imposed with respect to Posted Credit Support held by the Secured Party upon becoming aware of the same, regardless of whether any portion of that Posted Credit Support is subsequently disposed of under Paragraph 6(c), except for those taxes, assessments and charges that result from the exercise of the Secured Party's rights under Paragraph 6(c).

(c) *Liquidation/Application of Posted Credit Support.* All reasonable costs and expenses incurred by or on behalf of the Secured Party or the Pledgor in connection with the liquidation and/or application of any Posted Credit Support under Paragraph 8 will be payable, on demand and pursuant to the Expenses Section of this Agreement, by the Defaulting Party or, if there is no Defaulting Party, equally by the parties.

Paragraph 10. Expenses

Paragraph 10(a) is a simple statement that each party will pay its own expenses relating to its performance of its obligations under the New York Law CSA and will not be liable for any costs or expenses incurred by the other party.

Paragraph 10(b) clarifies that the Pledgor will be liable for taxes and other assessments with respect to the Posted Collateral, except for those taxes and assessments resulting from the Secured Party exercising its "use" rights under Paragraph 6(c).

When a Non-defaulting Party exercises its enforcement rights under Paragraph 8 all reasonable costs and expenses shall be borne by the Defaulting Party, or if there is none, by the parties equally.

Paragraph 11. Miscellaneous

(a) *Default Interest.* A Secured Party that fails to make, when due, any Transfer of Posted Collateral or the Interest Amount will be obligated to pay the Pledgor (to the extent permitted under applicable law) an amount equal to interest at the Default Rate multiplied by the Value of the items of property that were required to be Transferred, from (and including) the date that Posted Collateral or Interest Amount was required to be Transferred to (but excluding) the date of Transfer of that Posted Collateral or Interest Amount. This interest will be calculated on the basis of daily compounding and the actual number of days elapsed.

(b) *Further Assurances.* Promptly following a demand made by a party, the other party will execute, deliver, file and record any financing statement, specific assignment or other document and take any other action that may be necessary or desirable and reasonably requested by that party to create, preserve, perfect or validate any security interest or lien granted under Paragraph 2, to enable that party to exercise or enforce its rights under this Annex with respect to Posted Credit Support or an Interest Amount or to effect or document a release of a security interest on Posted Collateral or an Interest Amount.

(c) *Further Protection.* The Pledgor will promptly give notice to the Secured Party of, and defend against, any suit, action, proceeding or lien that involves Posted Credit Support Transferred by the Pledgor or that could adversely affect the security interest and lien granted by it under Paragraph 2, unless that suit, action, proceeding or lien results from the exercise of the Secured Party's rights under Paragraph 6(c).

(d) *Good Faith and Commercially Reasonable Manner.* Performance of all obligations under this Annex, including, but not limited to, all calculations, valuations and determinations made by either party, will be made in good faith and in a commercially reasonable manner.

(e) *Demands and Notices.* All demands and notices made by a party under this Annex will be made as specified in the Notices Section of this Agreement, except as otherwise provided in Paragraph 13.

(f) *Specifications of Certain Matters.* Anything referred to in this Annex as being specified in Paragraph 13 also may be specified in one or more Confirmations or other documents and this Annex will be construed accordingly.

Paragraph 11. Miscellaneous

Consistent with Section 2(e) of the ISDA Master Agreement, a Secured Party must pay interest at the Default Rate (i.e. 1% over the Pledgor's cost of funds) on the value of any Posted Collateral not transferred on the due date under the New York Law CSA. Paragraph 11 clarifies that the Default Interest accrued will be compounded daily from and including the due date to the day before the Transfer is actually made.

Paragraph 11(b) first obligates the Pledgor to co-operate with the Secured Party in the event that the Secured Party is having difficulty attaching, perfecting or enforcing its security interest in the Posted Collateral. The failure of the Pledgor to co-operate would constitute an Event of Default under Paragraph 7(iii).

Paragraph 11(b) then obligates the Secured Party to co-operate with the Pledgor in order to enable the Pledgor to obtain the release of a security interest in the Posted Collateral or an Interest Amount. The failure of the Secured Party to co-operate would also constitute an Event of Default under Paragraph 7(iii) because the New York Law CSA is a Credit Support Document for the Pledgor as well as for the Secured Party.

Paragraph 11(c) is helpful to the Secured Party in that it requires the Pledgor to defend any third party claims against the Posted Collateral. Again, failure to assist the Secured Party in such defence would constitute an Event of Default. However, there is no such obligation on the Pledgor where such legal action arises from the Secured Party's reuse of the Posted Collateral.

Paragraph 11(d) restates a party's obligations to act in good faith and in a commercially reasonable manner under the New York Law CSA.

Although Paragraph 11(e) is a mundane boilerplate provision, it is critical that a party understands how to make demands and give notice in order to ensure that it can exercise its rights and remedies under the New York Law CSA promptly. Parties should be sure to understand how to give notice properly in order to ensure that notice and cure periods are triggered promptly and effectively under this provision.

Paragraph 11(f) points out that the terms of the New York Law CSA can be amended through a Confirmation as well as through a formal amendment to the New York Law CSA itself.

Paragraph 12. Definitions

As used in this Annex:

"Cash" means the lawful currency of the United States of America.

"Credit Support Amount" has the meaning specified in Paragraph 3.

"Custodian" has the meaning specified in Paragraphs 6(b)(i) and 13.

"Delivery Amount" has the meaning specified in Paragraph 3(a).

"Disputing Party" has the meaning specified in Paragraph 5.

"Distributions" means with respect to Posted Collateral other than Cash, all principal, interest and other payments and distributions of cash or other property with respect thereto, regardless of whether the Secured Party has disposed of that Posted Collateral under Paragraph 6(c). Distributions will not include any item of property acquired by the Secured Party upon any disposition or liquidation of Posted Collateral or, with respect to any Posted Collateral in the form of Cash, any distributions on that collateral, unless otherwise specified herein.

"Eligible Collateral" means, with respect to a party, the items, if any, specified as such for that party in Paragraph 13.

"Eligible Credit Support" means Eligible Collateral and Other Eligible Support.

"Exposure" means for any Valuation Date or other date for which Exposure is calculated and subject to Paragraph 5 in the case of a dispute, the amount, if any, that would be payable to a party that is the Secured Party by the other party (expressed as a positive number) or by a party that is the Secured Party to the other party (expressed as a negative number) pursuant to Section 6(e)(ii)(2)(A) of this Agreement as if all Transactions (or Swap Transactions) were being terminated as of the relevant Valuation Time; provided that Market Quotation will be determined by the Valuation Agent using its estimates at mid-market of the amounts that would be paid for Replacement Transactions (as that term is defined in the definition of "Market Quotation").

"Independent Amount" means, with respect to a party, the amount specified as such for that party in Paragraph 13; if no amount is specified, zero.

Paragraph 12. Definitions

The following is a simplified glossary of all terms in the New York Law CSA.

GLOSSARY OF TERMS IN PARAGRAPH 12

Cash	Cash is always defined in the New York Law CSA to be US dollars.
Credit Support Amount	See annotation in Paragraph 3.
Custodian	See annotation in Paragraph 6(b).
Delivery Amount	See annotation in Paragraph 3.
Disputing Party	A party who disputes the other party's calculation of Transaction values in determining risk exposure and/or the value of any collateral held or to be returned.
Distributions	Distributions include any transfers of principal, interest or any other distributions made with respect to Posted Collateral except cash collateral.
Eligible Collateral	The types of collateral and their maturities that can be pledged by the Pledgor.
Eligible Credit Support	This includes Eligible Collateral and any other credit support designated by the parties such as letters of credit.
Exposure	The estimated termination value of all Transactions so as to calculate risk exposure. The calculation is made as if the Transactions were being closed out as of the Valuation Time.
Independent Amount	A term meaning either initial margin taken at the start of a collateral relationship and not counted in risk exposure calculations or a sum taken later in the relationship and which is counted in the risk exposure calculations.

"Interest Amount" means, with respect to an Interest Period, the aggregate sum of the amounts of interest calculated for each day in that Interest Period on the principal amount of Posted Collateral in the form of Cash held by the Secured Party on that day, determined by the Secured Party for each such day as follows:

(x) the amount of that Cash on that day; multiplied by

(y) the Interest Rate in effect for that day; divided by

(z) 360.

"Interest Period" means the period from (and including) the last Local Business Day on which an Interest Amount was Transferred (or, if no Interest Amount has yet been Transferred, the Local Business Day on which Posted Collateral in the form of Cash was Transferred to or received by the Secured Party) to (but excluding) the Local Business Day on which the current Interest Amount is to be Transferred.

"Interest Rate" means the rate specified in Paragraph 13.

"Local Business Day", unless otherwise specified in Paragraph 13, has the meaning specified in the Definitions Section of this Agreement, except that references to a payment in clause (b) thereof will be deemed to include a Transfer under this Annex.

"Minimum Transfer Amount" means, with respect to a party, the amount specified as such for that party in Paragraph 13; if no amount is specified, zero.

"Notification Time" has the meaning specified in Paragraph 13.

"Obligations" means, with respect to a party, all present and future obligations of that party under this Agreement and any additional obligations specified for that party in Paragraph 13.

"Other Eligible Support" means, with respect to a party, the items, if any, specified as such for that party in Paragraph 13.

"Other Posted Support" means all Other Eligible Support Transferred to the Secured Party that remains in effect for the benefit of that Secured Party.

"Pledgor" means either party, when that party (i) receives a demand for or is required to Transfer Eligible Credit Support under Paragraph 3(a) or (ii) has Transferred Eligible Credit Support under Paragraph 3(a).

Interest Amount	The aggregate sum of interest due on Cash collateral. The interest accrued during the interest period is not compounded (unless provided for in an amendment in Paragraph 13).
Interest Period	The period from the date when interest was last paid on Cash collateral to the date on which it is next due to be paid.
Interest Rate	The particular benchmark interest rate (e.g. Federal Funds (Effective)). In agreements involving US parties, it is typically based on Federal Funds (Effective). It may also include a spread.
Local Business Day	A normal business day in the location required for the valuation of Transactions and collateral under the New York Law CSA and also a normal business day for the party receiving a Transfer of collateral.
Minimum Transfer Amount	The minimum amount that the Delivery Amount or Return Amount must reach prior to a party being obligated to deliver or return collateral.
Notification Time	The agreed deadline for making a collateral call in order to receive a Transfer by the deadline specified in the New York Law CSA.
Obligations	The obligations of a party under the ISDA Master Agreement to be collateralllised under the New York Law CSA. The scope of obligations may be expanded under Paragraph 13.
Other Eligible Support	This constitutes credit support that the parties may agree to such as letters of credit or surety bonds.
Other Posted Support	Other Eligible Support that is actually provided by the Pledgor to the Secured Party (i.e. the delivery of a letter of credit).
Pledgor	The party that receives a demand requiring it to post collateral or the party who currently has pledged collateral.

"Posted Collateral" means all Eligible Collateral, other property, Distributions, and all proceeds thereof that have been Transferred to or received by the Secured Party under this Annex and not Transferred to the Pledgor pursuant to Paragraph 3(b), 4(d)(ii) or 6(d)(i) or released by the Secured Party under Paragraph 8. Any Interest Amount or portion thereof not Transferred pursuant to Paragraph 6(d)(ii) will constitute Posted Collateral in the form of Cash.

"Posted Credit Support" means Posted Collateral and Other Posted Support.

"Recalculation Date" means the Valuation Date that gives rise to the dispute under Paragraph 5; provided, however, that if a subsequent Valuation Date occurs under Paragraph 3 prior to the resolution of the dispute, then the *"Recalculation Date"* means the most recent Valuation Date under Paragraph 3.

"Resolution Time" has the meaning specified in Paragraph 13.

"Return Amount" has the meaning specified in Paragraph 3(b).

"Secured Party" means either party, when that party (i) makes a demand for or is entitled to receive Eligible Credit Support under Paragraph 3(a) or (ii) holds or is deemed to hold Posted Credit Support.

"Specified Condition" means, with respect to a party, any event specified as such for that party in Paragraph 13.

"Substitute Credit Support" has the meaning specified in Paragraph 4(d)(i).

"Substitution Date" has the meaning specified in Paragraph 4(d)(ii).

"Threshold" means, with respect to a party, the amount specified as such for that party in Paragraph 13; if no amount is specified, zero.

"Transfer" means, with respect to any Eligible Credit Support, Posted Credit Support or Interest Amount, and in accordance with the instructions of the Secured Party, Pledgor or Custodian, as applicable:

(i) in the case of Cash, payment or delivery by wire transfer into one or more bank accounts specified by the recipient;

(ii) in the case of certificated securities that cannot be paid or delivered by book-entry, payment or delivery in appropriate physical form to the recipient or its account accompanied by any duly executed instruments of transfer, assignments in blank, transfer tax stamps and any other documents necessary to constitute a legally valid transfer to the recipient;

(iii) in the case of securities that can be paid or delivered by book-entry, the giving of written instructions to the relevant depository institution or other entity specified by the recipient, together with a written copy thereof to the recipient, sufficient if complied with to result in a legally effective transfer of the relevant interest to the recipient; and

(iv) in the case of Other Eligible Support or Other Posted Support, as specified in Paragraph 13.

Posted Collateral	All collateral that has been pledged to, and is currently held by, the Secured Party.
Posted Credit Support	This includes Posted Collateral plus any Other Posted Support such as a letter of credit.
Recalculation Date	The Valuation Date that gave rise to the dispute.
Resolution Time	The deadline for resolving disputes, i.e. one Local Business Day after the date on which the party receives a notice that it disputes.
Return Amount	See annotation under Paragraph 3.
Secured Party	The party making a demand to receive collateral or the party holding Posted Collateral.
Specified Condition	A Termination Event such as Illegality or Credit Event Upon Merger designated by the parties in Paragraph 13 as a Specified Condition.
Substitute Credit Support	Collateral transferred to the Secured Party in substitution for previously pledged collateral.
Substitution Date	The date the Secured Party receives Substitute Credit Support.
Threshold	The unsecured risk exposure each party allows the other. Collateral may only be called or returned where the risk exposure exceeds the relevant party's Threshold and Minimum Transfer Amount.
Transfer	A Transfer occurs when collateral delivered to a Secured Party is deemed to be received by the Secured Party. For example, a Transfer of Cash occurs when the Cash is received in the Secured Party's bank account.

"Valuation Agent" has the meaning specified in Paragraph 13.

"Valuation Date" means each date specified in or otherwise determined pursuant to Paragraph 13.

"Valuation Percentage" means, for any item of Eligible Collateral, the percentage specified in Paragraph 13.

"Valuation Time" has the meaning specified in Paragraph 13.

"Value" means for any Valuation Date or other date for which Value is calculated and subject to Paragraph 5 in the case of a dispute, with respect to:

    (i)   Eligible Collateral or Posted Collateral that is:

        (A)   Cash, the amount thereof; and

        (B)   a security, the bid price obtained by the Valuation Agent multiplied by the applicable Valuation Percentage, if any;

    (ii)   Posted Collateral that consists of items that are not specified as Eligible Collateral, zero; and

    (iii) Other Eligible Support and Other Posted Support, as specified in Paragraph 13.

Valuation Agent	The Valuation Agent is the party calculating Exposure and the value of Posted Collateral. It is also the party that makes a request for collateral to be transferred or returned.
Valuation Date	The Local Business Day upon which risk exposure calculations and collateral valuations are made (based upon those amounts as of the Valuation Time) to determine if a collateral delivery or return is needed.
Valuation Percentage	The remaining value of collateral expressed in percentage terms after the agreed haircut has been deducted.
Valuation Time	The reference time at which calculations for collateral calls are made. They are often based on prices at the close of business on the Local Business Day before the Valuation Date.
Value	The agreed valuation bases for Cash and securities collateral in Paragraph 13(f).

Paragraph 13

This is the Elections and Variables Paragraph where the parties make their choices and amendments to the standard form of the New York Law CSA. Paragraph 13 is the New York Law CSA equivalent of the ISDA Master Agreement Schedule.

For the purpose of illustrating market practice on various choices made in Paragraph 13, I have reviewed over 25 versions of Paragraph 13 to the New York Law CSA used by various dealers, sophisticated end users and hedge funds which I consider to be a reasonable cross-section of the documentation seen in the market.

Below is an example of Paragraph 13 that reflects market practice. In addition to annotating the provisions, this section also illustrates variations of them.

Many of the provisions set out in Chapter 5 with respect to Paragraph 11 of the English Law CSA may also be applicable to Paragraph 13 of the New York CSA. These provisions have not been repeated here. The author has flagged throughout the following discussion where the reader should also consult Paragraph 11 of the English Law CSA for other relevant provisions.

Paragraph 13. Elections and Variables

(a) *Security Interest for "Obligations".* The term *"Obligations"* as used in this Annex includes the following additional obligations:

With respect to Party A: ....

With respect to Party B: ....

(b) *Credit Support Obligations*

    (i) *Delivery Amount, Return Amount and Credit Support Amount*

        (A) *"Delivery Amount"* has the meaning specified in Paragraph 3(a), unless otherwise specified here: ....

        (B) *"Return Amount"* has the meaning specified in Paragraph 3(b), unless otherwise specified here: ....

        (C) *"Credit Support Amount"* has the meaning specified in Paragraph 3, unless otherwise specified here: ....

    (ii) *Eligible Collateral.* The following items will qualify as *"Eligible Collateral"* for the party specified:

		Party A	Party B	Valuation Percentage
(A)	Cash	[ ]	[ ]	[ ]%
(B)	negotiable debt obligations issued by the US Treasury Department having an original maturity at issuance of not more than one year ("Treasury Bills")	[ ]	[ ]	[ ]%
(C)	negotiable debt obligations issued by the US Treasury Department having an original maturity at issuance of not more than one year but not more than 10 years ("Treasury Notes")	[ ]	[ ]	[ ]%
(D)	negotiable debt obligations by the US Treasury Department having an original maturity at issuance of more than 10 years ("Treasury Bonds")	[ ]	[ ]	[ ]%
(E)	other:	[ ]	[ ]	[ ]%

    (iii) *Other Eligible Support.* The following items will qualify as "*Other Eligible Support*" for the party specified:

		Party A	Party B
(A)	....	[ ]	[ ]
(B)	....	[ ]	[ ]

    (iv) *Thresholds*

        (A) *"Independent Amount"* means with respect to Party A: $....

            "Independent Amount" means with respect to Party B: $....

        (B) *"Threshold"* means with respect to Party A: $....................

            "Threshold" means with respect to Party B: $....................

        (C) *"Minimum Transfer Amount"* means with respect to Party A: $....................

            "Minimum Transfer Amount" means with respect to Party B: $....................

        (D) **Rounding.** The Delivery Amount and the Return Amount will be rounded [down to the nearest integral multiple of $.../up and down to the nearest integral multiple of $..., respectively*].

(c) *Valuation and Timing*

    (i) *"Valuation Agent"* means, for purposes of Paragraphs 3 and 5, the party making the demand under Paragraph 3, and, for purposes of Paragraph 6(d), the Secured Party receiving or deemed to receive the Distributions or the Interest. Amount, as applicable, unless specified here: ....

    (ii) *"Valuation Date"* means: ....

    (iii) *"Valuation Time"* means:

        [ ]   the close of business in the city of the Valuation Agent on the Valuation Date or date of calculation, as applicable;

        [ ]   the close of business on the Local Business Day before the Valuation Date or date of calculation, as applicable;

    provided that the calculations of Value and Exposure will be made as of approximately the same time on the same date.

    (iv) *"Notification Time"* means 1:00 p.m., New York time, on a Local Business Day, unless otherwise specified here: ....

(d) *Conditions Precedent and Secured Party's Rights and Remedies.* The following Termination Event(s) will be a *"Special Condition"* for the party specified (that party being the Affected Party if the Termination Event occurs with respect to that party):

	Party A	Party B
Illegality	[ ]	[ ]
Tax Event	[ ]	[ ]
Tax Event Upon Merger	[ ]	[ ]
Credit Event Upon Merger	[ ]	[ ]
Additional Termination Event(s):[1]	[ ]	[ ]
....	[ ]	[ ]
....	[ ]	[ ]

* Delete as applicable.

1 If the parties elect to designate an Additional Termination Event as a "Specified Condition", then they should only designate one or more Additional Termination Events that are designated as such in their Schedule.

(e) *Substitution.*

    (i) *"Substitution Date"* has the meaning specified in Paragraph 4(d)(ii), unless otherwise specified here: ....

    (ii) *Consent.* If specified here as applicable, then the Pledgor must obtain the Secured Party's consent for any substitution pursuant to Paragraph 4(d): [applicable/inapplicable*][2]

(f) *Dispute Resolution.*

    (i) *"Resolution Time"* means 1:00 p.m., New York time, on the Local Business Day following the date on which the notice is given that gives rise to a dispute under Paragraph 5, unless otherwise specified here: ....

    (ii) *Value.* For the purpose of Paragraphs 5(i)(C) and 5(ii), the Value of Posted Credit Support will be calculate as follows: ....

    (iii) *Alternative.* The provisions of Paragraph 5 will apply, unless an alternative dispute resolution procedure is specified here: ....

(g) *Holding and Using Posted Collateral.*

    (i) *Eligibility to Hold Posted Collateral; Custodians.* Party A and its Custodian will be entitled to hold Posted Collateral pursuant to Paragraph 6(b); *provided* that the following conditions applicable to it are satisfied:

        (1) Party A is not a Defaulting Party.

        (2) Posted Collateral may be held only in the following jurisdictions: ....

        (3) ....

        Initially, the **Custodian** for Party A is ....

        Party B and its Custodian will be entitled to hold Posted Collateral pursuant to Paragraph 6(b); *provided* that the following conditions applicable to it are satisfied:

        (1) Party B is not a Defaulting Party.

        (2) Posted Collateral may be held only in the following jurisdiction: ....

        (3) ....

        Initially, the **Custodian** for Party B is ....

    (ii) *Use of Posted Collateral.* The provisions of Paragraph 6(c) will not apply to the [party/parties*] specified here:

        [ ] Party A

        [ ] Party B

        and [that party/those parties*] will not be permitted to: ....

---

* Delete as applicable.

2 Parties should consider selecting "applicable" where substitution without consent could give rise to a registration requirement to perfect properly the security interest in Posted Collateral (e.g., where a party to the Annex is the New York branch of an English bank).

(h) *Distribution and Interest Amount.*

    (i) *Interest Rate.* The *"Interest Rate"* will be: ....

    (ii) *Transfer of Interest Amount.* The Transfer of the Interest Amount will be made on the last Local Business Day of each calendar month and on any Local Business Day that Posted Collateral in the form of Cash is Transferred to the Pledgor pursuant to Paragraph 3(b), unless otherwise specified here: ....

    (iii) *Alternative to Interest Amount.* The provisions of Paragraph 6(d)(ii) will apply, unless otherwise specified here: ....

(i) *Additional Representations(s).*

[Party A/Party B*] represents to the other party (which representation(s) will be deemed to be repeated as of each date on which it, as the Pledgor, Transfers Eligible Collateral) that:

    (i) ....

    (ii) ....

(j) *Other Eligible Support and Other Posted Support.*

    (i) *"Value"* with respect to Other Eligible Support and Other Posted Support means: ....

    (ii) *"Transfer"* with respect to Other Eligible Support and Other Posted Support means: ....

(k) *Demands and Notices.*

All demands, specifications and notices under this Annex will be made pursuant to the Notices Section of this Agreement, unless otherwise specified here: ....

    Party A ....
    ....

    Party B ....
    ....

(l) *Addresses for Transfers.*

    Party A ....
    ....

    Party B ....
    ....

(m) *Other Provisions.*

* Delete as applicable.

EXAMPLES OF PARAGRAPH 13 PROVISIONS

It is important to note that all calculations and amounts under the New York Law CSA are denominated in US dollars.

Obligations

    (a)   *Security Interest for "Obligations".* The term *"Obligations"* as used in this Annex includes no additional obligations with respect to Party A and Party B.

Parties generally do not expand the definition of "Obligations". However, some dealers have begun to expand the definition to include other obligations of their counterparty that fall outside of the ISDA Master Agreement. Many dealers, for example, may also lend securities or enter into repurchase agreements with their counterparty. By expanding the definition of Obligations to include these other obligations, in the event that their counterparty defaults, collateral could be applied not only against the early termination amount payable by the counterparty under the ISDA Master Agreement but also against the other obligations of the counterparty to the dealer. The following is an example of this type of provision:

    (a)   *Security Interest for "Obligations".* The term *"Obligations"* as used in this Annex means, with respect to a party, all present and future obligations under this Agreement or any other contractual arrangement between the Pledgor and the Secured Party or the Pledgor and any Affiliate of the Secured Party.

Credit Support Obligations

    (b)   *Credit Support Obligations.*
       (i)   *Delivery Amount, Return Amount and Credit Support Amount*
          (A) *"Delivery Amount"* has the meaning specified in Paragraph 3(a).

Return Amount

    (B) *"Return Amount"* has the meaning specified in Paragraph 3(b).

It is probably understood by the parties to the New York Law CSA that if the Credit Support Amount is zero, the Secured Party is obligated to return any Posted Collateral. Some Pledgors worry, however, that if the Return Amount is less than the Pledgor's Minimum Transfer Amount, that a Secured Party will not be obligated to return the remaining Posted Collateral. The following provision expressly eliminates that concern:

(B) *"Return Amount"* has the meaning specified in Paragraph 3(b), except that such definition is hereby amended by adding in the fifth line thereof after the words "(rounded pursuant to paragraph 13)" the words "; *provided* that if the Credit Support Amount is zero the Secured Party will, upon the Pledgor's request, Transfer to the Pledgor all Posted Credit Support".

Credit Support Amount

(C) *"Credit Support Amount"* has the meaning specified in Paragraph 3.

Similar to the changes suggested for the English Law CSA in Chapter 5 at p. 129 when dealing with hedge funds and other entities that are required to post Independent Amounts, the parties may want to amend the definition of Credit Support Amount and also add the "offset" provision in order to ensure that a Secured Party is always holding Posted Collateral equal to the Independent Amount regardless of its Credit Support Amount.

Eligible Collateral

(ii) *Eligible Collateral.* The following items will qualify as *"Eligible Collateral"* for the party specified, provided that the Secured Party shall be entitled at any time, and from time to time, not to accept as Eligible Collateral any of the following which constitute Ineligible Securities as defined below:

	Party A	Party B	Valuation Percentage
(A) *Cash*: US Dollars in depositary account form.	YES	YES	100%
(B) *Treasury Bills*: negotiable debt obligations issued by the US Treasury Department having a remaining maturity of not more than one year.	YES	YES	98%
(C) *Treasury Notes*: negotiable debt obligations issued by the US Treasury Department having a remaining maturity of more than one year but not more than 10 years.	YES	YES	98%
(D) *Treasury Bonds*: negotiable debt obligations issued by the US Treasury Department having a remaining maturity of more than 10 years but not more than 30 years.	YES	YES	98%

The above definition for Eligible Collateral is very common for US counterparties. Although some counterparties look to the "original" versus "remaining" maturity for applying the Valuation Percentage, "remaining" maturity would appear to be more useful given that the remaining maturity is typically what will determine the volatility in the value of the US Treasury security.

(E)	*Agency Securities:* negotiable debt obligations of the Federal National Mortgage Association (FNMA), Federal Home Loan Mortgage Corporation (FHLMC), Federal Home Loan Banks (FHLB), Federal Farm Credit Banks (FFCB), Student Loan Marketing Association (SLMA), Tennessee Valley Authority (TVA) having a remaining maturity of not more than 30 years.	YES	YES	92%

As the supply of US Treasury securities has tightened, parties have requested that they can pledge additional types of collateral. The most common of these have been debt securities of entities that are commonly referred to as "quasi-government" agencies or "government sponsored enterprises". The above provision lists the most common quasi-government agency securities that are requested for inclusion in the definition of Eligible Collateral. This list of possibilities, however, is often limited to the debt securities of the Federal National Mortgage Association and the Federal Home Loan Mortgage Corporation. These two agencies are most typically referred to as Fannie Mae and Freddie Mac, respectively.

Although the debt securities of quasi-government agencies do not have an express US government guarantee, quasi-government agencies are considered to be extremely creditworthy by the credit rating agencies and carry very high credit ratings. In agreeing to accept these securities, however, parties should be careful only to accept plain vanilla debt obligations and avoid debt securities that are principal or interest only, puttable or what are commonly referred to as "structured notes". The definition below of Ineligible Securities should cover any securities that would be inappropriate for a Secured Party to accept as collateral.

In addition to the debt obligations of quasi-government agency securities, US counterparties are now frequently requesting that mortgage-backed securities ("MBS") be added to the list of Eligible Collateral. Generally, US counterparties will only agree to include as eligible MBS certificates issued by FNMA, FHLMC and GNMA.

(F)	*FHLMC Certificates.* Mortgage participation certificates issued by FHLMC evidencing undivided interests or participations in pools of first lien conventional or FHA/VA residential mortgages or deeds of trust, guaranteed by FHLMC, and having a remaining maturity of not more than 30 years.	YES	YES	92%

(G)	***FNMA Certificates.*** Mortgage-backed pass-through certificates issued by FNMA evidencing undivided interests in pools of first lien mortgages or deeds of trust on residential properties, guaranteed by FNMA, and having a remaining maturity of not more than 30 years.	YES	YES	92%
(H)	***GNMA Certificates.*** Mortgage-backed pass-through certificates issued by private entities, evidencing undivided interests in pools of first lien mortgages or deeds of trust on single family residences, guaranteed by the Government National Mortgage Association (GNMA) with the full faith and credit of the United States, and having a remaining maturity of not more than 30 years.	YES	YES	92%

In addition, parties typically do not permit a party to pledge MBS collateral that constitutes an interest-only or principal only MBS, a real estate mortgage investment conduit or collateralised mortgage obligations. Structured notes and other similar securities are also usually not accepted. The following is an example of "ineligible securities" that a party would not be able to pledge:

> **"Ineligible Securities" means any obligations, securities, certificates or instruments that (i) are denominated in a currency other than US Dollars, (ii) are issued other than in Federal Reserve book entry form, or (iii) constitute or include structured notes or other structured debt instruments, real estate mortgage investment conduits, collateralized mortgage obligations, guaranteed mortgage certificates, interest-only securities, principal-only securities or any securities representing interests in, or are composed in whole or in part of, residual or high risk mortgage derivatives or other derivatives.**

Finally, you occasionally see general wording for other "Other Eligible Support". It is highly unusual, however, that Other Eligible Support (such as a letter of credit or a surety bond) would ever actually be used.

Such other Eligible Credit Support as the parties may from time to time agree in writing as being acceptable	To be agreed by the parties on a case by case basis.

In a bilateral New York Law CSA both boxes (for Party A and Party B) would be checked and the appropriate Valuation Percentage, determined by the credit function, entered alongside.

No haircut is normally applied to Cash and so its Valuation Percentage is usually 100%.

The Valuation Percentages for US Treasury securities and US Agency securities are similar to those set forth in Figure 5.2 in Chapter 5.

The normal Valuation Percentages for guaranteed US agencies is generally between 90% and 95%. The normal Valuation Percentages for MBS collateral are also generally between 90% and 95%. It is important to remember that the haircut is applied against the fair market value of the Posted Collateral, which is generally already at a discount from the face amount of the Posted Collateral.

Sometimes at the end of the Eligible Credit Support table the following wording will be added:

Notwithstanding the foregoing, the Valuation Percentage with respect to all Eligible Credit Support shall be deemed to be 100% with respect to a Valuation Date which is an Early Termination Date designated or deemed to have occurred as a result of an Event of Default.

The purpose of this is to limit the recovery of a Non-defaulting Party to 100% of what he is owed. Variations of this wording may be found on pp. 184–185.

Thresholds, Independent Amounts and Minimum Transfer Amounts

(iv) *Thresholds*

(A) *"Independent Amount"* means with respect to Party A: ....

"Independent Amount" means with respect to Party B: ....

As discussed earlier, less creditworthy parties are often required to post Independent Amounts before any trading takes place. In this case it is excluded from the Exposure calculations upon which any collateral call is based. Alternatively, it can be a sum which is callable after trading has occurred and may affect either party, possibly as a result of a credit ratings downgrade. This type of Independent Amount will be included in the calculation of Exposure for collateral call purposes.

An Independent Amount may be a fixed monetary sum or a percentage of the notional amount of an individual Transaction or Transactions. This is usually graduated according to the maturity of the individual Transaction. Moreover, Independent Amounts are typically lower for Transactions involving fixed income derivatives than those for equity or credit derivatives.

The discussion and examples of Independent Amount found in Chapter 5 are equally relevant to negotiations involving the New York Law CSA. (See pp. 137–139.)

Threshold

(B) *"Threshold"* means with respect to Party A: ....

 "Threshold" means with respect to Party B: ....

The Threshold is the level of unsecured exposure each party is content to allow the other before any collateral is called. This unsecured exposure will be increased by any Minimum Transfer Amount applying to the parties.

Generally speaking, Thresholds are recorded either as a monetary amount (or zero) or in the form of a credit ratings matrix. An example of the first is:

(B) *"Threshold"* means with respect to Party A: US$ 10,000,000

 "Threshold" means with respect to Party B: US$ 5,000,000

An example of the second kind is:

(B) *"Threshold"* means the amounts determined on the basis of the lower ratings assigned by either Standard & Poor's Ratings Group ("S&P"), a division of McGraw-Hill, Inc. or Moody's Investor Services, Inc. ("Moody's") to the long term, unsecured and unsubordinated debt of Party B; provided that if (x) Party B has no such ratings or (y) an Event of Default has occurred and is continuing, the Threshold with respect to the relevant party shall be zero:

S&P Rating	Moody's Rating	Threshold (US$ million)
AAA	Aaa	
AA+	Aa1	
AA	Aa2	
AA-	Aa3	
A+	A1	
A	A2	
A-	A3	
BBB+	Baa1	
BBB	Baa2	
BBB-	Baa3	
BB+	Ba1	
BB	Ba2	
BB- and below	Ba3 and below	

Again, the credit function would supply the necessary figures. Many US dealers will require that the threshold be zero below A- by S&P or below A3 by Moody's and almost all US dealers will require the threshold to be zero below BBB- by S&P or below Baa3 by Moody's. Anything below BBB- by S&P or Baa3 by Moody's is generally not considered to be investment grade.

As shown in the example provision above, a common amendment is to include a zero Threshold if a party suffers an Event of Default, or if a party is no longer rated by any credit rating agencies.

Although there are other credit rating agencies in the US such as Duff & Phelps Credit Rating Agency, Fitch, Inc. and A.M. Best, parties typically only reference S&P and Moody's. There may be situations, however, when a company may only be rated by one of the other credit rating agencies. A typical definition of a credit rating is as follows:

> "*Rating*" means the rating issued by either Moody's Investor Services ("Moody's") or Standard and Poor's Rating Group, a division of McGraw-Hill, Inc. ("S&P") in respect of either party's long term, unsecured and unsubordinated debt securities.

From previous discussion (see p. 69) you will recall that the New York Law CSA can be made unilateral by assigning a Threshold of Infinity to one of the parties.

Where the credit quality differential between the parties is broad, this can look quite stark:

(B) "*Threshold*" means with respect to Party A: Infinity

"*Threshold*" means with respect to Party B: Zero

You will also recall (see p, 66) that a zero Threshold is not only used where a counterparty is considered to be a weak credit but also to maximise regulatory capital savings because collateral is callable all the sooner where there is a zero Threshold.

Typically, Thresholds appear to be larger in the US than in Europe.

If a Threshold is not specified it is deemed to be zero.

Minimum Transfer Amount

(C) "*Minimum Transfer Amount*" means with respect to Party A: ....

"*Minimum Transfer Amount*" means with respect to Party B: ....

Minimum Transfer Amounts are designed to prevent costly transfers of low or "nuisance" amounts of collateral. Before a Delivery or Return Amount is required to be made under Paragraph 3, the amount must exceed the Minimum Transfer Amount.

Occasionally you see a Minimum Transfer Amount of zero which if combined with a zero Threshold means that you do not wish to take any unsecured risk on your counterparty.

Normally, the Minimum Transfer Amount is expressed in a fixed monetary sum (e.g. US$ 100,000) or linked to a credit ratings matrix as in the following example:

(C) *"Minimum Transfer Amount"* means with respect to Party A and Party B, the amount determined on the basis of the lower of the Long Term Debt Ratings in the table set forth below; provided however that if (i) a party has no Long Term Debt Ratings or (ii) an Event of Default has occurred and is continuing with respect to such party, such party's Minimum Transfer Amount shall be zero.

S&P Rating	Moody's Rating	Minimum Transfer Amount
AAA to A-	Aaa to A3	US$
BBB+ to BB	Baa1 to Ba2	US$
BB- and below	Ba3 and below	US$

Minimum Transfer Amounts tend to be larger in the US than in Europe. Many dealers will permit relatively large Minimum Transfer Amounts for parties that are rated AA- by S&P or Aa3 or above by Moody's. These amounts can range from $100,000 to several million dollars. Because the Minimum Transfer Amount has the indirect effect of extending additional unsecured credit to a Pledgor, the credit department will generally provide these numbers. Many US dealers will require that the Minimum Transfer Amount be zero below A- by S&P or A3 by Moody's and almost all US dealers will require the Minimum Transfer Amount to be zero below BBB- by S&P or Baa3 by Moody's.

As shown in the example above, a common amendment is to include a zero Minimum Transfer Amount if a party suffers an Event of Default. In addition, if a party is no longer rated by any credit rating agencies, the Minimum Transfer Amount will also go to zero.

The variations further discussed in Chapter 5 regarding Minimum Transfer Amounts are equally applicable to the New York Law CSA. See pp. 143–145.

A completely different approach towards permitting an unsecured amount of credit involves setting the Threshold for both parties at zero and providing the unsecured amount as part of the Minimum Transfer Amount. Under this approach, a party is provided an unsecured amount of credit until the Minimum Transfer Amount is exceeded. At this point, the Pledgor is then required to secure the entire Credit Support Amount since the Threshold is zero. The amounts set out for the Minimum Transfer Amount provisions typically parallel the amounts set out for the Threshold provisions in more traditional provisions. The following is a typical provision:

(C) *"Minimum Transfer Amount"* for purposes of computing a Delivery Amount pursuant to Paragraph 3(a), as of any date shall be as set forth in Schedule II hereto under the caption "Minimum Transfer Amount" and shall be, with respect to Party A, the amount set forth opposite the rating classification assigned to any long-term unsecured, unsubordinated debt securities of Party A, and, with respect to Party B, shall be the amount set forth opposite the rating classification assigned to any long-term unsecured unsubordinated debt securities of Party B by the Relevant Rating Agency. If at any time all outstanding long-term unsecured unsubordinated debt securities of Party A or Party B shall not be rated by either of the Relevant Rating Agencies, the Minimum Transfer Amount for such party shall be zero. In the event of a split rating classification by the Relevant Rating Agencies the Minimum Transfer Amount shall be the rating classification opposite the lowest of the ratings in Schedule II hereto. "Relevant Rating Agency" for purposes hereof means Moody's Investors Service, Inc. ("Moody's") and Standard & Poor's Ratings Group, a division of McGraw Hill, Inc. ("S&P"). The Minimum Transfer Amount for purposes of computing a Return Amount pursuant to Paragraph 3(b) shall be US$ 500,000. If an Event of Default occurs and is continuing with respect to a party as Pledgor, its Minimum Transfer Amount shall be zero.

Schedule II in this provision would resemble the Threshold Schedule based on credit ratings that are shown above. One difficulty with this approach is that if the Minimum Transfer Amount is the same for both the Delivery Amount and the Return Amount, if the Minimum Transfer Amount is large, such as $10 million, the Secured Party may end up being overcollateralised in the event that the Credit Support Amount were to decrease. This is because the Credit Support Amount would have to decrease by $10 million before the Secured Party was required to return Posted Collateral. In this example, the parties have resolved this concern by agreeing that the Minimum Transfer Amount for the purposes of a Return Amount is only $500,000, a number which is probably much lower than the amounts found in Schedule II.

Because the Minimum Transfer Amount only establishes a floor for transfers it does not avoid transfers of uneven amounts of collateral. Applying a rounding convention overcomes this.

Rounding

(D) *"Rounding"*. The Delivery Amount will be rounded up and the Return Amount will be rounded [down to the nearest integral multiple of ..../up and down to the nearest integral multiple of .... respectively].

One of the following options is usually selected:

● round the Delivery and Return Amount down to the nearest integral multiple specified; or

● round the Delivery Amount up and the Return Amount down to the nearest integral multiple specified. (This is the most common choice.)

If no rounding convention is specified, then the Delivery Amount and the Return Amount will not be rounded.

You would not normally specify that both Delivery and Return Amounts are to be rounded up, as this could leave a Transferee undercollateralised after transferring a Return Amount.

A typical example of a rounding provision is:

(D) *Rounding.* The Delivery Amount and the Return Amount will be rounded up and down respectively to the nearest integral multiple of US$ 10,000.

Although a rounding amount of $10,000 is most common, rounding amounts of $100,000 or even $250,000 are seen in the market.

Valuation Agent

(c) *Valuation and Timing.*

(i) *"Valuation Agent"* means: for purposes of Paragraphs 3 and 5, the party making the demand under Paragraph 3; for purposes of Paragraph 4(d)(ii), the Secured Party receiving the Substitute Credit Support; and, for purposes of Paragraph 6(d), the Secured Party receiving or deemed to receive the Distributions or the Interest Amount, as applicable;

The Valuation Agent calculates the Delivery Amount and the Return Amount and reports these calculations to the Pledgor and Secured Party so than they can fulfill their obligations under Paragraphs 3, 4, 5 and 6 of the New York Law CSA.

As described in the clause above, the party calling for the collateral (the Secured Party) under Paragraph 3(a) is the Valuation Agent. The Secured Party is also the Valuation Agent for transferring Distributions or Interest Amounts under Paragraph 6(d). The Pledgor would be the Valuation Agent if it were calling for a Return Amount under Paragraph 3(b). The standard wording is most commonly used.

In negotiations between US parties, it is relatively rare that a third party would ever be appointed as Valuation Agent. In fact, the author has never been involved with a negotiation where a third party was so appointed. Although a less sophisticated end user would probably be more comfortable with a third party acting as Valuation Agent, dealers have been reluctant to permit such a provision probably due to the fees a Valuation Agent would charge and probable operational and back-office headaches that would occur when involving a third party.

At times, one party will request that the other party act as the Valuation Agent for purposes of calculating Exposure and the Value of Posted Collateral. This situation would occur if one party did not have the ability or sophistication to make the necessary calculations itself. Many US dealers resist acting as Valuation Agent out of concern that they may be viewed as a fiduciary of the other party. They also are concerned about being liable for errors in making the required calculations.

The variations further discussed in Chapter 5 regarding Valuation Agents are equally applicable to the New York Law CSA. See pp. 149–151.

Valuation Date

(ii) *"Valuation Date"* means: ....

This item must be completed as there is no ISDA fallback position here.

Valuation Date states the frequency at which Exposure is calculated and collateral is revalued under the ISDA Master Agreement and the New York Law CSA. On each Valuation Date, the Valuation Agent must calculate the following and advise the other party/parties of:

- the Exposure
- the Value of the Pledgor's Posted Collateral (if any)
- the Credit Support Amount
- the Delivery Amount (if any) and
- the Return Amount (if any)

all as of the Valuation Time (see below).

A number of frequencies are, of course, possible, e.g. daily, weekly, monthly or on a particular day of each week or month.

The most common is:

(ii) *"Valuation Date"* means any Local Business Day.

This allows for daily exposure and collateral valuation. Most US dealers will calculate the Exposure and the Value of Posted Collateral each morning based on the close of business values on the previous day. Defining the Valuation Date to be any Local Business Day provides a dealer with the maximum amount of flexibility to call for a Delivery Amount.

The variations on the definition of Valuation Date set forth in Chapter 5 are equally applicable to the New York Law CSA. (See pp. 153–155.)

As described in Chapter 5, some parties may also request that a particular day also be expressly designated as a Valuation Date. This is particularly important for parties that are not operationally set up to do the necessary calculations and valuations and are dependent upon the other party to make certain calculations. These parties may need these calculations to close their books on a monthly basis, for example.

Valuation Time

(iii) *"Valuation Time"* means:

[ ] the close of business in the place of location of the Valuation Agent on the Valuation Date or date of calculation, as applicable;

[ ] the close of business on the Local Business Day immediately preceding the Valuation Date or date of calculation, as applicable;

provided that the calculations of Value and Exposure will, as far as practicable, be made as of approximately the same time on the same date.

The Valuation Time is the time at which the Valuation Agent calculates Exposure and the value of collateral held to determine if a Delivery Amount or Return Amount call is needed. The Valuation Agent will also factor in any Distributions or Interest Amounts due to the Transferor at the Valuation Time.

The parties have two main choices, viz:

- as at the close of business on the Valuation Date, or the date of calculation for Paragraph 6(d) payments to the Pledgor; or
- as at the close of business on the Local Business Day immediately before the Valuation Date, or the date of calculation for Paragraph 6(d) payments to the Pledgor.

They can, of course, choose another means for deciding the Valuation Time by amending this sub-paragraph.

Once they have made their choice, the New York Law CSA stipulates that the calculation of risk exposure and collateral values has to be made as of approximately at the same time on the selected date.

A Valuation Time as at the close of business on the Local Business Day immediately preceding the Valuation Date is the most common choice because collateral management units are then working from reports of exposure and collateral values at the close of that previous business day.

Notification Time

(iv) *"Notification Time"* means 1:00 p.m., New York time, on a Local Business Day, unless otherwise specified here: ....

This is the time by which, among other things, (1) the Valuation Agent must notify the parties of its calculations under Paragraph 4(b) on the Local Business Day following a Valuation Date and (2) a party must make a demand for a transfer of collateral so that the other party makes the appropriate transfer not later than the close of business on the next Local Business Day. If a demand for a transfer is made after the Notification Time then the transfer does not have to be made until the close of business on the second Local Business Day following the day on which the demand was made. Such transfers will be made if there is no dispute and no condition precedent being unfulfilled in Section 2(a)(iii) of the ISDA Master Agreement.

The Notification Time is specified to mean 1.00 p.m. New York time on the appropriate Local Business Day unless the parties agree otherwise. Sometimes parties arrange for the Notification Time for the Valuation Agent's Exposure calculations to be earlier than the Notification Time for collateral calls (at least where a third party acts as the Valuation Agent). In these circumstances, a party receiving notice of the Valuation Agent's calculations will be able to make a collateral call on the same day for a transfer to be made on the next Local Business Day.

Typically a Notification Time would not be later than 3.00 p.m. New York time in order to give the parties sufficient time to meet their collateral transfer deadlines.

The one exception to a collateral transfer on the following Local Business Day is with US$ Cash where I have seen the following language:

> (iv) *"Notification Time"* means 9:00 a.m. New York time on the Valuation Date provided, however, that, notwithstanding Paragraph 3(a), (x) with regard to Transfers of Eligible Credit Support in the form of US$ cash, if a request for delivery or return is made by the Notification Time, then the relevant Transfer shall be made not later than the close of business on the day on which such a request is received, or if such day is not a Local Business Day or if such request is made after the Notification Time, not later than the close of business on the next Local Business Day and (y) with regard to Transfers of other forms of Eligible Credit Support or posted credit support, the relevant Transfer shall be made in accordance with Paragraph 3(a).

Specified Conditions

(d) *Conditions Precedent and Secured Party's Rights and Remedies.* The following Termination Event(s) will be a *"Specified Condition"* for the party specified (that party being the Affected Party if the Termination Event occurs with respect to that party):

	Party A	Party B
Illegality	[X]	[X]
Tax Event	[ ]	[ ]
Tax Event Upon Merger	[ ]	[ ]
Credit Event Upon Merger	[X]	[X]
Additional Termination Event(s): . . .	[ ]	[ ]

By designating a Specified Condition, the parties agree that when it occurs:

- if the Affected Party (i.e. the condition has occurred to that party) is the Pledgor, the Secured Party's obligations to transfer collateral and interest payments to the Pledgor under Paragraphs 3, 4(d)(ii) and 6(d) are suspended;

- if the Affected Party is the Secured Party, the Pledgor's obligation to transfer collateral under Paragraphs 3 and 5 is suspended;

- if the Affected Party is the Pledgor, the Secured Party may exercise its rights and remedies under Paragraph 8(a).

The most common designated Specified Conditions are Illegality and Credit Event Upon Merger. Many parties are concerned about pledging collateral to a party that is affected by an Illegality through fears that the Pledgor may not be able to return the collateral pledged to it because of the Illegality.

Parties also do not want to pledge collateral to a party whose creditworthiness has become materially weaker due to a merger. They would be concerned that their counterparty might become insolvent because of the merger with the result that any pledged collateral might be trapped in an insolvency proceeding. Many parties also view the occurrence of a Credit Event Upon Merger as the fault of the Affected Party and think it should be treated in a similar way to an Event of Default for the purposes of the New York Law CSA.

Some dealers are reluctant, however, to agree to the designation of Specified Conditions (other than Illegality). The dealer is concerned about a scenario where a Specified Condition has occurred with respect to it while the dealer is also the Secured Party. If the dealer is exposed to the counterparty (i.e. the dealer is "in the money"), the dealer does not want the Pledgor's obligation to pledge collateral to be suspended because of the occurrence of the Specified Condition. The dealer is more concerned about the credit risk of its counterparty than the risk of having to pledge collateral to a counterparty that is subject to a Specified Condition.

Although a dealer may be willing to agree to designate Illegality as a Specified Condition, he is still concerned about being exposed to his counterparty due to the lengthy cure periods in the ISDA Master Agreement for Illegality. The following is a provision that limits the lengthy cure periods with respect to an Illegality that is also a Specified Condition:

(d) *Conditions Precedent and Secured Party's Rights and Remedies.* The following Termination Event(s) will be a *"Specified Condition"* for the party specified (that party being the Affected Party if the Termination Event occurs with respect to that party):

	Party A	Party B
Illegality	YES	YES

provided that if the Affected Party would be entitled to receive Eligible Credit Support or Posted Credit Support but for that Specified Condition, then notwithstanding Sections 6(b)(ii) and (iii) of this Agreement, the Affected Party may designate an Early Termination Date in respect of all Affected Transactions pursuant to Section 6(b)(iv) as the result of any such Termination Event(s) regardless of whether the condition set forth in Section 6(b)(iv)(1) has been satisfied.

Substitution

> (e) *Substitution.*
>> (i) *"Substitution Date"* has the meaning specified in Paragraph 4(d)(ii).
>> (ii) *Consent.* The Pledgor is not required to obtain the Secured Party's consent for any substitution.

The ability to substitute is an important right for Pledgors. Often a Pledgor requires the return of a particular security that was previously pledged to the Secured Party. For example, the security may be collateral that the Pledgor had repledged to the Secured Party. The Pledgor may then need to return that same security to its original pledgor. Please see the discussion regarding rehypothecation in Chapter 3, p. 55–56.

Many Secured Parties insist that they have the right to consent to a substitution. Even though the Secured Party will be receiving Substitute Credit Support, the substitution process is time consuming and uses up the limited back-office resources of the Secured Party. By having the right to consent, a Secured Party hopes to limit the number of substitutions that it will be required to perform by the Pledgor. A possible compromise could be to require consent, but to provide that such consent shall be not unreasonably withheld:

> (ii) *Consent.* The Pledgor is required to obtain the Secured Party's consent for any substitution pursuant to Paragraph 4(d), provided however, that such consent shall not be unreasonably withheld.

Some US dealers also believe that there are tax implications in dealing with UK counterparties if consent is not required:

> (ii) *Consent.* The Pledgor is not required to obtain the Secured Party's consent for any substitution pursuant to Paragraph 4(d) unless the Pledgor is organized under the laws of England or Wales, in which case such consent is not to be unreasonably withheld.

Resolution Time

> (f) *Dispute Resolution.*
>
> *"Resolution Time"* means 1:00 p.m., New York time, on the Local Business Day following the date on which the notice is given that gives rise to a dispute under Paragraph 5.

The Resolution Time is the deadline for the parties to resolve their dispute under Paragraph 5. If they fail, the Valuation Agent makes certain recalculations under Paragraph 5(i).

The fallback dispute Resolution Time is 1.00 p.m. New York time on the Local Business Day after the date notice is given that gives rise to a dispute under Paragraph 5 although this wording is sometimes changed to "the date on which notice of dispute is given under Paragraph 5" to avoid confusion with the Valuation Agent's notice of Exposure or collateral valuation.

US counterparties are often asked by European counterparties to agree to an earlier Resolution time due to the time difference between New York and Europe.

Value

(ii) *Value.* **For the purpose of Paragraphs 5(i)(C) and 5(ii), the Value of Posted Credit Support other than Cash will be calculated based upon the mid-point between the bid and offered purchase rates or prices for that Posted Credit Support as reported on the Bloomberg electronic service as of the Resolution Time, or if unavailable, as quoted to the Valuation Agent as of the Resolution Time by a dealer in that Posted Credit Support of recognized standing selected in good faith by the Valuation Agent, which calculation shall include any unpaid interest on that Posted Credit Support.**

Paragraph 5(ii) requires the parties to agree to a procedure to value Posted Collateral in the event that there is a dispute. Many US counterparties prefer to require the parties to look to published quotes for valuing Posted Collateral before going out to solicit quotes from dealers that trade in the disputed type of collateral. The most common and comprehensive source for published quotes is Bloomberg, L.P., a Delaware limited partnership ("Bloomberg").

Many parties, however, believe that if there were a dispute with respect to the Value of Posted Collateral, it is because the bid and offer prices are not available on Bloomberg or there is a disagreement over the quote that Bloomberg provides. In this case, the parties instead look directly to quotes:

If the dispute relates to the Value of a security, the Valuation Agent will use the arithmetic mean of the bid prices for the security obtained by it from Reference Dealers selected by it as provided in the final sentence of Section 4.14 of the 1991 Definitions, subject to the Valuation Percentage indicated in Paragraph 13(b)(ii) of this Annex. For these purposes, "Reference Dealers" means three leading dealers in the principal market for the relevant kind of security; provided, that if three quotations are not available for a particular security, then the number of quotations obtained with respect to such security will be used. If no quotations are available for a particular security, then the Valuation Agent's original calculation of Value thereof will be used – subject to agreement by both Parties – for that security, provided, that if the Parties remain unable to agree on a particular calculation after five (5) Local Business

Days for both Parties after the Party who is not the Valuation Agent has received notice that no quotations were available, another mutually acceptable Valuation Agent, which is a dealer in the relevant market, will be appointed to determine such calculation (the "Mutually Acceptable Valuation Agent"). The determination by the Mutually Acceptable Valuation Agent, shall be binding on Party A and Party B. The fees and expenses of the Mutually Acceptable Valuation Agent shall be borne by the Parties equally.

The discussion and example provisions of dispute resolution found in Chapter 5 at pp. 167–169 are also equally applicable to the New York Law CSA.

Alternative

(iii) *Alternative.* The provisions of Paragraph 5 will apply.

This provision enables the parties to adopt a different dispute resolution procedure to that contained in Paragraph 5. Normally, parties adopt Paragraph 5. See Chapter 5 at pp. 171–173 for a discussion of "Alternative" provisions.

Holding Posted Collateral

(g) *Holding and Using Posted Collateral.*

(i) *Eligibility to Hold Posted Collateral; Custodians.*

(A) Party A will be entitled to hold Posted Collateral itself or through a Custodian pursuant to Paragraph 6(b), *provided* that the following conditions applicable to it are satisfied:

(1) Party A is not a Defaulting Party.

(2) Posted Collateral may be held only in the following jurisdictions: New York.

(3) The party or entity holding the Posted Collateral maintains a Credit Rating of at least BBB+ from S&P and Baa1 from Moody's.

(4) The Custodian is a bank or trust company having total assets in excess of $10 billion.

(B) Party B will be entitled to hold Posted Collateral itself or through its Custodian pursuant to Paragraph 6(b), *provided* that the following conditions applicable to it are satisfied:

(1) Party B is not a Defaulting Party.

(2) Posted Collateral may be held only in the following jurisdictions: New York.

(3) **The party or entity holding the Posted Collateral maintains a Credit Rating of at least BBB+ from S&P and Baa1 from Moody's.**

(4) **The Custodian is a bank or trust company having total assets in excess of $10 billion.**

Parties frequently worry about the sophistication and credit quality of the Secured Party that is to hold the Posted Collateral. If the Secured Party itself is to hold the Posted Collateral, it is not permitted to be a Defaulting Party and often must have a high credit rating. Typically parties will request that a party or its Custodian have a credit rating of at least BBB+ from S&P and Baa1 from Moody's and hold either a certain amount of assets or have a certain net worth.

A Pledgor is concerned about pledging collateral to a party that is not creditworthy. This is because if the Secured Party were to become insolvent, it may be difficult for the Pledgor to obtain the return of the Posted Collateral. This is because the Pledgor would probably only be an unsecured creditor with respect to its contractual claim to the return of the collateral that it had pledged to the Secured Party.

As explained above in Paragraph 6(b), a custodian selected by the Secured Party is defined as an agent of the Secured Party and is not intended to have any fiduciary duties to the Pledgor. The parties would need to require that the Custodian enter into a custodial agreement with both the Pledgor and the Secured Party if the parties intend to create a fiduciary relationship between all three of them.

Paragraph 13(g)(i) also establishes where Posted Collateral can be held. As explained in Chapter 3 (see pp. 46–47 and 56–58), as long as the Posted Collateral is held in the US, the state laws governing the pledging and holding of collateral are consistent and uniform. However, many parties will still insist that Posted Collateral is held only in the State of New York. This is because parties are typically relying upon the ISDA collateral opinion given with respect to the State of New York or because they have only done due diligence with respect to the New York UCC.

Use of Posted Collateral

(ii) *Use of Posted Collateral.* **The provisions of Paragraph 6(c) will apply to Party A and will apply to Party B.**

Paragraph 6(c) assumes that the parties permit "rehypothecation" or use rights unless otherwise specified in Paragraph 13. See Chapter 3 (pp. 55–56) for a discussion of the issues involving rehypothecation.

The following provision provides additional protection for a Pledgor if it grants the Secured Party rehypothecation rights. The provision provides that a party must stop using the collateral if it no longer meets the eligibility requirements. A party may also want to consider a ratings trigger that would require the Secured Party to stop rehypothecating collateral in the event that its credit rating fell below a particular level.

(ii) *Use of Posted Collateral.* The provisions of Paragraph 6(c) will apply to both parties, and in addition to the other conditions set forth in Paragraph 6(c), the Secured Party's rights under Paragraph 6(c) are subject to the condition precedent that each of the conditions set forth in Paragraph 13(g)(i) is satisfied with respect to it.

Interest Amount

(h) *Distributions and Interest Amount.*

Interest Rate. The *"Interest Rate"* for any day will be the Federal Funds (Effective) rate published in N.Y. Federal Reserve Statistical Release H.15(519) for that day (or if that day is not a New York Business Day, then for the next preceding New York Business Day).

The Interest Rate is the interest which will be paid by the Secured Party on the Cash collateral received from the Pledgor plus or minus a spread. It will reflect the frequency of the Valuation Dates. This section must be completed as there is no ISDA fallback.

The Interest Rate between US parties is almost always based on the Federal Funds (Effective) rate. This represents the interest rate traditionally used when banks lend money on the interbank market overnight between themselves. Because this represents the rate of return anticipated by most banks on their overnight cash balances, they are generally reluctant to agree to other interest rates such as LIBOR because of a fear that LIBOR will diverge from Federal Funds (Effective).

The Federal Funds (Effective) rate is published in numerous other sources including Telerate and Bloomberg, among others. A different description of Federal Funds (Effective) could be expressed as follows:

Interest Rate. The *"Interest Rate"* on any day means the effective rate for Federal Funds as published on Telerate page 118, provided that if, for any reason, Telerate page 118 should be unavailable the Interest Rate shall be such rate as the Secured Party shall reasonably determine.

The actual interest rate charged will be the same, the provision simply referencing a different publication source.

Often a dealer will request that the rate be Federal Funds (Effective) less a spread such as 25 basis points. A dealer may ask for this because of difficulties the derivatives desk in particular may have in earning Federal Funds (Effective). Often the derivative desk will be charged a fee for having another part of the dealer invest the Cash collateral.

The calculation of the Interest Amount is based on "simple" as opposed to a "compounded" interest rate. The following provision provides for daily compounding if that is what the parties want:

For the purpose of computing the Interest Amount, the amount of interest computed for each day of the Interest Period shall be compounded daily.

Some parties also request that the Secured Party deliver a notice to the Pledgor with respect to the amount of interest that will be paid:

Notice of Interest Amount. A notice of the Interest Amount due to the Pledgor (or a statement that no such interest is due) shall be delivered to the Pledgor from the Secured Party on the next to last Local Business Day of each calendar month that Posted Collateral in the form of Cash is being held by the Secured Party.

Transfer of Interest Amount

(ii) *Transfer of Interest Amount.* The Transfer of the Interest Amount will be made on the first Local Business Day of each calendar month and on any Local Business Day that Posted Collateral in the form of Cash is Transferred to the Pledgor pursuant to Paragraph 3(b).

As long as the Secured Party does not become undersecured by transferring an Interest Amount, Paragraph 13(h)(ii) proposes that interest on cash collateral is transferred in arrears to the Secured Party on the first Local Business Day of each month and on any Local Business Day when a cash Return Amount is due to the Pledgor.

Whether this payment structure is acceptable will depend upon the parties' operational systems. Many parties prefer such interest transfers to take place on the second Local Business Day of the succeeding calendar month because they can spend the first Local Business Day of that month checking calculations and preparing the necessary electronic transfers.

There are not a large number of variations on this theme, but sometimes you see that the interest transfer date must be a Local Business Day in the cities where both parties are located. While it would be possible for the Secured Party to hold any Interest Amount as additional Posted Collateral as opposed to transferring it monthly, this is relatively uncommon. Most dealers are set up operationally to pay the Interest Amount monthly.

Alternative to Interest Amount

(iii) *Alternative to Interest Amount.* The provisions of Paragraph 6(d)(ii) will apply.

Although the drafters of Paragraph 6(d)(ii) anticipated that parties may want to diverge from the standard provisions, it is rarely used.

Additional Representations

(i) *Additional Representation(s)*. Not applicable.

Parties rarely add additional representations to the New York CSA. The following, however, is an example of a representation that was requested from a bank that has FDIC insurance for its deposits:

> *Additional Representation(s).* Party B represents to Party A (which representation(s) will be deemed to be repeated as of each date on which Party B, as the Pledgor, Transfers Eligible Collateral) that:
>
> The necessary action to authorize referred to in Section 3(a)(ii) of this Agreement includes all authorizations required under the Federal Deposit Insurance Act as amended (including amendments effected by the Financial Institutions Reform, Recovery, and Enforcement Act of 1989) and under any agreement, writ, decree or order entered into with the Pledgor's supervisory authorities; and at all times during the term of this Agreement, the Pledgor will continuously include and maintain as part of its official written books and records this Agreement, any Credit Support Document to which it is a party and all other exhibits, supplements and attachments hereto and documents incorporated by reference herein, including all Confirmations, and evidence of all necessary authorizations.
>
> This Agreement, any Credit Support Document to which the Pledgor is a party, each Confirmation, and any other documentation relating to this Agreement to which it is a party or that it is required to deliver will be executed and delivered by a duly appointed or elected and authorized officer of the Pledgor of the level of vice-president or higher. The Pledgor and the Secured Party agree that each Transaction and the Agreement are a "swap agreement" and a "qualified financial contract" and that the Agreement is a "master agreement", for purposes of Section 11(e)(8) of the Federal Deposit Insurance Act or any successor provisions.

This representation would normally be requested in the Schedule, but it could be added here. The representation is requested in order to ensure that the bank pledging the collateral is in compliance with Federal banking law.

Some parties also attempt to clarify that transfers made under the New York Law CSA are intended to qualify for special treatment under the US Bankruptcy Code:

> US Bankruptcy Code Provisions. (x) All Transfers of Posted Collateral hereunder (including the grant of a security interest in Posted Collateral hereunder) are "transfers" "under" the Agreement within the meaning of Section 546(g) of the United States Bankruptcy Code; and (y) to the extent any Transaction constitutes a "forward contract" within the meaning of the United States Bankruptcy Code, transfers of Posted Collateral under the Annex are intended to be "margin payments" within the meaning of Section 101(38) of the United States Bankruptcy Code.

Other Eligible Support

(j) *Other Eligible Support and Other Posted Support.* Not applicable.

This provision is also rarely used given that it is only applicable if the parties have agreed to include Other Posted Support. If Other Posted Support were pledged to the Secured Party, the parties may want to consider adding special provisions as to how to value or transfer that Other Posted Support.

Demands and Notices

(k) *Demands and Notices.* All demands, specifications and notices under this Annex will be made to a party as follows unless otherwise specified from time to time by that party for purposes of this Annex in a written notice given to the other party:

Party A: as set forth in the Notices section of the Agreement.

Party B: as set forth in the Notices section of the Agreement.

In large dealers, the collateral operation may be completely separate and administered apart from the derivatives desk or legal department. Accordingly, a party may want to designate additional addresses for notification if collateral is administered by another section of their operations.

A party may also want to clarify how notices can be given with respect to the transfer of collateral in order to conform the document to that party's practices in transferring collateral:

Notices. Notwithstanding Section 12 of the Agreement, any communication by a party ("X") to the other party ("Y") requesting the delivery or return of Eligible Credit Support or Posted Credit Support pursuant to Paragraph 3 of this Annex may be given orally (including telephonically to the telephone number of Y set forth in subparagraph (k) above, or any other telephone number Y may notify X of in writing) during normal business hours in the city in which Y is located on any Local Business Day to any officer, employee or agent of Y which identifies himself or herself as being permitted to receive oral communications on behalf of Y with respect to this Annex. Any such oral communication will be deemed received and effective when actually received by any such officer, employee or agent of Y. X shall deliver to Y, within one Local Business Day following receipt of an oral or written request by Y, a written confirmation of any such oral communication.

Addresses for Transfers

(l) *Addresses for Transfers.*

   (i) For each Transfer hereunder to Party A, instructions will be provided by Party A for that specific Transfer.

   (ii) For each Transfer hereunder to Party B, instructions will be provided by Party B for that specific Transfer.

This must be completed if collateral transfers and interest payments and Distributions are to be correctly routed to the recipient. Sometimes these details are spelt out by currency for cash and securities. In large dealers, the collateral operation will have standard accounts for Cash and securities that will not change on a day-to-day basis. Often these transfer instructions will be added directly to Paragraph 13.

Other provisions

(m) *Other provisions*

Paragraph 13(m) is similar to Part 5 of the ISDA Master Agreement Schedule – a place where other provisions may be inserted. There is no general market practice as to what should be added in Paragraph 13(m). There are, however, several general types of provisions that some parties will request to be added. Because these provisions are not market practice, they often will be difficult and time consuming to negotiate.

In addition to the provisions listed below, please also carefully review the miscellaneous provisions of Paragraph 11(h) of the English Law CSA that are discussed in Chapter 5 at pp. 183–193. Many of the provisions discussed there are equally applicable to the New York Law CSA.

Exposure

Some parties want to clarify the types of Transactions that will be included in the calculation of Exposure, the most common being the addition of Specified Transactions. Some parties also are unable or unwilling to collateralise certain types of Transactions such as credit derivatives. The following are some common provision examples:

> *Exposure.* All calculations of "Exposure" under this Annex shall *include* all Transactions, including all Specified Transactions that have been or will be entered into between the parties (whether or not evidenced by a Confirmation).

OR

Exposure. Without limiting the term "Obligations" as defined in this Annex, all calculations of "Exposure" under this Annex shall <u>exclude</u> the following:

(A) [All Transactions (including Specified Transactions) that are bond options.]

(B) [All Transactions (including Specified Transactions) that are FX Transactions maturing within _____ of their respective trade dates.]

(C) [All Transactions (including Specified Transactions) that are either FX Transactions or Currency Option Transactions.]

(D) _____.

OR

Exposure. The definition of "Exposure" in Paragraph 12 shall be amended by adding the following sentence at the end thereof: "For purpose of this definition, the term "Transaction" will only cover the following transactions: any rate swap transaction, basis-swap, forward rate transaction, bond option, interest rate option, cap transaction, floor transaction, collar transaction, cross-currency rate swap transaction (including any option with respect to any of these transactions), Equity Swap Transactions, Index Transactions, Share Transactions, Index Basket Transactions, Share Basket Transactions, Basket Option Transaction, and any Option Transaction (each as defined in the 1996 ISDA Equity Derivatives Definitions), any FX Transactions and Currency Options Transaction (each as defined in the 1998 FX and Currency Options Definitions). For the avoidance of doubt the term "Transaction" will not cover foreign exchange spot dealings.

Cure periods

Parties also often want to reduce the amount of time permitted to transfer collateral or to cure defaults.

The following provision reduces the cure period for failure to transfer collateral:

Grace Period. Clause (i) of Paragraph 7 is hereby amended by deleting the words "two Local Business Days" and substituting therefor "one Local Business Day".

OR

Events of Default. Paragraph 7 shall be amended so that the references in Paragraph 7(i), Paragraph 7(ii) and Paragraph 7(iii) to "two Local Business Days", "five Local Business Days", and "thirty days" respectively, shall instead be replaced by "one Local Business Day", "three Local Business Days" and "three Local Business Days" respectively.

OR

> *Events of Default.* Paragraph 7(i) shall be amended and restated in its entirety as follows: "(i) that party fails (or fails to cause its Custodian) to make, when due any Transfer of Eligible Collateral, Posted Collateral or the Interest Amount as applicable, required to be made by it and that failure continues for one Local Business Day after notice of that failure is given to that party;"

Transfer Timing

This provision adjusts the time for transfers of collateral in order to deal with a party's operational needs.

> *Transfer Timing.* Subject to Paragraphs 4(a) and 5 and unless otherwise specified, (i) if a demand for Transfer of Eligible Credit Support or Posted Credit Support is made by the Notification Time, then the Transfer of Eligible Credit Support or Posted Credit Support will be completed prior to 6:00 p.m., New York time, on the Local Business Day following the Local Business Day on which the demand is made, (ii) if a demand for Transfer of Eligible Credit Support or Posted Credit Support is made by the Notification Time with respect to a foreign currency exchange Transaction, such Transfer shall be completed prior to 6:00 p.m., New York time, on the third (3rd) Local Business Day following the Local Business Day on which the demand is made and (iii) if a demand for Transfer of Eligible Credit Support or Posted Credit Support is made subsequent to the Notification Time, then the relevant Transfer will be made in accordance with the rules provided in the immediately preceding subparagraphs (i) and (ii), except that the demand will be treated as if made on the Local Business Day following the day the demand was actually made.

OR

> *Transfer Timing.* Paragraph 4(b) is amended by (A) deleting the word "next" in the third line thereof and replacing it with the word "same"; and (B) deleting the words "second Local Business Day hereafter" in the fifth line thereof and replacing them with the words "next Local Business Day".

This provision makes timing adjustments with respect to the transfer of Distributions to the Pledgor:

> (iii) *Certain Distributions Received.* If a Secured Party receives or is deemed to receive Distributions on a day that is not a Local Business Day, or after its close of business on a Local Business Day, it will Transfer the Distributions to the Pledgor on the following Local Business Day, subject to Paragraph 4(a),

but only to the extent contemplated in Paragraph 6(d)(i) in connection with Distributions received or deemed received on a Local Business Day.

Remedies

Parties often request provisions that clarify and amplify a party's remedies under the New York Law CSA.

Rights and Remedies under Paragraph 8(a). The Secured Party will be entitled to exercise the rights and remedies provided for in Paragraph 8(a) if the Pledgor fails to pay when due any amount payable by it under Section 6 of this Agreement in connection with a Termination Event, even if the Pledgor is not the Affected Party.

AND

Set off. For purposes of Paragraphs 2 and 8(a)(iii) of this Annex, the reference to any amount payable under Section 6 of this Agreement in the definition of "Set-off" in this Agreement shall be deemed a reference to any amount payable with respect to any Obligation, as described in Paragraph 8(a)(iii) of this Annex.

AND

Secured Party's Rights and Remedies. (a) Supplementing the provisions of Paragraph 8(a), the Pledgor irrevocably appoints the Secured Party its attorney-in-fact, with full authority in its place and stead and in its name or otherwise, from time to time in the Secured Party's discretion, to take any action and to execute any instrument which the Secured Party may deem necessary or advisable to accomplish the purposes of this Annex, including without limitation:

(i) to ask, demand, collect, sue for, recover, compromise, receive and give acquittance and receipts for moneys due and to become due under or in respect of any Posted Collateral and to perform all other acts as fully as though the Secured Party were the absolute owner of the Posted Collateral for all purposes,

(ii) to receive, endorse, and collect any drafts or other instruments, documents and chattel paper, in connection with clause (i) above, and

(iii) to file any claims or take any action or institute any proceedings which the Secured Party may deem necessary or desirable for the collection of any of the Posted Collateral or otherwise to enforce the rights of the Secured Party with respect to any Posted Collateral.

(b) Further supplementing the provisions of Paragraphs 8(a) and 13(a), the Secured Party may apply Eligible Credit Support or Posted Credit Support to pay any amounts due by Pledgor to Secured Party pursuant to this Agreement, including any Transaction and any other amounts then due by Pledgor to Secured Party or its Affiliates under any other contractual arrangements between them.

Interest Amount and Taxes

Parties at times are concerned that the payment of the Interest Amount may trigger a Tax Event. Because the Interest Amount is typically insignificant in comparison with other payment obligations under the ISDA Master Agreement, the parties attempt to minimise any disruptions that such a Tax Event could cause on the parties:

> *Taxes in Connection with Interest Amounts:* Neither party will be entitled to designate an Early Termination Date on the ground of any Tax Event resulting from the party's obligation to pay additional amounts in respect of Indemnifiable Taxes imposed with respect to any Interest Amount it is required to Transfer under this Annex.

Dealings in Relation to Posted Collateral

Because US Treasury and quasi government agency securities no longer exist in certificate form, and because of the practice of rehypothecating collateral, parties are often concerned about whether they have breached the New York Law CSA when the collateral is returned. One approach has been to expressly approve the return of "fungible securities":

> *Fungible Securities.* In lieu of returning to the Pledgor pursuant to Paragraphs 3(b), 4(d), 5 and 8(d) any Posted Collateral comprising "securities" (as defined in the Uniform Commercial Code of the State of New York) the Secured Party may return "securities" that are "fungible" (as such term is used in that Code) for such securities.

Pledgors however, may be strongly resistant to that concept if a security with the same CUSIP number as the one that was pledged was not returned. This is because failure to receive back the same security with the same CUSIP number may trigger accounting consequences for the Pledgor.

Secured Parties also often seek additional assurances with respect to the Posted Collateral that they have received from the Pledgor:

> *No further dealings by Pledgor.* So long as the Agreement is in effect, the Pledgor covenants that it:

(i)   will keep the Posted Collateral free from all security interests or other encumbrances created by the Pledgor, except the security interest created hereunder and any security interests or other encumbrances created by the Secured Party;

(ii) will not sell, transfer, assign, deliver or otherwise dispose of, or grant any option with respect to any Posted Collateral or any interest therein, or create, incur or permit to exist any pledge, lien, mortgage, hypothecation, security interest, charge, option or any other encumbrance with respect to any Posted Collateral or any interest therein, without the prior written consent of the Secured Party.

Parties also attempt to further clarify the duty of care of a Secured Party:

Care of Posted Collateral. Supplementing the provisions of Paragraph 6(a), the Secured Party shall also be deemed to have exercised reasonable care if it takes such action for that purpose as the Pledgor shall reasonably request in writing (but no omission to comply with any such request shall of itself be deemed a failure to exercise reasonable care).

OR

Duty of Secured Party to Preserve Collateral; Limit on Secured Party's Liability: To the extent required by applicable law and subject to the remainder of this provision, the Secured Party will exercise reasonable care in the preservation of Posted Collateral held by it, and the parties agree that the Secured Party will be deemed to have exercised reasonable care if it exercises at least the same degree of care it would exercise with respect to its own property. However, without limiting the generality of the final sentence of paragraph 6(a), each party, as Pledgor, acknowledges that it has the means to monitor all matters relating to all valuations, payments, defaults and rights without need to rely on the other party, in its capacity as Secured Party, and that, given the provisions of this Annex on substitution, responsibility for the preservation of the rights of the Pledgor with respect to all such matters is reasonably allocated hereby to the Pledgor. The Secured Party will not be liable for any losses or damages that the Pledgor may suffer as a result of any failure by the Secured Party to perform, or any delay by it in performing, any of its obligations under this Annex if the failure or delay results from circumstances beyond the reasonable control of the Secured Party or its Custodian, such as interruption or loss of computer or communication devices, labor disturbance, natural disaster or local or national emergency.

ISDA elections and fallbacks

At this point it might be useful to summarise the ISDA fallbacks for Paragraph 13 and the provisions which must be completed for the Annex to be operative.

FIG. 6.1

ISDA fallbacks in the New York Law CSA

If no choice is made the following apply by default:

Provision	Fallback
Alternative	Paragraph 5 dispute resolution procedures apply
Consent for Substitution	No consent required
Eligibility to Hold Collateral	Secured Party cannot be a Defaulting Party
Independent Amount	Zero
Threshold	Zero
Minimum Transfer Amount	Zero
Notification Time	1.00 p.m. New York time
Notices	Pursuant to Notices Section of ISDA Master Agreement
Resolution Time	1.00 p.m. New York time
Rounding	No rounding
Specified Condition	No Specified Conditions apply
Substitution Date	Local Business Day following receipt of Substitute Credit Support
Transfer of Interest Amount	Last Local Business Day of a calendar month and any Local Business Day when a cash Return Amount is due to the Pledgor
Use or Rehypothecation of Posted Collateral	Use or rehypothecation permitted
Valuation Agent	The Secured Party for purposes of Paragraph 3(a) and the Pledgor for purposes of Paragraph 3(b).

Provisions which must be completed if there is no fallback are as follows:

● **Addresses for Transfers**

● **Eligible Collateral**

● **Interest Rate**

● **Other Eligible Support**

- Valuation Date
- Valuation Percentage
- Valuation Time
- Value.

COMPARISON OF THE NEW YORK LAW CSA WITH THE ENGLISH LAW CSA

The New York Law CSA and the English Law CSA are quite different conceptually as to how they secure and collateralise obligations under the ISDA Master Agreement. However, they share many common characteristics in their form, appearance and modus operandi.

Key similarities

There are several key similarities between the two documents. First, each document is an Annex to the ISDA Master Agreement Schedule and supplements, forms part of and is subject to the ISDA Master Agreement. Accordingly, they both conform much of their vocabulary and mechanics to the ISDA Master Agreement standard form and Schedule.

Second, the Transferee/Secured Party is free to use the collateral. For example, under the New York Law CSA, the Secured Party is often given use or rehypothecation rights. See Chapter 3 at pp. 55–56 for a discussion of these rights. Because the Transferee under the English Law CSA is treated as the owner of the collateral, it is also free to deal with the collateral as it sees fit. Of course, both the Secured Party and the Transferee have a contractual obligation to return the collateral upon the counterparty satisfying all its obligations under the ISDA Master Agreement.

Third, neither Annex requires any registration formalities. For example, because Eligible Collateral under the New York Law CSA is typically cash and securities, the Secured Party is not even required to make a UCC filing in order to perfect its security interest in the collateral.

Fourth, both Annexes use the same vocabulary and similar provisions whenever possible. Negotiators, however, should be careful to appreciate subtle differences between provisions that might otherwise appear identical in order to avoid drafting errors.

Principal differences

There are numerous important distinctions between the New York Law CSA and the English Law CSA that should be understood. Failure to appreciate these differences can result in drafting errors when a negotiator primarily using one form of the Annex negotiates an ISDA Master Agreement using the other Annex.

(i) In contrast to the New York Law CSA, the English Law CSA does not create a first priority security interest in and lien on the collateral transferred but transfers ownership outright to the Transferor.

(ii) The New York Law CSA enables a Pledgor to provide credit support in the form of a letter of credit or similar instrument. The English Law CSA contains no provision to include such other types of collateral when parties determine if any additional collateral is due on a Valuation Date.

(iii) The English Law CSA is intended to cover cash collateral and investment securities denominated in various currencies while the New York Law CSA is intended to be used primarily with US Dollars. This is why there are specific provisions to convert all values to a common Base Currency in the English Law CSA. There is no currency conversion mechanism in the New York Law CSA.

(iv) The English Law CSA contemplates taking investment securities located in various jurisdictions while the New York Law CSA is intended primarily to be used with US Treasury securities and quasi US government agency securities. Generally, in the New York Law CSA, transfers must occur within one Local Business Day. This is typically done easily because these types of US securities are always held through book entry at a Federal Reserve Bank. In the English Law CSA, transfers are required to occur as soon as practicable in accordance with custom in the relevant market. This is to allow, for example, for differences between settlement timing and practice in Euroclear as opposed to, say, a domestic settlement system for government bonds.

(v) The English Law CSA relies on netting and set-off. In the event of default collateral values are included within the close-out netting mechanism under the ISDA Master Agreement. The Transferor, therefore, takes the credit risk on the Transferee since, in contrast to the New York Law CSA's security interest, the Transferee has no continuing proprietary interest in the collateral provided.

(vi) Unlike the New York Law CSA, the English Law CSA is not a Credit Support Document to the ISDA Master Agreement. It constitutes a Confirmation to the relevant Transaction under the ISDA Master Agreement. This distinction could effect how events of default and other provisions operate under either Annex.

(vii) In determining if a Delivery Amount or a Return Amount has arisen, the English Law CSA provides an adjustment to the value of the collateral already held by a Transferee on the Valuation Date that takes into account incomplete transfers at that time. The New York Law CSA makes no such adjustment because collateral transfers generally take place within one Local Business Day.

(viii) The English Law CSA requires the receipt of the demand and transfer to take place in accordance with the Settlement Day on which such demand is received while the New York Law CSA only requires such demand to be made and the transfer to take place on the next Local Business Day.

(ix) The New York Law CSA provides that the parties may agree an event that constitutes a Specified Condition as a condition precedent with respect to the Pledgor's obligations. Under a Specified Condition the party affected by a stated Termination Event is not allowed to call for or substitute collateral nor receive dividends or interest on pledged collateral. The occurrence of a Specified Condition also permits a Secured Party to exercise its remedies under the New York Law CSA. The English Law CSA does not provide for a Specified Condition to be stated (in contrast to the English Law Deed).

(x) The English Law CSA provides that if the Transferor wishes to transfer New Credit Support the Transferee's consent is required. The New York Law CSA provides that the Pledgor may substitute credit support upon notice to the Secured Party. Paragraph 13 may provide for the Secured Party's consent to the substitution but it is not an absolute requirement of the terms of the New York Law CSA.

(xi) The English Law CSA requires that any Disputing Party must "reasonably" dispute the calculation of a Delivery or Return Amount or the value of a transfer. The New York Law CSA does not require this reasonableness standard. With respect to the transfer of the undisputed amount, the English Law CSA provides that the relevant transfer will be made not later than the close of business on the Settlement Day following the date the demand is received. The New York Law CSA, in contrast, provides for such transfer to take effect not later than the close of business on the Local Business Day following the call. This is because the New York Law CSA deals solely with US$ collateral.

(xii) The title transfer approach of the English Law CSA allows the Transferee to use the collateral. In contrast, subject to the New York Law CSA's rehypothecation rights, the Secured Party is required to exercise reasonable care in its custody arrangements for the posted collateral. It can appoint a custodian. The Transferee under the English Law CSA cannot appoint a custodian as this would destroy set-off mutuality.

(xiii) The English Law CSA requires the Transferee to transfer equivalent interest and dividend payments to the Transferor not later than the Settlement Day following each Distributions Date. Under the New York Law CSA the Secured Party must make such transfers on the Local Business Day following the one on which he received them.

(xiv) Close-out netting is the remedy for parties under the English Law CSA. A Secured Party under the New York Law CSA can look to rights under law as well as set off rights and the right to liquidate collateral through public or private sales. It can also buy it himself. In addition, the Pledgor can exercise similar rights if the Secured Party defaults.

(xv) The New York Law CSA obliges parties to file or deliver any document or perform any act to enable a valid, enforceable security interest to be created. The Pledgor must also give notice and defend any action that involves collateral except one arising from the Secured Party's reuse of it. The English Law CSA lacks these requirements.

(xvi) In Paragraph 7(i) of the New York Law CSA there is a two Local Business Day grace period following notice to remedy a failure to transfer collateral when due. There is no such grace period in the English Law CSA itself but Section 5(a)(i) of the ISDA Master Agreement would be invoked in these circumstances. That allows a three local Business Day grace period following notice to remedy the situation.

The ISDA English Law Credit Support Deed and the ISDA Japanese Law Credit Support Annex

7

In Chapter 1 (p. 7) it was mentioned that the *ISDA Collateral Survey 2000* estimated that both the English Law Credit Support Deed and the Japanese Law Credit Support Annex were then each used in only 1% of collateral arrangements.

Given this minority usage and space constraints in this book, it was considered appropriate to provide a summary treatment of each document rather than the type of extended expositions found in Chapters 5 and 6 on the English Law CSA and New York Law CSA respectively. Nonetheless, it is hoped that this chapter will still be useful.

The full texts of the English Law Credit Support Deed and the Japanese Law Credit Support Annex are reproduced in Annexes 6 and 7 by kind permission of the International Swaps and Derivatives Association, Inc.

PARAGRAPH BY PARAGRAPH SUMMARY OF THE ENGLISH LAW CREDIT SUPPORT DEED

The English Law Credit Support Deed (which we shall call the "Deed" from now on) was published by ISDA in autumn 1995.

It is a standalone document which relies for its effectiveness upon a security interest over the collateral received under it. It is also a Credit Support Document under the ISDA Master Agreement. This document is in the form of a deed because under its Paragraph 8(b) if a power of attorney has to be executed it must, under English law, be executed pursuant to a deed.

Let us now review the individual Paragraphs of the Deed.

Heading

Note that the Deed should be dated with the date it is actually executed and not the same date as the ISDA Master Agreement (unless that Agreement is executed on the same day).

In contrast, the English Law CSA is dated as of the same date as the ISDA Master Agreement itself which may have been executed some months or years before.

Paragraph 1. Interpretation

(a) Capitalised terms will have the same meanings in both the ISDA Master Agreement and the Deed. Where capitalised terms are not otherwise defined in the Deed or the Agreement they shall have the meanings given against them in Paragraph 12 of the Deed.

Where there is inconsistency, the Deed prevails over the Agreement and Paragraph 13 over the other provisions of the Deed.

The Deed covers payments of cash collateral and deliveries of securities and other assets.

(b) The Deed is structured as a bilateral document. Therefore either party may act as Secured Party or Chargor at different times during the life of the Deed. In respect of Other Posted Support the Secured Party will be considered to hold it as beneficiary rather than chargee.

Paragraph 2. Security

(a) Like any other English law security document, the Deed contains a covenant to perform the Obligations under the Agreement, the Deed or any other agreed relevant agreement referred to in Paragraph 13(b) of the Deed (see p. 302). This covenant is given by each party when acting as Chargor.

The purpose of this covenant is to provide a starting date for the limitation period in respect of any payment demand under the Deed. A deed executed under seal extends the limitation period to 12 years from the normal six years for contractual debt claims under English law.

It is possible to use the Deed to secure obligations of a third party, e.g. one of the Chargor's Affiliates by expanding the scope of the term "Obligations" in Paragraph 13(b). However, thought would need to be given as to whether the Chargor had received commercial consideration or benefit in these circumstances.

(b) This is the charging clause. In order to secure performance of its Obligations, the Chargor charges by way of first fixed legal mortgage all Posted Collateral in the form of cash and securities.

The Chargor also assigns the Assigned Rights to the Secured Party, under Paragraph 2(b)(iii). These are any rights (e.g. liens) which a securities clearance system, custodian or other third party may have over the Posted Collateral at any time.

As we saw in Chapter 3, the legal problems over the location of the collateral asset have been and are being clarified through Article 8 of the Uniform Commercial Code in the USA, Article 9(2) of the European Union Settlement Finality Directive, the European Union Directive on collateral financial arrangements and the Hague Convention on indirectly held securities.

As drafted, Paragraphs 2(b)(i) and (ii) deal respectively with non-cash Posted Collateral and Posted Collateral consisting of cash. This distinction was necessary at the time the Deed was drafted due to the 1986 *Re Charge Card Services Limited* case. This cast doubt on a chargor's ability to create a charge over cash in favour of a party holding that deposit. This is because the deposit represents a debt owed by the Secured Party to the Chargor and so it is "conceptually impossible" for the Secured Party to take a charge over a debt it owed. To avoid this problem cash collateral was often deposited with a third party bank and then assigned by way of security to the Secured Party – a circular route with the Secured Party ending up having a security interest in a debt owed by a third party rather than itself.

However, in 1997 in *Morris v Argrichemicals* Ltd the House of Lords overruled the *Charge Card* case. So now a cash depositor may charge its deposit to the deposit taker.

The granting of the charge is with full title guarantee. Up until July 1995, reference would have been made to the legal and beneficial owner granting the security interest.

However, there was a change in English statute law in 1994 in the Law of Property (Miscellaneous Provisions) Act 1994 to the effect that a legal and beneficial owner cannot give a full covenant for title to the property in question unless, from July 1995, the words "full title guarantee" are used instead of "legal and beneficial owner".

(c) Release of security

When the Obligations are extinguished or reduced below the Threshold or the Minimum Transfer Amount (if the Threshold is zero), Paragraph 2(c) makes clear that the Secured Party must transfer back the Posted Collateral to the Chargor, whereupon the security interest under the Deed is immediately released without further formality.

Paragraph 2(c) also makes clear that when securities are released, the Secured Party is obliged to return to the Chargor equivalent fungible securities (i.e. of the same type, class, issuer and issue) to the ones he received. The Secured Party does not have to return the identically numbered securities which might be impractical.

(d) Preservation of security

This is the continuing security provision and is designed under English law to avoid the operation of the Rule in *Clayton's Case* (1816). That Rule provides that payments into a current account discharge debts in the account in the order in which they were incurred. Any fresh advances under the account would therefore be unsecured.

In Paragraph 2(d) the security under the Deed is stated as unaffected by any intermediate payments in respect of the whole or part of the Obligations and shall continue to secure the outstanding Obligations.

However, even if the security ceases to be a continuing security, the Secured Party can open a new account or continue an existing account with the Chargor who will remain responsible for its Obligations regardless of any debits or credits to the account.

It is also stressed that security under the Deed is additional to and unaffected by any other security held or to be held by the Secured Party in respect of the Obligations.

(e) Waiver of defences

It is made clear that any acts or omissions which might in other circumstances give grounds to release the Chargor from its obligations under the Deed are waived and the Chargor will remain fully responsible under the Deed. These circumstances include:

- any time, indulgence or composition granted to the Chargor or a third party;
- any change in terms or inaction to perform or perfect any term of the ISDA Master Agreement or any security rights granted by the Chargor or a third party;
- any flaw in the regularity, validity or enforceability in the Chargor's obligations under the Agreement or any government action which results in this;
- any legal incapacity relating to the Chargor or any third party or any change to the terms of the Agreement or other document or security.

(f) Immediate recourse

The Chargor waives any right it has which obliges the Secured Party to claim payment first from any third party or to call on any guarantee or enforce any other security before enforcing its rights under the Deed.

(g) Reinstatement

If it should happen that any discharge of security is made following a payment or is made in reliance on a payment or arrangement which is avoided or vitiated by insolvency or some other event and the payment made has to be returned, the security under the Deed and the Chargor's liability thereunder shall continue as if no such discharge had been made.

Paragraph 3. Credit Support Obligations

Basically this Paragraph concerns collateral calls and returns and how they are calculated. Choices need to be made in Paragraph 13 to make the mechanism fully effective.

In Paragraph 3(a), the collateral taker (the Secured Party) can call for collateral from the collateral giver (the Chargor) where his derivatives risk exposure on the Chargor is greater than the Minimum Transfer Amount applicable to the Chargor.

The calculation of the Credit Support Amount will take into account:

(1) the net mark to market valuation of all Transactions under the Agreements plus or minus;

(2) the net Independent Amounts between the parties and

(3) any Threshold applicable to the Chargor.

When called upon, and assuming there is no dispute, the Chargor will transfer the requested amount of collateral (the "Delivery Amount") to the Secured Party. Any transfers already in transit in respect of previous collateral calls are also taken into account in the calculation of the Delivery Amount.

Paragraph 3(b) covers the position where the Secured Party holds surplus collateral which it must return to the Chargor if it is above the Secured Party's Minimum Transfer Amount *and* the Chargor calls for the return of the collateral. Please note that if the Chargor fails to make a call, the Secured Party is not obliged to transfer the collateral or point this out to the Chargor. However, if a third party Valuation Agent is involved this, of course, will not arise provided he is doing his job properly.

A Return Amount arises where the value of the collateral held by the Secured Party exceeds its risk exposure on the Chargor and is above the Secured Party's agreed Minimum Transfer Amount.

The Secured Party's obligations to repay cash collateral is subject not only to the security interest but also to the contractual set off provisions in Paragraph 8(a)(ii)(B) of the Deed.

Again with a Return Amount any collateral already in transit will be taken into account in the collateral amount to be returned.

Please note that collateral eligible for transfer is called Eligible Collateral or Other Eligible Support. When actually held by the Secured Party it is called Posted Collateral or other Posted Support.

Paragraph 4. Conditions Precedent, Transfers,

Calculations and Substitutions

A mixed bag of provisions appears in Paragraph 4.

(a) Conditions Precedent

Paragraph 4(a) is similar to the conditions precedent found in Section 2(a)(iii) of the ISDA Master Agreement in connection with payments or deliveries under it.

Each transfer obligation of the Chargor under Paragraph 3(a) (Delivery Amount) and 5 (in a dispute), or of the Secured Party under Paragraph 3(b) (Return Amounts), 4(d)(ii) (Substitutions), 5 (in a dispute) and 6(g) (payment of Interest Amounts or Distributions) is subject to the following pre-conditions:

- **no potential or actual Event of Default or Specified Condition (see pp. 227 and 262–263 for an explanation of this term) has occurred or is continuing;**

- **no Early Termination Date due to unsatisfied payments has occurred or been designated following an Event of Default or Specified Condition impacting the other party.**

(b) Transfers

Paragraph 4(b) describes how transfers are to be made under the Deed for cash, certificated securities and book entry securities charged under the Deed.

(i)   With cash, this is by transfer to the recipient's nominated bank account(s).

(ii) With securities certificates this will involve physical delivery to the recipient or its account, together with all necessary transfer documentation which will vest legal ownership with full title guarantee in the securities in the recipient.

(iii) With book entry or dematerialised securities, this entails the transferring party giving written instructions in a choice of media to the recipient's central securities depository system (e.g. Euroclear or Clearstream) where he holds his account. A copy of such instructions (which must be sufficient to transfer legal ownership with full title guarantee in the securities) must be sent to the recipient.

In the normal course (i.e. no dispute is in progress) if a collateral call notice is received for a Delivery Amount or a Return Amount before the deadline (Notification Time) agreed in Paragraph 13(d)(iv) then with securities, the transfer must be made no later than the close of business on the first trade settlement day thereafter in the relevant market. If the deadline is missed, transfer will occur on the next following trade settlement day in that market. With cash, the transfer must be made on the next Local Business Day if the call notice is received before the Notification Time and the following Local Business Day if not (see Paragraph 12, definition of Settlement Day).

(c) Calculations

Paragraph 4(c) provides for the calculation of exposure and the value of collateral held to be made by the relevant Valuation Agent specified in Paragraph 13 for the purposes of calculating Delivery Amounts and Return Amounts both in the normal course and in disputes. The Valuation Agent will notify its calculations to the other party (or to both parties if it is a third party) by the deadline (Notification Time) on the Local Business Day after it makes its calculations.

(d) Substitutions

Paragraph 4(d) is about substitutions of collateral.

(i) Unless stated otherwise in Paragraph 13(f), the Chargor may request by notice to the Secured Party a substitution of part or all of the collateral it has already transferred to the Secured Party in exchange for new collateral acceptable to the Secured Party.

(ii) If the Secured Party consents to this by written or oral notice to the Chargor, then the latter must transfer the substitute collateral to the Secured Party on the first trade settlement date thereafter. After it has received the new collateral, the Secured Party must return the original collateral which has been substituted no later than the trade settlement date after he has received the substitute collateral from the Chargor. This will usually be the following Local Business Day. In any case, on the transfer date the collateral must be worth the same or nearly the same and in no circumstances is he obliged to retransfer original collateral worth more than the new collateral. The consent point is important at least under English law because without it the Deed could constitute a floating charge which would, in a liquidation, rank behind other fixed charges and behind certain preferential creditors such as liquidators (for their charges), the Inland Revenue and HM Customs & Excise.

Unless already registered, if the Deed were to be recharacterised as a floating charge, it is likely to be void against a liquidator or other creditor of a Chargor because it failed to be registered at Companies House within 21 days of creation. Fines could be levied for this.

This would also mean that the debt secured by the Deed would become immediately payable and could trigger close-out under the ISDA Master Agreement.

Paragraph 5. Dispute resolution

(a) If a party disputes the Valuation Agent's calculation of exposure or the value of collateral held, Paragraph 5 provides a framework for resolving the dispute if it cannot be settled informally.

Collateral disputes *always* relate to these two matters and the calculation of exposure is the most common kind of dispute.

Please note in Paragraph 5(a) the Disputing Party has to observe a standard of reasonableness in initiating a dispute with its counterparty.

The steps are outlined in Paragraph 5(a)(1)–(4) and involve:

(1) a requirement for the Disputing Party to notify its counterparty or the third party Valuation Agent that it wishes to dispute the exposure calculation or collateral valuation not later than the close of business on the Local Business Day after either the date the collateral call notice is received or the date the collateral transfer has been made;

(2) in the case of disputes over exposure calculation for collateral calls, the Disputing Party agrees to transfer the undisputed amount to the other party not later than the close of business on the next trade settlement date following the date he receives the collateral call notice from the collateral giver;

(3) the parties will attempt to resolve the dispute by the deadline nominated in Paragraph 13(g)(i) – the Resolution Time;

(4) if they fail then:

    (i) (A) if the dispute involves the amount of collateral called for, the Valuation Agent will recalculate his figures for exposure and collateral value (including any haircut) by reusing any calculation of the undisputed part of the exposure.

          (B) It will then approach four Reference Market-makers for mid market quotations (i.e. the average of the bid and offer prices of the

Transactions concerned from four leading dealers). Provided four quotations are received the arithmetic mean of these quotations is used. To this is added the exposure calculation which is not in dispute. However, fewer than four quotations may be used in the recalculation of exposure but if no quotations are available for a particular Transaction then the Valuation Agent's original calculation will be used for that Transaction because it is the only reasonable thing to do in the circumstances.

(C) The Valuation Agent will also follow the method specified in Paragraph 13(g)(ii) for calculating the value of collateral held. This method has to be specified in Paragraph 13 or the dispute resolution provisions become inoperative. There is no fallback.

(ii) The Valuation Agent will directly focus on Paragraph 13(g)(ii) where the dispute solely involves the value of collateral held.

When all the recalculations have been done, the Valuation Agent will notify each party (if it is a third party) and the other party (if it is not) of the revised figures not later than the deadline (Notification Time) on the Local Business Day after the Resolution Time (i.e. the dispute resolution deadline agreed in the Deed).

Once all is agreed a revised collateral call notice is sent and the necessary collateral transfer is made.

(b) Paragraph 5(b) clarifies that failure to transfer a disputed amount does not constitute an Event of Default while the above process is being carried out. However, when the process is ended and the transfer is still not made then Paragraph 7 of the Deed comes into play and a Relevant Event will have occurred which could lead to an Event of Default being called under Section 5(a)(i) of the ISDA Master Agreement if the transfer is not made within three Local Business Days following notice to the Defaulting Party.

Paragraph 6. Holding Posted Collateral

(a) Care of Posted Collateral

The Secured Party has a duty of care to keep Posted Collateral in safe custody but has no obligation to collect interest or dividends or preserve or enforce any rights the Posted Collateral might have.

(b) Eligibility to Hold Posted Collateral: Custodians

The Secured Party can itself hold Posted Collateral or appoint a Custodian, subject to Paragraph 13 conditions, to do so. The Chargor can discharge its collateral transfer obligations when it transfers collateral to the appointed Custodian. Transfer to another Custodian is necessary within five Local Business Days if the first Custodian fails to fulfil Paragraph 13 conditions and the Chargor demands this. The Secured Party is liable for the Custodian's acts or omissions as he would be for his own under the Deed.

It is important that the Custodian is notified of the Charger's ownership interest in the Posted Collateral and, for the pledge to be perfected, the security interest in favour of the Secured Party.

(c) Segregated accounts

All non-cash Posted Collateral must be held in segregated accounts by the Secured Party or its Custodian. This protects the Secured Party, because if the non-cash Posted Collateral was commingled the Chargor's ownership interest in the securities would be lost because the Secured Party relies upon the Chargor's equity of redemption for its own continuing security interest in the collateral.

Segregation was considered unnecessary for cash collateral because the charge is over the Secured Party's contractual obligation to repay the correct amount of cash and not over tangible cash itself.

(d) No use of collateral

Paragraph 6(d) is a very strict prohibition on any sale, loan, repledging, assignment or other disposition by the Secured Party of the Posted Collateral it holds under the Deed. If it did any of these things it would wreck the security interest over the Posted Collateral.

(e) Rights accompanying Posted Collateral

(i) Provided no Paragraph 7 Relevant Event or Specified Condition has occurred, the Chargor is entitled to all interest and dividend payments on Posted Collateral securities and to have the Secured Party follow its voting instructions where such rights attach to the Posted Collateral. However, it must indemnify the Secured Party for any expense arising in doing so.

(ii) However, after a Relevant Event or Specified Condition has happened, the Secured Party may exercise its rights, voting or otherwise, over the Posted Collateral without the Chargor's consent although he must notify the Chargor of such exercise.

(f) Calls and other obligations

(i) The Chargor is obliged to pay all calls in respect of the Posted Collateral securities and, if it fails to do so, must reimburse the Secured Party if it decides to pay the call on the Chargor's behalf. Before reimbursement such additional securities will form part of the Chargor's Obligations and will bear interest at the Default Rate from the date the Secured Party pays the call.

(ii) In addition, the Chargor is responsible for supplying the Secured Party with such information as it has in respect of a notice issued by a securities issuer under s 212 of the Companies Act 1985. Such notices are normally issued by public companies wanting to find out the exact identity of holders of their securities. The sub-paragraph also extends to similar inquiries arising under Articles of Association or constituting documents. Where the Chargor fails to do this, the Secured Party may choose to volunteer such information as it has on the Chargor's behalf.

(iii) The Chargor has a continuing liability to perform and observe all the terms, conditions and obligations it has in relation to the collateral it has charged.

(iv) Paragraph 6(f)(iv) is a general disclaimer by the Secured Party. It is not liable to perform or fulfil any of the Chargor's obligations in relation to the collateral. It is not obliged to make any payment in connection with the collateral nor to file any claim or take any other action to collect or enforce any payment due to it under the Deed.

(g) Distributions and Interest Amount

(i) The Secured Party must transfer to the Chargor any distribution he receives from a securities issuer not later than the Settlement Day following its receipt provided that there are no collateral implications in doing so.

(ii) Interest Amount is the interest payable by the Secured Party on cash deposits he holds as collateral from the Chargor. The frequency at which cash interest is paid over to the Chargor is stated in Paragraph 13(i)(ii). It is usually monthly. Again it will not be paid over if it creates or increases a collateral call and will continue to be held as part of the Chargor's collateral balance in those circumstances.

Indeed, if any distributions on securities or interest on cash collateral is not paid over to the Chargor by the Secured Party it will form part of the Posted Collateral balance or be set off in accordance with Paragraph 8(a)(ii) as described below.

Paragraph 7. Default

This Paragraph is also important and sets out the events which can trigger the Secured Party's enforcement rights under the Deed. These can arise if an Event of Default occurs or there is a failure to perform any obligation under the Deed. There is a grace period of two Local Business Days where the failure relates to collateral or interest/distribution transfers and 30 days in respect of any other obligation under the Deed. Both grace periods commence from the issue of a notice by the non-Defaulting Party to the Defaulting Party. These failures are individually called a "Relevant Event".

The term "Relevant Event" refers to both parties, but in fact the Deed fails to specify any consequences of a Relevant Event impacting a Secured Party. A Paragraph 13 amendment is sometimes made to address this.

Paragraph 8. Rights of enforcement

(a) Secured Party's rights

Paragraph 8 is the most important part of the Deed as it details the Secured Party's enforcement rights. These arise from a Relevant Event, Specified Condition (see pp. 227 and 262–263) or the designation of an Early Termination Date happening to the Chargor.

Paragraph 8(a)(i) deals with the Secured Party's enforcement rights with non-cash Posted Collateral.

If the Chargor fails to pay its Obligations in full when they are due, the Secured Party may immediately without notice exercise all its powers under the Deed, e.g.:

(A) **to sell all or part of the Posted Collateral by any legal means and at its absolute discretion; and**

(B) **to receive payments or moneys due to the Chargor in respect of the Posted Collateral and to hold on to them.**

Sections 93 (partial redemption of charges) and 103 (regulation of the exercise of a power of sale) of the Law of Property Act 1925 are stated as not applying under the Deed. These exclusions commonly appear in other English law governed charge documentation.

Paragraph 8(a)(ii) gives the Secured Party the right to realise cash collateral by the following means:

(A) **To discharge the Obligations due in any order it sees fit; or**

(B) **To offset the Chargor's payment of Obligations against any Return Amount owed by the Secured Party to the Chargor; or**

(C) **To debit any sole or joint accounts of the Chargor held at any of the Secured Party's offices with all or any part of amounts owing by the Chargor under its Obligations to the Secured Party; or**

(D) **To combine any such account referred to in (C) above with the account holding the Posted Collateral making any currency conversions, transfers or bookkeeping entries on the Chargor's account(s) as the Secured Party thinks are proper.**

Finally, the Secured Party may also exercise all applicable rights and remedies it has in respect of Other Posted Collateral specified in Paragraph 13(c)(iii).

(b) Power of attorney

Paragraph 8(b) gives the Secured Party a power of attorney exclusively for the purpose of securing performance of the Obligations. As attorney, the Secured Party can act in its own name or in the name of the Chargor to:

(i) **execute any transfer in relation to the Posted Collateral;**

(ii) **exercise all the Chargor's powers and rights in the same;**

(iii) take various actions in relation to moneys due or arising out of the Posted Collateral and to give a good discharge for the same;

(iv) endorse cheques or similar instruments in relation to the Posted Collateral; and

(v) institute such proceedings, actions or claims as the Secured Party thinks necessary to protect or enforce the security interest under the Deed.

As mentioned before, the Secured Party can only execute a document as a deed under this power of attorney if the power of attorney is itself granted pursuant to a deed. This is why it is sensible to execute the Deed itself as a deed in its signing block.

(c) Protection of purchaser

(i) Third parties purchasing collateral from an enforcing Secured Party are protected by this provision. Such a third party purchaser need not concern itself with:

- whether any of the Secured Party's powers has become exercisable;
- whether any Obligation is due;
- whether the Secured Party has acted properly or regularly; or
- how the Secured Party has dealt with any money paid to it.

(ii) Provided the third party purchaser has not acted in bad faith, it may assume that the Secured Party has dealt with the above matters in a valid manner under the Deed. If, however, the Chargor considers that the Secured Party has acted improperly, it may sue but, if successful, it may only claim damages and not receive back any collateral sold to the third party.

As well as protecting the third party collateral purchaser, this provision also indirectly shields the Secured Party from possible liabilities to the collateral purchaser which could otherwise arise.

(d) Deficiencies and excess proceeds

When all proceeds from collateral realisations have been received by the Secured Party, he must return any surplus to the Chargor (subject to any further set off or counterclaim rights the Secured Party may have). In any case where there is any shortfall in the amount raised by the collateral to cover the Obligations, the Chargor remains liable for that shortfall.

(e) Final returns

When the Chargor owes nothing under any present or future Obligations (any liability to withholding tax under Section 2(d) of the ISDA Master Agreement is excluded from this), the Secured Party must return any collateral it is still holding to the Chargor.

Paragraph 9. Representations

In this Paragraph standard representations are made by each party when acting in the capacity of Chargor under the Deed in respect of the following matters:

- it has power to grant a security interest over the collateral and has taken all necessary authorising action;
- it has full legal title to the collateral charged under the Deed and such collateral is free from all encumbrances apart from securities liens in a clearing system;
- following the Chargor's transfer of the collateral to the Secured Party, the Secured Party will have a valid security interest over the collateral;
- no competing third party security interests (except for securities liens in a clearing system) will be created over the collateral following the performance of the Chargor's obligations under the Deed.

The New York CSA includes within its third representation, a representation covering the perfection or priority of the security interest created under it. This is fine as far as New York law is concerned, but is less practical with the Deed where the security interest could be taken over collateral in various countries and currencies and give rise to conflict of laws issues.

Paragraph 10. Expenses

This is a simple but comprehensive expenses provision.

Each party will pay its own costs and expenses arising from performing its obligations under the Deed.

However, the Chargor shall be liable for any taxes or charges imposed upon the collateral held by the Secured Party as soon as it becomes aware of them.

Following realisation or set off of collateral, the Defaulting Party will pay the liquidation costs unless there is no Defaulting Party in which case both parties will share them equally.

Paragraph 11. Other provisions

This Paragraph brings together a number of "boilerplate" provisions which give additional protections to the parties.

(a) Default Interest

Where the Secured Party fails to transfer Posted Collateral or an Interest Amount promptly, it will be obliged to pay compensation to the Chargor at the Default Rate (1% over the Chargor's cost of funds). The default interest period includes the date on which such return or payment was due to but excluding the date on which it is actually made (in accordance with the normal practice in the derivatives markets). In addition daily compounding of interest will also apply.

(b) Further assurances

Promptly following a demand from the Secured Party, the Chargor will take any necessary action to ensure the security interest is validly created and perfected over the collateral. In addition, the Secured Party undertakes to arrange the release of the charge over any collateral to be returned or paid over to the Chargor under the Deed.

(c) Further protection

The Chargor will promptly notify the Secured Party of any lawsuit or attachment relating to the collateral it has charged to the Secured Party and defend the same.

(d) Good faith and commercially reasonable manner

This describes the standard required of both parties for their performance under the Deed including any calculations or valuations they may make.

(e) Demands and notices

Self-explanatory provision. All demands and notices under the Deed will be given in one of the traditional or electronic means stated in Section 12 of the Master Agreement unless provided otherwise under Paragraph 13.

(f) Specifications of certain matters

This provision states that any matter referred to in the Deed as being specified in Paragraph 13 could alternatively be referred to in a Confirmation or other document and, if so, the Deed will be interpreted accordingly.

(g) Governing law and jurisdiction

The Deed is a standalone document and it is appropriate for it to have a separate governing law and jurisdiction clause.

Page 12 of *The User's Guide to the ISDA Credit Support Documents under English Law* points out that under English law there is no objection per se why the Deed cannot be used in conjunction with an ISDA Master Agreement subject to New York law. However, if this is done, greater expense and inconvenience could arise in litigation where two documents under different governing laws are involved.

However, it would be inadvisable to make the Deed subject to New York law because:

● **English and New York law have important differences over taking security interests; and**

● **the Deed was composed with English law principles in mind.**

Paragraph 12. Definitions: Glossary of Terms

Assigned Rights	The Chargor's rights to collateral transferred to or present in a securities clearance system or with a third party.
Base Currency	The currency into which exposure and collateral is converted to calculate if a collateral call needs to be made.
Base Currency Equivalent	If collateral is denominated in another currency, the amount in the Base Currency needed to buy the other currency at the spot rate of exchange so as to convert it into the Base Currency.
Chargor	The party charging the collateral under the Deed.
Credit Support Amount	The net risk exposure the Secured Party has on the Chargor and which needs to be collateralised.
Custodian	A third party who holds securities in a clearing system and administers them.
Delivery Amount	The amount of collateral the Chargor needs to deliver if he agrees a collateral call from the Secured Party.
Disputing Party	A party who disputes the other party's calculation of Transaction values in determining risk exposure and/or the value of any collateral held or to be returned.
Distributions	Periodic payments of interest or dividends on bonds or shares by issuers of the same to their holders.
Distributions Date	The date upon which holders of bonds or shares are entitled to receive interest or dividends from their issuers.
Eligible Collateral	The collateral types and maturities agreed by the parties to be subject to the Deed.
Eligible Credit Support	Eligible Collateral plus Other Eligible Support specified in Paragraph 13(c)(iii) of the Deed including securities redeemed by their issuer.
Eligible Currency	The agreed currency or currencies for cash collateral transferred under the Deed.

Exposure	The estimated replacement value of all Transactions (using mid market quotations from dealers) so as to calculate risk exposure. The calculation is made as if the Transactions were being closed out on the basis described in the definition.
Independent Amount	A confusing term meaning either initial margin taken at the start of a collateral relationship and not counted in risk exposure calculations or a sum taken later in the relationship and which is counted in the risk exposure calculations.
Interest Amount	The aggregate sum of interest due on cash collateral including its conversion into the Base Currency Equivalent where interest is due on cash collateral in various currencies.
Interest Period	The period from the date when interest was last paid on cash collateral to the date on which it is next due to be paid.
Interest Rate	The particular benchmark interest rate (e.g. EONIA, Fed Funds) which the parties agree shall be paid on cash deposited as collateral. It may include a spread.
Local Business Day	A normal business day for commercial banks in the location required for the valuation of Transactions and collateral under the Deed. With securities transfers, a normal business day for securities clearance systems.
Minimum Transfer Amount	The agreed minimum level that the Credit Support Amount must reach before a party is obliged to deliver or return collateral.
Notification Time	The agreed deadline for making a collateral call.
Obligations	All obligations of either party under the ISDA Master Agreement and the Deed.
Other Eligible Support	Additional or alternative collateral specified in Paragraph 13(c)(iii) of the Deed.
Other Posted Support	Other Eligible Support when transferred and charged to the Secured Party.

Posted Collateral	All Eligible Collateral and Distributions transferred under the Deed to the Secured Party or received by it and under its control. Includes Distributions and Interest Amounts not yet paid over to the Chargor.
Posted Credit Support	The totality of collateral charged to and held by or on behalf of the Secured Party.
Recalculation Date	In a dispute the date or dates upon which recalculation of Transaction and collateral values are made.
Relevant Event	An Event of Default under the ISDA Master Agreement or a performance failure under the terms of the Deed.
Resolution Time	The agreed deadline for resolving disputes.
Return Amount	The collateral amount to be returned by the secured party to the chargor because it is surplus to the secured party's risk exposure on the chargor.
Secured Party	The party benefiting from the charging of the collateral under the Deed.
Settlement Day	For cash collateral transfers, the following Local Business Day. For securities collateral the next Local Business Day when transfer of such securities can be completed in the normal course.
Specified Condition	A pre-condition under which the party affected by a stated Termination Event cannot call for or substitute collateral nor receive dividends or interest on pledged collateral.
Substitute Credit Support	Where agreed by the secured party, collateral transferred by the chargor in substitution for other collateral already held by the secured party.
Substitution Date	The deadline for the secured party to return designated previously delivered collateral to the chargor following an agreed substitution.
Substitution Notice	The notice given by the Chargor to the Secured Party requesting the substitution of collateral previously charged with new collateral of equivalent value.

Threshold	The unsecured risk exposure each party allows the other. Collateral may only be called or returned where the risk exposure exceeds the relevant party's Threshold and Minimum Transfer Amount.
Valuation Agent	Either each party to the Deed performing their own valuations of Transactions and collateral and making collateral calls as appropriate or a third party doing this for them both.
Valuation Date	The Local Business Day upon which risk exposure calculations and collateral valuations are made to determine if a collateral call is needed.
Valuation Percentage	The remaining value of collateral expressed in percentage terms after the agreed haircut has been deducted.
Valuation Time	The reference time as at which calculations for collateral calls are made. They are often based on prices at the close of business on the Local Business Day before the Valuation Date.
Value	The agreed valuation bases in Paragraph 13(g)(ii) of the Deed for cash and securities collateral required to value collateral in a dispute.

Paragraph 13. Elections and Variables

In order to avoid repetition, I do not propose to go over the same ground covered in Chapter 5 relating to matters already covered in respect of Paragraph 11 of the English Law CSA. However, the following provisions are not found in that document:

(b) Security interest for "Obligations"

Paragraph 13(b) allows the parties to expand the Paragraph 12 definition of Obligations (i.e. all obligations of either party under the ISDA Master Agreement and the Deed) to be covered by the security interest. This means that liabilities outside the ISDA Master Agreement and the Deed can be specified and brought within the ambit of the security interest under the Deed. This would, of course, require a legal analysis that such an arrangement would be enforceable under insolvency laws in the Chargor's jurisdiction of incorporation.

(c)(iii) Other Eligible Support

This allows the parties to specify other acceptable collateral for a Chargor to supply, e.g. bank letters of credit, third party guarantees, investment grade corporate bonds or even gold. If Other Eligible Support applies, then the parties must in Paragraph 13(j) describe how Value is to be calculated for these items. Any grace periods or Events of Default in the documentation for such assets/instruments should also be taken into account in the Deed provisions.

(e) Conditions precedent and secured party's rights and remedies

Paragraph 4(a) sets out the pre-conditions for the parties' collateral call, substitution and distribution transfer rights under the Deed. If an Event of Default is called, an Early Termination Date designated, or a Specified Condition occurs the normal run of things is interrupted.

Paragraph 13(e) enables the parties to specify one or more Termination Events as Specified Conditions. If these occur, then the Affected Party cannot call for or substitute collateral nor receive dividends or interest on pledged collateral until the position is cured. This is because a non-Affected Party would not wish, inter alia, to have to release collateral or distributions to an Affected Party in these circumstances. This is a useful protection for a Secured Party.

Amendments can be made to the Termination Events for this purpose, e.g. Credit Event Upon Merger impacts below a certain credit rating. Any Termination Event may be designated as a Specified Condition but Additional Termination Events should only be nominated as Specified Conditions if these mirror Additional Termination Events in the ISDA Master Agreement.

(h) Eligibility to hold Posted Collateral; Custodians

This provision usefully sets out conditions for the parties to hold collateral themselves and to use custodians. As for the parties themselves, they must not have defaulted. As for the Posted Collateral, it is likely to be held only in specified jurisdictions. The custodian is identified and often there is wording added, stating minimum asset size or formal credit rating before the Custodian is eligible for appointment. The following is a full example of this:

> Party A and its Custodian will be entitled to hold Posted Collateral pursuant to Paragraph 6(b); provided that the following conditions applicable to it are satisfied:
>
> (1) Party A is not a Defaulting Party nor is subject to a Specified Condition which has occurred and is continuing.
>
> (2) Party A or its Custodian (as the case may be) has US$10 billion in assets.
>
> (3) Party A or its Custodian (as the case may be) has a Rating of Baa1 or better from Moody's and BBB+ or better from S&P.

(4)   The Custodian is not an Affiliate of Party A.

(5)   Posted Collateral may only be held in the following jurisdictions: Germany, United Kingdom, The State of New York.

Initially, the Custodian for Party A is [*name of institution*].

The specifications for Party B's Custodian are usually the same.

(j)(i) Other Eligible Support and Other Posted Support

The definition of Value in Chapter 12 is inadequate to cover valuation of these items and so the necessary modus operandi needs to be specified here. Sometimes this might just be expressed as "as agreed between the parties from time to time".

Signing block

The footnotes on page 24 of the Deed give guidance on how it should be executed – under seal or under hand, as appropriate. In addition, Appendix D to the *User's Guide to the ISDA Credit Support Documents under English Law* sets out the normal requirements to executing a deed under English law as at when it was published in 1999.

PRINCIPAL DIFFERENCES BETWEEN THE ENGLISH LAW CSA AND THE ENGLISH LAW DEED

The English law CSA differs from the English law Deed in the following main ways:

1.   It is a title transfer agreement while the English law Deed creates a security interest over the collateral.

2.   It requires very few formalities for its perfection. The English law Deed needs to be registered at Companies House in the UK.

3.   The Transferee has unfettered rights to use the collateral under the CSA. This is expressly forbidden under Paragraph 6(d) of the English law Deed.

4.   The English law Deed is a standalone document (a Credit Support Document under the ISDA Master Agreement) while the CSA forms part of the ISDA Master Agreement itself.

5.   The CSA relies for its effectiveness on the close-out netting provisions of the ISDA Master Agreement. The English law Deed relies upon the enforcement of a security interest.

6.   The English law Deed allows for a number of Termination Events to be added as Specified Conditions (i.e. extra events which can trigger the enforcement of a Secured Party's close-out rights). If a Specified Condition applies to a party he cannot call for collateral, substitute it or receive Distributions or interest on collateral posted by it while it lasts. The English law CSA lacks Specified Conditions.

7. The English law Deed imposes a duty of care on the Secured Party in holding collateral and allows him to use custodians. This is not permitted in the CSA as it would destroy the mutuality of the set off arrangements.

8. Under the English law Deed the Chargor appoints the Secured Party as its power of attorney to complete any necessary documents in a close-out situation. There is no such arrangement in the CSA because it is not by nature a deed.

9. The English law Deed contains a governing law clause (as it is a standalone document) while the CSA does not (as it is part of the ISDA Master Agreement).

10. The English law Deed allows a separate category of collateral entitled Other Eligible Support to be specified in the Variables Paragraph. This could be a guarantee or letter of credit. The CSA has no such provision.

11. Undoubtedly it would be costlier and more time consuming to enforce collateral under the English law Deed than the English law CSA.

ISDA Fallbacks for the English law Deed

Fig. 7.1

If no choice is made the following apply by default:

Provision	Fallback
Base Currency	US Dollars
Eligible Currency	Base Currency
Independent Amount	Zero
Threshold	Zero
Minimum Transfer Amount	Zero
Rounding	No rounding
Valuation Agent	The party making demand under Paragraph 3 and the Transferee for Paragraph 6 payments.
Substitution Date	The Settlement Date following the Transferee's receipt of New Credit Support
Specified Condition	Does not apply if not specified.
Alternative	Paragraph 5 dispute resolution procedures apply.
Eligibility to Hold Posted Collateral: Custodians	Secured Party not a Defaulting Party.
Transfer of Interest Amount	Last Local Business Day of a calendar month and any Local Business Day when a cash Return Amount is due to the Transferor.
Alternative to Interest Amount	Paragraph 6(g)(ii) and Paragraph 12 definition of Interest Amount applies.

FIG. 7.2 Provisions which must be completed as there is no fallback

Eligible Collateral
Other Eligible Support
Valuation Date
Valuation Time
Notification Time
Resolution Time
Value
Interest Rate
Value and Transfer of Other Eligible Support and Other Posted Support.
Addresses for Transfers.

ISDA JAPANESE LAW CREDIT SUPPORT ANNEX

Introduction

The 1995 ISDA Credit Support Annex (Security Interest subject to Japanese Law) (the "Japanese CSA") is according to the *ISDA Collateral Survey 2000* only used in 1% of cases (see p. 7). Hence, the description of it here will be in very summary form. The text of the Japanese CSA is reproduced in full in Annex 7 by kind permission of the International Swaps and Derivatives Association, Inc.

The Japanese CSA is for use with collateral arrangements in Japan involving assets located there. It is subject to Japanese law (Paragraph 11(g)).

Security interests are taken over collateral in one of two ways under Japanese law, viz:

- **Pledging Collateral; or**
- **Lending Collateral with a right of set off.**

Eligible collateral is mostly cash, cash deposits, Japanese Government bonds ("JGBs") or other readily marketable Japanese securities.

The Japanese CSA closely resembles the New York CSA in many of its terms. However, it is different structurally in that it is a standalone Credit Support Document and like the English Law Deed is not incorporated into the ISDA Master Agreement. It falls within the compass of Section 5(a)(iii) of the ISDA Master

Agreement so that any Credit Support Default will count as an Event of Default under the ISDA Master Agreement.

As with the other ISDA Credit Support Documents, the Japanese CSA is a bilateral document so that, during its life, either party could be the Obligor (pledgor) or the Obligee (secured party), although it is likely that only one of them will be the Obligor at any particular time.

As mentioned above, there are two main ways of creating a security interest under Japanese law, either via a pledge or through a loan of collateral to the Obligee with a right of set off.

The Obligee's rights and obligations and the degree of care and other duties required of the Obligee or its custodian holding the collateral will differ depending upon which arrangement is used. This will also affect the method of enforcement upon an Event of Default or Termination Event. Each method has certain advantages and drawbacks over the other. The Japanese CSA lets the parties use either or both methods and incorporates provisions which reflect the different rights, obligations and enforcement methods.

Assignment by way of security is a third method of establishing a valid form of security arrangement under Japanese law. However, it was not adopted in the Japanese Law CSA for tax reasons, and because under such an arrangement, the assignor may not be entitled to the return of the assigned collateral if the assignee goes bust.

(a) Pledge method

Under Japanese law, pledges are governed by the terms of the Civil Code of Japan which outlines the requirements for their creation and the respective rights and the obligations of the pledgor and the pledgee. In general, there are three categories of assets that can be subject to pledge under Japanese law, viz:

- **moveables (similar to chattel – a term which means personal property)**;
- **immoveables (similar to real estate)**;
- **intangible property such as intellectual property and obligation rights (similar to choses in action, i.e. an asset which a person has the right to recover (if withheld) through action, e.g. money in a bank account).**

For the purposes of the Japanese CSA, a pledge over JGBs in bearer form or in the book entry transfer system, which are considered to be moveables, would take the form of a pledge over chattel, and a pledge over JGBs in registered form or Cash Deposits would be a pledge over choses in action.

Creation and perfection of pledge

A pledge over a chattel is created when the pledgee takes possession of the pledged asset, including possession by an agent, and perfection is achieved by the continuing possession of it. Book entry JGBs can be pledged by instructing the Bank of Japan (the "BOJ") to transfer them to the pledgee's designated "collateral account". The BOJ is deemed to hold such JGBs on behalf of the pledgee.

With JGBs held in registered form, the security interest must be created and perfected by registration of the pledge. This involves the pledgor and the pledgee signing and sealing a request for pledge which is then submitted to the BOJ. The BOJ registers the contents of the request, normally a description of the pledged JGBs, the amount of the claim and the name of the pledgor and the pledgee. Since February 1996, this can be done electronically.

A pledge over a Cash Deposit is created by an agreement and is perfected by either a notarised notice from the pledgor to the Obligor of the pledged claim (i.e. the bank holding the deposit) or a notarised acknowledgement by such bank. If a physical certificate exists for the pledged claim, it must be given to the pledgee in order for the pledge to be validly created. ISDA's *User's Guide to the Japanese Credit Support Annex* advises parties taking a pledge over a Cash Deposit to consult their Japanese lawyers because many leading scholars believe that a pledge may not be created over a demand deposit account whose balance fluctuates. Others disagree with this view.

Enforcement of pledge

A pledgee of a chattel may enforce the pledge by selling the pledged asset by public sale and applying the proceeds in satisfaction of its claim. If such collateral consists of book entry JGBs, the pledgee may instruct the BOJ to transfer such JGBs from his "collateral account" into his own "proprietary account". A pledgee of a chose in action may enforce the pledge by directly collecting the pledged claim from the Obligor. This demand will be made to the bank which maintains the pledged account, in the case of Cash Deposit, or the BOJ, in the case of JGBs in registered form. This difference in the method of enforcement is reflected in Paragraph 8(a) of the Japanese CSA.

Any enforcement methods other than those envisaged by the Civil Code of Japan are generally invalid. For example, any type of private sale, including an agreement to transfer ownership of the pledged asset, is invalid unless it involves a commercial merchant who pledges assets in the normal course of its business. A pledgor may demand the release of its pledge if the pledgee, in violation of the statute, disposes of the pledged asset or rehypothecates it without the pledgor's consent. The pledgee will also be liable for damages resulting from the breach of specified duties of care. Although a pledgee can enforce its pledge during a bankruptcy proceeding it cannot do so if a corporate reorganisation or administration is involved.

Repledge

Collateral can be repledged under Paragraph 6(d)(i) of the Japanese CSA with the pledgor's consent. Without such consent, the Obligee may, at its own risk, repledge the collateral, but if a *force majeure* event occurs and the repledged collateral is destroyed, the Obligee is still liable to the Obligor for such collateral but would have discharged its responsibility in such instance had consent been obtained. In either case, the Obligor's rights to the return of the collateral in certain situations when mark to market values fluctuate may be junior to the rights of the repledgee. Moreover, since the Obligee is required to return Posted Pledging Collateral in the form of the exact pledged assets, it will automatically breach its agreement with the repledgee when a Return Amount is due on the Valuation Date in respect of the Posted Pledging Collateral it has repledged. Of course, the repledgee can agree to release the repledge in the Return Amount. The rights of an innocent repledgee will prevail over the Obligor's right to return of the pledged asset or to demand the release of the pledge.

Pros and cons of the pledge method

Pros

(i)   It is well established legally that the pledge can secure all claims even if their balances fluctuate over time;

(ii) less likelihood that the parties will be subject to Securities Transfer Tax (unless the collateral is realised because of enforcement of the security interest).

Cons

(i)   Significant costs could be incurred by the regular return of previously pledged collateral due to the mark to market values of Transactions moving in favour of the Obligor;

(ii) more limited scope for repledging collateral under the Pledge than under the loan and set off method;

(iii) enforcement of a pledge is prohibited in a corporate restructuring.

Loan and set off method

As an alternative to a pledge, a security interest can be created by loaning collateral to an Obligee and granting a right to set off this loan against the Obligor's Obligations under the ISDA Master Agreement. This is akin to the title transfer approach. Cash, JGBs, listed stocks and other readily available securities are eligible for this type of loan. For example, JGBs can be lent on the understanding that the borrower will return JGBs of the same type and value. Under Paragraph 2(a) of the Japanese CSA, the parties agree to set off the Obligor's Obligations against the Obligee's obligation to "repay" the Posted Lending Collateral.

The Obligee owns the loaned assets and may exercise all rights of an owner (including sale or repledge), subject only to the obligation to transfer the Posted Lending Collateral or Equivalent Collateral under Paragraph 3(b) when a Return Amount arises, and the obligation to return Posted Lending Collateral upon the termination of the ISDA Master Agreement under Paragraph 2(a). Paragraph 8(b)(iv) grants the Obligor comparable set off rights if the Obligee fails to return Posted Collateral whenever a Return Amount is due.

Registered JGBs may be lent by sending an electronic request for transfer through the BOJ which then makes entries on its books to reflect the borrower as the new owner. Book entry JGBs can be lent by instructing the BOJ to transfer JGBs from the lender's proprietary account to the borrower's proprietary account.

Enforceability of set off

In order for this arrangement to create a first priority interest, the set off provision must be enforceable. In respect of attachments by the Obligor's creditors on the Obligor's claim to the return of loaned collateral, the Civil Code of Japan establishes that set off by an Obligee of an obligation is not effective against a counter claim by the Obligor's creditors which is obtained after an attachment takes effect in respect of that obligation. Therefore, an Obligee generally must acquire the claim before an attaching creditor. Although such attachments would breach Paragraph 7 of the Japanese CSA and would be an Event of Default if not cured within 30 days after notice, if the claim is perfected in accordance with the Civil Code of Japan, the creditor will prevail over the Obligee's right of set off. Similar concerns exist if the Obligor assigns or pledges his claim to the return of the loaned assets to a third party. If the Obligor gives notice to the Obligee, the third party pledgee will prevail over the Obligee's right of set off.

These considerations led to the inclusion of Paragraph 13(m), which establishes that such attachment, assignment or pledge constitutes an Additional Event of Default and will trigger an Automatic Early Termination of the Agreement. Therefore, set off takes effect as of the occurrence of these events, establishing a first priority security interest vis-à-vis attaching creditors or assignees. Even without such a provision, the Obligee's set off right could prevail over attaching creditors and assignees (see the *User's Guide to the Japanese Credit Support Annex* for further details).

A second requirement for a valid set off is that the claim and counterclaim to be set off must be of the same kind. To the extent JGBs or other securities are used as Posted Lending Collateral, this requirement would not be met because such securities are different in kind from the Obligations, which are a money claim. Therefore, the Japanese CSA provides that the obligation of the Obligee to return Posted Lending Collateral in the form of securities is made subject to an option for the Obligee to return Equivalent Collateral or the Cash equivalent under Paragraphs 2(a) and 3(b). However, such an election may have certain tax consequences.

Insolvency close-out netting is well established as effective in Japan. The Japanese Bankruptcy Law generally allows set off outside the bankruptcy proceedings, and the Corporate Reorganisation Law allows set off if both claims mature before the deadline for filing proof of claims. However, the restrictions on set off contained in the insolvency laws provide that claims acquired or obligations assumed or owed after a creditor becomes aware that there has been a suspension of payments or an insolvency filing shall not be available for set off unless such claims or obligations arose by operation of law or by a cause which arose before these events or by a cause which arose one year or more before the declaration of bankruptcy or commencement of corporate reorganisation proceedings by the court. Furthermore, claims acquired or obligations assumed or owed after there has been a declaration of bankruptcy or commencement of corporate reorganisation proceedings by the court will not be available for set off. Therefore, if the loan is made in violation of the above, set off will not be enforceable. However, the loan envisaged under the Japanese CSA should not be treated as voidable unless made after there has been a declaration of bankruptcy or a commencement of corporate reorganisation proceedings by the court since, on any Valuation Date, the Obligor effectively receives an extension of credit in exchange for the Posted Lending Collateral and the obligation to make such loan is typically created before a suspect period.

Pros and cons of the loan method

Pros

(i)   Repledging of collateral is allowed;

(ii) set off is available, subject to conditions, in insolvency and corporate reorganisation situations.

Cons

(i)   The only priority the Obligor has if an Obligee defaults is in respect of surplus collateral. Otherwise, he ranks with the general creditors. The pledge method is better in this respect as it gives a general right of redemption to the Obligor;

(ii) possible tax consequences arise in using this method where the Obligee sets off the cash equivalent of Lending Collateral in the form of securities. This will result in the Securities Transaction Tax being levied because the set off of the cash equivalent instead of returning or selling off the securities themselves is deemed to be a sale (see page 14 of the *User's Guide to the Japanese Credit Support Annex*).

The main differences between the Japanese CSA and the New York CSA are as follows:

- the terms Pledgor and Secured Party are replaced by Obligor and Obligee;
- posted Collateral is split into Posted Lending Collateral and Posted Pledging Collateral;
- different treatment of security interest creation in Paragraph 2;
- different treatment in holding and using collateral in Paragraph 6;
- different rights and remedies for the Obligor and Obligee in Paragraph 8;
- different Paragraph 13 provisions for designating Lending Collateral and Pledging Collateral (13(b)(ii)) and assignment or pledge of Posted Lending Collateral as an Event of Default (13(m));
- modification of notice provisions and time of day conventions to suit Japanese business practices.

It is worth noting several things about the registration of JGBs.

Transfer of title in or perfection of a pledge over JGBs held in registered form will be reflected in the registry on the next Local Business Day if the necessary documents are received by the BOJ by 3 p.m. on a Local Business Day. However, any application for registration will not be accepted during the period commencing on the seventh Local Business Day before each payment day of principal or interest on the relevant bonds and ending on the Local Business Day immediately before such payment day. The transfer of JGBs on the electronic transfer system will be made at the time the relevant message is sent via the system. However, no change in an account will be accepted by the system during the two Local Business Day period before an interest payment date or on the date of redemption of the relevant bonds.

PARAGRAPH BY PARAGRAPH SUMMARY OF THE ISDA JAPANESE LAW CREDIT SUPPORT ANNEX

Heading

The Japanese CSA is dated on the day it is created but refers to an ISDA Master Agreement which already exists and is probably dated as of another date.

Preamble

The Japanese CSA is a Credit Support Document in relation to the ISDA Master Agreement.

Paragraph 1

Where there is inconsistency, the Japanese CSA prevails over the Schedule and its Paragraph 13 over the Japanese CSA as a whole.

Either party may act as Obligee or Obligor at different times during the life of the Japanese CSA.

Paragraph 2

The security interest is split between the Loan and Set Off and Pledge arrangements.

(a) Loan

Each party, in the capacity of Obligor, lends Lending Collateral to the other as security for its Obligations under the ISDA Master Agreement and grants the Obligee a right of set off. Such Posted Lending Collateral will be returned to the Obligor as a Return Amount or if a substitution request is granted or as surplus collateral in an enforcement situation. If the Posted Lending Collateral is securities, then the Obligee can cash settle instead if it wishes.

(b) Pledge

The Obligor grants the Obligee a first priority continuing security interest (including a statutory pledge) in, and right of set off against all Posted Pledging Collateral. The security interest will be in the form of a statutory pledge (*Shichiken*). When that Posted Pledging Collateral is returned to the Obligor, the security interest is immediately released.

Paragraph 3

This Paragraph concerns collateral calls and returns and how they are calculated. Basically the Obligee compares his exposure to the collateral he holds and calls for more, returns any excess or does nothing, depending upon the calculations after taking into account Independent Amounts, Thresholds and/or Minimum Transfer Amounts.

Paragraph 4

(a) Collateral transfers are only made if no Event of Default, Potential Event of Default, Specified Condition or Early Termination Date exists.

(b) Transfers are to be made by close of business on the third Local Business Day if the demand is made by the Notification Time. If not, transfers are delayed by one Local Business Day.

(c) Calculations of exposure and collateral values to be made by the Valuation Agent as of the Valuation Time for each Valuation Date. Calculations to be notified to parties not later than the Notification Time on the Local Business Day following the applicable Valuation Date.

(d) The Obligor may substitute collateral upon giving notice to the Obligee. The Obligee must transfer back the original collateral not later than three Local Business Days after he received the substitute collateral. He is only obliged to return collateral of equal value to the substitute collateral.

Paragraph 5

If a dispute arises on exposure or collateral value calculations, the Disputing Party will notify the other party and the Valuation Agent by specified deadlines and will transfer the undisputed amount. The parties consult to resolve the dispute. If the dispute relates to exposure, the Valuation Agent tries to obtain four Market Quotations. If it relates to collateral values, the Valuation Agent follows the process stipulated in Paragraph 13(f).

Following recalculation, the Valuation Agent notifies the parties not later than the Notification Time on the Local Business Day following the Resolution Time and the transfer is then made within three Local Business Days of such notice.

Paragraph 6

(a) Until it has to return the Posted Lending Collateral, the Obligee shall have full ownership and usage rights to it.

(b) The Obligee has a duty of care to keep Posted Pledging Collateral in safe custody but has no duty to collect interest or dividends.

(c) The Obligee can hold Posted Pledging Collateral or appoint a custodian subject to Paragraph 13 conditions to do so. The Obligor will discharge its collateral transfer obligations when it transfers collateral to the appointed custodian. Transfer to another custodian or to the Obligee is necessary within seven Local Business Days if the custodian fails to fulfil Paragraph 13 conditions and the Obligor demands this. The Obligee is liable for the custodian's acts or omissions.

(d) The use of Posted Pledging Collateral by the Obligee is permitted in the absence of close-out events.

The Obligee will transfer distributions it receives to the Obligor not later than the third Local Business Day after receipt unless this creates or causes an increase in its Exposure on the Obligor which could give rise to a collateral call. The same applies to Interest. Untransferred Interest will form part of the Posted Lending Collateral.

Paragraph 7

Three Events of Default are stated:

- **failure to post or return collateral or to pay distributions or interest when due for three Local Business Days after notice;**
- **failure to comply with provisions for use of collateral three Local Business Days after notice;**
- **failure to perform any other agreement or obligation under the Japanese CSA for 30 days after notice.**

Paragraph 8

(a) The Obligee's rights and remedies are triggered by the occurrence or designation of an Early Termination Date as a result of an Event of Default or Specified Condition in respect of the Obligor. If this happens the Obligee can exercise:

- **rights available under applicable law;**
- **rights under terms of Posted Other Support;**
- **right to set off (including conversion of securities' values into cash and taking account of currency conversions where necessary);**
- **right to liquidate Posted Pledging Collateral by public or private sale. The Obligee can purchase the Posted Pledging Collateral himself. No notice is necessary to the Obligor unless required by law;**
- **in the case of Posted Pledging Collateral, the right to attach a cash deposit pledged by the Obligor and apply the proceeds to the Obligor's obligations.**

(b) The Obligor's rights and remedies are triggered by the occurrence and continuation of an Event of Default or Specified Condition in respect of the Secured Party or the occurrence or designation of an Early Termination Date. If this occurs the Obligor can exercise:

- **rights available under applicable law;**
- **rights under terms of Posted Other Support;**
- **rights requiring the Obligee immediately to transfer all Posted Credit Support and the Interest Amount to the Obligor;**
- **right to set off or withhold payment of remaining amounts if such transfer is not made.**

(c) Obligee to transfer any surplus proceeds to Obligor from collateral liquidation post realisation. Obligor remains liable for any shortfall.

(d) When all the Obligor's liabilities are paid, Obligee will transfer back all remaining Posted Credit Support and Interest to Obligor.

Paragraph 9

Three Representations are stated viz:

- The Obligor has power and is authorised to grant a security interest on its collateral and has taken all necessary authorising action;
- it is sole owner of the collateral which is free of encumbrances;
- upon transfer the Obligee will have a valid and perfected first priority security interest in the collateral.

Paragraph 10

(a)   Each party pays its own costs for its obligations under the Japanese CSA;

(b)   the Obligor will pay all taxes and charges due on Posted Credit Support unless they arise from the Obligee's sale or re-use of the collateral;

(c)   all collateral liquidation costs to be paid on demand by the Defaulting Party or equally if there is no Defaulting Party.

Paragraph 11

(a)   Interest on failed transfers by the Obligee will be at the Default Rate (i.e. 1% over the Obligor's cost of funds);

(b)   parties agree to execute all necessary documentation to create, perfect, enforce or release a security interest;

(c)   The Obligor will notify the Obligee and defend any third party suit against the Posted Credit Support except where that suit arises from the Obligee's sale or use of the collateral;

(d)   each party will perform its obligations in good faith;

(e)   demands and notices to be made as per Paragraph 13;

(f)   Paragraph 13 matters can be repeated in Confirmations or other documents;

(g)   the Japanese CSA is governed by Japanese law and is subject to the jurisdiction of the Japanese courts.

Paragraph 12

Definitions.

Paragraph 13

Elections and Variables.

In this connection Paragraph 13(m) includes an additional Event of Default in respect of other financial crisis.

There is no signing block at the end of the Japanese CSA because this is normal Japanese practice. However, there is nothing to stop parties adding an additional signature page to the document for this. This is frequently done.

Given the very specific nature of Japanese security interest creation requirements, it is vital that parties consult their legal advisers when contemplating taking a security interest over Japanese collateral and not rely upon the brief summary above.

The 2001 ISDA Margin Provisions

8

Introduction

Similarities and differences with the other ISDA
Credit Support Documents

Structure of the 2001 ISDA Margin Provisions

Section by section commentary on the 2001 ISDA
Margin Provisions and Supplement

INTRODUCTION

After some two years of discussions, the *2001 ISDA Margin Provisions* (the "Margin Provisions") were published in May 2001. Historically they arose to address concerns from the Asian and Russian financial crises of 1997 and 1998 which led major market players to propose the following changes to the existing ISDA Credit Support Document regime:

- tighter timing for completing margin calls, returns and substitutions;
- tighter timing and procedural mechanics for resolving disputes;
- simpler, brief documentation in plainer English which would make collateral trades cheaper to document and lower market entry barriers for new counterparties;
- possibility to use Margin Provisions to collateralise exposure under non-ISDA agreements too (see p. 324).

SIMILARITIES AND DIFFERENCES WITH THE OTHER ISDA CREDIT SUPPORT DOCUMENTS

While quite radical, in some ways there are great similarities between the Margin Provisions and the existing ISDA Credit Support Documents, viz:

- each document is designed to secure or support the net risk exposure a collateral taker (Taker) has on a collateral giver (Provider);
- each document is bilateral in nature so that either party could potentially be a Taker or a Provider as exposure changes due to market price or rate movements;
- each document provides for periodic mark to market valuation of net exposure and collateral (margin);
- each document is designed primarily for use with cash or securities margin.

However, there are differences too, viz:

- the Margin Provisions provide in one document key operational provisions with a choice of different governing law approaches for taking margin (see p. 324);
- tighter operational timescales for margin calls, substitutions and dispute resolutions;
- a clearer concept of initial margin in the term Lock-Up Margin;
- different terminology for similar concepts in the ISDA Credit Support Documents.

If one has a good grounding in the other ISDA Credit Support Documents there is no real need to be nervous of the Margin Provisions. Indeed, ISDA states on page 8 of its *User's Guide to the 2001 ISDA Margin Provisions* that existing collateral arrangements under one of the current ISDA Credit Support Documents are not affected by the publication of the Margin Provisions. However, market players can amend and restate their current ISDA Credit Support Document as a Supplement by incorporating the Margin Provisions through the Form of Amendment in Appendix A to the Margin Provisions. I know of no one who has yet done so.

Indeed, so far there has been very little, if any, usage of the Margin Provisions for documenting collateralised transactions for four main reasons, viz:

- market players lacking the high class systems needed to cope with the tight operational timescales for margining, substitutions and dispute resolutions;

- lack of a full set of ISDA legal opinions on the effectiveness of the Margin Provisions in various jurisdictions (so far ten have been published);

- potential risk that moving from a collateral arrangement under an ISDA Credit Support Document to a new arrangement under the Margin Provisions could in some jurisdictions trigger bankruptcy law preference or suspect period rules;

- lack of training in the Margin Provisions for collateral management or documentation personnel.

Despite this, the Margin Provisions are seen by ISDA as the collateral document of the future, especially with their versatile cross margining possibilities with other agreements.

The Margin Provisions take the form of a five-part definitional booklet structured as shown in Figure 8.1.

FIG. 8.1

Structure of Margin Provisions

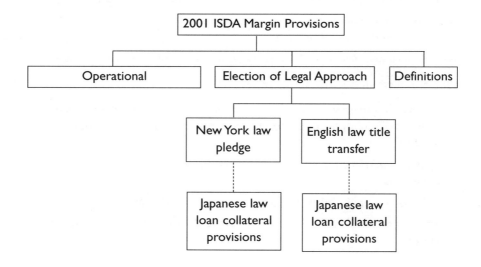

STRUCTURE OF THE 2001 ISDA MARGIN PROVISIONS

Part 1: Operational Provisions

This Part contains the non-legal, operational provisions that are essentially common whether an outright title transfer or security interest approach to taking margin is adopted. These include transfer timing, dispute resolution and substitutions.

Part 2: Security Interest Approach (New York law)

Necessary provisions for creating a security interest in margin under New York law.

Part 3: Title Transfer Approach (English law)

Necessary provisions for a title transfer approach to taking margin under English law.

Part 4: Local Law Annex

Provisions added to address local legal requirements relevant to the chosen method of taking margin. Section 4.1 allows the parties to use the Provisions when taking certain Japanese Margin but this assumes that either Part 2 or Part 3 has been selected to govern the overall margin arrangement. In due course, other jurisdictions could be added to this Part to cover the specific ways margin is taken in them.

Part 5: Definitions (51 of them)

2001 ISDA Margin Supplement

The core definitional booklet document is supplemented by a Margin Supplement (the "Supplement") which allows the parties to make various choices and amendments to the Margin Provisions and in this way is similar to the Elections and Variables Paragraphs of the ISDA Credit Support Documents. The Supplement essentially gives effect to a margin arrangement under the Margin Provisions. It forms part of and is governed by the Agreement and, because it incorporates the Margin Provisions, it is relatively short. Of course, this structure is similar to a Confirmation incorporating the terms of one of ISDA's Definitions booklets.

The Margin Provisions and the Supplement are reproduced as Annex 9 with the kind permission of the International Swaps and Derivatives Association, Inc.

There are also six Appendices suggesting the format of various notices which can be given under the Margin Provisions. Finally, there is an Annex dealing with various additional definitions applying to margin subject to Article 8 of the New York Uniform Commercial Code.

So to recap, the Margin Provisions contain the governing text and the Supplement is exchanged between the parties. It becomes part of the ISDA Master Agreement and incorporates the Margin Provisions. It also states the elections and variables chosen from the Margin Provisions in the Supplement. It is important that new users receive not only the Supplement but a copy of the Margin Provisions too when considering the documentation.

The Supplement has its own signature block not because it is mandatory but because some ISDA members wanted it.

The Margin Provisions are versatile. They can also be used with non-ISDA agreements subject to appropriate drafting to collateralise the aggregate net exposure of a party under more than one ISDA Master Agreement. In addition, different Parts of the Margin Provisions can be applied to different types of margin.

The *User's Guide to the 2001 ISDA Margin Provisions* (page 13) confirms that it is possible to have different governing laws for an ISDA Master Agreement and its related margin arrangements. It quotes three examples:

● **a choice of the New York law security approach under Part 2 of the Margin Provisions in conjunction with an ISDA Master Agreement governed by English law or vice versa;**

● **a different legal approach and governing law for each party as Margin Provider. For instance a New York bank might want to provide margin under the New York law security interest of Part 2 of the Margin Provisions while its counterparty, an English bank, might want to provide margin using the English law title transfer approach under Part 3 of the Margin Provisions. This arrangement is possible with appropriate drafting probably in Part 1 of the Supplement;**

● **different governing laws for different types of margin assets, e.g. New York law for US Treasuries and English law for European government securities provided legal advice in the jurisdiction where the assets are located is positive. Again this should be possible with the additional wording suggested in footnotes 1 and 2 to the Supplement in Appendix A of the Margin Provisions.**

The Margin Provisions cannot be used with the English Law Deed or Pledging Collateral under the Japanese CSA.

Please note that in the Margin Provisions, the term "Margin" is used throughout rather than "collateral" or "credit support".

The Margin Provisions are available for use, but because of their challenging deadlines, market players need to be very sure of the quality of their systems before moving over to them. Clearly at this stage this is not the case.

As a preliminary to examining the Margin Provisions it may be useful to become more comfortable with some of the terms by comparing them to their counterparts in the other ISDA Credit Support Documents. By and large, the terms used in the Margin Provisions are simpler to define than in the latter.

Comparison of Terms

FIG. 8.2

Margin Provisions	English Law CSA	New York Law CSA
Additional Margin Amount	Independent Amount	Independent Amount
Base Currency	Base Currency	N/A
Call Recipient	N/A	N/A
Calling Party	N/A	N/A
Eligible Margin	Eligible Credit Support	Eligible Credit Support
Equivalent Margin	Equivalent Credit Support	Posted Credit Support
Lock-Up Margin	N/A	N/A
Margin Business Day	Local Business Day	Local Business Day
Margin Received	Credit Support Balance	Posted Credit Support
Margin Required	Credit Support Amount	Credit Support Amount
Margin Supplement	Credit Support Annex	Credit Support Annex
Provider	Transferor	Pledgor
Taker	Transferee	Secured Party

If you wish to compare the key elements of the Margin Provisions with those in the New York Law CSA and the English Law CSA, ISDA usefully outlines them in Appendices G and H of its *User's Guide to the 2001 ISDA Margin Provisions*.

Part 1: Operational Provisions

Part 1 of the Margin Provisions sets out:

- the basic exposure and margin valuation mechanics;
- transfer timing;
- margin-related Events of Default;
- dispute resolution procedures;
- margin substitutions;
- income and distribution rights;
- cash margin interest;
- expenses;
- default interest;
- demands;
- notices.

First of all, it is worth saying something about the Taker of margin under the Margin Provisions. The Taker is basically the party with a net risk exposure on the other party (the Provider) which he wants covered by margin.

Under the Margin Provisions the functions of the Taker are:

- to demand Eligible Margin;
- to hold Margin Received;
- to demand Lock-Up Margin;
- to return surplus margin;
- to receive and respond to Substitution Notices.

Either party can be a Taker or Provider under the Margin Provisions at any time. It is also possible for neither party to be the Taker if:

- no Lock-Up Margin is needed under the Supplement;
- neither party is holding Margin Received;
- neither party is entitled to call for Eligible Margin because its net exposure does not exceed the Provider's Threshold or Minimum Transfer Amount.

Operational Provisions

Section 1.1 Margin Transfer Obligations.

(a) *Delivery Amount.* Upon a demand made by the Taker on or promptly following a Valuation Date, if the Delivery Amount for that Valuation Date equals or exceeds the Provider's Minimum Transfer Amount, then the Provider will Transfer to the Taker Eligible Margin having a Value as of the date that the Transfer is Initiated at least equal to the applicable Delivery Amount (rounded as specified in the Supplement). The Delivery Amount (adjusted as referred to in the definition of such term) applicable to the Provider for any Valuation Date will equal the amount by which:

  (i) the Margin Required exceeds

  (ii) the Value as of that Valuation Date of all Margin Received held by the Taker.

(b) *Return Amount.* Upon a demand made by the Provider on or promptly following a Valuation Date, if the Return Amount for that Valuation Date equals or exceeds the Taker's Minimum Transfer Amount, then the Taker will Transfer to the Provider Equivalent Margin having a Value as of the date that the Transfer is Initiated as close as practicable to the applicable Return Amount (rounded as specified in the Supplement). The Return Amount (adjusted as referred to in the definition of such term) applicable to the Taker for any Valuation Date will equal the amount by which:

  (i) the Value as of that Valuation Date of all Margin Received held by the Taker exceeds

  (ii) the Margin Required.

In no circumstances shall the Taker be required to Transfer Equivalent Margin with a Value in excess of the Return Amount. The Provider may specify in a demand the Equivalent Margin to be Transferred by the Taker to the extent the Value of such Equivalent Margin is equal to or less than the Return Amount.

SECTION BY SECTION COMMENTARY ON THE 2001 ISDA MARGIN PROVISIONS AND SUPPLEMENT

Section 1.1 (a) and (b)

This important section sets out the Provider's delivery obligations and the Taker's return obligations.

While the terminology may differ, the process is much the same as in the other ISDA Credit Support Documents.

If the Margin Required is greater than the Value of the Margin Received, the Taker can call for more Margin if this exceeds the Provider's Minimum Transfer Amount.

If the Value of the Margin Received is greater than the Margin Required, the Taker returns the surplus Margin to the Provider if it exceeds his Minimum Transfer Amount. The Provider has to demand this Return Amount.

This top-up or variation margin aims to cover current exposure.

(c) ***Lock-up Margin.***

  (i)   If Lock-up Margin is specified with respect to a party as Provider, it will not be taken into account in, is separate from, and is in addition to, any calculation of Margin Required with respect to the Provider, but will be Transferred by the Provider to the Taker on the date of the Supplement, or on such date as the parties may agree as specified in the Supplement or otherwise.

  (ii) A Provider may demand the return of Lock-up Margin (if Part 2 applies) or Cash, securities or other property of the same type, nominal value, description and amount as such Lock-up Margin (if Part 3 applies) from Taker in any circumstances specified in the Supplement. Once the specified circumstances are no longer continuing, the Taker may demand delivery of new Lock-up Margin.

  (iii) Notice of a demand will be given by the Taker, and Lock-up Margin will be Transferred by the Provider, as if it were a demand for Transfer of a Delivery Amount. Notice of a demand will be given by the Provider, and Lock-up Margin (if Part 2 applies) or Cash, securities or other property of the same type, nominal value, description and amount as such Lock-up Margin (if Part 3 applies) will be Transferred by the Taker, as if it were a demand for Transfer of a Return Amount.

(d) ***No Offset.*** Except as otherwise provided in these Provisions or in the Supplement, if either party is required to make a Transfer of Lock-up Margin, then that Transfer will be made free of any set-off (as defined in Section 14 of the ISDA Master Agreement), lien or withholding whatsoever, including in respect of any Delivery Amount or Return Amount to be Transferred on the same date or Margin Received held by either party.

(c) Lock-up Margin

In contrast, initial margin or Lock-up Margin is intended to cover possible future exposure between Valuation Dates and the next delivery of variation margin. Lock-up Margin may be provided by one or both parties. In the latter case, a party might be a Taker in respect of one pool of margin assets and a Provider in relation to another.

Lock-up Margin is effectively initial margin although the Margin Provisions give no guidance on how it should be calculated. The Supplement (Paragraph 5) suggests a fixed monetary sum in the Base Currency but it could also be calculated as a percentage of the Notional Amount of a Transaction or some other formula. It could also be linked to formal credit ratings.

Section 1.1(c)(i) makes it clear that Lock-up Margin is totally outside any calculations for Margin Required. Even if the Taker has no current risk Exposure on the Provider at a particular time, the Taker may still demand delivery of Lock-up Margin.

Section 1.1(c)(ii) of the Margin Provisions allows the Provider of Lock-up Margin to demand its return in accordance with defined circumstances in the Supplement. This may arise if the Taker has no risk exposure on the Provider and none is likely to arise in the future. Then the Lock-up Margin itself (if Part 2 of the Margin Provisions applies) or equivalent fungible assets (if Part 3 applies) will be returned by the Taker. If, however, a new Transaction occurs then the Provider must return the Lock-up Margin.

Section 1.1(c)(iii) states that demands for delivery or return of Lock-up Margin will be made by notices between the parties.

Section 1.1(d) makes clear that such transfers are to be made clear of any set off, liens or withholding unless otherwise agreed. This includes any set off against any Delivery Amounts or Return Amounts being made contemporaneously.

Even though a Taker may have no risk exposure on a Provider it will want to keep the Lock-up Margin as long as there is a chance of potential future exposure. The Supplement will, therefore, only usually allow return of Lock-up Margin where there is no current or potential exposure for the Taker on the Provider.

Returns of Lock-up Margin are possible where they are linked to formal credit ratings and the Provider's debt obligations are upgraded. The Lock-up Margin would be transferred again if the Provider's rating was subsequently downgraded. The same could happen if the Taker agreed to a Threshold on its Exposure.

Please note that neither Minimum Transfer Amount nor Rounding applies to Lock-up Margin.

Section 1.2 Conditions Precedent. Each Transfer obligation of the Provider and of the Taker under Part 1 of these Provisions is subject to the conditions precedent that:

(a) no Event of Default (or event which, with the giving of Notice or the lapse of time or both, would constitute an Event of Default) or Specified Condition has occurred and is continuing with respect to the other party; and

(b) no date on which all outstanding Transactions under the Agreement have been or will be accelerated, terminated, liquidated or cancelled and for which any unsatisfied payment obligations exist has occurred or been designated as the result of an Event of Default or Specified Condition with respect to the other party.

Section 1.2. Conditions Precedent

Here the Margin Provisions lay out conditions precedent for the performance of both parties' obligations under them. These are similar to the conditions precedent in Section 2(a)(iii) of the ISDA Master Agreement.

If an actual or potential Event of Default has occurred to a party or it has had its obligations under the Agreement accelerated through the designation of an Early Termination Date (close-out date) then the other party does not have to deliver Margin to it.

Another pre-condition is that no Specified Condition (typically a Termination Event specified in the Supplement) has impacted the other party.

Section 1.3 Transfer Timing.

(a) Each reference in this Section 1.3 to a time or to a Margin Business Day is a reference to that time or Margin Business Day in the location of the Call Recipient.

(b) If a Call Recipient receives a demand for the Transfer of Eligible Margin or Equivalent Margin by the Notification Time on a Margin Business Day, then by 5:00 p.m. on that Margin Business Day, the Call Recipient must Initiate the Transfer and provide Notice (such Notice may be in the form of Appendix B) to the Calling Party of:

   (i)   the type of Eligible Margin or Equivalent Margin that it will deliver; and

   (ii) the Settlement Date for such Eligible Margin or Equivalent Margin.

(c) If a Call Recipient receives a demand for the Transfer of Eligible Margin or Equivalent Margin after the Notification Time, the demand will be deemed to have been received at the Notification Time on the next Margin Business Day, unless a subsequent demand is received prior to such Notification Time, in which case such subsequent demand will govern.

(d) Any Transfer contemplated by this Section 1.3 must be completed by 5:00 p.m. in the location of the account of the Calling Party on the Settlement Date.

(e) If a Transfer of Eligible Margin or Equivalent Margin is not completed in accordance with Section 1.3(d), or the Notice required by Section 1.3(b) is not provided by 5:00 p.m. in the location of the Call Recipient, then:

   (i)   Without prejudice to the rights of the Calling Party under sub-Section 1.3(e)(ii) below, the Calling Party may elect to notify the Call Recipient of its failure to Transfer Eligible Margin or Equivalent Margin or its failure to give such Notice (such Notice of failure may be in the form of Appendix C) and request that the Call Recipient remedy such failure by such time and on such day as the Calling Party shall specify in such Notice of failure.

   (ii) The Calling Party may give the Notice provided for under Section 1.4(b)(i), in the event of a failure to Transfer Eligible Margin or Equivalent Margin, or give the Notice provided for under Section 1.4(b)(ii), in the event of a failure to give the Notice required by Section 1.3(b).

Section 1.3. Transfer Timing

High operational standards are set for the transfer of collateral by shortening the call cycle. The basic rule is that if a call is received by 10:00 a.m. (the "Notification Time") the Transfer must be initiated by 5:00 p.m. that same day and the Call Recipient has to notify the Calling Party at that time of the type of Eligible Margin it will deliver and when. Failure to provide the notice or the collateral one Margin Business Day after a failure notice sent by the other party will result in an Event of Default. Compare this to the current situation under the New York Law CSA where transfer must take place not later than the close of business on the Local Business Day after the day on which the call is made. While this new rule has a tighter timeframe, it is more closely tied to the settlement cycles of the main types of collateral (particularly cash).

References to a time or a Margin Business Day are to those in the place where the Call Recipient is located.

Initiation of a transfer means taking all necessary steps to ensure the transfer takes place by the Settlement Date.

The Call Recipient must send a notice to the Calling Party when it has initiated the transfer. This notice will describe the type of margin which it will deliver and the Settlement Date. This notice will trigger an investigation by the Calling Party if the margin is not delivered. The Settlement Date will vary according to whether cash or securities are being transferred and with securities it will be in line with market practice for their delivery.

In any case the transfer must be completed by 5:00 p.m. on the Settlement Date in the location of the Calling Party. If this does not happen the Calling Party can give one of the following notices:

(1) **it may notify the Call Recipient and ask for the failure to be remedied by a certain date and time; or**

(2) **it may give a notice declaring an Event of Default.**

If the Calling Party gives the notice in (1) and the margin is still not delivered it can still subsequently give the notice in (2).

If the Call Recipient fails to give the notice that it has initiated transfer of the margin, the Calling Party also has the right to give either of the notices in (1) or (2) above.

There are certain practical points here. First, unrealistic timescales for margin delivery should not be set where the parties or the margin are located in countries with significantly different time zones. Second, any transfer timing amendments made to the Supplement to accommodate this, e.g. altering the Notification Time, could entail changes to other provisions, e.g. dispute resolution procedures.

It should be borne in mind that daily calling for margin could result in two calls being received by the Call Recipient – one after the Notification Time on the first Margin Business Day and the second before the Notification Time on the next Margin Business Day. In these circumstances the second call supersedes the first.

Section 1.4 Additional Events of Default.

(a) Each reference in this Section 1.4 to a Margin Business Day is a reference to that Margin Business Day in the location of the recipient of the related Notice.

(b) In addition to the Events of Default specified in an Agreement, an Event of Default will exist with respect to a party if:

   (i)   that party fails (or fails to cause its Custodian) to make, when due, a Transfer of:

      (A) Lock-up Margin or Cash, securities or other property of the same type, nominal value, description and amount as any Lock-up Margin; or

      (B) Eligible Margin or Equivalent Margin; or

      (C) Equivalent Distributions or any Interest Amount;

   and such failure is not remedied on or before the first Margin Business Day after Notice to that party of such failure;

   (ii) that party fails to provide the Notice required by Section 1.3(b) below and such failure is not remedied on or before the first Margin Business Day after Notice to that party of such failure; or

   (iii) that party fails (or fails to cause its Custodian) to comply with or perform any agreement or obligation under these Provisions or a Supplement (other than any obligations referenced in sub-Section 1.4(b)(i) and sub-Section 1.4(b)(ii) above and Section 2.3 below) to be complied with or performed by the party in accordance with these Provisions if such failure is not remedied on or before the thirtieth day after Notice to that party of such failure.

(c) The failure by a party to make a Transfer of any amount which is the subject of a dispute will not be considered a failure to make, when due, a Transfer for purposes of sub-Section 1.4(b)(i) above for so long as such party is performing its obligations in accordance with the dispute resolution procedures set out in Section 1.6 below.

(d) Any Notice given pursuant to Section 1.4(b) may be in the form of Appendix D.

Section 1.4. Additional Events of Default

For this Section, reference to a Margin Business Day is to one in the place where the recipient of a notice is located.

In addition to the Events of Default stated in an Agreement incorporating the Margin Provisions, Section 1.4 specifies the following or further Events of Default, viz:

(1) **failure by a party (or its Custodian) to pay, deliver or perform its obligations under the Margin Provisions. This will include not transferring Lock-up Margin or fungible assets for previously lodged Lock-up Margin, Eligible Margin or Equivalent Margin or payments of interest on cash margin and distributions on margin securities;**

(2) **failure by the Call Recipient to give a notice that it has initiated the transfer of margin following a call.**

These failures only have a short grace period of one Margin Business Day to remedy.

In Section 1.4(b)(iii), there is also a 30-day cure period following notice for a breach of any other obligations under the Margin Provisions.

Section 1.4(c) provides a carve-out from an Event of Default being declared where the failure to pay or deliver stems from a dispute and the Section 1.6 dispute resolution procedures are being followed.

Section 1.5. Calculations as of Valuation Time. All calculations of Value and Exposure for purposes of Section 1.1 and Section 1.6 will be based on information obtained as of the Valuation Time.

Section 1.5. Calculations as of Valuation Time

This is meant to ensure that all Transaction exposure and margin valuations for the purposes of calling or returning margin in the normal course or in a dispute are undertaken as of the Valuation Time based on information obtained then.

Section 1.6 Procedures for Dispute Resolution.

(a) *General.*

    (i) Each party agrees to attempt to resolve any dispute as quickly as possible following Notice of the dispute being given or received.

    (ii) If either party fails to comply with any of the requirements for delivery of Notices stated below in this Section 1.6, the failure will not be deemed an Event of Default. However, the party that fails to comply with such requirements for delivery of Notices will, for the purpose of determining the Delivery Amount, the Return Amount or any Value, no longer be able to dispute the information contained in the Notice most recently provided by the other party. Any Delivery Amount, Return Amount or Value will be calculated based on such information and any information previously agreed or notified by the parties.

(b) *Dispute of Delivery Amount or Return Amount.*

    (i) Each reference in this sub-Section 1.6(b) to a time or to a Margin Business Day is a reference to that time or Margin Business Day in the location of the Call Recipient.

    (ii) If a Call Recipient disputes a demand to Transfer a Delivery Amount or a Return Amount, it must, as Disputing Party, on the same Margin Business Day the demand is received or deemed received, as relevant:

        (A) transmit a Notice of dispute (such Notice of dispute may be in the form of Appendix E) for receipt by the Calling Party by 1:00 p.m. that day;

        (B) Initiate Transfer to the Calling Party by 5:00 p.m. in accordance with Section 1.3(b) of Eligible Margin having a Value as of the date Transfer is Initiated equal to the Undisputed Amount, if the Undisputed Amount equals or exceeds the Disputing Party's Minimum Transfer Amount; and

        (C) transmit Portfolio Information for receipt by the Calling Party by 5:00 p.m. that day.

    (iii) The Calling Party must review the Portfolio Information and information held by it regarding the relevant portfolio of Transactions between the parties. The Calling Party will transmit Notice to the Disputing Party by 10:00 a.m. on the next Margin Business Day (the *"Second Day"*) in the location of the Call Recipient of:

Section 1.6. Procedures for dispute resolution

A completely revamped and detailed dispute resolution procedure with operationally challenging deadlines has been set. This has the dual aims of speeding up the process and reducing opportunities for a party to use the dispute resolution procedure as a delaying tactic.

First of all, the parties undertake to try and resolve any dispute as quickly as possible following notice of one. The process varies according to whether the dispute is about the level of a margin call or the value of the margin transferred. All timings in respect of margin call disputes are in the location of the Call Recipient. Timing references for all disputes involving valuation of margin are in the location where the margin was delivered.

If the Call Recipient disputes a demand to transfer or return collateral, it must send the Calling Party a dispute notice by 1:00 p.m. on the same day and initiate transfer of any undisputed amount (provided it is above the Disputing Party's Minimum Transfer Amount) by 5:00 p.m. that day and, at the same time, send the Calling Party Portfolio Information (i.e. Transaction details) so as to resolve the dispute.

The undisputed amount could be zero where it is below the Minimum Transfer Amount, or where there is a disagreement over which party has an Exposure on the other.

The Calling Party must review the Portfolio Information and notify the Call Recipient of any discrepancies in the Transaction population by 10:00 a.m. on the next Margin Business Day. The Calling Party must also send the Call Recipient its Valuation Data so that any discrepancies in Exposure calculations can be identified. This could be difficult to achieve if the information sent by both parties is configured in different ways.

By 1:00 p.m. on that day the Disputing Party must respond to the Calling Party with any information requested and supply its own Valuation Data.

If the dispute is not resolved by 5:00 p.m. that day each party then selects one independent leading dealer to determine the Exposure relating to any disputed Transaction or the Value of any Margin Received. They have until 5:00 p.m. on the next Margin Business Day to report back.

In the normal course, parties would accept the arithmetic mean received from each independent source.

However, if two quotations are not provided or there is a material disagreement on the facts, the parties can choose to continue the negotiations, find some other remedy or close-out the disputed Transactions if they have chosen to apply Dispute Termination Event in the Supplement which will terminate all Transactions under the Agreement at mid-market on a no fault basis.

Once the dispute is resolved, the Disputing Party must transfer the agreed residual collateral (ignoring any Minimum Transfer Amount) by the Notification Time on the next Margin Business Day. Failure to do so will result in an Event of Default.

Please note that if during the process a party fails to comply with the delivery of notice requirements, this will not count as an Event of Default (at least not until notice expires following a failure notice from the other party), but it will not be able to dispute the Delivery Amount, Return Amount or Value figures in the notice most recently given by the other party.

(A) the details of any differences between the Disputing Party's Portfolio Information and information held by the Calling Party regarding the Transactions, including a description of all available evidence (which must be transmitted with such Notice, to the extent practicable), as relevant, of Transactions the Calling Party considers outstanding or a request for evidence of the execution and detailed particulars of relevant Transactions, in the case of differences as to the existence or characteristics of any Transaction; and

(B) the Calling Party's Valuation Data in the case of a difference as to calculation of the Exposure or the Value of Margin Received.

(iv) By 1:00 p.m. on the Second Day, the Disputing Party must by Notice to the Calling Party provide any evidence or information requested by the Calling Party, the Disputing Party's relevant Valuation Data and such other information as the Disputing Party considers appropriate.

(v) In the case of any dispute as to Exposure or Value of Margin Received, if the dispute has not been resolved by 5:00 p.m. on the Second Day, each party must in good faith select one independent reference source and the following procedures shall apply:

(A) Each independent reference source will be instructed to determine the Exposure associated with any disputed Transaction or the Value of any Margin Received (or determine any constituent element within the calculation of Exposure or Value that has been isolated by the parties as an element in dispute) as of the Valuation Date relating to the relevant demand.

(B) The independent reference sources will be instructed to report to both parties their determinations by 5:00 p.m. on the Margin Business Day following the Second Day (the *"Third Day"*).

(C) Each independent reference source will be instructed to use the same methods, practices and degree of care that it would use to establish any facts and make any calculations were it required to do so in its own business.

(D) Each independent reference source must be a leading dealer in the particular type of Transaction in dispute or any entity that provides valuation services with respect to such type of Transaction in the general course of its business and must be independent of each of the parties, which independence will not be deemed diminished solely because the independent reference source is active in the same market in which either of the parties is active or has entered into transactions with either of the parties.

(E) The parties agree that the arithmetic average of the determinations from each independent reference source will prevail.

(F) If by 5:00 p.m. on the Third Day:

(1) the parties are unable to obtain quotes from two independent reference sources; or

(2) the independent reference sources disagree on any material facts, the parties may choose (x) to continue the negotiations, (y) to seek such other remedy as each in its discretion determines or (z) if Dispute Termination Event is specified as applicable in the Supplement and the dispute relates to the Exposure associated with specific disputed Transactions, to terminate such disputed Transactions in accordance with the procedures, and in pursuit of such remedies, set forth in the Agreement as they relate to a Dispute Termination Event.

(vi) In the case of a dispute as to the existence or agreed characteristics of a Transaction, if the dispute has not been resolved by 5:00 p.m. on the Second Day, the parties may choose to continue the negotiations or to seek such other remedy as each in its discretion determines.

(vii) Following the resolution or deemed resolution of a dispute, the Disputing Party must Transfer Eligible Margin or Equivalent Margin to the Calling Party in satisfaction of the demand for such margin that gave rise to the dispute as if in response to a demand received by the Notification Time on the Margin Business Day following the resolution, subject to Section 1.3 above and without regard to the Minimum Transfer Amount, after taking into account any prior Transfer of any relevant Undisputed Amount and any adjustment agreed between the parties or determined by the independent reference sources in accordance with sub-Section 1.6(b)(v) above (and no further obligations will arise on the part of either party in respect of the dispute).

(c) *Dispute of Value of Transfer.*

(i)   Each reference in this sub-Section to a time or to a Margin Business Day is a reference to that time or Margin Business Day in the location of the Calling Party.

(ii) If a Calling Party (which term includes a Taker of Substitute Margin for purposes of this sub-Section 1.6(c) disputes the Value of a Transfer of Eligible Margin, Lock-up Margin (or Cash, securities or other property of the same type, nominal value, description and amount as such Lock-up Margin), Substitute Margin or Equivalent Margin it must, as Disputing Party, on the Margin Business Day following the Margin Business Day Transfer is Initiated, transmit a Notice of dispute (such Notice of dispute may be in the form of Appendix F) for receipt by the other party by 1:00 p.m. on that day.

(iii) Before 10:00 a.m. on the Margin Business Day immediately following the Margin Business Day on which the Notice of dispute was received, the Call Recipient (which term includes a Provider of Substitute Margin for purposes of this sub-Section 1.6(c) will recalculate the Value of the relevant margin, using any undisputed values set forth in the Notice of dispute, as of the date the Transfer was Initiated and in accordance with the procedures (if any) in the Supplement.

(iv) Immediately following a recalculation, the Call Recipient must notify the Disputing Party of the results of the recalculation. The Call Recipient must Initiate Transfer by 5:00 p.m. on the Margin Business Day immediately following the Margin Business Day on which the Notice of dispute was received of any additional Eligible Margin, additional Lock-up Margin (or Cash, securities or other property of the same type, nominal value, description and amount as such Lock-up Margin), additional Substitute Margin or Equivalent Margin required based on such recalculation. The Minimum Transfer Amount shall not apply to margin to be Transferred pursuant to this sub-Section 1.6(c)(iv).

(v)   If:

(A) the Call Recipient is unable, due to circumstances beyond its control, to recalculate the Value of the relevant margin; or

(B) the Disputing Party disputes the recalculated Value of the relevant margin,

Section 1(6)(c). Dispute of Value of Transfer

Where the Disputing Party disputes the value of margin transferred it must send a dispute notice to the other party to reach them by 1.00 p.m. on the Margin Business Day following the one the margin transfer was set in motion.

The Call Recipient then has until 10.00 a.m. on the next Margin Business Day to recalculate the value of the Margin Received making use of any undisputed values in the dispute notice. He then reports his results to the Disputing Party. If the Disputing Party agrees these recalculations then the Call Recipient must initiate the transfer of the additional margin by 5.00 p.m. on that same Margin Business Day.

If the Call Recipient cannot recalculate the value of the margin or the Disputing Party still disputes it then the parties have the same three choices as in the other type of dispute, viz:

- continue negotiations;
- seek another remedy;
- call a Dispute Termination Event if this has been selected in Paragraph 6 of the Supplement.

So, in both cases, the rules are more strict and the timescale more pacey than before.

the parties may choose (x) to continue the negotiations, (y) to seek such other remedy as each in its discretion determines or (z) if Dispute Termination Event is specified as applicable in the Supplement and the dispute relates to the Value associated with the Transfer of Eligible Margin, Lock-up Margin (or Cash, securities or other property of the same type, nominal value, description and amount as such Lock-up Margin), Substitute Margin or Equivalent Margin, to terminate the Agreement in accordance with the procedures, and in pursuit of such remedies, set forth in the Agreement as they relate to a Dispute Termination Event.

Section 1.7 Substitutions.

(a) *Times.* Each reference in this Section 1.7 to a time or to a Margin Business Day is a reference to that time or Margin Business Day in the location of the Taker.

(b) *Delivery of Substitution Notice.* Unless otherwise specified in the Supplement, the Provider may deliver a Substitution Notice (such Substitution Notice may be in the form of Appendix G) to the Taker.

(c) *Timing of Delivery of Substitution Notice.* If the Taker receives a Substitution Notice after 5:00 p.m. or other than on a Margin Business Day, it will be deemed to have been received by the Taker on the next Margin Business Day. References to receipt of a Substitution Notice in this Section 1.7 are references to both actual receipt and deemed receipt, as relevant.

(d) *Consent to Substitution.* Each substitution pursuant to a Substitution Notice will be subject to Paragraph 8 of the Supplement.

(e) *Substitute Margin.* The Provider will Initiate Transfer of Substitute Margin having a Value as of the date Transfer is Initiated as close as practicable to, but in any event not less than, the amount specified in the Substitution Notice by 1:00 p.m. on any Margin Business Day on or after the date the Substitution Notice is effective.

(f) *Timing of Substitutions.*

   (i) If the Taker is able to confirm, to its reasonable satisfaction, that it has received the Substitute Margin by 1:00 p.m. on a Margin Business Day, then the Taker will Initiate Transfer to the Provider of the Equivalent Margin specified in the Substitution Notice by 5:00 p.m. on the same day.

   (ii) If the Taker is able to confirm, to its reasonable satisfaction, that it has received the Substitute Margin after 1:00 p.m. on a Margin Business Day, then the Taker will Initiate Transfer to the Provider of the Equivalent Margin specified in the Substitution Notice by 5:00 p.m. on the next Margin Business Day.

(g) *Value of Equivalent Margin.* In any substitution pursuant to this Section 1.7, the Taker must Transfer Equivalent Margin with a Value as close as practicable to, but in any event not greater than, the Value of the Substitute Margin as of the date Transfer of the Equivalent Margin is Initiated.

Section 1.7. Substitutions

Timescales for substitutions have also been tightened up under the Margin Provisions. All timing references are in those of the margin Taker.

The first point to consider is whether the Taker's consent is needed for the substitution and a choice is made in Paragraph 8 of the Supplement on this point. There is a possible recharacterisation risk if consent is not selected and the Provider is an English incorporated company and the Part 2 New York law security interest approach is chosen in the Supplement. Page 31 of the *User's Guide to the 2001 ISDA Margin Provisions* elaborates on this. However, this is not a problem if the Part 3 English title transfer approach is chosen as there is then no question of a security interest being created.

This done, the Provider needs to send a Substitution Notice (possibly in the form of Appendix G of the Margin Provisions) to the Taker by 5.00 p.m on the day it initiates the transfer of the Substitute Margin. If the Provider does not make this deadline, the Taker is deemed to receive the notice on the following Margin Business Day.

The Provider, however, must take all necessary steps to make the transfer by 1.00 p.m. on the day it issues the Substitution Notice and/or it is effective. If the Provider wants to effect the transfer on the same Margin Business Day on which the Substitution Notice becomes effective, it needs the Taker's consent by 1.00 p.m. on that day.

Let us assume that the transfer is made as planned. If the Taker can confirm that he has received the Substitute Margin by 1.00 p.m. on a Margin Business Day he must take all the necessary steps to initiate the transfer back to the Provider of Equivalent Margin by 5.00 p.m. on that same Margin Business Day. If, however, he cannot confirm his position by 1.00 p.m. he has until 5.00 p.m. on the next Margin Business Day to return the Equivalent Margin to the Provider. Its value on the day of the transfer is initiated must be no greater than the value of the Substitute Margin.

The *User's Guide to the 2001 ISDA Margin Provisions* (page 32) gives an interesting example of the fast track margin substitution taking place on the same Margin Business Day.

Section 1.8 Distributions and Interest Amounts.

(a) *Times.* Each reference in this Section 1.8 to a time or to a Margin Business Day is a reference to that time or Margin Business Day in the location of the Taker.

(b) *Distributions.* If, with respect to any Margin Received (and without regard to any use or disposition of Margin Received by the Taker), the Taker is deemed to receive Distributions on a Distributions Date, it will Transfer Equivalent Distributions to the Provider. The Transfer must be Initiated by 5:00 p.m. on the Margin Business Day immediately following the Distributions Date. The Taker is required to Transfer Equivalent Distributions only to the extent that a Delivery Amount would not be created or increased by that Transfer, as calculated by the Taker (and the date of calculation will be deemed to be a Valuation Date for this purpose).

(c) *Interest Amount.*

   (i) In lieu of any interest or other amounts paid or deemed to have been paid with respect to Margin Received in the form of Cash (all of which may be retained by the Taker), the Taker will Transfer the Interest Amount to the Provider. The Transfer of an Interest Amount will be Initiated no later than two Margin Business Days after the end of the relevant Interest Period. The Interest Amount will be determined by the Taker based on the principal amount of Margin Received in the form of Cash held by the Taker on each day in an Interest Period. The Interest Amount will be computed for each Interest Period on a simple basis, unless otherwise provided for in the Supplement. The Taker is required to Transfer the Interest Amount only to the extent that a Delivery Amount would not be created or increased by that Transfer, as calculated by the Taker (and the date of calculation will be deemed to be a Valuation Date for this purpose).

   (ii) If Eligible Margin in the form of Cash is received after 5:00 p.m. in the location of the Taker, the Taker will have no obligation to pay interest for that day and interest will begin to accrue on the following Margin Business Day, unless that Taker is, in the ordinary course of business, able to invest the Cash so received on an overnight basis.

Section 1.8. Distributions and Interest Amount

First of all, all timings are in the Taker's location. Section 1.8 first concerns itself with income payments or distributions made by issuers of securities used as margin. This income will be passed through by the Taker to the Provider and will include any income paid on Lock-up Margin too. The Taker has until 5.00 p.m. on the Margin Business Day following the date upon which general holders of the securities are entitled to receive income or distributions on them. The Taker does not transfer the actual income remittance received but makes its own cheque or electronic transfer to the Provider. This is technically termed an Equivalent Distribution under the Margin Provisions. However, if the transfer of such Equivalent Distribution will cause or increase a margin call it is not made and the income is added to the balance of Margin Received held by the Taker.

The Taker has to pay up anyway, even if he has sold the securities on to a third party.

Section 1.8(c) concerns interest on cash margin. The Interest Period and Rate and whether it is to be calculated on a simple or compounded basis are all selected in Paragraph 9 of the Supplement. The underlying assumption in the Supplement is that the Interest Amount will be calculated on a simple basis.

Interest accrues on each day of an Interest Period which extends from and including the date when an Interest Amount was last paid to the Provider to the day before the current period end date. If no previous Interest Amount has been paid, the Interest Period would be the date on which the cash collateral was first received by the Taker.

The Supplement posits two possibilities for Interest Period end dates, viz:

- **the first calendar day of each month; and**
- **any Margin Business Day on which a Cash Return Amount is paid to the Provider.**

Either or both of these could apply or some other date. This will usually depend on the capabilities of each party's systems. Interest Amounts for cash margin in different currencies are calculated using the relevant day count fractions.

An Interest Amount must be transferred no later than two Margin Business Days after the end of the relevant Interest Period unless it causes or increases a margin call whereupon it is added to the balance of Margin Received held by the Taker.

If a transfer of cash margin is received by the Taker after 5.00 p.m. in its location it will not have to pay interest on the cash margin for that day and interest will only start to accrue on the following Margin Business Day unless the Taker is ordinarily in the position of being able to invest such late receipts overnight in the money market.

Section 1.9 Additional Definitions With Respect to Margin Subject to Article 8 of the New York Uniform Commercial Code. In the event that Margin Received or Equivalent Margin is of a type and subject to circumstances to which Article 8 of the New York Uniform Commercial Code would apply, Article 8 of the New York Uniform Commercial Code will apply and the definitions set forth in Annex A to these Provisions will be deemed to be incorporated into these Provisions.

Section 1.9. Additional Definitions With Respect to

Article 8 of the New York Uniform Commercial Code

This deals specifically with US dollar securities collateral subject to Article 8 of the NYUCC. This applies to securities held by the Taker as margin in an account in the State of New York irrespective of which governing law or legal approach is chosen in the Supplement. It is possible to exclude this in the Supplement, but if this is not done and it is included then the definitions in Annex A of the Margin Provisions are deemed incorporated in them.

Section 1.10 Miscellaneous.

(a) *Expenses*. Each party will be liable for and pay its own costs and expenses (including, without limitation, any stamp, transfer or similar transaction tax or duty payable on any Transfer that it is required to make) in connection with performing its obligations in relation to any margin arrangements under these Provisions.

(b) *Default Interest*. A Taker that fails to make, when due, any Transfer of Equivalent Margin, Substitute Margin, Equivalent Distributions or an Interest Amount will be obligated to compensate the Provider. The Taker must pay the Provider (to the extent permitted under applicable law) interest on the Value of the Cash or items of property that were required to be Transferred, from (and including) the date that the Equivalent Margin, Substitute Margin, Equivalent Distributions or Interest Amount was required to be Transferred to (but excluding) the date of Transfer of that Equivalent Margin, Equivalent Distributions or Interest Amount, at a rate per annum equal to the Default Rate. The Value of these items will be calculated as of the relevant Valuation Date and as if all items are Eligible Margin. Such interest will be calculated on the basis of daily compounding and the actual number of days elapsed.

(c) *Demands*. All demands referenced in these Provisions may be made or given substantially in the form, if any, attached hereto, and will be effective if delivered in a manner and at the time set forth in the Notices Section, except as otherwise provided in these Provisions or in the Supplement. References in these Provisions to receipt of a demand are references to both actual receipt and deemed receipt, as relevant.

(d) *Notices*. All Notices referenced in these Provisions may be made or given substantially in the form, if any, attached hereto, and will be effective if delivered in a manner and at the time set forth in the Notices Section, except as otherwise provided in these Provisions or in the Supplement. The place for delivery of any Notice is the place specified as the Calling Party's or Call Recipient's address or contact details for Notices in the Supplement (or if no such details are provided in the Supplement, such details as are provided in the Agreement) or such other address or contact details as has been notified to the other party at least five Margin Business Days (by reference to the location of the party to which the Notice is sent) prior to the relevant demand being made.

Section 1.10. Miscellaneous

These concluding provisions in Section 1 are boilerplate in nature. They are:

(a) *Expenses*

Each party will pay its own costs in relation to margin arrangements under the Margin Provisions.

(b) *Default Interest*

If the Taker fails to make any of the various payments it is obliged to make to the Provider, then Default Interest at the Default Rate (i.e. 1% over the Provider's cost of funds) will be payable by the Taker on a daily compounded basis from and including the date the payment was originally due to be made to and including the day before it is actually made.

(c) *Demands*

All demands can be made in the form of the various Notices shown in Appendices B–G of the Margin Provisions and, as regards the ISDA Master Agreement will be effective if delivered in the ways described in its Section 12, unless otherwise specified in the Margin Provisions or agreed by the parties in the Supplement.

(d) Notices

This is basically repeated in the first sentence of this provision. The delivery address for any notice will be that given for the parties in the Supplement, failing which that in Part 4(a) of the ISDA Master Agreement Schedule. If these are out of date it shall be at the address notified by the addressee in its place of business at least five Margin Business Days before the relevant demand is made.

(e) **_Specifications of Certain Matters._** Anything referred to in these Provisions as being specified in the Supplement also may be specified in one or more Confirmations or other documents, and these Provisions will be construed accordingly.

(f) **_Good Faith and Commercially Reasonable Manner._** Performance of all obligations under these Provisions, including, but not limited to, all calculations, valuations and determinations made by either party, will be made or conducted in good faith and in a commercially reasonable manner.

(e) Specifications of certain matters

Any matters which the Margin Provisions state should be specified in the Supplement could alternatively be referred to in a Confirmation or in any other document agreed by the parties. Where this is done, it should be made clear that the election or amendment will survive the termination of the Transaction under the Confirmation. In my opinion, it is better to make such choices in the master documentation rather than under a Confirmation.

(f) Good faith and commercially reasonable manner

Each party must behave in this manner in respect of all its obligations under the Margin Provisions.

Figure 8.3 tabulates the operative locations for the various timing references alluded to in this Part 1.

Timing references in the Margin Provisions

FIG. 8.3

Section No.	Item	Operative Place
1.3	Transfer Timing	Margin Business Day in the location of the Call Recipient.
1.4	Additional Events of Default	Margin Business Day in the Notice recipient's location.
1.6	Disputes	Margin Business Day in the location of the Call Recipient except for margin valuation when it is the location of the Calling Party.
1.7	Substitutions	Margin Business Day in the Taker's location.
1.8	Distributions and Interest Amounts	Margin Business Day in the Taker's location.
1.10	Notices	Margin Business Day in the Recipient's location.

Part 2: Security interest approach (New York law)

The next two parts of the Margin Provisions give the parties the choice between the New York security interest approach or the English law title transfer approach to govern their collateral arrangement. These approaches should be clear to you from reading Chapters 3, 5 and 6.

The New York security interest approach is set out in Part 2 of the Margin Provisions. This is substantially the same as the approach adopted in the New York CSA.

Figure 8.4 illustrates where the provisions may be found in each document. An explanation of the various Sections of Part 2 is set out overleaf.

FIG. 8.4

Location of provisions in the New York Law CSA and the Margin Provisions

Nature of Item	Paragraph in New York Law CSA	Section reference in the Margin Provisions
Security Interest and Set Off	2	2.1
Credit Support Obligations	3	1.1
Conditions Precedent	4(a)	1.2
Transfer Timing	4(b)	1.3
Calculations	4(c)	1.5
Substitutions	4(d)	1.7
Dispute Resolution	5	1.6
Holding and using Posted Collateral	6(a)–(c)	2.2
Distributions and Interest Amount	6(d)–(e)	1.8
Event of Default re margin transfer	7(i)	1.4(b)(i)
Event of Default re use of margin	7(ii)	2.3
Other Event of Default	7(iii)	1.4(b)(iii)
Taker's rights and remedies	8(a)	2.4(a)
Market Risk	8(a)(iv)	2.4(b)
Provider's rights and remedies	8(b)	2.4(c)
Deficiencies and Excess Proceeds	8(c)	2.4(d)
Final Returns	8(d)	2.4(e)
Representations	9	2.5
Expenses	10	1.10(a) and 2.7
Default Interest	11(a)	1.8(b)
Further Assurances	11(b)	2.8(a)

Nature of Item	Paragraph in New York Law CSA	Section reference in the Margin Provisions
Further Protection	11(c)	2.8(b)
Good faith	11(d)	1.10(f)
Demands and Notices	11(e)	1.10(c)–(d)
Specifications of certain matters	11(f)	1.10(e)
Definitions	12	5
Elections and Variables	13	Supplement

PART 2

ELECTIVE PROVISIONS – SECURITY INTEREST APPROACH (NEW YORK LAW)

The parties may elect, by incorporation of this Part 2 into the Supplement, to have the following provisions apply to Transfers of Cash or other property under these Provisions, in which case the provisions of this Part 2 shall be construed in accordance with New York law.

Section 2.1 Security Interest and Set-off. Each party, as the Provider, hereby pledges to the other party, as the Taker, as security for its Obligations, and grants to the Taker a first priority continuing security interest in, lien on and right of set-off in, on or against all Margin Received received by the Taker. Upon the Transfer by the Taker to the Provider of Margin Received, the security interest, lien and right of set-off granted under this Section 2.1 in, on and against that Margin Received will be released immediately and, to the fullest extent possible, without any further action by either party. The Interest Amount or portion thereof not Transferred pursuant to Section 1.8(c) will constitute Margin Received in the form of Cash and will be subject to the security interest, lien and right of set-off granted under this Section 2.1.

Section 2.1. Security interest and set off

When acting as Provider, each party pledges Eligible Margin to the Taker to secure its obligations under the ISDA Master Agreement (or any other agreement where obligations are being collateralised) by way of a first priority continuing security and lien. The security interest only covers margin actually received by the Taker and not any margin which is in transit to him. Allied to this is a right of set off which technically can only attach to debt claims and not property claims under New York law. As the *User's Guide to the 2001 ISDA Margin Provisions* explains, the combination of a security interest and set off right covers both the Taker's property claims over securities he holds but has not reused and his debt liability in respect of accrued but unpaid Interest Amounts on cash margin he holds.

Where margin is returned to the Provider, the security interest is automatically released. Where any Interest Amount on cash margin is not released because it would cause or increase a margin call on the Provider, it will remain Margin Received subject to the security interest.

Section 2.2 Holding and Using Margin Received.

(a) *Care of Margin Received.* Without limiting the Taker's rights under Section 2.2(c), the Taker will exercise reasonable care to assure the safe custody of all Margin Received to the extent required by applicable law. In any event, the Taker will be deemed to have exercised reasonable care if it exercises at least the same degree of care as it would exercise with respect to its own property. Except as specified in the preceding sentence, the Taker will have no duty with respect to Margin Received, including, without limitation, any duty to collect any Distributions, or enforce or preserve any rights pertaining thereto.

(b) *Eligibility to Hold Margin Received; Custodians.*

 (i) Upon Notice by the Taker to the Provider of the appointment of a Custodian, the Provider's obligations to make any Transfer will be discharged by making the Transfer to that Custodian. The holding of Margin Received by a Custodian will be deemed to be the holding of that Margin Received by the Taker for which the Custodian is acting.

 (ii) If the Taker or its Custodian fails to satisfy any conditions specified in the Supplement for holding Margin Received, then upon a demand made by the Provider, the Taker will, not later than five Margin Business Days after the demand, Transfer or cause its Custodian to Transfer all Margin Received held by it to a Custodian that satisfies those conditions or, if no such Custodian is specified, to the Taker.

 (iii) The Taker will be liable for the acts or omissions of its Custodian to the same extent that the Taker would be liable for its own acts or omissions.

(c) *Use of Margin Received*

 (i) Unless otherwise specified in the Supplement and without limiting the rights and obligations of the parties under Sections 1.1 to 1.8 or Section 2.4, if no Event of Default with respect to the Taker has occurred and is continuing, and if no Specified Condition has occurred with respect to the Taker (or with respect to which Specified Condition the Taker is an Affected Party, in the case of an ISDA Master Agreement), and if no date has occurred or been designated on which all outstanding Transactions have been or will be accelerated, terminated, liquidated or cancelled as a result of an Event of Default or

Section 2.2. Holding and using Margin Received

(a)   The security interest, of course, only gives the Taker a partial interest in the Margin Received and the Provider retains conditional ownership rights. However, while holding the Margin Received, the Taker must look after it as this is required by the New York Uniform Commercial Code. He must also hold the margin in safe custody or treat it with the same measure of care as he would his own property.

However, the Taker is not obliged to exercise any voting rights of the securities or preserve any of the holder's rights against the issuer nor even to collect Distributions. However, on this last point, he is not excused from paying over Equivalent Distributions to the Provider as required by Section 1.8 of the Margin Provisions, whether or not he holds the securities at the time the Distribution is paid.

Finally, the Taker's rights under Section 2.2(c), i.e. use of margin, are not to be prejudiced by the manner in which he exercises his duty of care for the securities.

(b)   (i)   The Taker may use a Custodian to hold Margin Received and when the Provider transfers margin to the Custodian, following a margin call from the Taker, then his duty is deemed to be discharged.

(ii)   However, the Provider as conditional owner of Equivalent Securities also has a say here if any conditions in Paragraph 14 of the Supplement are breached in connection with a custodian's eligibility (e.g. credit ratings or an asset test). Then upon giving the Taker five Margin Business Days' prior notice, it can demand that the margin is transferred to another custodian who can meet these criteria and if none is found, to the Taker himself.

(iii)   It is confirmed that the Taker is as liable for its custodian's acts and omissions as it is for its own.

(c)   Unlike in most of Europe, a New York law pledge of securities permits the pledgee to use the securities if the pledgor agrees. This is not usually possible in Europe, because free use of an asset is incompatible with the partial nature of the pledgee's security interest.

(i)   Here, provided an Event of Default, Specified Condition or Early Termination Date has not occurred to the Taker, he can use the collateral in any of the ways described in Section 2.2(c)(i)(A) which covers all likely options and (in B) register its interest in the Margin Received in its own or its custodian's or nominee's name. The equity of redemption or ownership rights of the Provider are ignored in this case because the Provider agrees to this right of the Taker.

The detailed provisions of Section 9-207 of the NYUCC concern the rights and duties of a Secured Party having possession or control of margin and are expressly excluded here.

Specified Condition with respect to the Taker (or with respect to which Specified Condition the Taker is an Affected Party, in the case of an ISDA Master Agreement), then the Taker will, notwithstanding Section 9-207 of the New York Uniform Commercial Code, have the right to:

(A) sell, pledge, rehypothecate, assign, invest, use, commingle or otherwise dispose of, or otherwise use in its business, any Margin Received it holds, free from any claim or right of any nature whatsoever of the Provider, including any equity or right of redemption by the Provider; and

(B) register any Margin Received in the name of the Taker, its Custodian or a nominee for either.

(ii) For purposes of the obligation to Transfer Eligible Margin or Equivalent Margin pursuant to Sections 1.1, 1.3, 1.6 and 1.7 and any rights or remedies authorized under these Provisions, the Taker will be deemed to continue to hold all Margin Received and receive Distributions made thereon, regardless of whether the Taker has exercised any rights with respect to any Margin Received pursuant to sub-Section 2.2(c)(i) above.

(ii) For the purpose of margin calls, transfer timing, disputes and substitutions and receipt of Distributions under Section 1.8, the Taker will still be deemed to hold the Margin Received even if he has disposed of it under one of the permissible methods here.

Note that this right of use will be considered to apply unless the parties choose otherwise in Paragraph 15 of the Supplement. Conditions for use of the margin can also be imposed by agreement in Paragraph 15.

Section 2.3 Additional Event of Default. An Event of Default will exist with respect to a party (including for purposes of Section 5(a)(iii)(I) of the ISDA Master Agreement) if that party fails to comply with any restriction or prohibition specified in these Provisions with respect to any of the rights specified in Section 2.2(c) and that failure continues for five Margin Business Days after Notice of that failure is given to that party.

Section 2.3. Additional Event of Default

If a party fails to comply with the conditions stipulated for the use of margin more than five Margin Business Days after the other party has given it notice of such failure, it will constitute an Event of Default against the first party. Section 5(a)(iii)(1) of the ISDA Master Agreement relates to Credit Support Default. This Event of Default is triggered if (i) a party or any Credit Support Provider of a party breaches a Credit Support Document and the breach is continuing following any applicable grace period, (ii) the Credit Support Document is not in effect before satisfaction of all obligations under related Transactions without the written consent of the other party, or (iii) a party, or a Credit Support Provider, among other things, repudiates its Credit Support Document.

Section 2.4 Certain Rights and Remedies.

(a) *Taker's Rights and Remedies.* If at any time (1) an Event of Default or Specified Condition with respect to the Provider (or with respect to which Specified Condition the Provider is an Affected Party, in the case of an ISDA Master Agreement) has occurred and is continuing or (2) a date on which all outstanding Transactions have been or will be accelerated, terminated, liquidated or cancelled has occurred or been designated as the result of an Event of Default or Specified Condition with respect to the Provider (or with respect to which Specified Condition the Provider is an Affected Party, in the case of an ISDA Master Agreement), then, unless the Provider has paid in full all its Obligations that are then due, the Taker may exercise one or more of the following rights and remedies:

(i) all rights and remedies available to a secured party under applicable law with respect to Margin Received held by the Taker;

(ii) the right to set-off any amounts payable by the Provider with respect to any Obligations against any Margin Received or the Cash equivalent of any Margin Received held by the Taker (or any obligation of the Taker to Transfer that Margin Received); and

(iii) the right to liquidate any Margin Received held by the Taker through one or more public or private sales or other dispositions with such prior Notice, if any, as may be required and cannot be waived under applicable law, free from any claim or right of any nature whatsoever of the Provider, including any equity or right of redemption by the Provider (with the Taker having the right to purchase any or all of the Margin Received to be sold) and to apply the proceeds (or the Cash equivalent of the proceeds) from the liquidation of the Margin Received to any amounts payable by the Provider with respect to any Obligations in such order as the Taker may elect.

(b) *Market Risk.* Each party acknowledges and agrees that Margin Received in the form of securities may decline rapidly in value or is of a type customarily sold on a recognized market and, accordingly, the Provider is not entitled to prior Notice of any sale of that Margin Received by the Taker, except any Notice that is required under applicable law and cannot be waived.

Section 2.4. Certain Rights and Remedies

(a) Assuming that the Provider has not paid in full all its Obligations under its ISDA Master Agreement with the Taker and that it is afflicted by an Event of Default, Specified Condition or Early Termination Date then the Taker has the following rights:

- all legal rights of a secured party in respect of Margin Received held by it;

- a right to set off any payments due from the Provider in respect of the Obligations and against any debt claim (e.g. Interest Amounts) which the Taker owes the Provider;

- the public or private sale of securities without notice to the Provider (unless required by law). Such a sale is to be free of any claim by the Provider to an equity of redemption (i.e. right of return) in the Margin Received. The Taker is also given the right to buy the Margin Received itself but subject to the Section 1.10(f) requirement to act in good faith and in a commercially reasonable manner. It can also apply the sales proceeds to the Provider's Obligations in the order it thinks fit.

(b) This acknowledges that market values of securities can fluctuate rapidly and gives the Taker the right to sell the Margin Received promptly without previous notice to the Provider unless this is required by law.

This provision might be useful even in an administration situation where a freeze will catch security interests. A court might be persuaded to allow a swift sale if this is likely to be in the interest of the creditors as a whole.

(c) ***Provider's Rights and Remedies.*** If at any time a date on which all outstanding Transactions have been or will be accelerated, terminated, liquidated or cancelled has occurred or been designated as the result of an Event of Default or Specified Condition with respect to the Taker (or with respect to which Specified Condition the Taker is an Affected Party, in the case of an ISDA Master Agreement), then, except in the case of a date on which less than all outstanding Transactions have been or will be accelerated, terminated, liquidated or cancelled where the Taker has paid in full all of its Obligations that are then due with respect to payments upon early termination of those Transactions:

(i)   the Provider may exercise all rights and remedies available to a pledgor under applicable law with respect to Margin Received held by the Taker;

(ii) the Taker will be obligated immediately to Transfer all Margin Received and any Interest Amount to the Provider; and

(iii) to the extent that Margin Received or the Interest Amount is not so Transferred pursuant to sub-Section 2.4(c)(ii) above, the Provider may:

   (A) set-off any amounts payable by the Provider with respect to any Obligations against any Margin Received or the Cash equivalent of any Margin Received held by the Taker (or any obligation of the Taker to Transfer that Margin Received); and

   (B) to the extent that the Provider does not set-off under sub-Section 2.4(c)(iii)(A) above, withhold payment of any remaining amounts payable by the Provider with respect to any Obligations, up to the Value of any remaining Margin Received held by the Taker, until that Margin Received is Transferred to the Provider.

(c) Of course, a Taker can also be subject to an Event of Default, Specified Condition or Early Termination Date and if this happens the Provider has the following rights:

- all the legal rights of a pledgor against Margin Received and held by its pledgee;
- the immediate return of all Margin Received and Interest Amounts from the Taker;

If this does not happen the Provider can:

(A) set off any of its Obligation payments against the cash equivalent of the margin held by the Taker, thus skilfully rendering both items debt claims eligible for set off against one another; and

(B) withhold payment of any Obligations to the Taker up to the value of the margin held by the Taker. It can only do this up to the time the Taker actually returns the margin to it.

(d) ***Deficiencies and Excess Proceeds.*** When no amounts are or thereafter may become payable by the Provider with respect to any Obligations (other than with respect to a contingent tax gross-up or similar ancillary contingent obligation or any contingent obligation under Section 2.6 or Section 1.10(a)), the Taker will Transfer to the Provider any proceeds and Margin Received remaining after liquidation, set-off and/or application under this Section 2.4. The Provider in all events will remain liable for any amounts remaining unpaid after any liquidation, set-off and/or application under this Section 2.4.

(e) ***Final Returns.*** When no amounts are or thereafter may become payable by the Provider with respect to any Obligations (other than with respect to a contingent tax gross-up or similar ancillary contingent obligation or any contingent obligation under Section 2.6 and Section 1.10(a)), the Taker will Transfer to the Provider all Margin Received.

Section 2.4(d). Deficiencies and Excess Proceeds and Final Returns

(d) This essentially provides that upon close-out, the Taker will transfer any surplus net proceeds to the Provider. However, the Provider remains liable for any shortfall that remains. Section 1.10(a) relates to either the party's expenses and Section 2.6 relates to Distributions.

(e) If at any point the Provider has no outstanding Obligations whatever to the Taker, the latter must return all the margin he holds to the Provider.

Section 2.5 Representations. Each party represents to the other party (which representations will be deemed to be repeated as of each date on which it, as the Provider, Transfers Margin Received) that:

(a) it has the power to grant a security interest in and lien on any Margin Received it Transfers as the Provider and has taken all necessary actions to authorize the granting of that security interest and lien;

(b) it is the sole owner of or otherwise has the right to Transfer all Margin Received it Transfers to the Taker pursuant to these Provisions, free and clear of any security interest, lien, encumbrance, claim of a property interest or restriction (including without limitation any restriction or requirement imposed by any securities law or regulation) other than the security interest and lien granted under Section 2.1;

(c) upon the Transfer of any Margin Received to the Taker under the terms of these Provisions, the Taker will have a valid and perfected first priority security interest in such Margin Received (assuming that any central clearing corporation or any third-party financial intermediary or other entity not within the control of the Provider involved in the Transfer of that Margin Received gives the Notices and takes the action required of it under applicable law for perfection of that interest); and

(d) the performance by it of its obligations as set out in these Provisions will not result in the creation of any security interest, lien, encumbrance, claim of a property interest or restriction (including without limitation any restriction or requirement imposed by any securities law or regulation) on any Margin Received other than the security interest, lien and right of set-off granted under Section 2.1.

Section 2.5. Representations

These are the standard representations made by the Provider every time it transfers margin to the Taker, viz:

- it is empowered to grant a security interest in the margin and has taken all necessary authorising action;

- it is the sole owner of and has the sole right to transfer the margin free and clear of any encumbrance or third party interest. The security interest under Section 2.1 is, of course, excluded;

- the security interest conferred upon the Taker will be a valid and perfected first priority security interest provided that, where involved, any third party securities clearance system or similar intermediary performs all necessary acts to effect this;

- the performance of the Provider's Obligations hereunder will not lead to the creation of any other security interest in the margin given to the Taker apart from the one granted under Section 2.1;

The Provider will need to check that he is not breaking any negative pledges by entering into this security interest.

Section 2.6 Distributions. Without prejudice to Section 2.2(b), on each Distributions Date the Taker will be deemed, for purposes of Section 1.8(b), to have received Distributions in respect of Margin Received.

Section 2.7 Expenses.

(a) *Margin Received.* Section 1.10(a) notwithstanding, the Provider will promptly pay when due all taxes, assessments or charges of any nature that are imposed with respect to Margin Received held by the Taker upon becoming aware of them, regardless of whether any portion of that Margin Received is subsequently disposed of under Section 2.2(c), except for those taxes, assessments and charges that result from the exercise of the Taker's rights under Section 2.2(c).

(b) *Liquidation and/or Application of Margin Received.* Section 1.10(a) notwithstanding, all reasonable costs and expenses incurred by or on behalf of the Taker or the Provider in connection with the liquidation and/or application of any Margin Received under Section 2.4 will be payable, on demand and pursuant to the Expenses Section, by the party in respect of which an Event of Default has occurred. If there is no party to which an Event of Default has occurred, each party is liable for its own costs and expenses.

Section 2.6. Distributions

This just underlines the fact that the Taker will be deemed to have received coupon payments on securities from their issuer and obliged to pass these on to the Provider (Section 1.8), even though he has no obligation to collect these distributions (Section 2.2(a)) or he may have disposed of the securities (Section 2.2(c)).

Section 2.7. Expenses

Section 2.7 modifies Section 1.10(a) in the following ways:

(a) the Provider has to bear any taxes or other charges which are disposed on the margin transferred to the Taker unless these are due to the latter's use of the margin;

(b) any enforcement expenses arising from an Event of Default will be promptly paid by the Defaulting Party. If there is no Defaulting Party, these costs are individually borne by the parties.

Section 2.8 Miscellaneous.

(a) *Further Assurances.* Promptly following a demand made by a party, the other party will execute, deliver, file and record any financing statement, specific assignment or other document and take any other action that may be necessary or desirable and reasonably requested by that party to create, preserve, perfect or validate any security interest, lien or right of set-off created or granted under Section 2.1, to enable that party to exercise or enforce its rights with respect to Margin Received or to effect or document a release of a security interest in or lien on Margin Received.

(b) *Further Protection.* The Provider will promptly give Notice to the Taker of, and defend against, any suit, action, proceeding or lien, encumbrance, claim of a property interest or restriction that involves Margin Received Transferred by the Provider or that could adversely affect the security interest, lien or right of set-off created or granted by it under Section 2.1, unless that suit, action, proceeding or lien, encumbrance, claim of a property interest or restriction results from the exercise of the Taker's rights under Section 2.2(c).

Section 2.8. Miscellaneous

These are further boilerplate provisions. Section 2.8(a) requires each party to co-operate fully in any formalities required to perfect, enforce or release the margin arrangement.

Section 2.8(b) requires the Provider promptly to notify the Taker of any legal action actually or potentially affecting the margin delivered or the security interest, and to defend itself against such action unless it arises from the Taker's use of the margin under Section 2.2(c) hereof.

Part 3: Title transfer approach (English law)

Introduction

The English law title transfer approach is set out in the much shorter Part 3 of the Margin Provisions. Again, it is largely the same as the approach taken in the English Law CSA.

Figure 8.5 illustrates where the provisions may be found in each document.

FIG. 8.5

Location of provisions in the English Law CSA and the Margin Provisions

Nature of Item	Paragraph in English Law CSA	Section reference in the Margin Provisions
Preamble	Preamble	N/A
Interpretation	1	N/A
Credit Support Obligations	2	1.1
Transfer Timing	3(a)	1.3
Calculations	3(b)	1.5
Exchanges	3(c)	1.7
Dispute Resolution	4	1.6
Transfer of Title	5(a)	3.1(a)
No Security Interest	5(b)	3.1(b)
Distributions and Interest Amount	5(c)	1.8 and 3.4
Default	6	3.2
Representation	7	3.3
Expenses	8	1.10(a) and 2.7
Default Interest	9(a)	1.8(b)
Good faith	9(b)	1.10(f)
Demands and Notices	9(c)	1.10(c)–(d)
Specification of certain matters	9(d)	1.10(e)
Definitions	10	5
Elections and Variables	11	Supplement

As mentioned in Chapter 3 (p. 35), assuming the Margin Provisions are being used with an ISDA Master Agreement, the title transfer approach relies on the Agreement's Section 6 close-out netting provisions. Where the title transfer approach of Part 3 of the Margin Provisions is used with a non-ISDA agreement, a contractual set off provision must be included.

One major difference from the English Law CSA is that, unlike the CSA the Supplement is not treated as a Transaction (see Paragraph 6 of the English Law CSA) under the ISDA Master Agreement, because the treatment is amended to the modus operandi of Section 3.2 of the Margin Provisions.

Just to recap, the title transfer approach was developed in the derivatives, repo and stocklending markets to permit the Taker to use the Margin Received without the restrictions normally applying to a pledge. The legal approach here is one of outright transfer of title to the Taker which, when achieved, leaves the Provider with no continuing ownership interest in the margin. All it has is a conditional right to receive Equivalent Margin back from the Taker. If the Taker goes bust, then the Provider ranks only as an unsecured creditor. This is the risk he takes in entering into the arrangement.

PART 3
ELECTIVE PROVISIONS – TITLE TRANSFER APPROACH (ENGLISH LAW)

The parties may elect, by incorporation of this Part 3 into the Supplement, to have the following provisions apply to Transfers of Cash or other property under these Provisions, in which case the provisions of this Part 3 shall be construed in accordance with English law.

Section 3.1 Transfer of Title and No Security Interest.

(a) *Transfer of Title.* Each party agrees that all right, title and interest in and to any Lock-up Margin, Eligible Margin, Equivalent Margin, Substitute Margin, Equivalent Distributions or Interest Amount which it Transfers to the other party under these Provisions will vest in the recipient free and clear of any liens, claims, charges or encumbrances or any other interest of the Transferring party or of any third person (other than a lien routinely imposed on all securities in a relevant clearance system). Each Transfer under these Provisions will be made so as to constitute or result in a valid and legally effective transfer of the Transferring party's legal and beneficial title to the recipient.

(b) *No Security Interest.* The parties do not intend to create in favor of either party any mortgage, charge, lien, pledge, encumbrance or other security interest in any Cash or other property, to which this Part 3 applies, Transferred by one party to the other party under these Provisions.

Section 3.1. Transfer of Title and No Security Interest

(a)   Each transfer made by either party (whether of margin of various sorts or interest on cash or bonds) is a full transfer of ownership in such assets and free and clear of third party claims except for liens or charges routinely imposed by a securities clearance system.

(b)   This is a clear statement that neither party proposes to create any security interest in the margin transferred under this Section of the Margin Provisions.

Section 3.2 Default.

(a) If at any time a date on which all outstanding Transactions have been or will be accelerated, terminated, liquidated or cancelled has occurred or been designated as a result of an Event of Default or Specified Condition in relation to either party (an "*Early Termination Date*" in the case of an ISDA Master Agreement):

(i) in the case of an ISDA Master Agreement for which Market Quotation is the applicable payment measure for purposes of Section 6(e) of the ISDA Master Agreement, an amount equal to the Value of the Margin Received held by the Taker will be an Unpaid Amount due from the Taker to the Provider for purposes of Section 6(e) of the ISDA Master Agreement; and

(ii) in the case of an ISDA Master Agreement for which Loss is the applicable payment measure for purposes of Section 6(e) of the ISDA Master Agreement, Loss shall include an amount equal to the Value of the Margin Received held by the Taker (expressed as a negative number) for purposes of Section 6(e) of the ISDA Master Agreement.

(iii) in the case of an Agreement which is not in the form of an ISDA Master Agreement:

(A) if the Provider is the defaulting party or the party impaired by the relevant Specified Condition, then the Taker has the right, without prior notice to the Provider, to set-off any amounts payable by the Provider with respect to any Obligations against an amount equal to the Value of the Margin Received by the Taker; and

(B) if the Taker is the defaulting party, then the Provider has the right, without prior Notice to the Taker, to set-off the Value of the Margin Received by the Taker against any amounts payable by the Provider with respect to any Obligations.

(b) For purposes of effecting any set-off permitted by this Section 3.2, the party exercising the right of set-off may convert any obligation to another currency at a market rate determined by that party.

(c) The Taker will Transfer to the Provider any Equivalent Margin relating to Margin Received remaining after any application of this Section 3.2 after satisfaction in full of all amounts payable by the Provider with respect to any Obligations. The Provider in any event will remain liable for any amounts remaining unpaid by it after any application of this Section 3.2.

Section 3.2. Default

(a)   This is a very important provision which gives effect to close-out under the title transfer approach.

If a right to close-out all Transactions under an ISDA Master Agreement occurs then:

(i)   **if Market Quotation is the payment measure, then the value of the margin held by the Taker will be treated as an Unpaid Amount due from the Taker to the Provider;**

(ii)   **if Loss is the payment measure, then the value of the Margin Received by the Taker will be deducted from the other elements of the Loss calculation;**

(iii)   **where a non-ISDA Master agreement is involved, the non-defaulting party has the right to set off its obligations against those of its counterparty.**

For the purposes of this Section, Margin Received includes Lock-up Margin and accrued but unpaid Interest Amounts and Distributions. The references to such margin being "held" by the Taker in Section 3.2(a)(i) and (ii) should not be taken literally. He could have sold or repledged the securities. He is only deemed to hold them. In fact the Taker does not hold any assets of the Provider as such, but merely has a conditional contractual obligation to return fungible Equivalent Margin to the Provider up to the value of the margin received from him.

(b)   Currency conversion is possible if necessary.

(c)   Surplus proceeds from margin realisations will be returned to the Provider after all his Obligations have been fully discharged. Conversely the Provider will remain responsible to the Taker for any shortfall.

Section 3.3 Representation. Each party represents to the other party (which representation will be deemed to be repeated as of each date on which it Transfers Eligible Margin, Equivalent Margin, Substitute Margin or Equivalent Distributions or any other Cash, securities or other property under these Provisions) that it is the sole owner of or otherwise has the right to Transfer all Eligible Margin, Equivalent Margin, Substitute Margin or Equivalent Distributions or any other Cash, securities or other property it Transfers to the other party under these Provisions, free and clear of any security interest, lien, encumbrance or other restriction (other than a lien routinely imposed on all securities in a relevant clearance system).

Section 3.4 Distributions. Without prejudice to Section 3.1, on each Distributions Date the Taker will be deemed, for purposes of Section 1.8(b), to have received Distributions in respect of Margin Received.

Section 3.3. Representation

Each party represents to the other that each time it makes a margin transfer or income pass-through to the other it is the sole owner of and entitled to make such transfers free and clear of any third party security interest or lien (apart from securities clearance systems liens). This reinforces Section 3.1(a) and should protect the Taker from any claims from third parties that it was aware of their security interests.

Section 3.4. Distributions

This is akin to the situation in Section 2.6 of Part 2 of the Margin Provisions. However, it is also different because, under title transfer, the Taker becomes owner of the margin transferred and can sell it. Speaking very strictly, the margin under the title approach consists not of the transfer of assets but of a contractual obligation of the Taker to redeliver equivalent fungible margin assets to the Provider if the latter fulfils its Obligations under the ISDA Master Agreement.

The Taker is deemed to be the receiver of Distributions paid by the securities issuer and must pay these on to the Provider under Part 1, Section 1.8(b) so as to preserve the Provider's traditional rights to such income.

Part 4: Additional Elective Provisions

Introduction

Part 4 of the Margin Provisions is where jurisdiction specific issues can be included either by themselves or more likely under the umbrella of an overarching choice of Part 2 or Part 3 as the legal approach and governing law under the Margin Provisions.

At the time the Margin Provisions were being composed, only parties in Japan were sufficiently active in establishing collateralised arrangements to justify the inclusion of jurisdiction specific Provisions for them in Part 4. Other jurisdictions may be added in due course were this is important for legal or operational reasons. Where this happens such provisions will be automatically incorporated into this Part 4.

It is possible for the local law to govern the Margin Provisions as a carve-out from the overarching governing law but this would lead to different governing laws applying to different parts of the contractual relationship and the desirability of this would have to be checked out with the parties' lawyers. However, if Japanese Margin is the only margin being taken, it is possible to apply Part 4 as the governing law and add in Parts 1 and 5 of the Margin Provisions, plus the Supplement to complete the contractual agreements.

Section 4.1 sets out the Japanese law loan collateral approach which is essentially the same as corresponding provisions in the Japanese CSA.

PART 4

ELECTIVE PROVISIONS

The parties may elect, by incorporation of either Part 2 or Part 3 and the relevant Section of this Part 4 into the Supplement, to have one or more of the following Sections apply to Transfers of Cash or other property under these Provisions, in which case the provisions of this Part 4 shall be construed in accordance with Japanese law.

Section 4.1 Japanese Credit Support Provisions – Loan and Deposit.

Provisions for Parties using Japanese Margin.

(a) *Characterization of the Arrangement.* Solely for the purposes of determining each Party's rights and obligations with respect to the Transfer of Eligible Margin or Equivalent Margin consisting of Japanese Margin, and without prejudice to other provisions of these Provisions or the Agreement, each Party agrees as follows:

  (i) The term *"Transfer"* under Section 1.1(a) means a loan (for the avoidance of doubt, if these Provisions are governed by Japanese law or if the term *shohi-taishaku* is to be construed under Japanese law) of Japanese Margin held in the form of securities and a deposit (for the avoidance of doubt, if these Provisions are governed by Japanese law or if the term *shohi-kitaku* is to be construed under Japanese law) of Japanese Margin held in the form of Cash.

  (ii) Until the Taker is required, pursuant to the terms of these Provisions, to return the Japanese Margin Received, as long as (A) no Event of Default with respect to the Taker has occurred and is continuing, (B) no Specified Condition has occurred with respect to the Taker and (C) no date has occurred or been designated on which all outstanding Transactions have been or will be accelerated, terminated, liquidated or cancelled as a result of an Event of Default or Specified Condition (with respect to which Specified Condition the Taker is an Affected Party, in the case of an ISDA Master Agreement), the Taker shall be entitled to have all the incidents of ownership of such Japanese Margin, including without limitation, the right to sell, transfer, lend or otherwise dispose of, pledge, assign, invest, use, commingle or otherwise use in its business and register or record in the name of the Taker, its Custodian or nominee for the Japanese Margin Received.

Section 4.1(a)

Japanese law regards transfers of Japanese Margin in the form of securities as a loan and transfers of cash as a deposit. This entitles a non-defaulting Taker to use the margin as if it were its outright owner. Section 4.1 establishes a margin arrangement akin to the English law title transfer approach in Part 3 of the Margin Provisions, except that in Section 4.1(a)(iii) the Taker may, with the Provider's prior written consent, instead of returning Equivalent Securities repay the equivalent in Japanese Yen cash. This right is important to the close-out mechanism in Section 4.1(b).

(iii) Where the Japanese Margin is in the form of securities, the Taker may repay the Japanese Yen Cash equivalent of such Japanese Margin. The Transfer of Equivalent Margin or repayment of the Japanese Yen Cash equivalent shall be deemed to be a return of the Japanese Margin under Section 1.1(b). However, solely for the purpose of Section 1.1(b), and as long as an Early Termination Date has not occurred (in the case of an ISDA Master Agreement) or no date has occurred or been designated on which all outstanding Transactions have been or will be accelerated, terminated, liquidated or cancelled, the Taker's option to repay such Japanese Yen Cash equivalent is subject to the prior written consent of the Provider.

(b) *Event of Default or Specified Condition.* If a date has occurred or been designated on which all outstanding Transactions have been or will be accelerated, terminated, liquidated or cancelled (in the case of an ISDA Master Agreement, an Event of Default) as a result of an Event of Default or Specified Condition in relation to a Party (with respect to which Specified Condition, such Party is an Affected Party), the Non-Defaulting Party or the Party which is not the Affected Party, as the case may be, has the right specified below. If such Event of Default is an event to which the Parties specified the Automatic Early Termination provision of Section 6(a) of the ISDA Master Agreement or any provision in an Agreement, other than the ISDA Master Agreement, of like effect, to be applicable, or is one of the Other Japanese Events of Default, then, in any such case, without regard to the intention of either of the Parties, the following shall be deemed to occur automatically as of the time specified in Section 6(a) of the ISDA Master Agreement and, in all other cases, as of the time immediately preceding the occurrence of the relevant event(s):

(i) Where the Japanese Margin Received is held in the form of securities, the Taker, without any action on the part of either Party, will be deemed to have elected to repay the Japanese Yen Cash equivalent (computed by reference to the actual interest rates, quotations on the relevant exchanges and other indices or market prices) and together with the Japanese Margin Received in the form of Cash, such amounts will be immediately due and payable to the Provider.

(ii) Any such amounts due under sub-Section (b)(i) above shall be set-off against any Obligations of the Provider, without prior Notice or formalities which might otherwise be required, and if necessary, such amounts are deemed to have been converted into the currency of such Obligations at the relevant rate prevailing on the date when such set-off is effected or deemed to have been exercised.

(iii) The Taker will Transfer to the Provider an amount, if any, remaining after the application of the foregoing. The Provider in all events will remain liable for any amounts, including, but not limited to, the Obligation under other part(s) of these Provisions to immediately Transfer Margin Received and any Interest Amount under such Part(s) (in the event it is, at such time the Taker of any Margin Received) to the Taker, remaining unpaid or undelivered, if any, after such application. Either or both of such amounts shall be subject to set-off hereunder or the general

Section 4.1(b)

If a close-out date occurs the Taker will be deemed to have chosen to repay the Yen cash equivalent of the value of any Japanese Margin securities he holds. This conversion into a money sum helps the Taker's set off rights.

Upon close-out, the actions taken are of immediate effect and the Non-defaulting Party can set off the Obligations against the value of the Japanese Margin Received. If Automatic Early Termination applies under an ISDA Master Agreement, the set off will be automatically triggered. Currency conversions are possible. The Taker will transfer any surplus realisations to the Provider after all the latter's liabilities have been discharged subject to any other set off rights the Taker may have. The Provider remains liable for any residual shortfall.

The Defaulting Party shall be liable for all reasonable enforcement costs or expenses subject to any legal set off rights available to the parties.

The Provider is responsible for promptly paying taxes or other charges levied on it by the government or its tax authority in respect of Japanese Margin held by the Taker.

rights of set-off available to the Parties under the relevant laws. For purposes of effecting any set-off, the amount of an Obligation to Transfer Margin Received shall be equal to the Value of such Margin Received and the party exercising the right of set-off may, together with any other amounts owing to it, convert such amount into another currency at a market rate determined by that party.

(iv) All reasonable costs and expenses incurred by or on behalf of the Non-Defaulting Party in connection with the liquidation and/or application of any Japanese Margin above will be payable on demand by the Defaulting Party and shall be subject to the general rights of set-off available to the Parties under the relevant laws.

(v) The Provider shall promptly pay when due taxes, assessments or charges of any nature that are imposed on the Taker by any government or other taxing authority with respect to Japanese Margin Received held by the Taker upon becoming aware of the same.

(c) *Additional Events of Default.* The following shall be Additional Events of Default:

(ix) *Other Japanese Events of Default.* A Party:

(1) has a pre-judgment attachment (*karisasiosae*), post-judgment attachment (*sashiosae*) or other court order of enforcement issued in respect of any of its rights to receive the Japanese Margin Received or the Obligations; or

(2) transfers, assigns or pledges any of its rights to receive the Japanese Margin Received or the Obligations to a third Party.

In the case of an ISDA Master Agreement, Section 6(a) of the ISDA Master Agreement is amended by inserting after the words, "or, to the extent analogous thereto, (8)" at the end thereof the words "or specified in Section 5(a)(ix)(1) or (2) of the 2001 ISDA Margin Provisions".

Section 4.1(c)

These additional Events of Default mirror those in Paragraph 13(m) of the Japanese CSA. They concern pre- and post-judgement asset attachments and enforcement court orders on both Japanese Margin Received and Obligations and the transfer, assignment or pledge to a third party of such rights. This would destroy the set off mutuality. Appropriate amendments are made to the ISDA Master Agreement by reference.

(d) *Governing Law and Jurisdiction.* The Transaction(s) under this Section 4.1 shall be governed by and construed in accordance with the laws of Japan or, if another governing law is specified as applying for purposes of this Section 4.1, such other governing law. If the laws of Japan apply for purposes of this Part 4, the following shall apply:

Where an election (*sentaku*) to repay in Cash is made or deemed made under Section 4.1(b)(i), the Taker's obligation (such obligation is intended by the Parties to be a *sentaku-saimu* under Japanese laws) to return the Japanese Margin Received will be deemed to be an obligation to return the Japanese Yen Cash equivalent from the time of receipt of the relevant Japanese Margin.

With respect to any suit, action or proceedings relating to Margin Received to which this Part 4 applies and to which Japanese law is applicable, each Party irrevocably submits to the jurisdiction of the Japanese courts in addition to the submission to other courts provided in the Agreement.

(e) *Definitions.* Part 5 is amended to include the following additional definitions (which will replace any inconsistent definitions of the same terms that may exist in Part 5):

(i) *Equivalent Margin.* "*Equivalent Margin*" means in relation to Japanese Margin, securities of the same type, nominal value, description and amount and issuer, class, series, maturity, coupon rate and principal amount as that Japanese Margin or new or if different securities which have been exchanged for, converted into or substituted for that Japanese Margin.

(ii) *Japanese Margin.* "*Japanese Margin*" means Eligible Margin consisting of negotiable debt obligations of the Government of Japan and/or Cash denominated in Japanese Yen and such other items specified for a Party as Japanese Margin which is Eligible Margin in the Supplement.

(iii) *Japanese Margin Received.* "*Japanese Margin Received*" means Margin Received which is Japanese Margin.

Section 4.1(d) and (e)

(d) Japanese law will govern unless another governing law is specified (due to juris-diction specific provisions being outlined for that other jurisdiction in this Section 4.1).

If Japanese law applies then:

- the Taker's option to return Yen cash for the value of Japanese Margin Received is repeated;

- each party irrevocably submits to the Japanese courts in respect of actions involving the Japanese Margin Received and the other courts specified in the ISDA Master Agreement.

(e) Additional definitions to go in Part 5 relating to Japanese Margin.

Part 5: Definitions

As Part 5 is already a simplified list of definitions. I do not propose to redefine them here for reasons of space and inutility. However, they are worth reading in their original form which is reproduced in Annex 9.

Supplement

The Supplement is the engine of the Margin Provisions. In it the parties agree their choices for operating the margin arrangements and can also amend the other provisions, if required. In this way the Supplement is similar to Paragraph 11 of the English Law CSA and Paragraph 13 of the New York Law CSA.

The format of the Supplement is not compulsory but is likely to be followed by the markets. The Supplement contains a number of fallbacks if no choice is made by the parties, but some provisions have no fallback and the Supplement would be inoperative if no choice is made. This is unlikely to be a problem in practice as no party is likely to fall at this hurdle after negotiating a margin arrangement this far.

Figures 8.6 and 8.7 respectively describe the fallback and non-fallback provisions. If no choice is made the following apply by default in the Supplement:

FIG. 8.6

ISDA Fallbacks in the Margin Provisions

Provision	Fallback
Base Currency	US Dollars
Lock-up Margin	Zero
Valuation Percentage	100%
Additional Margin Amount	Zero
Independent Amount	Zero
Threshold	Zero
Minimum Transfer Amount	Zero
Rounding	No rounding
Dispute Termination Event	Will not apply
Consent to Substitution	Will not apply
Interest Amount	Simple accrual basis
Obligations	Only those in the ISDA Master Agreement if no others stated
Use of Margin Received	Will apply

Provisions in the Supplement which must be completed as there is no fallback

FIG. 8.7

Margin Approach
Exposure
Eligible Margin
Interest Rate, Interest Amount and Interest Period
Demands and Notices
Transfer Information
Other Provisions

Appendix A
NOTE: THIS SUPPLEMENT IS DESIGNED FOR USE WITH THE 2001 ISDA MARGIN PROVISIONS. THIS SUPPLEMENT MUST BE READ IN CONJUNCTION WITH THOSE PROVISIONS.

ISDA

International Swaps and Derivatives Association, Inc.

2001 ISDA MARGIN SUPPLEMENT, dated as of _____

to the following Agreements: dated as of _____

_____ dated as of _____

_____ dated as of _____

_____ dated as of _____

between

_____ and _____

("Party A")   ("Party B")

This 2001 ISDA Margin Supplement (this "Supplement") supplements, forms part of, and is subject to, the above-referenced Agreements and the 2001 ISDA Margin Provisions (the "Provisions"), as published by the International Swaps and Derivatives Association, Inc. The Provisions are incorporated into this Supplement to the extent set out below. In the event of any inconsistency between this Supplement and the Provisions or the provisions of the above-referenced Agreements, this Supplement will prevail. In the event of any inconsistency between the provisions of any Confirmation and the Provisions (including the Supplement), such Confirmation will prevail for purposes of the relevant Transaction or Transactions.

Preamble

Not only is it possible to use the Supplement with an agreement other than the ISDA Master Agreement, but it can also be used with two or more ISDA Master Agreements simultaneously, where the net exposure under each Agreement is added together. Hence, the Supplement gives itself to cross margining across various trading relationships the parties may have with each other.

The Preamble makes it clear that the Supplement "supplements, forms part of, and is subject to" the Agreements to which it relates and which are specified by their effective dates.

The Preamble stipulates that where there is any inconsistency between the Supplement and the Margin Provisions or any terms in any of the agreements referred to in its heading, the Supplement will prevail. Where there is any conflict between the Supplement and a Confirmation, the Confirmation prevails in respect of the particular Transaction.

Supplement

Paragraph 1. Margin Approach. Part [2] [3] [and Section _____ of Part 4] of the Provisions [is] [are] hereby incorporated into this Supplement.]

Paragraph 2. Exposure. Transactions or classes of Transactions which are not to be taken into account when calculating Exposure: _____.

Paragraph 3. Base Currency. Base Currency has the following meaning: _____, if such currency is freely available.

Paragraph 1: Margin Approach

This is where the parties must choose the Supplement's legal approach and governing law: the New York law security interest approach, the English law title transfer approach and/or the Japanese law loan collateral approach (with other possible local law provisions in future editions of the Margin Provisions). Each approach is intended to work in conjunction with the Margin Provisions' Part 1 Operational Provisions and Part 5 Definitions.

Sometimes, for legal reasons, the parties may want to apply one legal approach to a particular class of margin (e.g. Japanese Margin) and another legal approach to the rest of the margin it holds. Where this is the case, the *User's Guide to the 2001 ISDA Margin Provisions* (page 30) in footnote 1 to the Supplement suggests the following language to achieve this:

> **In respect of any Eligible Margin specified in Paragraph 4 below, the relevant part of the Provisions corresponding to such Eligible Margin (as detailed in Paragraph 4 below) is hereby incorporated into this Supplement in respect of such Eligible Margin.**

Paragraph 2: Exposure

The Margin Provisions start from the position of assuming that all the Transactions under the agreements will be taken into account in calculating Exposure. This is based on market practice and concern that omitting Transactions from the Exposure calculation will result in a two-tiered structure of collateralised and uncollateralised trades which might make close-out netting problematical.

Still, if you want to do this, Paragraph 2 is the place. The parties have freedom of choice in determining which Transactions are to be excluded whether for example by product or branch (if the party concerned is multibranch). The exclusion must be very clearly drafted if misunderstandings are to be avoided.

The exclusion relates purely to the calculation of Margin Required. If the Provider defaults, all margin held by the Taker would be available for it to set off against the Obligations of the Provider.

Paragraph 3: Base Currency

The parties need to choose a Base Currency. The fallback is US Dollars.

Paragraph 4. Margin.

Eligible Margin for Party A	Valuation Percentage
(A) Cash (denominated in the currencies specified here)	
(B) Securities (listed by issuer and with any conditions as to remaining maturity)	

Eligible Margin for Party B	Valuation Percentage
(A) Cash (denominated in the currencies specified here)	
(B) Securities (listed by issuer and with any conditions as to remaining maturity)	

Paragraph 4: Margin

Here you must state the types of Eligible Margin that may be delivered to meet a margin call. The table assumes that Eligible Margin will be either cash or securities. Securities should be identified by the issuer and with any conditions as to residual maturity agreed between the parties. There is no fallback for types of Eligible Margin. They must be specified. The parties also need to agree Valuation Percentages for each type of Eligible Margin. If no Valuation Percentage is stated the fallback is 100%.

As mentioned in the commentary on Paragraph 1 above, where different legal approaches are to apply to different types of Eligible Margin, the Part of the Provisions concerned should be specified against each type of Eligible Margin.

The Valuation Percentage is the residual value of the security after the haircut has been deducted, e.g. a 5% haircut gives a 95% Valuation Percentage.

Paragraph 5. Structural Parameters.

Party A	Fixed amount in Base Currency
Lock-up Margin	
Additional Margin Amount	
Threshold	
Minimum Transfer Amount	

Party A may make a demand under Section 1.1(c)(ii) in the following circumstances:

[ ] if no Transactions are outstanding between the parties and Party A has no payment obligations, absolute or contingent, other than with respect to a tax gross-up or similar ancillary contingent obligation or any contingent obligation under Section 1.10(a) and Section 2.6, if applicable, pursuant to any Agreement.

[ ] if Party B's Exposure is equal to or less than _____.

Party B	Fixed amount in Base Currency
Lock-up Margin	
Additional Margin Amount	
Threshold	
Minimum Transfer Amount	

Party B may make a demand under Section 1.1(c)(ii) in the following circumstances:

[ ] if no Transactions are outstanding between the parties and Party B has no payment obligations, absolute or contingent, other than with respect to a tax gross-up or similar ancillary contingent obligation or any contingent obligation under Section 1.10(a) and Section 2.6, if applicable, pursuant to any Agreement.

[ ] if Party A's Exposure is equal to or less than _____.

Paragraph 5: Structural Parameters

Paragraph 5 sets out a "Structural Parameters" table describing the level of Lock-up Margin, Additional Margin Amount, Threshold and Minimum Transfer Amount applicable to each party.

(a) Lock-up Margin

Lock-up Margin is essentially initial margin due from a Provider to cover potential future risk exposure between Valuation Dates. It may be due from the Provider even when the Taker has no current risk exposure on the Provider.

Lock-up Margin may be a fixed monetary sum in the Base Currency or it may be calculated by way of a formula or a credit rating. This formula may simply be the sum of a fixed amount per Transaction entered into, excluding those like options where the Taker has no ongoing risk exposure because he has received a full upfront premium from the Provider.

If Lock-up Margin is not stated it is considered to be zero.

Lock-up Margin is transferred independently of the Margin Required calculation and is not included in it.

Paragraph 5 also gives two choices in a tick box format to a Provider to demand return of Lock-up Margin it previously transferred, viz:

- **when the Taker has no actual or potential, present or future risk exposure whatsoever on the Provider;**
- **where the Taker's risk exposure has fallen below an agreed monetary figure or a level linked to a formula.**

It is also possible for Lock-up Margin not to be required at all under the Supplement where neither party holds any margin nor has any right to call perhaps because their net exposure is below the other party's Threshold and/or Minimum Transfer Amount.

(b) Additional Margin Amount

The Additional Margin Amount applying to each party is normally a fixed amount in the Base Currency but could be calculated by a formula and vary with the size and/or number of Transactions entered into under the Agreement(s). If an Additional Margin Amount is not stated, it is deemed to be zero.

The Additional Marginal Amount is part of the calculation of Margin Required and, therefore, forms part of the top up margin mechanics of Sections 1.1(a) and (b) of the Margin Provisions. The Additional Margin Amount is essentially the same as the concept of Independent Amount in the New York Law CSA and English Law CSA.

(c) Threshold

As stated before, a party's Threshold is the unsecured risk exposure you are willing to allow them before you consider calling margin.

The Threshold is usually a fixed monetary figure or linked to a party's senior unsecured debt credit rating which may fluctuate. Where the fluctuation results in the Threshold falling to zero, legal advice should previously have been taken that this will not be seen as a preference under the insolvency laws of the party suffering the downgrading.

Once the margin calculations are done, the Margin Required is the excess over the Threshold level. The Taker remains exposed to the Provider up to the Threshold level. However, it is possible for the parties to agree by appropriate drafting that once the Threshold has been exceeded, full margining is triggered which will reduce the Taker's Exposure to zero.

(d) Minimum Transfer Amount

To avoid transfers of small amounts parties can agree a Minimum Transfer Amount for each of them. This will normally be a fixed amount in the Base Currency or it can be linked to credit ratings.

The Minimum Transfer Amount need not be the same for each party if one party is much less creditworthy. Then its Minimum Transfer Amount will be set at a lower level. Minimum Transfer Amounts will usually reduce to zero if an Event of Default occurs or a party's debt obligations are downgraded below investment grade or cease to be rated at all. Again it would be wise to establish with lawyers that no preference is likely to take place under the insolvency laws of the downgraded party's jurisdiction of incorporation.

If no Minimum Transfer Amount is stated, it is deemed to be zero. The Minimum Transfer Amount is not part of the calculation of Margin Required. Rather it is applied once a Delivery Amount or Return Amount is calculated in order to ascertain if margin needs to be delivered at all.

Please note that Minimum Transfer Amount does not apply to transfers of Lock-up Margin or Substitutions, Distributions, Interest Amounts or amounts to be transferred under the dispute resolution process except for an undisputed amount.

Because the use of Minimum Transfer Amount only establishes a "floor", it does not eliminate the possibility that parties will be required to deliver uneven amounts of margin which is instead dealt with by use of a rounding convention as provided in Paragraph 5(e).

Rounding. [The Delivery Amount and the Return Amount will each be rounded down to the nearest integral multiple of .../up and down to the nearest integral multiple of ..., respectively]

(e) Rounding

You can devise your own rounding convention or choose one of two suggested here, i.e. (i) round each Delivery Amount and Return Amount down to the nearest integral multiple specified; or (ii) round each Delivery Amount up and each Return Amount down to the nearest integral multiple specified.

If no rounding convention is specified, then the Delivery Amount and the Return Amount will not be rounded.

For the reasons stated in Chapter 5 (p. 147) you would not normally round both Amounts up, as this would leave a Taker undercollateralised. Some market players use a rounding convention instead of specifying a Minimum Transfer Amount. It works but can be inconvenient operationally.

Note again that any agreed rounding convention does not apply to transfers of margin in relation to Lock-up Margin, Additional Margin Amounts, Substitutions, Distributions, Interest Amounts or amounts to be transferred under the dispute resolution process (other than an undisputed amount).

Paragraph 6. Dispute Resolution – Dispute Termination Event. For purposes of sub-Sections 1.6(b)(v)(F) and 1.6(c)(v), Dispute Termination Event is not applicable between the parties, unless otherwise stated here:

Paragraph 7. Dispute Resolution – Value. For the purpose of sub-Section 1.6(c)(iii), the Value of Eligible Margin or Margin Received will be re-calculated based on the higher of the bid price quoted by the Call Recipient or the offer price quoted by the Calling Party, in each case on the basis of a purchase by the Call Recipient from or a sale by the Calling Party to, independent third party dealers in the relevant security.

Paragraph 6: Dispute Resolution — Dispute Termination Event

Under each of the two dispute resolution procedures outlined in Section 1.6(b) (value of transactions) and Section 1.6(c) (value of collateral) one possible result of a failure to resolve the dispute is that either party may declare a Dispute Termination Event, leading to the early termination of all Transactions under the Agreement(s) on a no-fault basis. This allows each Transaction to be closed out at mid-market valuations. A Dispute Termination Event may only be declared, however, if it is stated as applicable in the Supplement.

Paragraph 6 of the Supplement is drafted so that Dispute Termination Event will not apply, unless the parties state otherwise. In other words, if they do not deal with this point in the Supplement, then it is assumed that Dispute Termination Event does not apply.

Paragraph 7: Dispute Resolution — Value

If a Calling Party disputes the value of any margin transferred to it following a margin call, Section 1.6(c)(ii) of the Margin Provisions requires the Call Recipient to recalculate the value of the margin transferred using any undisputed values quoted in the dispute notice and in accordance with the procedures (if any) laid down in the Supplement.

Paragraph 7 of the Supplement sets out a possible procedure, namely that the value of the margin will be recalculated "based on the higher of the bid price quoted by the Call Recipient or the offer price quoted by the Calling Party, in each case on the basis of a purchase by the Call Recipient from, or a sale by the Calling Party to, independent third party dealers in the relevant security.

This method of calculating the price is thought to be fair because it counterbalances (a) the Call Recipient's normal motivation to claim the highest possible Value for a transfer of a particular security as margin against (b) the Call Recipient's normal modus operandi, when buying the same security from an independent third party, to pay the lowest possible purchase price for the security. In the same way, this approach balances the Calling Party's usual incentive to ascribe the lowest possible value to a transfer of margin it has received against the Calling Party's normal position when selling the same security to an independent third party to sell it at the highest sale price it can get.

As between the Call Recipient's bid price and the Calling Party's offer price, the working group that prepared the Margin Provisions considered that the higher of the two prices was fair to both parties, but this does not preclude parties from taking another approach. This manner of calculating the price only apples to securities margin and works best if each of the parties trades securities in the normal course of its business. The values ascribed by each party to the margin are thus tested against the market which, therefore, assures the fairness of the final result.

In using the wording set out in Paragraph 7 parties may wish, for the sake of clarity, to delete the words "Eligible Margin or Margin Received" in the second line and to replace them with the words "any relevant margin in the form of a security".

Paragraph 8. Consent to Substitution. If specified here as applicable, then the Provider must obtain the Taker's consent for any substitution pursuant to Section 1.7(d): [applicable/inapplicable].

Paragraph 8: Consent to Substitution

The Provider must obtain the Taker's consent to any substitution under Section 1.7(d) of the Margin Provisions if such a consent requirement is stated as applying in the Supplement. Where nothing is stated, the consent requirement will not apply. Consent may be given in any reasonable form agreed by the parties who will need to take account of legal requirements in this respect in the jurisdictions where they are located.

The *User's Guide to the 2001 ISDA Margin Provisions* helpfully points out that Paragraph 8 is the only Paragraph of the Supplement referred to by number in the Margin Provisions and that if parties decide to depart from the Paragraph numbering of the Supplement, they may want to delete the words "Paragraph 8 of" in Section 1.7(d).

Paragraph 8 should, of course, be chosen to apply where automatic consent could lead to a Transaction or agreement being recharacterised and/or for the collateral to be ineffective for want of registration before a liquidation (see Chapter 3, pp. 36–37).

Paragraph 9. Interest Rate, Interest Amount and Interest Period. The Interest Rate in relation to Eligible Margin comprised of Cash in each currency will be:

Cash (specify currency)	Interest Rate

The Interest Amount will be computed for each Interest Period on a simple basis, pursuant to Section 1.8(c), unless otherwise stated here: _____.

The Interest Period end dates will be [the first calendar day of each month] [any date on which a Return Amount consisting wholly or partly of Cash is Transferred to the Provider pursuant to Section 1.1(b)] [specify other Interest Period end dates].

Paragraph 9: Interest Rate, Interest Amount and Interest Period

The parties can specify in Paragraph 9 of the Supplement the Interest Rate that will apply to the cash margin in each currency and, subject to certain conditions, paid to the Provider under Section 1.8(c) of the Margin Provisions.

Of course, it is possible for the parties to agree for no Interest Amounts to be paid on cash margin by applying a zero Interest Rate.

Interest Amounts are assumed to be calculated on a simple basis unless the parties state another basis here. The parties also specify in this Paragraph the Interest Period end dates. Two possibilities are suggested, one being the first calendar day of each month and the other being any date on which a Return Amount consisting wholly or partly of cash is transferred back to the Provider. Either or both of these could apply or the parties could state other alternatives. What is possible will depend on the parties' systems.

Paragraph 10. Demands and Notices.

Addresses for Demands and Notice:

Party A: _____.

Party B: _____.

Paragraph 11. Transfer Information.

Party A: _____.

Party B: _____.

Paragraph 12. Conditions Precedent and Rights and Remedies. The following events will be a Specified Condition for the party specified:

_____.

Paragraph 13. Obligations. The term "Obligations" as used in the Provisions includes the following additional obligations:

With respect to Party A: _____.

With respect to Party B: _____.

Paragraph 10: Demands and Notices

All demands and notices to be made under the Supplement are to be made pursuant to the Notices Section(s) of the various Agreement(s), unless otherwise stated in the Margin Provisions or in the Supplement. This would be Section 12 in the ISDA Master Agreement.

Paragraph 11: Transfer Information

This is where identification should be made of where transfers of Eligible Margin, Interest Amount (if applicable) and Equivalent Margin are to be paid or delivered.

Paragraph 12: Conditions Precedent and Rights and Remedies

Parties may specify Specified Conditions in connection with the conditions precedent in Section 1.2, the Use of the Margin Received provision in Section 2.2 and the enforcement provisions of Parts 2 and 3 and Section 4.1 of the Margin Provisions. With an ISDA Master Agreement, for example, this could include any of its Termination Events. Any Additional Termination Events specified should mirror those in the ISDA Master Agreement.

Paragraph 13: Obligations

"Obligations" is the term used in the Margin Provisions to describe all present and future obligations of a party under the Agreement(s), including under the Supplement itself.

The scope of the "Obligations" can be expanded to include obligations arising under agreements other than the ISDA Master Agreement(s) covered by the Supplement. Although the calculation of the Margin Required would remain limited to the Exposure of each party as Taker under the Agreement(s), the expansion of "Obligations" means that a Taker could apply any Margin Received against the additional obligations specified. In practice, the Taker would apply Margin Received first to its net risk exposure on the Provider and afterwards to the additional obligations. The Margin Provisions, however, do not require that the Obligations are actually discharged in this order.

Paragraph 14. Eligibility to Hold Margin Received; Custodians. Party A and its Custodian will be entitled to hold Margin Received pursuant to Section 2.2(b); *provided* that the following conditions applicable to Party A are satisfied:

    (i)   An Event of Default with respect to Party A has not occurred and is then continuing.

    (ii) Margin Received may be held only in the following jurisdictions:

                       _____.

              Initially, the Custodian for Party A is

                       _____.

Party B and its Custodian will be entitled to hold Margin Received pursuant to Section 2.2(b); *provided* that the following conditions applicable to Party B are satisfied:

    (i)   An Event of Default with respect to Party B has not occurred and is then continuing.

    (ii) Margin Received may be held only in the following jurisdictions:

                       _____.

              Initially, the Custodian for Party B is

                       _____.

Paragraph 14: Eligibility to hold Margin Received; Custodians

This Paragraph only applies to the New York law security interest approach set out in Part 2 of the Margin Provisions.

Under Section 2.2(b), the Taker and its specified Custodian (if any) will be entitled to hold Margin Received provided that the conditions stated in the Supplement are satisfied. Two such conditions are set out in Paragraph 14 of the Supplement in a "tick box" choice.

One condition is that no Event of Default has occurred in respect of Party A or Party B. This condition is usually chosen as a matter of course. The other condition is that Margin Received may be held in certain specified jurisdictions which are chosen by the parties according to their own circumstances. These may be specific countries (or specific legal jurisdictions within those countries, e.g. New York in relation to the US). Other conditions may be applied, e.g. financial eligibility tests.

The identity of the Custodian may be stated in the Supplement, if desired.

Paragraph 15. Use of Margin Received. The provisions of Section 2.2(c) will not apply to the [party/parties] specified here:

[ ] Party A

[ ] Party B

and [that party/those parties] will not be permitted to: _____.

Paragraph 16. Other Provisions.

IN WITNESS WHEREOF the parties have executed this document on the respective dates set forth below with effect from the date of the Supplement referenced on the first page of this document.

_____	_____
(Name of Party)	(Name of Party)

By: _____   By: _____
Name: Name:
Title: Title:
Date: Date:

Paragraph 15: Use of Margin Received

Again this Paragraph only applies to the New York Law security interest approach set out in Part 2 of the Margin Provisions.

Under Section 2.2(c) the Taker has the right to use Margin Received as set forth in Section 2.2(c)(i) and (ii) unless otherwise provided in the Supplement. In other words, the Taker's right to use its margin is assured unless the parties specifically choose the opposite.

Paragraph 15 of the Supplement sets out in a "tick box" format the possibility of disapplying this right of use in relation to one or both parties. In addition, the parties may specify certain limitations or conditions on the use of any Margin Received to either party in its capacity as Taker.

Paragraph 16: Other Provisions

Paragraph 16 is the place to include modifications to specific clauses of the Margin Provisions as well as additional provisions. This is very similar to the function of the ISDA Master Agreement Schedule.

Signature Block

The Supplement includes a signing block. Where the Supplement is used with an ISDA Master Agreement, it forms part of the ISDA Master Agreement and, therefore, does not really need to be signed separately although local legal advice should be taken on this point in each jurisdiction where margin assets are located. Many parties sign ISDA Master Agreement Schedules nowadays and may prefer to do the same with the Supplement even though it is not strictly necessary.

Hopefully if there is another edition of this book, we can study a completed Supplement and variants of wording and provisions used in it.

New developments　9

The world of collateral continues alive and dynamic on all sides. On the documentation front the initiatives over the past 18 months have been and are:

- the European Directive on collateral financial arrangements;
- the draft Hague Convention on indirectly held securities;
- the ISDA 2001 Credit Support Protocol (now closed);
- ISDA bilateral Amendment Agreement;
- ISDA Collateral Asset Definitions project;
- ISDA electronic data interchange project;
- 2002 Margin Survey;
- changes to US Insolvency laws.

Taking each of these in turn:

Progress on the European Directive on collateral financial arrangements and the draft Hague Convention on indirectly held securities have already been discussed in Chapter 3 on pp. 44–45. These are highly significant initiatives in the legal framework of the future European collateral market for derivatives products.

ISDA 2001 CREDIT SUPPORT PROTOCOL

The term "Margin" which features prominently in the *2001 ISDA Margin Provisions* gave way to Credit Support here because the Protocol offered the chance to amend certain provisions in existing Credit Support Annexes.

On 1 August 2001, ISDA published this Protocol which through the selection of ten Annexes (five each for the English Law CSA and the New York Law CSA) allowed parties to amend certain provisions in their CSAs on a multilateral basis.

ISDA had used this Protocol route twice before with European Monetary Union in 1998 and in 2000 before the entry of the Greek drachma into the EU single currency regime.

The 10 Annexes were:

English Law CSA	New York Law CSA
Annex 1 Transfer Timing	Annex 1 Transfer Timing
Annex 2 Dispute Resolution	Annex 2 Dispute Resolution
Annex 3 Dispute Termination Event	Annex 3 Dispute Termination Event
Annex 4 Exchanges	Annex 4 Substitutions
Annex 5 Definitions	Annex 5 Definitions

The wording of the *2001 ISDA Margin Provisions* is closely followed in relation to all these matters.

The Protocol was open for adherence from 1 August 2001 until 28 February 2002. Unfortunately, only one party registered as an Adhering Party and as two are needed to tango, the Protocol closed ineffective.

It is possible that the Protocol will be revived in the future when the Margin Provisions are more in use and, if so, it is worth mentioning its principal features. Under such a Protocol, parties choose which Annexes they will adopt and state this in a letter to ISDA in a prescribed form. ISDA registers their choices on its website. The Annexes chosen are matched with those of other Adhering Parties and where they correspond the CSAs between them are deemed amended from the date the later Adhering Party's choices are registered by ISDA.

Please note that:

- the Protocol cannot be negotiated or have terms added to or deleted from it;

- the underlying ISDA Master Agreement and CSA remain in full force and effect after the Protocol Annexes are adopted;

- the Protocol and Adherence Letter are governed by the same governing law as the CSA;

- ISDA had obtained clean English and New York law opinions on the Protocol's enforceability.

ISDA BILATERAL AMENDMENT AGREEMENT

As an alternative, ISDA has also published a form of bilateral Amendment Agreement with the same Annexes which parties can complete with certain of their counterparties if they preferred not to follow the Protocol route. This Amendment Agreement is reproduced as Annex 8 by kind permission of the International Swaps and Derivatives Association, Inc.

So, in summary, ISDA offered four ways of dealing with collateral documentation, viz:

Whole relationship
- Use of existing ISDA credit support documentation;
- use of 2001 ISDA Margin Provisions and Supplement.

Part of relationship
- Adherence to the 2001 ISDA Credit Support Protocol for certain matters on a multilateral basis (now closed);

- negotiation of an Amendment Agreement for the same matters on a bilateral basis.

The choice is yours!

ISDA COLLATERAL ASSET DEFINITIONS PROJECT

At its AGM in Berlin in April 2001, ISDA announced a new project to produce a definitions booklet for collateral assets which will complement the existing ISDA Credit Support Documents.

Among the reasons given for doing this were:

- to make market practice more predictable;
- to use a greater range of assets;
- to establish central valuation guidelines;
- to improve control over the collateral pool;
- to supplement the range of useful ISDA definitions booklets.

One of the problems which has arisen in the market is that even eligible collateral descriptions in Credit Support Annexes can have unintended delivery consequences.

The following example was quoted in the presentation:

The CSA may state:

negotiable debt obligations issued by the Government of the United States of America having a remaining maturity of more than one year but not more than 10 years.

One imagines a delivery of US Treasury bills, notes or bonds depending upon tenor. However, a counterparty could deliver TIPS within this description and are US government agencies altogether excluded?

TIPS are Treasury Inflation Protected Securities issued by the US Treasury through auctions three times a year. Fixed interest is paid twice yearly upon the inflation adjusted principal of the bonds. Principal adjusted for inflation is paid out upon the maturity of these bonds after ten years. With inflation adjustment to these securities every six months at coupon payment times, valuation of them for haircutting purposes is a little more complex than usual.

The *Collateral Asset Definitions* will strive to clarify this and similar issues for the market by proposing a standard set of terms and definitions for collateral assets. The aim is to include eligible collateral lists in ISDA Credit Support Documents by making reference to the *Collateral Asset Definitions*. With existing counterparties, it is proposed that the updating of eligible collateral lists between them should be done in a way which limits the need to renegotiate existing documentation. It is anticipated that the *Collateral Asset Definitions* will include definitions of commonly used asset groups, standard valuation percentages for given holding periods and defined price sources.

Benefits arising from the use of the greater range of assets could be better use of the diversity of potential collateral assets which a firm may have, cross-product margining and access to new market players who may not hold significant amounts of government securities. However, they may have asset backed securities, mortgage backed securities, equities, corporate bonds or commodities, for example, all of which could be offered as collateral with appropriate haircuts.

As regards asset valuations, the *Collateral Asset Definitions* would seek to provide sufficient information so that pricing and reference sources can be respectively agreed for securities and interest rates. A haircut methodology is also being explored which, inter alia, will define holding periods and a process for changing haircuts where they are outdated or where a security, for instance, becomes illiquid or in periods of high price volatility in the market. Formal reviews of haircuts may be at regular intervals or upon the triggering of certain events, e.g. credit rating downgrades.

Improvements in controls could include:

- criteria for rejecting collateral;
- amending a Credit Support Annex without renegotiation through adoption of relevant parts of the *Collateral Asset Definitions*;
- possible easier communications with traders, credit officers and regulators through the use of common terms.

The *Collateral Asset Definitions* project is advancing well and the aim is to produce a booklet defining debt and equity securities and cash in the main collateral centres in Europe, the US and Asia by the time of ISDA's next AGM in Tokyo in April 2003.

ISDA ELECTRONIC DATA INTERCHANGE PROJECT

ISDA has formed a working group to design standard formats for portfolio information notices in Excel and XML to make reconciliations easier both at the start of a collateralised relationship and in dispute situations.

The working group is also exploring the establishment of a automatic data feed between collateral agreement legal databases and collateral operating systems.

Some consideration is being given to proposing a standard format for margin call notices.

2002 MARGIN SURVEY

A new ISDA Margin Survey convering 2002 is due to be published at the start of 2003. This should be an even more useful reflection of the collateral market than previous surveys because twice as many firms have participated than in the *ISDA Margin Survey 2001*.

CHANGES TO US INSOLVENCY LAWS

The US Congress is currently attempting to amend several Federal statutes that affect the insolvency treatment of over-the-counter derivative transactions. While not specifically treating collateralisation issues, they do clarify and eliminate several ambiguities in Federal statutes. Unfortunately, many of these changes are still bottled up in Congressional committees, although it is anticipated that they will be approved sooner rather than later.

For example, Congress is attempting to broaden the derivative friendly US Bankruptcy Code provisions that provide special treatment to creditors who have entered into over-the-counter derivative transactions with now insolvent debtors. Many of these changes expand the number and type of transactions that are eligible for special treatment under various Federal insolvency statutes. These changes would provide additional legal certainty as creditors exercise their rights under Credit Support Documents.

Congress is also attempting to strengthen the statutory protections extended to netting agreements between "financial institutions" under FDICIA. For example, currently only netting agreements governed by US law are covered by the statute. Congress is trying to extend that to include those agreements governed by laws other than US law.

THE FUTURE

In Chapter 4, I foreshadowed a likely trend of concentration and centralisation of collateral activities within firms and a break up of separate product fiefdoms which have developed over the years but which essentially do the same thing *vis-à-vis* collateralisation. If implemented successfully, this should optimise the use of collateral and lead to improvements in operational efficiencies and, of course, staff allocation. Doubtless, it will need a high IT content to develop the necessary systems.

Some banks are already offering Collateral Management services to customers but clearly there is scope to expand this to a management service across various derivatives and securities products. Such a service would provide customers with a single contact point for common reporting and position management for many different products. The service would, of course, need secure electronic information delivery systems. It would also offer enhanced payment netting opportunities across products.

It would require increased analysis of the legal impact of each of its constituents, better training of collateral management staff given the likely increased complexity of their roles and need for greater product knowledge and enhanced risk management systems to monitor and control the various inherent risks, both old and new.

The motivations of this are, therefore, better use of collateral resources within firms and better focus on customer needs.

As far as firms are concerned, it is not just a question of if it moves collateralise it, but if it is collateralised, move it. The dynamic environment outlined above is, I think, one which is full of opportunity for those who want to embrace it.

Now is a good time to be a collateral manager!

Annexes

We have provided these nine Annexes in the hope that they might provide useful reference material in one place.

Annex 1

A facsimile of the ISDA Credit Support Annex (Bilateral Form – Transfer. Subject to English Law) (reproduced with the kind permission of the International Swaps and Derivatives Association, Inc.).

Annex 2

A facsimile of the ISDA Credit Support Annex (Bilateral Form. Subject to New York Law) (reproduced with the kind permission of the International Swaps and Derivatives Association, Inc.).

Annex 3

List of countries where ISDA has obtained collateral legal opinions.

Annex 4

Relevant extracts from the New York Uniform Commercial Code.

Annex 5

Form of Amendment Agreement from Appendix A of the *User's Guide to the ISDA Credit Support Documents under English Law.*

Annex 6

A facsimile of the ISDA Credit Support Deed (Bilateral Form – Security Interest. Subject to English Law) (reproduced with the kind permission of the International Swaps and Derivatives Association, Inc.).

Annex 7

A facsimile of the ISDA Credit Support Annex (Bilateral Form – Loan and Pledge. Subject to Japanese Law) (reproduced with the kind permission of the International Swaps and Derivatives Association, Inc.).

Annex 8

Two Amendment Agreements for agreeing certain provisions in the *2001 ISDA Margin Provisions* on a bilateral basis.

Annex 9

A facsimile of the *2001 ISDA Margin Provisions* (reproduced with the kind permission of the International Swaps and Derivatives Association, Inc.).

ANNEX I
ISDA CREDIT SUPPORT ANNEX SUBJECT TO ENGLISH LAW

(Bilateral Form - Transfer)[1]   (ISDA Agreements Subject to English Law)[2]

International Swaps and Derivatives Association, Inc.

CREDIT SUPPORT ANNEX

to the Schedule to the

ISDA Master Agreement

dated as of ....

between

.... and ....
("Party A")   ("Party B")

This Annex supplements, forms part of, and is subject to, the ISDA Master Agreement referred to above and is part of its Schedule. For the purposes of this Agreement, including, without limitation, Sections 1(c), 2(a), 5 and 6, the credit support arrangements set out in this Annex constitute a Transaction (for which this Annex constitutes the Confirmation).

Paragraph 1. Interpretation

Capitalised terms not otherwise defined in this Annex or elsewhere in this Agreement have the meanings specified pursuant to Paragraph 10, and all references in this Annex to Paragraphs are to Paragraphs of this Annex. In the event of any inconsistency between this Annex and the other provisions of this Schedule, this Annex will prevail, and in the event of any inconsistency between Paragraph 11 and the other

---

[1] This document is not intended to create a charge or other security interest over the assets transferred under its terms. Persons intending to establish a collateral arrangement based on the creation of a charge or other security interest should consider using the ISDA Credit Support Deed (English law) or the ISDA Credit Support Annex (New York law), as appropriate.

[2] This Credit Support Annex has been prepared for use with ISDA Master Agreements subject to English law. Users should consult their legal advisers as to the proper use and effect of this form and the arrangements it contemplates. In particular, users should consult their legal advisers if they wish to have the Credit Support Annex made subject to a governing law other than English law or to have the Credit Support Annex subject to a different governing law than that governing the rest of the ISDA Master Agreement (e.g., English law for the Credit Support Annex and New York law for the rest of the ISDA Master Agreement).

provisions of this Annex, Paragraph 11 will prevail. For the avoidance of doubt, references to "transfer" in this Annex mean, in relation to cash, payment and, in relation to other assets, delivery.

Paragraph 2. Credit Support Obligations

(a)   *Delivery Amount.* Subject to Paragraphs 3 and 4, upon a demand made by the Transferee on or promptly following a Valuation Date, if the Delivery Amount for that Valuation Date equals or exceeds the Transferor's Minimum Transfer Amount, then the Transferor will transfer to the Transferee Eligible Credit Support having a Value as of the date of transfer at least equal to the applicable Delivery Amount (rounded pursuant to Paragraph 11(b)(iii)(D)).   Unless otherwise specified in Paragraph 11(b), the "Delivery Amount" applicable to the Transferor for any Valuation Date will equal the amount by which:

(i)   the Credit Support Amount

exceeds

(ii)   the Value as of that Valuation Date of the Transferor's Credit Support Balance (adjusted to include any prior Delivery Amount and to exclude any prior Return Amount, the transfer of which, in either case, has not yet been completed and for which the relevant Settlement Day falls on or after such Valuation Date).

(b)   *Return Amount.* Subject to Paragraphs 3 and 4, upon a demand made by the Transferor on or promptly following a Valuation Date, if the Return Amount for that Valuation Date equals or exceeds the Transferee's Minimum Transfer Amount, then the Transferee will transfer to the Transferor Equivalent Credit Support specified by the Transferor in that demand having a Value as of the date of transfer as close as practicable to the applicable Return Amount (rounded pursuant to Paragraph 11(b)(iii)(D)) and the Credit Support Balance will, upon such transfer, be reduced accordingly.   Unless otherwise specified in Paragraph 11(b), the "Return Amount" applicable to the Transferee for any Valuation Date will equal the amount by which:

(i)   the Value as of that Valuation Date of the Transferor's Credit Support Balance (adjusted to include any prior Delivery Amount and to exclude any prior Return Amount, the transfer of which, in either case, has not yet been completed and for which the relevant Settlement Day falls on or after such Valuation Date)

exceeds

(ii)   the Credit Support Amount.

Paragraph 3. Transfers, Calculations and Exchanges

(a)   *Transfers.* All transfers under this Annex of any Eligible Credit Support, Equivalent Credit Support, Interest Amount or Equivalent Distributions shall be made in accordance with the instructions of the Transferee or Transferor, as applicable, and shall be made:

(i)   in the case of cash, by transfer into one or more bank accounts specified by the recipient;

(ii)   in the case of certificated securities which cannot or which the parties have agreed will not be delivered by book-entry, by delivery in appropriate physical form to the recipient or its account accompanied by any duly executed instruments of transfer, transfer tax stamps and any other documents necessary to constitute a legally valid transfer of the transferring party's legal and beneficial title to the recipient; and

(iii)   in the case of securities which the parties have agreed will be delivered by book-entry, by the giving of written instructions (including, for the avoidance of doubt, instructions given by telex, facsimile transmission or electronic messaging system) to the relevant depository institution or other entity specified by the recipient, together with a written copy of the instructions to the recipient, sufficient, if complied with, to result in a legally effective transfer of the transferring party's legal and beneficial title to the recipient.

Subject to Paragraph 4 and unless otherwise specified, if a demand for the transfer of Eligible Credit Support or Equivalent Credit Support is received by the Notification Time, then the relevant transfer will be made not later than the close of business on the Settlement Day relating to the date such demand is received; if a demand is received after the Notification Time, then the relevant transfer will be made not later than the close of business on the Settlement Day relating to the day after the date such demand is received.

(b)   **Calculations.** All calculations of Value and Exposure for purposes of Paragraphs 2 and 4(a) will be made by the relevant Valuation Agent as of the relevant Valuation Time. The Valuation Agent will notify each party (or the other party, if the Valuation Agent is a party) of its calculations not later than the Notification Time on the Local Business Day following the applicable Valuation Date (or, in the case of Paragraph 4(a), following the date of calculation).

(c)   **Exchanges.**

(i)   Unless otherwise specified in Paragraph 11, the Transferor may on any Local Business Day by notice inform the Transferee that it wishes to transfer to the Transferee Eligible Credit Support specified in that notice (the "New Credit Support") in exchange for certain Eligible Credit Support (the "Original Credit Support") specified in that notice comprised in the Transferor's Credit Support Balance.

(ii)   If the Transferee notifies the Transferor that it has consented to the proposed exchange, (A) the Transferor will be obliged to transfer the New Credit Support to the Transferee on the first Settlement Day following the date on which it receives notice (which may be oral telephonic notice) from the Transferee of its consent and (B) the Transferee will be obliged to transfer to the Transferor Equivalent Credit Support in respect of the Original Credit Support not later than the Settlement Day following the date on which the Transferee receives the New Credit Support, unless otherwise specified in Paragraph 11(d) (the "Exchange Date"); *provided* that the Transferee will only be obliged to transfer Equivalent Credit Support with a Value as of the date of transfer as close as practicable to, but in any event not more than, the Value of the New Credit Support as of that date.

3

Paragraph 4. Dispute Resolution

(a)   *Disputed Calculations or Valuations.* If a party (a "Disputing Party") reasonably disputes (I) the Valuation Agent's calculation of a Delivery Amount or a Return Amount or (II) the Value of any transfer of Eligible Credit Support or Equivalent Credit Support, then:

(1)   the Disputing Party will notify the other party and the Valuation Agent (if the Valuation Agent is not the other party) not later than the close of business on the Local Business Day following, in the case of (I) above, the date that the demand is received under Paragraph 2 or, in the case of (II) above, the date of transfer;

(2)   in the case of (I) above, the appropriate party will transfer the undisputed amount to the other party not later than the close of business on the Settlement Day following the date that the demand is received under Paragraph 2;

(3)   the parties will consult with each other in an attempt to resolve the dispute; and

(4)   if they fail to resolve the dispute by the Resolution Time, then:

(i)   in the case of a dispute involving a Delivery Amount or Return Amount, unless otherwise specified in Paragraph 11(c), the Valuation Agent will recalculate the Exposure and the Value as of the Recalculation Date by:

(A)   utilising any calculations of that part of the Exposure attributable to the Transactions that the parties have agreed are not in dispute;

(B)   calculating that part of the Exposure attributable to the Transactions in dispute by seeking four actual quotations at mid-market from Reference Market-makers for purposes of calculating Market Quotation, and taking the arithmetic average of those obtained; *provided* that if four quotations are not available for a particular Transaction, then fewer than four quotations may be used for that Transaction, and if no quotations are available for a particular Transaction, then the Valuation Agent's original calculations will be used for the Transaction; and

(C)   utilising the procedures specified in Paragraph 11(e)(ii) for calculating the Value, if disputed, of the outstanding Credit Support Balance;

(ii)   in the case of a dispute involving the Value of any transfer of Eligible Credit Support or Equivalent Credit Support, the Valuation Agent will recalculate the Value as of the date of transfer pursuant to Paragraph 11(e)(ii).

Following a recalculation pursuant to this Paragraph, the Valuation Agent will notify each party (or the other party, if the Valuation Agent is a party) as soon as possible but in any event not later than the Notification Time on the Local Business Day following the Resolution Time. The appropriate party will, upon demand following such notice given by the Valuation Agent or a resolution pursuant to (3) above and subject to Paragraph 3(a), make the appropriate transfer.

4

(b)   *No Event of Default.* The failure by a party to make a transfer of any amount which is the subject of a dispute to which Paragraph 4(a) applies will not constitute an Event of Default for as long as the procedures set out in this Paragraph 4 are being carried out. For the avoidance of doubt, upon completion of those procedures, Section 5(a)(i) of this Agreement will apply to any failure by a party to make a transfer required under the final sentence of Paragraph 4(a) on the relevant due date.

Paragraph 5. Transfer of Title, No Security Interest, Distributions and Interest Amount

(a)   *Transfer of Title.* Each party agrees that all right, title and interest in and to any Eligible Credit Support, Equivalent Credit Support, Equivalent Distributions or Interest Amount which it transfers to the other party under the terms of this Annex shall vest in the recipient free and clear of any liens, claims, charges or encumbrances or any other interest of the transferring party or of any third person (other than a lien routinely imposed on all securities in a relevant clearance system).

(b)   *No Security Interest.* Nothing in this Annex is intended to create or does create in favour of either party any mortgage, charge, lien, pledge, encumbrance or other security interest in any cash or other property transferred by one party to the other party under the terms of this Annex.

(c)   *Distributions and Interest Amount.*

(i)   *Distributions.* The Transferee will transfer to the Transferor not later than the Settlement Day following each Distributions Date cash, securities or other property of the same type, nominal value, description and amount as the relevant Distributions ("Equivalent Distributions") to the extent that a Delivery Amount would not be created or increased by the transfer, as calculated by the Valuation Agent (and the date of calculation will be deemed a Valuation Date for this purpose).

(ii)   *Interest Amount.* Unless otherwise specified in Paragraph 11(f)(iii), the Transferee will transfer to the Transferor at the times specified in Paragraph 11(f)(ii) the relevant Interest Amount to the extent that a Delivery Amount would not be created or increased by the transfer, as calculated by the Valuation Agent (and the date of calculation will be deemed a Valuation Date for this purpose).

Paragraph 6. Default

If an Early Termination Date is designated or deemed to occur as a result of an Event of Default in relation to a party, an amount equal to the Value of the Credit Support Balance, determined as though the Early Termination Date were a Valuation Date, will be deemed to be an Unpaid Amount due to the Transferor (which may or may not be the Defaulting Party) for purposes of Section 6(e). For the avoidance of doubt, if Market Quotation is the applicable payment measure for purposes of Section 6(e), then the Market Quotation determined under Section 6(e) in relation to the Transaction constituted by this Annex will be deemed to be zero, and, if Loss is the applicable payment measure for purposes of Section 6(e), then the Loss determined under Section 6(e) in relation to the Transaction will be limited to the Unpaid Amount representing the Value of the Credit Support Balance.

Paragraph 7. Representation

Each party represents to the other party (which representation will be deemed to be repeated as of each date on which it transfers Eligible Credit Support, Equivalent Credit Support or Equivalent Distributions) that it is the sole owner of or otherwise has the right to transfer all Eligible Credit Support, Equivalent Credit Support or Equivalent Distributions it transfers to the other party under this Annex, free and clear of any security interest, lien, encumbrance or other restriction (other than a lien routinely imposed on all securities in a relevant clearance system).

Paragraph 8. Expenses

Each party will pay its own costs and expenses (including any stamp, transfer or similar transaction tax or duty payable on any transfer it is required to make under this Annex) in connection with performing its obligations under this Annex, and neither party will be liable for any such costs and expenses incurred by the other party.

Paragraph 9. Miscellaneous

(a)   *Default Interest.* Other than in the case of an amount which is the subject of a dispute under Paragraph 4(a), if a Transferee fails to make, when due, any transfer of Equivalent Credit Support, Equivalent Distributions or the Interest Amount, it will be obliged to pay the Transferor (to the extent permitted under applicable law) an amount equal to interest at the Default Rate multiplied by the Value on the relevant Valuation Date of the items of property that were required to be transferred, from (and including) the date that the Equivalent Credit Support, Equivalent Distributions or Interest Amount were required to be transferred to (but excluding) the date of transfer of the Equivalent Credit Support, Equivalent Distributions or Interest Amount.   This interest will be calculated on the basis of daily compounding and the actual number of days elapsed.

(b)   *Good Faith and Commercially Reasonable Manner.* Performance of all obligations under this Annex, including, but not limited to, all calculations, valuations and determinations made by either party, will be made in good faith and in a commercially reasonable manner.

(c)   *Demands and Notices.* All demands and notices given by a party under this Annex will be given as specified in Section 12 of this Agreement.

(d)   *Specifications of Certain Matters.* Anything referred to in this Annex as being specified in Paragraph 11 also may be specified in one or more Confirmations or other documents and this Annex will be construed accordingly.

Paragraph 10. Definitions

As used in this Annex:

"Base Currency" means the currency specified as such in Paragraph 11(a)(i).

"Base Currency Equivalent" means, with respect to an amount on a Valuation Date, in the case of an amount denominated in the Base Currency, such Base Currency amount and, in the case of an amount denominated in a currency other than the Base Currency (the "Other Currency"), the amount of Base Currency required to purchase such amount of the Other Currency at the spot exchange rate determined by the Valuation Agent for value on such Valuation Date.

"Credit Support Amount" means, with respect to a Transferor on a Valuation Date, (i) the Transferee's Exposure plus (ii) all Independent Amounts applicable to the Transferor, if any, minus (iii) all Independent Amounts applicable to the Transferee, if any, minus (iv) the Transferor's Threshold; *provided, however,* that the Credit Support Amount will be deemed to be zero whenever the calculation of Credit Support Amount yields a number less than zero.

"Credit Support Balance" means, with respect to a Transferor on a Valuation Date, the aggregate of all Eligible Credit Support that has been transferred to or received by the Transferee under this Annex, together with any Distributions and all proceeds of any such Eligible Credit Support or Distributions, as reduced pursuant to Paragraph 2(b), 3(c)(ii) or 6. Any Equivalent Distributions or Interest Amount (or portion of either) not transferred pursuant to Paragraph 5(c)(i) or (ii) will form part of the Credit Support Balance.

"Delivery Amount" has the meaning specified in Paragraph 2(a).

"Disputing Party" has the meaning specified in Paragraph 4.

"Distributions" means, with respect to any Eligible Credit Support comprised in the Credit Support Balance consisting of securities, all principal, interest and other payments and distributions of cash or other property to which a holder of securities of the same type, nominal value, description and amount as such Eligible Credit Support would be entitled from time to time.

"Distributions Date" means, with respect to any Eligible Credit Support comprised in the Credit Support Balance other than cash, each date on which a holder of such Eligible Credit Support is entitled to receive Distributions or, if that date is not a Local Business Day, the next following Local Business Day.

"Eligible Credit Support" means, with respect to a party, the items, if any, specified as such for that party in Paragraph 11(b)(ii) including, in relation to any securities, if applicable, the proceeds of any redemption in whole or in part of such securities by the relevant issuer.

"Eligible Currency" means each currency specified as such in Paragraph 11(a)(ii), if such currency is freely available.

"Equivalent Credit Support" means, in relation to any Eligible Credit Support comprised in the Credit Support Balance, Eligible Credit Support of the same type, nominal value, description and amount as that Eligible Credit Support.

"Equivalent Distributions" has the meaning specified in Paragraph 5(c)(i).

"Exchange Date" has the meaning specified in Paragraph 11(d).

ISDA® 1995

451

"Exposure" means, with respect to a party on a Valuation Date and subject to Paragraph 4 in the case of a dispute, the amount, if any, that would be payable to that party by the other party (expressed as a positive number) or by that party to the other party (expressed as a negative number) pursuant to Section 6(e)(ii)(1) of this Agreement if all Transactions (other than the Transaction constituted by this Annex) were being terminated as of the relevant Valuation Time, on the basis that (i) that party is not the Affected Party and (ii) the Base Currency is the Termination Currency; *provided* that Market Quotations will be determined by the Valuation Agent on behalf of that party using its estimates at mid-market of the amounts that would be paid for Replacement Transactions (as that term is defined in the definition of "Market Quotation").

"Independent Amount" means, with respect to a party, the Base Currency Equivalent of the amount specified as such for that party in Paragraph 11(b)(iii)(A); if no amount is specified, zero.

"Interest Amount" means, with respect to an Interest Period, the aggregate sum of the Base Currency Equivalents of the amounts of interest determined for each relevant currency and calculated for each day in that Interest Period on the principal amount of the portion of the Credit Support Balance comprised of cash in such currency, determined by the Valuation Agent for each such day as follows:

(x)   the amount of cash in such currency on that day; multiplied by

(y)   the relevant Interest Rate in effect for that day; divided by

(z)   360 (or, in the case of pounds sterling, 365).

"Interest Period" means the period from (and including) the last Local Business Day on which an Interest Amount was transferred (or, if no Interest Amount has yet been transferred, the Local Business Day on which Eligible Credit Support or Equivalent Credit Support in the form of cash was transferred to or received by the Transferee) to (but excluding) the Local Business Day on which the current Interest Amount is transferred.

"Interest Rate" means, with respect to an Eligible Currency, the rate specified in Paragraph 11(f)(i) for that currency.

"Local Business Day", unless otherwise specified in Paragraph 11(h), means:

(i)   in relation to a transfer of cash or other property (other than securities) under this Annex, a day on which commercial banks are open for business (including dealings in foreign exchange and foreign currency deposits) in the place where the relevant account is located and, if different, in the principal financial centre, if any, of the currency of such payment;

(ii)   in relation to a transfer of securities under this Annex, a day on which the clearance system agreed between the parties for delivery of the securities is open for the acceptance and execution of settlement instructions or, if delivery of the securities is contemplated by other means, a day on which commercial banks are open for business (including dealings in foreign exchange and foreign currency deposits) in the place(s) agreed between the parties for this purpose;

8

ISDA® 1995

(iii)   in relation to a valuation under this Annex, a day on which commercial banks are open for business (including dealings in foreign exchange and foreign currency deposits) in the place of location of the Valuation Agent and in the place(s) agreed between the parties for this purpose; and

(iv)   in relation to any notice or other communication under this Annex, a day on which commercial banks are open for business (including dealings in foreign exchange and foreign currency deposits) in the place specified in the address for notice most recently provided by the recipient.

"Minimum Transfer Amount" means, with respect to a party, the amount specified as such for that party in Paragraph 11(b)(iii)(C); if no amount is specified, zero.

"New Credit Support" has the meaning specified in Paragraph 3(c)(i).

"Notification Time" has the meaning specified in Paragraph 11(c)(iv).

"Recalculation Date" means the Valuation Date that gives rise to the dispute under Paragraph 4; *provided, however,* that if a subsequent Valuation Date occurs under Paragraph 2 prior to the resolution of the dispute, then the *"Recalculation Date"* means the most recent Valuation Date under Paragraph 2.

"Resolution Time" has the meaning specified in Paragraph 11(c)(i).

"Return Amount" has the meaning specified in Paragraph 2(b).

"Settlement Day" means, in relation to a date, (i) with respect to a transfer of cash or other property (other than securities), the next Local Business Day and (ii) with respect to a transfer of securities, the first Local Business Day after such date on which settlement of a trade in the relevant securities, if effected on such date, would have been settled in accordance with customary practice when settling through the clearance system agreed between the parties for delivery of such securities or, otherwise, on the market in which such securities are principally traded (or, in either case, if there is no such customary practice, on the first Local Business Day after such date on which it is reasonably practicable to deliver such securities).

"Threshold" means, with respect to a party, the Base Currency Equivalent of the amount specified as such for that party in Paragraph 11(b)(iii)(B); if no amount is specified, zero.

"Transferee" means, in relation to each Valuation Date, the party in respect of which Exposure is a positive number and, in relation to a Credit Support Balance, the party which, subject to this Annex, owes such Credit Support Balance or, as the case may be, the Value of such Credit Support Balance to the other party.

"Transferor" means, in relation to a Transferee, the other party.

"Valuation Agent" has the meaning specified in Paragraph 11(c)(i).

"Valuation Date" means each date specified in or otherwise determined pursuant to Paragraph 11(c)(ii).

"Valuation Percentage" means, for any item of Eligible Credit Support, the percentage specified in Paragraph 11(b)(ii).

"Valuation Time" has the meaning specified in Paragraph 11(c)(iii).

"Value" means, for any Valuation Date or other date for which Value is calculated, and subject to Paragraph 4 in the case of a dispute, with respect to:

(i)   Eligible Credit Support comprised in a Credit Support Balance that is:

    (A)   an amount of cash, the Base Currency Equivalent of such amount multiplied by the applicable Valuation Percentage, if any; and

    (B)   a security, the Base Currency Equivalent of the bid price obtained by the Valuation Agent multiplied by the applicable Valuation Percentage, if any; and

(ii)   items that are comprised in a Credit Support Balance and are not Eligible Credit Support, zero.

ISDA® 1995

Paragraph 11. Elections and Variables

(a) *Base Currency and Eligible Currency.*

   (i) "Base Currency" means United States Dollars unless otherwise specified here:

   ....

   (ii) "Eligible Currency" means the Base Currency and each other currency specified here:

   ....
   ....

(b) *Credit Support Obligations.*

   (i) *Delivery Amount, Return Amount and Credit Support Amount.*

   (A) *"Delivery Amount"* has the meaning specified in Paragraph 2(a), unless otherwise specified here: ....

   (B) *"Return Amount"* has the meaning specified in Paragraph 2(b), unless otherwise specified here: ....

   (C) *"Credit Support Amount"* has the meaning specified in Paragraph 10, unless otherwise specified here: ....

   (ii) *Eligible Credit Support.* The following items will qualify as *"Eligible Credit Support"* for the party specified:

		Party A	Party B	Valuation Percentage
(A)	cash in an Eligible Currency	[ ]	[ ]	[ ]%
(B)	negotiable debt obligations issued by the Government of [ ] having an original maturity at issuance of not more than one year	[ ]	[ ]	[ ]%
(C)	negotiable debt obligations issued by the Government of [ ] having an original maturity at issuance of more than one year but not more than 10 years	[ ]	[ ]	[ ]%

ISDA® 1995

(D)   negotiable debt obligations issued by the   [ ]   [ ]   [ ]%
        Government of [   ] having an
        original maturity at issuance of more than
        10 years

(E)   other: ....   [ ]   [ ]   [ ]%

(iii)   *Thresholds.*

(A)   *"Independent Amount"* means with respect to Party A: ....
        "Independent Amount" means with respect to Party B: ....

(B)   *"Threshold"* means with respect to Party A: ....
        "Threshold" means with respect to Party B: ....

(C)   *"Minimum Transfer Amount"* means with respect to Party A: ....
        "Minimum Transfer Amount" means with respect to Party B: ....

(D)   *Rounding.* The Delivery Amount and the Return Amount will be rounded [down to the
nearest integral multiple of ..../up and down to the nearest integral multiple of ...., respectively[3]].

(c)   *Valuation and Timing.*

(i)   *"Valuation Agent"* means, for purposes of Paragraphs 2 and 4, the party making the
demand under Paragraph 2, and, for purposes of Paragraph 5(c), the Transferee, as applicable,
unless otherwise specified here: ....

(ii)   *"Valuation Date"* means: ....

(iii)   *"Valuation Time"* means:

        [ ]   the close of business in the place of location of the Valuation Agent on the
                Valuation Date or date of calculation, as applicable;

        [ ]   the close of business on the Local Business Day immediately preceding the
                Valuation Date or date of calculation, as applicable;

provided that the calculations of Value and Exposure will, as far as practicable, be made as of
approximately the same time on the same date.

(iv)   *"Notification Time"* means 1:00 p.m., London time, on a Local Business Day, unless
otherwise specified here: ....

---

[3] Delete as applicable.

(d)   *Exchange Date.*   "*Exchange Date*" has the meaning specified in Paragraph 3(c)(ii), unless otherwise specified here: ....

(e)   *Dispute Resolution.*

    (i)   "*Resolution Time*" means 1:00 p.m., London time, on the Local Business Day following the date on which the notice is given that gives rise to a dispute under Paragraph 4, unless otherwise specified here: ....

    (ii)   *Value.* For the purpose of Paragraphs 4(a)(4)(i)(C) and 4(a)(4)(ii), the Value of the outstanding Credit Support Balance or of any transfer of Eligible Credit Support or Equivalent Credit Support, as the case may be, will be calculated as follows: ....

    (iii)   *Alternative.* The provisions of Paragraph 4 will apply, unless an alternative dispute resolution procedure is specified here: ....

(f)   *Distributions and Interest Amount.*

    (i)   *Interest Rate.* The "Interest Rate" in relation to each Eligible Currency specified below will be:

Eligible Currency	*Interest Rate*
....	....
....	....
....	....

    (ii)   *Transfer of Interest Amount.* The transfer of the Interest Amount will be made on the last Local Business Day of each calendar month and on any Local Business Day that a Return Amount consisting wholly or partly of cash is transferred to the Transferor pursuant to Paragraph 2(b), unless otherwise specified here:..

    (iii)   *Alternative to Interest Amount.* The provisions of Paragraph 5(c)(ii) will apply, unless otherwise specified here: ....

(g)   *Addresses for Transfers.*

Party A: ....
....

Party B: ....
....

(h)   *Other Provisions.*

ISDA® 1995

ANNEX 2
ISDA CREDIT SUPPORT ANNEX SUBJECT TO NEW YORK LAW

(Bilateral Form)   (ISDA Agreements Subject to New York Law Only)

International Swaps and Derivatives Association, Inc.

CREDIT SUPPORT ANNEX

to the Schedule to the

. . . .

dated as of . . . .

between

. . . .   and   . . . .

("Party A")   ("Party B")

This Annex supplements, forms part of, and is subject to, the above-referenced Agreement, is part of its Schedule and is a Credit Support Document under this Agreement with respect to each party.

Accordingly, the parties agree as follows:—

Paragraph 1. Interpretation

(a)   *Definitions and Inconsistency.* Capitalized terms not otherwise defined herein or elsewhere in this Agreement have the meanings specified pursuant to Paragraph 12, and all references in this Annex to Paragraphs are to Paragraphs of this Annex. In the event of any inconsistency between this Annex and the other provisions of this Schedule, this Annex will prevail, and in the event of any inconsistency between Paragraph 13 and the other provisions of this Annex, Paragraph 13 will prevail.

(b)   *Secured Party and Pledgor.* All references in this Annex to the "Secured Party" will be to either party when acting in that capacity and all corresponding references to the "Pledgor" will be to the other party when acting in that capacity; *provided, however,* that if Other Posted Support is held by a party to this Annex, all references herein to that party as the Secured Party with respect to that Other Posted Support will be to that party as the beneficiary thereof and will not subject that support or that party as the beneficiary thereof to provisions of law generally relating to security interests and secured parties.

Paragraph 2. Security Interest

Each party, as the Pledgor, hereby pledges to the other party, as the Secured Party, as security for its Obligations, and grants to the Secured Party a first priority continuing security interest in, lien on and right of Set-off against all Posted Collateral Transferred to or received by the Secured Party hereunder. Upon the Transfer by the Secured Party to the Pledgor of Posted Collateral, the security interest and lien granted hereunder on that Posted Collateral will be released immediately and, to the extent possible, without any further action by either party.

Paragraph 3. Credit Support Obligations

(a)   *Delivery Amount.* Subject to Paragraphs 4 and 5, upon a demand made by the Secured Party on or promptly following a Valuation Date, if the Delivery Amount for that Valuation Date equals or exceeds the Pledgor's Minimum Transfer Amount, then the Pledgor will Transfer to the Secured Party Eligible Credit Support having a Value as of the date of Transfer at least equal to the applicable Delivery Amount (rounded pursuant to Paragraph 13). Unless otherwise specified in Paragraph 13, the *"Delivery Amount"* applicable to the Pledgor for any Valuation Date will equal the amount by which:

(i) the Credit Support Amount

exceeds

(ii) the Value as of that Valuation Date of all Posted Credit Support held by the Secured Party.

(b)   *Return Amount.* Subject to Paragraphs 4 and 5, upon a demand made by the Pledgor on or promptly following a Valuation Date, if the Return Amount for that Valuation Date equals or exceeds the Secured Party's Minimum Transfer Amount, then the Secured Party will Transfer to the Pledgor Posted Credit Support specified by the Pledgor in that demand having a Value as of the date of Transfer as close as practicable to the applicable Return Amount (rounded pursuant to Paragraph 13). Unless otherwise specified in Paragraph 13, the *"Return Amount"* applicable to the Secured Party for any Valuation Date will equal the amount by which:

(i) the Value as of that Valuation Date of all Posted Credit Support held by the Secured Party

exceeds

(ii) the Credit Support Amount.

"Credit Support Amount" means, unless otherwise specified in Paragraph 13, for any Valuation Date (i) the Secured Party's Exposure for that Valuation Date plus (ii) the aggregate of all Independent Amounts applicable to the Pledgor, if any, minus (iii) all Independent Amounts applicable to the Secured Party, if any, minus (iv) the Pledgor's Threshold; *provided, however,* that the Credit Support Amount will be deemed to be zero whenever the calculation of Credit Support Amount yields a number less than zero.

Paragraph 4. Conditions Precedent, Transfer Timing, Calculations and Substitutions

(a)   *Conditions Precedent.* Each Transfer obligation of the Pledgor under Paragraphs 3 and 5 and of the Secured Party under Paragraphs 3, 4(d)(ii), 5 and 6(d) is subject to the conditions precedent that:

(i) no Event of Default, Potential Event of Default or Specified Condition has occurred and is continuing with respect to the other party; and

(ii) no Early Termination Date for which any unsatisfied payment obligations exist has occurred or been designated as the result of an Event of Default or Specified Condition with respect to the other party.

(b)   *Transfer Timing.* Subject to Paragraphs 4(a) and 5 and unless otherwise specified, if a demand for the Transfer of Eligible Credit Support or Posted Credit Support is made by the Notification Time, then the relevant Transfer will be made not later than the close of business on the next Local Business Day; if a demand is made after the Notification Time, then the relevant Transfer will be made not later than the close of business on the second Local Business Day thereafter.

(c)   *Calculations.* All calculations of Value and Exposure for purposes of Paragraphs 3 and 6(d) will be made by the Valuation Agent as of the Valuation Time. The Valuation Agent will notify each party (or the other party, if the Valuation Agent is a party) of its calculations not later than the Notification Time on the Local Business Day following the applicable Valuation Date (or in the case of Paragraph 6(d), following the date of calculation).

ISDA® 1994

(d) **Substitutions.**

(i) Unless otherwise specified in Paragraph 13, upon notice to the Secured Party specifying the items of Posted Credit Support to be exchanged, the Pledgor may, on any Local Business Day, Transfer to the Secured Party substitute Eligible Credit Support (the "Substitute Credit Support"); and

(ii) subject to Paragraph 4(a), the Secured Party will Transfer to the Pledgor the items of Posted Credit Support specified by the Pledgor in its notice not later than the Local Business Day following the date on which the Secured Party receives the Substitute Credit Support, unless otherwise specified in Paragraph 13 (the "Substitution Date"); *provided* that the Secured Party will only be obligated to Transfer Posted Credit Support with a Value as of the date of Transfer of that Posted Credit Support equal to the Value as of that date of the Substitute Credit Support.

Paragraph 5. Dispute Resolution

If a party (a "Disputing Party") disputes (I) the Valuation Agent's calculation of a Delivery Amount or a Return Amount or (II) the Value of any Transfer of Eligible Credit Support or Posted Credit Support, then (1) the Disputing Party will notify the other party and the Valuation Agent (if the Valuation Agent is not the other party) not later than the close of business on the Local Business Day following (X) the date that the demand is made under Paragraph 3 in the case of (I) above or (Y) the date of Transfer in the case of (II) above, (2) subject to Paragraph 4(a), the appropriate party will Transfer the undisputed amount to the other party not later than the close of business on the Local Business Day following (X) the date that the demand is made under Paragraph 3 in the case of (I) above or (Y) the date of Transfer in the case of (II) above, (3) the parties will consult with each other in an attempt to resolve the dispute and (4) if they fail to resolve the dispute by the Resolution Time, then:

(i) In the case of a dispute involving a Delivery Amount or Return Amount, unless otherwise specified in Paragraph 13, the Valuation Agent will recalculate the Exposure and the Value as of the Recalculation Date by:

(A) utilizing any calculations of Exposure for the Transactions (or Swap Transactions) that the parties have agreed are not in dispute;

(B) calculating the Exposure for the Transactions (or Swap Transactions) in dispute by seeking four actual quotations at mid-market from Reference Market-makers for purposes of calculating Market Quotation, and taking the arithmetic average of those obtained; *provided* that if four quotations are not available for a particular Transaction (or Swap Transaction), then fewer than four quotations may be used for that Transaction (or Swap Transaction); and if no quotations are available for a particular Transaction (or Swap Transaction), then the Valuation Agent's original calculations will be used for that Transaction (or Swap Transaction); and

(C) utilizing the procedures specified in Paragraph 13 for calculating the Value, if disputed, of Posted Credit Support.

(ii) In the case of a dispute involving the Value of any Transfer of Eligible Credit Support or Posted Credit Support, the Valuation Agent will recalculate the Value as of the date of Transfer pursuant to Paragraph 13.

Following a recalculation pursuant to this Paragraph, the Valuation Agent will notify each party (or the other party, if the Valuation Agent is a party) not later than the Notification Time on the Local Business Day following the Resolution Time. The appropriate party will, upon demand following that notice by the Valuation Agent or a resolution pursuant to (3) above and subject to Paragraphs 4(a) and 4(b), make the appropriate Transfer.

ISDA® 1994

Paragraph 6. Holding and Using Posted Collateral

(a)   *Care of Posted Collateral.* Without limiting the Secured Party's rights under Paragraph 6(c), the Secured Party will exercise reasonable care to assure the safe custody of all Posted Collateral to the extent required by applicable law, and in any event the Secured Party will be deemed to have exercised reasonable care if it exercises at least the same degree of care as it would exercise with respect to its own property. Except as specified in the preceding sentence, the Secured Party will have no duty with respect to Posted Collateral, including, without limitation, any duty to collect any Distributions, or enforce or preserve any rights pertaining thereto.

(b)   *Eligibility to Hold Posted Collateral; Custodians.*

(i) *General.* Subject to the satisfaction of any conditions specified in Paragraph 13 for holding Posted Collateral, the Secured Party will be entitled to hold Posted Collateral or to appoint an agent (a "Custodian") to hold Posted Collateral for the Secured Party. Upon notice by the Secured Party to the Pledgor of the appointment of a Custodian, the Pledgor's obligations to make any Transfer will be discharged by making the Transfer to that Custodian. The holding of Posted Collateral by a Custodian will be deemed to be the holding of that Posted Collateral by the Secured Party for which the Custodian is acting.

(ii) *Failure to Satisfy Conditions.* If the Secured Party or its Custodian fails to satisfy any conditions for holding Posted Collateral, then upon a demand made by the Pledgor, the Secured Party will, not later than five Local Business Days after the demand, Transfer or cause its Custodian to Transfer all Posted Collateral held by it to a Custodian that satisfies those conditions or to the Secured Party if it satisfies those conditions.

(iii) *Liability.* The Secured Party will be liable for the acts or omissions of its Custodian to the same extent that the Secured Party would be liable hereunder for its own acts or omissions.

(c)   *Use of Posted Collateral.* Unless otherwise specified in Paragraph 13 and without limiting the rights and obligations of the parties under Paragraphs 3, 4(d)(ii), 5, 6(d) and 8, if the Secured Party is not a Defaulting Party or an Affected Party with respect to a Specified Condition and no Early Termination Date has occurred or been designated as the result of an Event of Default or Specified Condition with respect to the Secured Party, then the Secured Party will, notwithstanding Section 9-207 of the New York Uniform Commercial Code, have the right to:

(i) sell, pledge, rehypothecate, assign, invest, use, commingle or otherwise dispose of, or otherwise use in its business any Posted Collateral it holds, free from any claim or right of any nature whatsoever of the Pledgor, including any equity or right of redemption by the Pledgor; and

(ii) register any Posted Collateral in the name of the Secured Party, its Custodian or a nominee for either.

For purposes of the obligation to Transfer Eligible Credit Support or Posted Credit Support pursuant to Paragraphs 3 and 5 and any rights or remedies authorized under this Agreement, the Secured Party will be deemed to continue to hold all Posted Collateral and to receive Distributions made thereon, regardless of whether the Secured Party has exercised any rights with respect to any Posted Collateral pursuant to (i) or (ii) above.

(d)   *Distributions and Interest Amount.*

(i) *Distributions.* Subject to Paragraph 4(a), if the Secured Party receives or is deemed to receive Distributions on a Local Business Day, it will Transfer to the Pledgor not later than the following Local Business Day any Distributions it receives or is deemed to receive to the extent that a Delivery Amount would not be created or increased by that Transfer, as calculated by the Valuation Agent (and the date of calculation will be deemed to be a Valuation Date for this purpose).

4   ISDA® 1994

(ii) *Interest Amount.* Unless otherwise specified in Paragraph 13 and subject to Paragraph 4(a), in lieu of any interest, dividends or other amounts paid or deemed to have been paid with respect to Posted Collateral in the form of Cash (all of which may be retained by the Secured Party), the Secured Party will Transfer to the Pledgor at the times specified in Paragraph 13 the Interest Amount to the extent that a Delivery Amount would not be created or increased by that Transfer, as calculated by the Valuation Agent (and the date of calculation will be deemed to be a Valuation Date for this purpose). The Interest Amount or portion thereof not Transferred pursuant to this Paragraph will constitute Posted Collateral in the form of Cash and will be subject to the security interest granted under Paragraph 2.

Paragraph 7. Events of Default

For purposes of Section 5(a)(iii)(1) of this Agreement, an Event of Default will exist with respect to a party if:

(i) that party fails (or fails to cause its Custodian) to make, when due, any Transfer of Eligible Collateral, Posted Collateral or the Interest Amount, as applicable, required to be made by it and that failure continues for two Local Business Days after notice of that failure is given to that party;

(ii) that party fails to comply with any restriction or prohibition specified in this Annex with respect to any of the rights specified in Paragraph 6(c) and that failure continues for five Local Business Days after notice of that failure is given to that party; or

(iii) that party fails to comply with or perform any agreement or obligation other than those specified in Paragraphs 7(i) and 7(ii) and that failure continues for 30 days after notice of that failure is given to that party.

Paragraph 8. Certain Rights and Remedies

(a) *Secured Party's Rights and Remedies.* If at any time (1) an Event of Default or Specified Condition with respect to the Pledgor has occurred and is continuing or (2) an Early Termination Date has occurred or been designated as the result of an Event of Default or Specified Condition with respect to the Pledgor, then, unless the Pledgor has paid in full all of its Obligations that are then due, the Secured Party may exercise one or more of the following rights and remedies:

(i) all rights and remedies available to a secured party under applicable law with respect to Posted Collateral held by the Secured Party;

(ii) any other rights and remedies available to the Secured Party under the terms of Other Posted Support, if any;

(iii) the right to Set-off any amounts payable by the Pledgor with respect to any Obligations against any Posted Collateral or the Cash equivalent of any Posted Collateral held by the Secured Party (or any obligation of the Secured Party to Transfer that Posted Collateral); and

(iv) the right to liquidate any Posted Collateral held by the Secured Party through one or more public or private sales or other dispositions with such notice, if any, as may be required under applicable law, free from any claim or right of any nature whatsoever of the Pledgor, including any equity or right of redemption by the Pledgor (with the Secured Party having the right to purchase any or all of the Posted Collateral to be sold) and to apply the proceeds (or the Cash equivalent thereof) from the liquidation of the Posted Collateral to any amounts payable by the Pledgor with respect to any Obligations in that order as the Secured Party may elect.

Each party acknowledges and agrees that Posted Collateral in the form of securities may decline speedily in value and is of a type customarily sold on a recognized market, and, accordingly, the Pledgor is not entitled to prior notice of any sale of that Posted Collateral by the Secured Party, except any notice that is required under applicable law and cannot be waived.

5

(b)   *Pledgor's Rights and Remedies.* If at any time an Early Termination Date has occurred or been designated as the result of an Event of Default or Specified Condition with respect to the Secured Party, then (except in the case of an Early Termination Date relating to less than all Transactions (or Swap Transactions) where the Secured Party has paid in full all of its obligations that are then due under Section 6(e) of this Agreement):

(i) the Pledgor may exercise all rights and remedies available to a pledgor under applicable law with respect to Posted Collateral held by the Secured Party;

(ii) the Pledgor may exercise any other rights and remedies available to the Pledgor under the terms of Other Posted Support, if any;

(iii) the Secured Party will be obligated immediately to Transfer all Posted Collateral and the Interest Amount to the Pledgor; and

(iv) to the extent that Posted Collateral or the Interest Amount is not so Transferred pursuant to (iii) above, the Pledgor may:

(A) Set-off any amounts payable by the Pledgor with respect to any Obligations against any Posted Collateral or the Cash equivalent of any Posted Collateral held by the Secured Party (or any obligation of the Secured Party to Transfer that Posted Collateral); and

(B) to the extent that the Pledgor does not Set-off under (iv)(A) above, withhold payment of any remaining amounts payable by the Pledgor with respect to any Obligations, up to the Value of any remaining Posted Collateral held by the Secured Party, until that Posted Collateral is Transferred to the Pledgor.

(c)   *Deficiencies and Excess Proceeds.* The Secured Party will Transfer to the Pledgor any proceeds and Posted Credit Support remaining after liquidation, Set-off and/or application under Paragraphs 8(a) and 8(b) after satisfaction in full of all amounts payable by the Pledgor with respect to any Obligations; the Pledgor in all events will remain liable for any amounts remaining unpaid after any liquidation, Set-off and/or application under Paragraphs 8(a) and 8(b).

(d)   *Final Returns.* When no amounts are or thereafter may become payable by the Pledgor with respect to any Obligations (except for any potential liability under Section 2(d) of this Agreement), the Secured Party will Transfer to the Pledgor all Posted Credit Support and the Interest Amount, if any.

Paragraph 9. Representations

Each party represents to the other party (which representations will be deemed to be repeated as of each date on which it, as the Pledgor, Transfers Eligible Collateral) that:

(i) it has the power to grant a security interest in and lien on any Eligible Collateral it Transfers as the Pledgor and has taken all necessary actions to authorize the granting of that security interest and lien;

(ii) it is the sole owner of or otherwise has the right to Transfer all Eligible Collateral it Transfers to the Secured Party hereunder, free and clear of any security interest, lien, encumbrance or other restrictions other than the security interest and lien granted under Paragraph 2;

(iii) upon the Transfer of any Eligible Collateral to the Secured Party under the terms of this Annex, the Secured Party will have a valid and perfected first priority security interest therein (assuming that any central clearing corporation or any third-party financial intermediary or other entity not within the control of the Pledgor involved in the Transfer of that Eligible Collateral gives the notices and takes the action required of it under applicable law for perfection of that interest); and

(iv) the performance by it of its obligations under this Annex will not result in the creation of any security interest, lien or other encumbrance on any Posted Collateral other than the security interest and lien granted under Paragraph 2.

ISDA® 1994

Paragraph 10. Expenses

(a)   *General.* Except as otherwise provided in Paragraphs 10(b) and 10(c), each party will pay its own costs and expenses in connection with performing its obligations under this Annex and neither party will be liable for any costs and expenses incurred by the other party in connection herewith.

(b)   *Posted Credit Support.* The Pledgor will promptly pay when due all taxes, assessments or charges of any nature that are imposed with respect to Posted Credit Support held by the Secured Party upon becoming aware of the same, regardless of whether any portion of that Posted Credit Support is subsequently disposed of under Paragraph 6(c), except for those taxes, assessments and charges that result from the exercise of the Secured Party's rights under Paragraph 6(c).

(c)   *Liquidation/Application of Posted Credit Support.* All reasonable costs and expenses incurred by or on behalf of the Secured Party or the Pledgor in connection with the liquidation and/or application of any Posted Credit Support under Paragraph 8 will be payable, on demand and pursuant to the Expenses Section of this Agreement, by the Defaulting Party or, if there is no Defaulting Party, equally by the parties.

Paragraph 11. Miscellaneous

(a)   *Default Interest.* A Secured Party that fails to make, when due, any Transfer of Posted Collateral or the Interest Amount will be obligated to pay the Pledgor (to the extent permitted under applicable law) an amount equal to interest at the Default Rate multiplied by the Value of the items of property that were required to be Transferred, from (and including) the date that Posted Collateral or Interest Amount was required to be Transferred to (but excluding) the date of Transfer of that Posted Collateral or Interest Amount. This interest will be calculated on the basis of daily compounding and the actual number of days elapsed.

(b)   *Further Assurances.* Promptly following a demand made by a party, the other party will execute, deliver, file and record any financing statement, specific assignment or other document and take any other action that may be necessary or desirable and reasonably requested by that party to create, preserve, perfect or validate any security interest or lien granted under Paragraph 2, to enable that party to exercise or enforce its rights under this Annex with respect to Posted Credit Support or an Interest Amount or to effect or document a release of a security interest on Posted Collateral or an Interest Amount.

(c)   *Further Protection.* The Pledgor will promptly give notice to the Secured Party of, and defend against, any suit, action, proceeding or lien that involves Posted Credit Support Transferred by the Pledgor or that could adversely affect the security interest and lien granted by it under Paragraph 2, unless that suit, action, proceeding or lien results from the exercise of the Secured Party's rights under Paragraph 6(c).

(d)   *Good Faith and Commercially Reasonable Manner.* Performance of all obligations under this Annex, including, but not limited to, all calculations, valuations and determinations made by either party, will be made in good faith and in a commercially reasonable manner.

(e)   *Demands and Notices.* All demands and notices made by a party under this Annex will be made as specified in the Notices Section of this Agreement, except as otherwise provided in Paragraph 13.

(f)   *Specifications of Certain Matters.* Anything referred to in this Annex as being specified in Paragraph 13 also may be specified in one or more Confirmations or other documents and this Annex will be construed accordingly.

ISDA® 1994

Paragraph 12. Definitions

As used in this Annex:—

"Cash" means the lawful currency of the United States of America.

"Credit Support Amount" has the meaning specified in Paragraph 3.

"Custodian" has the meaning specified in Paragraphs 6(b)(i) and 13.

"Delivery Amount" has the meaning specified in Paragraph 3(a).

"Disputing Party" has the meaning specified in Paragraph 5.

"Distributions" means with respect to Posted Collateral other than Cash, all principal, interest and other payments and distributions of cash or other property with respect thereto, regardless of whether the Secured Party has disposed of that Posted Collateral under Paragraph 6(c). Distributions will not include any item of property acquired by the Secured Party upon any disposition or liquidation of Posted Collateral or, with respect to any Posted Collateral in the form of Cash, any distributions on that collateral, unless otherwise specified herein.

"Eligible Collateral" means, with respect to a party, the items, if any, specified as such for that party in Paragraph 13.

"Eligible Credit Support" means Eligible Collateral and Other Eligible Support.

"Exposure" means for any Valuation Date or other date for which Exposure is calculated and subject to Paragraph 5 in the case of a dispute, the amount, if any, that would be payable to a party that is the Secured Party by the other party (expressed as a positive number) or by a party that is the Secured Party to the other party (expressed as a negative number) pursuant to Section 6(e)(ii)(2)(A) of this Agreement as if all Transactions (or Swap Transactions) were being terminated as of the relevant Valuation Time; *provided* that Market Quotation will be determined by the Valuation Agent using its estimates at mid-market of the amounts that would be paid for Replacement Transactions (as that term is defined in the definition of "Market Quotation").

"Independent Amount" means, with respect to a party, the amount specified as such for that party in Paragraph 13; if no amount is specified, zero.

"Interest Amount" means, with respect to an Interest Period, the aggregate sum of the amounts of interest calculated for each day in that Interest Period on the principal amount of Posted Collateral in the form of Cash held by the Secured Party on that day, determined by the Secured Party for each such day as follows:

> (x) the amount of that Cash on that day; multiplied by

> (y) the Interest Rate in effect for that day; divided by

> (z) 360.

"Interest Period" means the period from (and including) the last Local Business Day on which an Interest Amount was Transferred (or, if no Interest Amount has yet been Transferred, the Local Business Day on which Posted Collateral in the form of Cash was Transferred to or received by the Secured Party) to (but excluding) the Local Business Day on which the current Interest Amount is to be Transferred.

"Interest Rate" means the rate specified in Paragraph 13.

"Local Business Day", unless otherwise specified in Paragraph 13, has the meaning specified in the Definitions Section of this Agreement, except that references to a payment in clause (b) thereof will be deemed to include a Transfer under this Annex.

ISDA® 1994

"Minimum Transfer Amount" means, with respect to a party, the amount specified as such for that party in Paragraph 13; if no amount is specified, zero.

"Notification Time" has the meaning specified in Paragraph 13.

"Obligations" means, with respect to a party, all present and future obligations of that party under this Agreement and any additional obligations specified for that party in Paragraph 13.

"Other Eligible Support" means, with respect to a party, the items, if any, specified as such for that party in Paragraph 13.

"Other Posted Support" means all Other Eligible Support Transferred to the Secured Party that remains in effect for the benefit of that Secured Party.

"Pledgor" means either party, when that party (i) receives a demand for or is required to Transfer Eligible Credit Support under Paragraph 3(a) or (ii) has Transferred Eligible Credit Support under Paragraph 3(a).

"Posted Collateral" means all Eligible Collateral, other property, Distributions, and all proceeds thereof that have been Transferred to or received by the Secured Party under this Annex and not Transferred to the Pledgor pursuant to Paragraph 3(b), 4(d)(ii) or 6(d)(i) or released by the Secured Party under Paragraph 8. Any Interest Amount or portion thereof not Transferred pursuant to Paragraph 6(d)(ii) will constitute Posted Collateral in the form of Cash.

"Posted Credit Support" means Posted Collateral and Other Posted Support.

"Recalculation Date" means the Valuation Date that gives rise to the dispute under Paragraph 5; *provided, however*, that if a subsequent Valuation Date occurs under Paragraph 3 prior to the resolution of the dispute, then the "Recalculation Date" means the most recent Valuation Date under Paragraph 3.

"Resolution Time" has the meaning specified in Paragraph 13.

"Return Amount" has the meaning specified in Paragraph 3(b).

"Secured Party" means either party, when that party (i) makes a demand for or is entitled to receive Eligible Credit Support under Paragraph 3(a) or (ii) holds or is deemed to hold Posted Credit Support.

"Specified Condition" means, with respect to a party, any event specified as such for that party in Paragraph 13.

"Substitute Credit Support" has the meaning specified in Paragraph 4(d)(i).

"Substitution Date" has the meaning specified in Paragraph 4(d)(ii).

"Threshold" means, with respect to a party, the amount specified as such for that party in Paragraph 13; if no amount is specified, zero.

"Transfer" means, with respect to any Eligible Credit Support, Posted Credit Support or Interest Amount, and in accordance with the instructions of the Secured Party, Pledgor or Custodian, as applicable:

> (i) in the case of Cash, payment or delivery by wire transfer into one or more bank accounts specified by the recipient;

> (ii) in the case of certificated securities that cannot be paid or delivered by book-entry, payment or delivery in appropriate physical form to the recipient or its account accompanied by any duly executed instruments of transfer, assignments in blank, transfer tax stamps and any other documents necessary to constitute a legally valid transfer to the recipient;

> (iii) in the case of securities that can be paid or delivered by book-entry, the giving of written instructions to the relevant depository institution or other entity specified by the recipient, together with a written copy thereof to the recipient, sufficient if complied with to result in a legally effective transfer of the relevant interest to the recipient; and

> (iv) in the case of Other Eligible Support or Other Posted Support, as specified in Paragraph 13.

ISDA® 1994

"Valuation Agent" has the meaning specified in Paragraph 13.

"Valuation Date" means each date specified in or otherwise determined pursuant to Paragraph 13.

"Valuation Percentage" means, for any item of Eligible Collateral, the percentage specified in Paragraph 13.

"Valuation Time" has the meaning specified in Paragraph 13.

"Value" means for any Valuation Date or other date for which Value is calculated and subject to Paragraph 5 in the case of a dispute, with respect to:

(i) Eligible Collateral or Posted Collateral that is:

(A) Cash, the amount thereof; and

(B) a security, the bid price obtained by the Valuation Agent multiplied by the applicable Valuation Percentage, if any;

(ii) Posted Collateral that consists of items that are not specified as Eligible Collateral, zero; and

(iii) Other Eligible Support and Other Posted Support, as specified in Paragraph 13.

Paragraph 13. Elections and Variables

(a)   *Security Interest for "Obligations"*. The term *"Obligations"* as used in this Annex includes the following additional obligations:

   With respect to Party A: . . . .

   With respect to Party B: . . . .

(b)   *Credit Support Obligations.*

   (i) *Delivery Amount, Return Amount and Credit Support Amount.*

      (A) *"Delivery Amount"* has the meaning specified in Paragraph 3(a), unless otherwise specified here: . . . .

      (B) *"Return Amount"* has the meaning specified in Paragraph 3(b), unless otherwise specified here: . . . .

      (C) *"Credit Support Amount"* has the meaning specified in Paragraph 3, unless otherwise specified here: . . . .

   (ii) *Eligible Collateral*. The following items will qualify as *"Eligible Collateral"* for the party specified:

		Party A	Party B	Valuation Percentage
(A)	Cash	[ ]	[ ]	[ ]%
(B)	negotiable debt obligations issued by the U.S. Treasury Department having an original maturity at issuance of not more than one year ("Treasury Bills")	[ ]	[ ]	[ ]%
(C)	negotiable debt obligations issued by the U.S. Treasury Department having an original maturity at issuance of more than one year but not more than 10 years ("Treasury Notes")	[ ]	[ ]	[ ]%
(D)	negotiable debt obligations issued by the U.S. Treasury Department having an original maturity at issuance of more than 10 years ("Treasury Bonds")	[ ]	[ ]	[ ]%
(E)	other:	[ ]	[ ]	[ ]%

   (iii) *Other Eligible Support*. The following items will qualify as *"Other Eligible Support"* for the party specified:

		Party A	Party B
(A)	. . . .	[ ]	[ ]
(B)	. . . .	[ ]	[ ]

ISDA® 1994

(iv) *Thresholds.*

    (A)   *"Independent Amount"* means with respect to Party A: $ ....
            "Independent Amount" means with respect to Party B: $ ....

    (B)   *"Threshold"* means with respect to Party A: $ ....
            "Threshold" means with respect to Party B: $ ....

    (C)   *"Minimum Transfer Amount"* means with respect to Party A: $ ....
            "Minimum Transfer Amount" means with respect to Party B: $ ....

    (D)   **Rounding.** The Delivery Amount and the Return Amount will be rounded [down to the nearest integral multiple of $. . . ./up and down to the nearest integral multiple of $. . . ., respectively].

(c)   *Valuation and Timing.*

    (i)   *"Valuation Agent"* means, for purposes of Paragraphs 3 and 5, the party making the demand under Paragraph 3, and, for purposes of Paragraph 6(d), the Secured Party receiving or deemed to receive the Distributions or the Interest Amount, as applicable, unless otherwise specified here: ....

    (ii)   *"Valuation Date"* means: ....

    (iii)   *"Valuation Time"* means:

        [ ]   the close of business in the city of the Valuation Agent on the Valuation Date or date of calculation, as applicable;

        [ ]   the close of business on the Local Business Day before the Valuation Date or date of calculation, as applicable;

provided that the calculations of Value and Exposure will be made as of approximately the same time on the same date.

    (iv) *"Notification Time"* means 1:00 p.m., New York time, on a Local Business Day, unless otherwise specified here: ....

(d)   *Conditions Precedent and Secured Party's Rights and Remedies.* The following Termination Event(s) will be a *"Specified Condition"* for the party specified (that party being the Affected Party if the Termination Event occurs with respect to that party):

	Party A	Party B
Illegality	[ ]	[ ]
Tax Event	[ ]	[ ]
Tax Event Upon Merger	[ ]	[ ]
Credit Event Upon Merger	[ ]	[ ]
Additional Termination Event(s):[1]		
....	[ ]	[ ]
....	[ ]	[ ]

---

* Delete as applicable.

[1] If the parties elect to designate an Additional Termination Event as a "Specified Condition", then they should only designate one or more Additional Termination Events that are designated as such in their Schedule.

(e)   *Substitution.*

(i) *"Substitution Date"* has the meaning specified in Paragraph 4(d)(ii), unless otherwise specified here: . . . .

(ii) *Consent.* If specified here as applicable, then the Pledgor must obtain the Secured Party's consent for any substitution pursuant to Paragraph 4(d): [applicable/inapplicable*]²

(f)   *Dispute Resolution.*

(i) *"Resolution Time"* means 1:00 p.m., New York time, on the Local Business Day following the date on which the notice is given that gives rise to a dispute under Paragraph 5, unless otherwise specified here: . . . .

(ii) *Value.* For the purpose of Paragraphs 5(i)(C) and 5(ii), the Value of Posted Credit Support will be calculated as follows: . . . .

(iii) *Alternative.* The provisions of Paragraph 5 will apply, unless an alternative dispute resolution procedure is specified here: . . . .

(g)   *Holding and Using Posted Collateral.*

(i) *Eligibility to Hold Posted Collateral; Custodians.* Party A and its Custodian will be entitled to hold Posted Collateral pursuant to Paragraph 6(b); *provided* that the following conditions applicable to it are satisfied:

(1) Party A is not a Defaulting Party.

(2) Posted Collateral may be held only in the following jurisdictions: . . . .

(3) . . . .

Initially, the **Custodian** for Party A is . . . .

Party B and its Custodian will be entitled to hold Posted Collateral pursuant to Paragraph 6(b); *provided* that the following conditions applicable to it are satisfied:

(1) Party B is not a Defaulting Party.

(2) Posted Collateral may be held only in the following jurisdictions: . . . .

(3) . . . .

Initially, the **Custodian** for Party B is . . . .

(ii) *Use of Posted Collateral.* The provisions of Paragraph 6(c) will not apply to the [party/parties*] specified here:

[ ] Party A

[ ] Party B

and [that party/those parties*] will not be permitted to: . . . .

---

* Delete as applicable.

² Parties should consider selecting "applicable" where substitution without consent could give rise to a registration requirement to perfect properly the security interest in Posted Collateral (*e.g.*, where a party to the Annex is the New York branch of an English bank).

13   **ISDA® 1994**

471

(h)   ***Distributions and Interest Amount.***

       (i) ***Interest Rate.*** The ***"Interest Rate"*** will be: ....

       (ii) ***Transfer of Interest Amount.*** The Transfer of the Interest Amount will be made on the last Local Business Day of each calendar month and on any Local Business Day that Posted Collateral in the form of Cash is Transferred to the Pledgor pursuant to Paragraph 3(b), unless otherwise specified here: .. ..

       (iii) ***Alternative to Interest Amount.*** The provisions of Paragraph 6(d)(ii) will apply, unless otherwise specified here: ....

(i)   ***Additional Representation(s).***

[Party A/Party B*] represents to the other party (which representation(s) will be deemed to be repeated as of each date on which it, as the Pledgor, Transfers Eligible Collateral) that:

       (i) ....

       (ii) ....

(j)   ***Other Eligible Support and Other Posted Support.***

       (i) ***"Value"*** with respect to Other Eligible Support and Other Posted Support means: ....

       (ii) ***"Transfer"*** with respect to Other Eligible Support and Other Posted Support means: ....

(k)   ***Demands and Notices.***

All demands, specifications and notices under this Annex will be made pursuant to the Notices Section of this Agreement, unless otherwise specified here:

       Party A: ....
       ....

       Party B: ....
       ....

(l)   ***Addresses for Transfers.***

       Party A: ....
       ....

       Party B: ....
       ....

(m)   ***Other Provisions.***

---

* Delete as applicable.

14   **ISDA® 1994**

ANNEX 3
LIST OF COUNTRIES WHERE ISDA HAS OBTAINED COLLATERAL LEGAL OPINIONS

List of jurisdictions where ISDA has obtained completed collateral legal opinions on the English Law CSA and the New York Law CSA (as at October 2002)

Australia	Mallesons Stephens Jaques
Austria	Weiss-Tessbach
Belgium	De Bandt, van Hecke & Lagae
Bermuda	Conyers, Dill & Pearman
Canada	Stikeman, Elliott
Cayman Islands	Maples & Calder
Denmark	Gorrissen Federspiel Kierkegaard
England	Allen & Overy
Finland	Peltonen, Ruokonen & Itainen
France	Gide Loyrette Nouel
Germany	Hengeler Mueller Weitzel Wirtz
Hong Kong	Allen & Overy Hong Kong
Indonesia	Ali Budjiardo, Nugroho, Reksodiputro
Ireland	McCann Fitzgerald
Italy	Brosio Casati e Associati and Ughi e Nunziate
Japan	Mitsui, Yasuda, Wani & Maeda
Luxembourg	Loesch & Wolter
Malaysia	Shearn Delamore & Co
Netherlands	Nauta Dutilh
New Zealand	Bell Gully
Portugal	Abreu, Cardigos & Partners
Singapore	Allen & Gledhill
South Korea	Kim & Chang
Sweden	Mannheimer Swartling Advokatbyra AB
Switzerland	Lenz & Staehelin
Taiwan	Lee & Li
Thailand	Baker & McKenzie
United States	Cravath, Swaine & Moore

ANNEX 4
RELEVANT EXTRACTS FROM THE NEW YORK UNIFORM COMMERCIAL CODE

EXTRACTS FROM THE NEW YORK UNIFORM COMMERCIAL CODE

Section 8–102. Definitions.

(a) In this Article:

(1) "Adverse claim" means a claim that a claimant has a property interest in a financial asset and that it is a violation of the rights of the claimant for another person to hold, transfer, or deal with the financial asset.

(2) "Bearer form", as applied to a certificated security, means a form in which the security is payable to the bearer of the security certificate according to its terms but not by reason of an indorsement.

(3) "Broker" means a person defined as a broker or dealer under the federal securities laws, but without excluding a bank acting in that capacity.

(4) "Certificated security" means a security that is represented by a certificate.

(5) "Clearing corporation" means:

(i) a person that is registered as a "clearing agency" pursuant to 15 United States Code S 78-c(a)(23), as from time to time amended;

(ii) a federal reserve bank; or

(iii) any other person that provides clearance or settlement services with respect to financial assets that would require it to register as a clearing agency under the federal securities laws but for an exclusion or exemption from the registration requirement, if its activities as a clearing corporation, including promulgation of rules, are subject to regulation by a federal or state governmental authority.

(6) "Communicate" means to:

(i) send a signed writing; or

(ii) transmit information by any mechanism agreed upon by the persons transmitting and receiving the information.

(7) "Entitlement holder" means a person identified in the records of a securities intermediary as the person having a security entitlement against the securities intermediary. If a person acquires a security entitlement by virtue of Section 8–501(b)(2) or (3), that person is the entitlement holder.

(8) "Entitlement order" means a notification communicated to a securities intermediary directing transfer or redemption of a financial asset to which the entitlement holder has a security entitlement.

(9) "Financial asset", except as otherwise provided in Section 8–103, means:

(i) a security;

(ii) an obligation of a person or a share, participation, or other interest in a person or in property or an enterprise of a person, which is, or is of a type, dealt in or traded on financial markets, or which is recognized in any area in which it is issued or dealt in as a medium for investment; or

(iii) any property that is held by a securities intermediary for another person in a securities account if the securities intermediary has expressly agreed with the other person that the property is to be treated as a financial asset under this Article. As context requires, the term means either the interest itself or the means by which a person's claim to it is evidenced, including a certificated or uncertificated security, a security certificate, or a security entitlement.

(10) "Good faith", for purposes of the obligation of good faith in the performance or enforcement of contracts or duties within this Article, means honesty in fact and the observance of reasonable commercial standards of fair dealing.

(11) "Indorsement" means a signature that alone or accompanied by other words is made on a security certificate in registered form or on a separate document for the purpose of assigning, transferring, or redeeming the security or granting a power to assign, transfer, or redeem it.

(12) "Instruction" means a notification communicated to the issuer of an uncertificated security which directs that the transfer of the security be registered or that the security be redeemed.

(13) "Registered form", as applied to a certificated security, means a form in which:

(i) the security certificate specifies a person entitled to the security; and

(ii) a transfer of the security may be registered upon books maintained for that purpose by or on behalf of the issuer, or the security certificate so states.

(14) "Securities intermediary" means:

(i) a clearing corporation; or

(ii) a person, including a bank or broker, that in the ordinary course of its business maintains securities accounts for others and is acting in that capacity.

(15) "Security", except as otherwise provided in Section 8–103, means an obligation of an issuer or a share, participation, or other interest in an issuer or in property or an enterprise of an issuer:

(i)   which is represented by a security certificate in bearer or registered form, or the transfer of which may be registered upon books maintained for that purpose by or on behalf of the issuer;

(ii)   which is one of a class or series or by its terms is

divisible into a class or series of shares, participations, interests, or obligations; and

(iii) which:

(A) is, or is of a type, dealt in or traded on securities exchanges or securities markets; or

(B) is a medium for investment and by its terms expressly provides that it is a security governed by this Article.

(16) "Security certificate" means a certificate representing a security.

(17) "Security entitlement" means the rights and property interest of an entitlement holder with respect to a financial asset specified in Part 5.

(18) "Uncertificated security" means a security that is not represented by a certificate.

(b) Other definitions applying to this Article and the sections in which they appear are:

"Appropriate person".	Section 8–107.
"Control".	Section 8–106.
"Delivery".	Section 8–301.
"Investment company security".	Section 8–103.
"Issuer". Section 8–201.	
"Overissue".	Section 8–210.
"Protected purchaser".	Section 8–303.
"Securities account".	Section 8–501.

(c) In addition, Article 1 contains general definitions and principles of construction and interpretation applicable throughout this Article.

(d) The characterization of a person, business, or transaction for purposes of this Article does not determine the characterization of the person, business, or transaction for purposes of any other law, regulation, or rule.

(e) The following definitions in Article 9 apply to this article:

Cooperative interest	Section 9–102(a)(27-b)
Cooperative organization	Section 9–102(a)(27-c)
Cooperative record	Section 9–102(a)(27-e)

Section 8–104. Acquisition of Security or Financial Asset or Interest Therein.

(a)   A person acquires a security or an interest therein, under this Article, if:

(1)   the person is a purchaser to whom a security is delivered pursuant to Section 8–301; or

(2)   the person acquires a security entitlement to the security pursuant to Section 8–501.

(b)   A person acquires a financial asset, other than a security, or an interest therein, under this Article, if the person acquires a security entitlement to the financial asset.

(c)   A person who acquires a security entitlement to a security or other financial asset has the rights specified in Part 5, but is a purchaser of any security, security entitlement, or other financial asset held by the securities intermediary only to the extent provided in Section 8–503.

(d)   Unless the context shows that a different meaning is intended, a person who is required by other law, regulation, rule, or agreement to transfer, deliver, present, surrender, exchange, or otherwise put in the possession of another person a security or financial asset satisfies that requirement by causing the other person to acquire an interest in the security or financial asset pursuant to subsection (a) or (b).

Section 8–106. Control.

(a)   A purchaser has "control" of a certificated security in bearer form if the certificated security is delivered to the purchaser.

(b)   A purchaser has "control" of a certificated security in registered form if the certificated security is delivered to the purchaser, and:

(1)   the certificate is indorsed to the purchaser or in blank by an effective indorsement; or

(2)   the certificate is registered in the name of the purchaser, upon original issue or registration of transfer by the issuer.

(c)   A purchaser has "control" of an uncertificated security if:

(1)   the uncertificated security is delivered to the purchaser; or

(2)   the issuer has agreed that it will comply with instructions originated by the purchaser without further consent by the registered owner.

(d)   A purchaser has "control" of a security entitlement if:

(1)   the purchaser becomes the entitlement holder;

(2)   the securities intermediary has agreed that it will comply with entitlement orders originated by the purchaser without further consent by the entitlement holder; or

(3)   another person has control of the security entitlement on behalf of the purchaser or, having previously acquired control of the security entitlement, acknowledges that it has control on behalf of the purchaser.

(e)   If an interest in a security entitlement is granted by the entitlement holder to the entitlement holder's own securities intermediary, the securities intermediary has control.

(f)   A purchaser who has satisfied the requirements of subsection (c) or (d) has control even if the registered owner in the case of subsection (c) or the entitlement holder in the case of subsection (d) retains the right to make substitutions for the uncertificated security or security entitlement, to originate instructions or entitlement orders to the issuer or securities intermediary, or otherwise to deal with the uncertificated security or security entitlement.

(g)   An issuer or a securities intermediary may not enter into an agreement of the kind described in subsection (c)(2) or (d)(2) without the consent of the registered owner or entitlement holder, but an issuer or a securities intermediary is not required to enter into such an agreement even though the registered owner or entitlement holder so directs. An issuer or securities intermediary that has entered into such an agreement is not required to confirm the existence of the agreement to another party unless requested to do so by the registered owner or entitlement holder.

Section 8–110. Applicability; Choice of Law.

(a) The local law of the issuer's jurisdiction, as specified in subsection (d), governs:

(1)   the validity of a security;

(2)   the rights and duties of the issuer with respect to registration of transfer;

(3)   the effectiveness of registration of transfer by the issuer;

(4)   whether the issuer owes any duties to an adverse claimant to a security; and

(5)   whether an adverse claim can be asserted against a person to whom transfer of a certificated or uncertificated security is registered or a person who obtains control of an uncertificated security.

(b)   The local law of the securities intermediary's jurisdiction, as specified in subsection (e), governs:

(1)   acquisition of a security entitlement from the securities intermediary;

(2)   the rights and duties of the securities intermediary and entitlement holder arising out of a security entitlement;

(3)   whether the securities intermediary owes any duties to an adverse claimant to a security entitlement; and

(4) whether an adverse claim can be asserted against a person who acquires a security entitlement from the securities intermediary or a person who purchases a security entitlement or interest therein from an entitlement holder.

(c) Except with respect to cooperative interests, the local law of the jurisdiction in which a security certificate is located at the time of delivery governs whether an adverse claim can be asserted against a person to whom the security certificate is delivered.

(d) "Issuer's jurisdiction" means the jurisdiction under which the issuer of the security is organized or, if permitted by the law of that jurisdiction, the law of another jurisdiction specified by the issuer. An issuer organized under the law of this State may specify the law of another jurisdiction as the law governing the matters specified in subsection (a)(2) through (5).

(e) The following rules determine a "securities intermediary's jurisdiction" for purposes of this section:

(1) If an agreement between the securities intermediary and its entitlement holder governing the securities account expressly provides that a particular jurisdiction is the securities intermediary's jurisdiction for purposes of this part, this article, or this act, that jurisdiction is the securities intermediary's jurisdiction.

(2) If paragraph (1) does not apply and an agreement between the securities intermediary and its entitlement holder governing the securities account expressly provides that the agreement is governed by the law of a particular jurisdiction, that jurisdiction is the securities intermediary's jurisdiction.

(3) If neither paragraph (1) nor paragraph (2) apply and an agreement between the securities intermediary and its entitlement holder governing the securities account expressly provides that the securities account is maintained at an office in a particular jurisdiction, that jurisdiction is the securities intermediary's jurisdiction.

(4) If none of the preceding paragraphs apply, the securities intermediary's jurisdiction is the jurisdiction in which the office identified in an account statement as the office serving the entitlement holder's account is located.

(5) If none of the preceding paragraphs apply, the securities intermediary's jurisdiction is the jurisdiction in which the chief executive office of the securities intermediary is located.

(f) A securities intermediary's jurisdiction is not determined by the physical location of certificates representing financial assets, or by the jurisdiction in which is organized the issuer of the financial asset with respect to which an entitlement holder has a security entitlement, or by the location of facilities for data processing or other record keeping concerning the account.

Section 8–301. Delivery.

(a) Delivery of a certificated security to a purchaser occurs when:

(1) the purchaser acquires possession of the security certificate;

(2) another person, other than a securities intermediary, either acquires possession of the security certificate on behalf of the purchaser or, having previously acquired possession of the certificate, acknowledges that it holds for the purchaser; or

(3) a securities intermediary acting on behalf of the purchaser acquires possession of the security certificate, only if the certificate is in registered form and is (i) registered in the name of the purchaser, (ii) payable to the order of the purchaser, or (iii) specially indorsed to the purchaser by an effective indorsement and has not been indorsed to the securities intermediary or in blank.

(b) Delivery of an uncertificated security to a purchaser occurs when:

(1) the issuer registers the purchaser as the registered owner, upon original issue or registration of transfer; or

(2) another person, other than a securities intermediary, either becomes the registered owner of the uncertificated security on behalf of the purchaser or, having previously become the registered owner, acknowledges that it holds for the purchaser.

Section 8–501. Securities Account; Acquisition of Security Entitlement from Securities Intermediary.

(a) "Securities account" means an account to which a financial asset is or may be credited in accordance with an agreement under which the person maintaining the account undertakes to treat the person for whom the account is maintained as entitled to exercise the rights that comprise the financial asset.

(b) Except as otherwise provided in subsections (d) and (e), a person acquires a security entitlement if a securities intermediary:

(1) indicates by book entry that a financial asset has been credited to the person's securities account;

(2) receives a financial asset from the person or acquires a financial asset for the person and, in either case, accepts it for credit to the person's securities account; or

(3) becomes obligated under other law, regulation, or rule to credit a financial asset to the person's securities account.

(c) If a condition of subsection (b) has been met, a person has a security entitlement even though the securities intermediary does not itself hold the financial asset.

(d) If a securities intermediary holds a financial asset for another person, and the financial asset is registered in the name of, payable to the order of, or specially indorsed to the other person, and has not been indorsed to the securities intermediary or in blank, the other person is treated as holding the financial asset directly rather than as having a security entitlement with respect to the financial asset.

(e) Issuance of a security is not establishment of a security entitlement.

Section 8–503. Property Interest of Entitlement Holder in Financial Asset held by Securities Intermediary.

(a) To the extent necessary for a securities intermediary to satisfy all security entitlements with respect to a particular financial asset, all interests in that financial asset held by the securities intermediary are held by the securities intermediary for the entitlement holders, are not property of the securities intermediary, and are not subject to claims of creditors of the securities intermediary, except as otherwise provided in Section 8–511.

(b) An entitlement holder's property interest with respect to a particular financial asset under subsection (a) is a pro rata property interest in all interests in that financial asset held by the securities intermediary, without regard to the time the entitlement holder acquired the security entitlement or the time the securities intermediary acquired the interest in that financial asset.

(c) An entitlement holder's property interest with respect to a particular financial asset under subsection (a) may be enforced against the securities intermediary only by exercise of the entitlement holder's rights under Sections 8–505 through 8–508.

(d) An entitlement holder's property interest with respect to a particular financial asset under subsection (a) may be enforced against a purchaser of the financial asset or interest therein only if:

(1) insolvency proceedings have been initiated by or against the securities intermediary;

(2) the securities intermediary does not have sufficient interests in the financial asset to satisfy the security entitlements of all of its entitlement holders to that financial asset;

(3) the securities intermediary violated its obligations under Section 8–504 by transferring the financial asset or interest therein to the purchaser; and

(4) the purchaser is not protected under subsection (e). The trustee or other liquidator, acting on behalf of all entitlement holders having security entitlements with respect to a particular financial asset, may recover the financial asset, or interest therein, from the purchaser. If the trustee or other liquidator elects not to pursue that right, an entitlement holder whose security entitlement remains unsatisfied has the right to recover its interest in the financial asset from the purchaser.

(e)   An action based on the entitlement holder's property interest with respect to a particular financial asset under subsection (a), whether framed in conversion, replevin, constructive trust, equitable lien, or other theory, may not be asserted against any purchaser of a financial asset or interest therein who gives value, obtains control, and does not act in collusion with the securities intermediary in violating the securities intermediary's obligations under Section 8–504.

Section 8–504. Duty of Securities Intermediary to Maintain Financial Asset.

(a)   A securities intermediary shall promptly obtain and thereafter maintain a financial asset in a quantity corresponding to the aggregate of all security entitlements it has established in favor of its entitlement holders with respect to that financial asset. The securities intermediary may maintain those financial assets directly or through one or more other securities intermediaries.

(b)   Except to the extent otherwise agreed by its entitlement holder, a securities intermediary may not grant any security interests in a financial asset it is obligated to maintain pursuant to subsection (a).

(c)   A securities intermediary satisfies the duty in subsection (a) if:

(1)   the securities intermediary acts with respect to the duty as agreed upon by the entitlement holder and the securities intermediary; or

(2)   in the absence of agreement, the securities intermediary exercises due care in accordance with reasonable commercial standards to obtain and maintain the financial asset.

(d)   This section does not apply to a clearing corporation that is itself the obligor of an option or similar obligation to which its entitlement holders have security entitlements.

Section 8–505. Duty of Securities Intermediary with Respect to Payments and Distributions.

(a)   A securities intermediary shall take action to obtain a payment or distribution made by the issuer of a financial asset. A securities intermediary satisfies the duty if:

(1)   the securities intermediary acts with respect to the duty as agreed upon by the entitlement holder and the securities intermediary; or

(2)   in the absence of agreement, the securities intermediary exercises due care in accordance with reasonable commercial standards to attempt to obtain the payment or distribution.

(b)   A securities intermediary is obligated to its entitlement holder for a payment or distribution made by the issuer of a financial asset if the payment or distribution is received by the securities intermediary.

Section 8–506. Duty of Securities Intermediary to Exercise Rights as Directed by Entitlement Holder.

A securities intermediary shall exercise rights with respect to a financial asset if directed to do so by an entitlement holder. A securities intermediary satisfies the duty if:

(1) the securities intermediary acts with respect to the duty as agreed upon by the entitlement holder and the securities intermediary; or

(2) in the absence of agreement, the securities intermediary either places the entitlement holder in a position to exercise the rights directly or exercises due care in accordance with reasonable commercial standards to follow the direction of the entitlement holder.

Section 8–507. Duty of Securities Intermediary to Comply with Entitlement Order.

(a) A securities intermediary shall comply with an entitlement order if the entitlement order is originated by the appropriate person, the securities intermediary has had reasonable opportunity to assure itself that the entitlement order is genuine and authorized, and the securities intermediary has had reasonable opportunity to comply with the entitlement order. A securities intermediary satisfies the duty if:

(1) the securities intermediary acts with respect to the duty as agreed upon by the entitlement holder and the securities intermediary; or

(2) in the absence of agreement, the securities intermediary exercises due care in accordance with reasonable commercial standards to comply with the entitlement order.

(b) If a securities intermediary transfers a financial asset pursuant to an ineffective entitlement order, the securities intermediary shall reestablish a security entitlement in favor of the person entitled to it, and pay or credit any payments or distributions that the person did not receive as a result of the wrongful transfer. If the securities intermediary does not reestablish a security entitlement, the securities intermediary is liable to the entitlement holder for damages.

Section 8–508. Duty of Securities Intermediary to Change Entitlement Holder's Position to Other Form of Security Holding.

A securities intermediary shall act at the direction of an entitlement holder to change a security entitlement into another available form of holding for which the entitlement holder is eligible, or to cause the financial asset to be transferred to a securities account of the entitlement holder with another securities intermediary. A securities intermediary satisfies the duty if:

(1) the securities intermediary acts as agreed upon by the entitlement holder and the securities intermediary; or

(2)   in the absence of agreement, the securities intermediary exercises due care in accordance with reasonable commercial standards to follow the direction of the entitlement holder.

Section 8–511. Priority Among Security Interests and Entitlement Holders.

(a)   Except as otherwise provided in subsections (b) and (c), if a securities intermediary does not have sufficient interests in a particular financial asset to satisfy both its obligations to entitlement holders who have security entitlements to that financial asset and its obligation to a creditor of the securities intermediary who has a security interest in that financial asset, the claims of entitlement holders, other than the creditor, have priority over the claim of the creditor.

(b)   A claim of a creditor of a securities intermediary who has a security interest in a financial asset held by a securities intermediary has priority over claims of the securities intermediary's entitlement holders who have security entitlements with respect to that financial asset if the creditor has control over the financial asset.

(c)   If a clearing corporation does not have sufficient financial assets to satisfy both its obligations to entitlement holders who have security entitlements with respect to a financial asset and its obligation to a creditor of the clearing corporation who has a security interest in that financial asset, the claim of the creditor has priority over the claims of entitlement holders.

Section 9–103. Purchase-money Security Interest; Application of Payments; Burden of Establishing.

(a)   Definitions. In this section:

(1)   "purchase-money collateral" means goods or software that secures a purchase-money obligation incurred with respect to that collateral; and

(2)   "purchase-money obligation" means an obligation of an obligor incurred as all or part of the price of the collateral or for value given to enable the debtor to acquire rights in or the use of the collateral if the value is in fact so used.

(b)   Purchase-money security interest in goods. A security interest in goods is a purchase-money security interest:

(1)   to the extent that the goods are purchase-money collateral with respect to that security interest;

(2)   if the security interest is in inventory that is or was purchase-money collateral, also to the extent that the security interest secures a purchase-money obligation incurred with respect to other inventory in which the secured party holds or held a purchase-money security interest; and

(3) also to the extent that the security interest secures a purchase-money obligation incurred with respect to software in which the secured party holds or held a purchase-money security interest.

(c) Purchase-money security interest in software. A security interest in software is a purchase-money security interest to the extent that the security interest also secures a purchase-money obligation incurred with respect to goods in which the secured party holds or held a purchase-money security interest if:

(1) the debtor acquired its interest in the software in an integrated transaction in which it acquired an interest in the goods; and

(2) the debtor acquired its interest in the software for the principal purpose of using the software in the goods.

(d) Consignor's inventory purchase-money security interest. The security interest of a consignor in goods that are the subject of a consignment is a purchase-money security interest in inventory.

(e) Application of payment in non-consumer-goods transaction. In a transaction other than a consumer-goods transaction, if the extent to which a security interest is a purchase-money security interest depends on the application of a payment to a particular obligation, the payment must be applied:

(1) in accordance with any reasonable method of application to which the parties agree;

(2) in the absence of the parties' agreement to a reasonable method, in accordance with any intention of the obligor manifested at or before the time of payment; or

(3) in the absence of an agreement to a reasonable method and timely manifestation of the obligor's intention, in the following order:

(A) to obligations that are not secured; and

(B) if more than one obligation is secured, to obligations secured by purchase-money security interests in the order in which those obligations were incurred.

(f) No loss of status of purchase-money security interest in non-consumer-goods transaction. In a transaction other than a consumer-goods transaction, a purchase-money security interest does not lose its status as such, even if:

(1) the purchase-money collateral also secures an obligation that is not a purchase-money obligation;

(2) collateral that is not purchase-money collateral also secures the purchase-money obligation; or

(3) the purchase-money obligation has been renewed, refinanced, consolidated, or restructured.

(g)   Burden of proof in non-consumer-goods transaction. In a transaction other than a consumer-goods transaction, a secured party claiming a purchase-money security interest has the burden of establishing the extent to which the security interest is a purchase-money security interest.

(h)   Non-consumer-goods transactions; no inference. The limitation of the rules in subsections (e), (f), and (g) to transactions other than consumer-goods transactions is intended to leave to the court the determination of the proper rules in consumer-goods transactions. The court may not infer from that limitation the nature of the proper rule in consumer-goods transactions and may continue to apply established approaches.

Section 9–104. Control of Deposit Account.

(a)   Requirements for control. A secured party has control of a deposit account if:

(1)   the secured party is the bank with which the deposit account is maintained;

(2)   the debtor, secured party, and bank have agreed in an authenticated record that the bank will comply with instructions originated by the secured party directing disposition of the funds in the deposit account without further consent by the debtor; or

(3)   the secured party becomes the bank's customer with respect to the deposit account.

(b)   Debtor's right to direct disposition. A secured party that has satisfied subsection (a) has control, even if the debtor retains the right to direct the disposition of funds from the deposit account.

Section 9–105. Control of Electronic Chattel Paper.

A secured party has control of electronic chattel paper if the record or records comprising the chattel paper are created, stored, and assigned in such a manner that:

(1)   a single authoritative copy of the record or records exists which is unique, identifiable and, except as otherwise provided in paragraphs (4), (5), and (6), unalterable;

(2)   the authoritative copy identifies the secured party as the assignee of the record or records;

(3)   the authoritative copy is communicated to and maintained by the secured party or its designated custodian;

(4)   copies or revisions that add or change an identified assignee of the authoritative copy can be made only with the participation of the secured party;

(5)   each copy of the authoritative copy and any copy of a copy is readily identifiable as a copy that is not the authoritative copy; and

(6)   any revision of the authoritative copy is readily identifiable as an authorized or unauthorized revision.

Section 9–203. Attachment and Enforceability of Security Interest; Proceeds; Supporting Obligations; Formal Requisites.

(a)   Attachment. A security interest attaches to collateral when it becomes enforceable against the debtor with respect to the collateral, unless an agreement expressly postpones the time of attachment.

(b)   Enforceability. Except as otherwise provided in subsections (c) through (i), a security interest is enforceable against the debtor and third parties with respect to the collateral only if:

(1)   value has been given;

(2)   the debtor has rights in the collateral or the power to transfer rights in the collateral to a secured party; and

(3)   one of the following conditions is met:

(A)   the debtor has authenticated a security agreement that provides a description of the collateral and, if the security interest covers timber to be cut, a description of the land concerned;

(B)   the collateral is not a certificated security and is in the possession of the secured party under Section 9–313 pursuant to the debtor's security agreement;

(C)   the collateral is a certificated security in registered form and the security certificate has been delivered to the secured party under Section 8–301 pursuant to the debtor's security agreement; or

(D)   the collateral is deposit accounts, electronic chattel paper, investment property, or letter-of-credit rights, and the secured party has control under Section 9–104, 9–105, 9–106, or 9–107 pursuant to the debtor's security agreement.

(c)   Other UCC provisions. Subsection (b) is subject to Section 4–210 on the security interest of a collecting bank, Section 5–118 on the security interest of a letter-of-credit issuer or nominated person, Section 9–110 on a security interest arising under Article 2 or 2-A, and Section 9–206 on security interests in investment property.

(d)   When a person becomes bound by another person's security agreement. A person becomes bound as debtor by a security agreement entered into by another person if, by operation of law other than this article or by contract:

(1)   the security agreement becomes effective to create a security interest in the person's property; or

(2)   the person becomes generally obligated for the obligations of the other person, including the obligation secured under the security agreement, and acquires or succeeds to all or substantially all of the assets of the other person.

(e)   Effect of new debtor becoming bound. If a new debtor becomes bound as debtor by a security agreement entered into by another person:

(1)   the agreement satisfies subsection (b)(3) with respect to existing or after-acquired property of the new debtor to the extent the property is described in the agreement; and

(2)   another agreement is not necessary to make a security interest in the property enforceable.

(f)   Proceeds and supporting obligations. The attachment of a security interest in collateral gives the secured party the rights to proceeds provided by Section 9–315 and is also attachment of a security interest in a supporting obligation for the collateral.

(g)   Lien securing right to payment. The attachment of a security interest in a right to payment or performance secured by a security interest or other lien on personal or real property is also attachment of a security interest in the security interest, mortgage, or other lien.

(h)   Security entitlement carried in securities account. The attachment of a security interest in a securities account is also attachment of a security interest in the security entitlements carried in the securities account.

(i)   Commodity contracts carried in commodity account. The attachment of a security interest in a commodity account is also attachment of a security interest in the commodity contracts carried in the commodity account.

Section 9–204. After-acquired Property; Future Advances.

(a)   After-acquired collateral. Except as otherwise provided in subsection (b), a security agreement may create or provide for a security interest in after-acquired collateral.

(b)   When after-acquired property clause not effective. A security interest does not attach under a term constituting an after-acquired property clause to:

(1)   consumer goods, other than an accession when given as additional security, unless the debtor acquires rights in them within 10 days after the secured party gives value; or

(2)   a commercial tort claim.

(c)   Future advances and other value. A security agreement may provide that collateral secures, or that accounts, chattel paper, payment intangibles, or promissory notes are sold in connection with, future advances or other value, whether or not the advances or value are given pursuant to commitment.

Section 9–207. Rights and Duties of Secured Party Having Possession or Control of Collateral.

(a)   Duty of care when secured party in possession. Except as otherwise provided in subsection (d), a secured party shall use reasonable care in the custody and preservation of collateral in the secured party's possession. In the case of chattel paper or an instrument, reasonable care includes taking necessary steps to preserve rights against prior parties unless otherwise agreed.

(b)   Expenses, risks, duties, and rights when secured party in possession. Except as otherwise provided in subsection (d), if a secured party has possession of collateral:

(1)   reasonable expenses, including the cost of insurance and payment of taxes or other charges, incurred in the custody, preservation, use, or operation of the collateral are chargeable to the debtor and are secured by the collateral;

(2)   the risk of accidental loss or damage is on the debtor to the extent of a deficiency in any effective insurance coverage;

(3)   the secured party shall keep the collateral identifiable, but fungible collateral may be commingled; and

(4)   the secured party may use or operate the collateral:

(A)   for the purpose of preserving the collateral or its value;

(B)   as permitted by an order of a court having competent jurisdiction; or

(C)   except in the case of consumer goods, in the manner and to the extent agreed by the debtor.

(c)   Duties and rights when secured party in possession or control.

Except as otherwise provided in subsection (d), a secured party having possession of collateral or control of collateral under Section 9–104, 9–105, 9–106, or 9–107:

(1)   may hold as additional security any proceeds, except money or funds, received from the collateral;

(2)   shall apply money or funds received from the collateral to reduce the secured obligation, unless remitted to the debtor; and

(3)   may create a security interest in the collateral.

(d)   Buyer of certain rights to payment. If the secured party is a buyer of accounts, chattel paper, payment intangibles, or promissory notes or a consignor:

(1)   subsection (a) does not apply unless the secured party is entitled under an agreement:

(A)   to charge back uncollected collateral; or

    (B)   otherwise to full or limited recourse against the debtor or a secondary obligor based on the nonpayment or other default of an account debtor or other obligor on the collateral; and

(2)   subsections (b) and (c) do not apply.

Section 9–304. Law Governing Perfection and Priority of Security Interests in Deposit Accounts

(a)   Law of bank's jurisdiction governs. The local law of a bank's jurisdiction governs perfection, the effect of perfection or nonperfection, and the priority of a security interest in a deposit account maintained with that bank.

(b)   Bank's jurisdiction. The following rules determine a bank's jurisdiction for purposes of this part:

    (1)   If an agreement between the bank and the debtor governing the deposit account expressly provides that a particular jurisdiction is the bank's jurisdiction for purposes of this part, this article, or this chapter, that jurisdiction is the bank's jurisdiction.

    (2)   If paragraph (1) does not apply and an agreeemnt between the bank and its customer governing the deposit account expressly provides that the agreement is governed by the law of a particular jurisdiction, that jurisdiction is the bank's jurisdiction.

    (3)   If neither paragraph (1) nor paragraph (2) applies and an agreement betwen the bank and its customer governing the deposit account expressly provides that the deposit account is maintained at an office in a particular jurisdiction, that jurisdiction is the bank's jurisdiction.

    (4)   If none of the preceding paragraphs apply, the bank's jurisdiction is the jurisdiction in which the office identified in an account statement as the office serving the customer's account is located.

    (5)   If none of the preceding paragraphs apply, the bank's jurisdiction is the jurisdiction in which the chief executive office of the bank is located.

Section 9–305. Law Governing Perfection and Priority of Security Interests in Investment Property.

(a)   Governing law: general rules. Except as otherwise provided in subsections (c) and (d), the following rules apply:

    (1)   While a security certificate is located in a jurisdiction, the local law of that jurisdiction governs perfection, the effect of perfection or nonperfection, and the priority of a security interest in the certificated security represented thereby.

    (2)   The local law of the issuer's jurisdiction as specified in Section 8–110(d) governs perfection, the effect of perfection or nonperfection, and the priority of a security interest in an uncertificated security.

(3)   The local law of the securities intermediary's jurisdiction as specified in Section 8–110(e) governs perfection, the effect of perfection or nonperfection, and the priority of a security interest in a security entitlement or securities account.

(4)   The local law of the commodity intermediary's jurisdiction governs perfection, the effect of perfection or nonperfection, and the priority of a security interest in a commodity contract or commodity account.

(b)   Commodity intermediary's jurisdiction. The following rules determine a commodity intermediary's jurisdiction for purposes of this part:

(1)   If an agreement between the commodity intermediary and commodity customer governing the commodity account expressly provides that a particular jurisdiction is the commodity intermediary's jurisdiction for purposes of this part, this article, or this chapter, that jurisdiction is the commodity intermediary's jurisdiction.

(2)   If paragraph (1) does not apply and an agreement between the commodity intermediary and commodity customer governing the commodity account expressly provides that the agreement is governed by the law of a particular jurisdiction, that jurisdiction is the commodity intermediary's jurisdiction.

(3)   If neither paragraph (1) nor paragraph (2) applies and an agreement between the commodity intermediary and commodity customer governing the commodity account expressly provides that the commodity account is maintained at an office in a particular jurisdiction, that jurisdiction is the commodity intermediary's jurisdiction.

(4)   If none of the preceding paragraphs apply, the commodity intermediary's jurisdiction is the jurisdiction in which the office identified in an account statement as the office serving the commodity customer's account is located.

(5)   If none of the preceding paragraphs apply, the commodity intermediary's jurisdiction is the jurisdiction in which the chief executive office of the commodity intermediary is located.

(c)   When perfection governed by law of jurisdiction where debtor located. The local law of the jurisdiction in which the debtor is located governs:

(1)   perfection of a security interest in investment property by filing;

(2)   automatic perfection of a security interest in investment property created by a broker or securities intermediary; and

(3)   automatic perfection of a security interest in a commodity contract or commodity account created by a commodity intermediary.

(d)   Cooperative interests. Subsections (a) through (c) do not apply to cooperative interests.

Section 9–504. Indication of Collateral.

A financing statement sufficiently indicates the collateral that it covers if the financing statement provides:

(1) a description of the collateral pursuant to Section 9–108; or

(2) an indication that the financing statement covers all assets or all personal property.

Section 9–505. Filing and Compliance with Other Statutes and Treaties for Consignments, Leases, Other Bailments, and Other Transactions.

(a) Use of terms other than "debtor" and "secured party". A consignor, lessor, or other bailor of goods, a licensor, or a buyer of a payment intangible or promissory note may file a financing statement, or may comply with a statute or treaty described in Section 9–311(a), using the terms "consignor", "consignee", "lessor", "lessee", "bailor","bailee", "licensor", "licensee", "owner", "registered owner", "buyer", "seller", or words of similar import, instead of the terms "secured party" and "debtor".

(b) Effect of financing statement under subsection (a). This part applies to the filing of a financing statement under subsection (a) and, as appropriate, to compliance that is equivalent to filing a financing statement under Section 9–311(b), but the filing or compliance is not of itself a factor in determining whether the collateral secures an obligation. If it is determined for another reason that the collateral secures an obligation, a security interest held by the consignor, lessor, bailor, licensor, owner, or buyer which attaches to the collateral is perfected by the filing or compliance.

Section 9–506. Effect of Errors or Omissions.

(a) Minor errors and omissions. A financing statement substantially satisfying the requirements of this part is effective, even if it has minor errors or omissions, unless the errors or omissions make the financing statement seriously misleading.

(b) Financing statement seriously misleading. Except as otherwise provided in subsection (c), a financing statement that fails sufficiently to provide the name of the debtor in accordance with Section 9–503(a) is seriously misleading.

(c) Financing statement not seriously misleading. If a search of the records of the filing office under the debtor's correct name, using the filing office's standard search logic, if any, would disclose a financing statement that fails sufficiently to provide the name of the debtor in accordance with Section 9–503(a), the name provided does not make the financing statement seriously misleading.

(d) "Debtor's correct name". For purposes of Section 9–508(b), the "debtor's correct name" in subsection (c) means the correct name of the new debtor.

ANNEX 5
AMENDMENT AGREEMENT

APPENDIX A

FORM OF AMENDMENT TO ISDA MASTER AGREEMENT TO ADD
THE 1995 ISDA CREDIT SUPPORT ANNEX (TRANSFER)[1]

Parties should consult with their legal advisers and any other adviser they deem appropriate prior to using this form of Amendment. Because of the varied documentation structures in the marketplace, modifications to this form of Amendment may be necessary or an entirely different form of amendment may be appropriate.

AMENDMENT TO ISDA MASTER AGREEMENT

dated as of ....

.... and ....

have entered into an ISDA Master Agreement dated as of ...., as amended and supplemented from time to time (the "Agreement").

The parties have agreed to amend the Agreement as follows:

1.   Amendment of the Agreement

Upon execution of this Amendment by both parties, the Agreement is amended to add as part of the Schedule to the Agreement the 1995 ISDA Credit Support Annex (Transfer) (the "Annex") in the form set out in the Exhibit attached to this Amendment.

2.   Representations

Each party represents to the other party that all representations contained in the Agreement (including all representations set out in the Annex) are true and accurate as of the date of this Amendment and that such representations are deemed to be given or repeated, as the case may be, by each party on the date of this Amendment.

3.   Miscellaneous

(a)   **Definitions.** Capitalised terms used in this Amendment and not otherwise defined shall have the meanings specified for such terms in the Agreement.

(b)   **Entire Agreement.** This Amendment constitutes the entire agreement and understanding of the parties with respect to its subject matter and supersedes all oral communication and prior writings (except as otherwise provided in this Amendment) with respect to its subject matter.

---

[1]   As the Deed is a stand-alone document, it is not necessary to amend the related ISDA Master Agreement in order to put it in place.

(c)   **Counterparts.** This Amendment may be executed and delivered in counterparts (including by facsimile transmission), each of which will be deemed an original.

(d)   **Headings.** The headings used in this Amendment are for convenience of reference only and are not to affect the construction of or to be taken into consideration in interpreting this Amendment.

(e)   **Governing Law.** This Amendment will be governed by and construed in accordance with English law/the laws of the State of New York (without reference to choice of law doctrine).[2]

IN WITNESS WHEREOF the parties have executed this Amendment on the respective dates specified below with effect from the date specified on the first page of this Amendment.

....
            (Name of Party)   (Name of Party)

By:...   By...

Name: Name:
Title: Title:
Date: Date:

---

[2]   Delete as applicable.

ANNEX 6
ISDA CREDIT SUPPORT DEED SUBJECT TO ENGLISH LAW

(Bilateral Form - Security Interest)[1] (ISDA Agreements Subject to English Law)[2]

International Swaps and Derivatives Association, Inc.

CREDIT SUPPORT DEED

between

.... and ....
("Party A") ("Party B")

made on ....[3]

relating to the

ISDA Master Agreement

dated as of ....between Party A and Party B.

This Deed is a Credit Support Document with respect to both parties in relation to the ISDA Master Agreement referred to above (as amended and supplemented from time to time, the "Agreement").

Accordingly, the parties agree as follows:

Paragraph 1. Interpretation

(a) *Definitions and Inconsistency.* Unless otherwise defined in this Deed, capitalised terms defined in the Agreement have the same meaning in this Deed. Capitalised terms not otherwise defined in this Deed or in the Agreement have the meanings specified pursuant to Paragraph 12, and all references in this Deed to Paragraphs are to Paragraphs of this Deed. In the event of any inconsistency between this Deed and the provisions of the Agreement, this Deed will prevail, and in the event of any inconsistency between Paragraph 13 and the other provisions of this Deed, Paragraph 13 will prevail. For the avoidance of doubt,

---

[1] This document is intended to create a charge or other security interest over the assets transferred under its terms. Persons intending to establish a collateral arrangement based on a full transfer should consider using the ISDA Credit Support Annex (English law).

[2] This Credit Support Deed has been prepared for use with ISDA Master Agreements subject to English law. Users should consult their legal advisers as to the proper use and effect of this form and the arrangements it contemplates. In particular, users should consult their legal advisers if they wish to have the Credit Support Deed made subject to a governing law other than English law.

[3] The parties should insert here the date this Deed is actually executed and not the effective ("as of") date of the related ISDA Master Agreement, if different.

references to "transfer" in this Deed mean, in relation to cash, payment and, in relation to other assets, delivery.

(b)   *Secured Party and Chargor.* All references in this Deed to the "Secured Party" will be to either party when acting in that capacity and all corresponding references to the "Chargor" will be to the other party when acting in that capacity; *provided, however,* that if Other Posted Support is held by a party to this Deed, all references in this Deed to that party as the Secured Party with respect to that Other Posted Support will be to that party as the beneficiary of that Other Posted Support and will not subject that support or that party as the beneficiary of that Other Posted Support to provisions of law generally relating to security interests and secured parties.

Paragraph 2. Security

(a)   *Covenant to Perform.* Each party as the Chargor covenants with the other party that it will perform the Obligations in the manner provided in the Agreement, this Deed or any other relevant agreement.

(b)   *Security.* Each party as the Chargor, as security for the performance of the Obligations: (i) mortgages, charges and pledges and agrees to mortgage, charge and pledge, with full title guarantee, in favour of the Secured Party by way of first fixed legal mortgage all Posted Collateral (other than Posted Collateral in the form of cash), (ii) to the fullest extent permitted by law, charges and agrees to charge, with full title guarantee, in favour of the Secured Party by way of first fixed charge all Posted Collateral in the form of cash; and (iii) assigns and agrees to assign, with full title guarantee, the Assigned Rights to the Secured Party absolutely.

(c)   *Release of Security.* Upon the transfer by the Secured Party to the Chargor of Posted Collateral, the security interest granted under this Deed on that Posted Collateral will be released immediately, and the Assigned Rights relating to that Posted Collateral will be re-assigned to the Chargor, in each case without any further action by either party. The Chargor agrees, in relation to any securities comprised in Posted Collateral released by the Secured Party under this Deed, that it will accept securities of the same type, nominal value, description and amount as those securities.

(d)   *Preservation of Security.* The security constituted by this Deed shall be a continuing security and shall not be satisfied by any intermediate payment or satisfaction of the whole or any part of the Obligations but shall secure the ultimate balance of the Obligations. If for any reason this security ceases to be a continuing security, the Secured Party may open a new account with or continue any existing account with the Chargor and the liability of the Chargor in respect of the Obligations at the date of such cessation shall remain regardless of any payments into or out of any such account. The security constituted by this Deed shall be in addition to and shall not be affected by any other security now or subsequently held by the Secured Party for all or any of the Obligations.

(e)   *Waiver of Defences.* The obligations of the Chargor under this Deed shall not be affected by any act, omission or circumstance which, but for this provision, might operate to release or otherwise exonerate the Chargor from its obligations under this Deed or affect such obligations including (but without limitation) and whether or not known to the Chargor or the Secured Party:

ISDA ®1995

(i)   any time or indulgence granted to or composition with the Chargor or any other person;

(ii)   the variation, extension, compromise, renewal or release of, or refusal or neglect to perfect or enforce, any terms of the Agreement or any rights or remedies against, or any security granted by, the Chargor or any other person;

(iii)   any irregularity, invalidity or unenforceability of any obligations of the Chargor under the Agreement or any present or future law or order of any government or authority (whether of right or in fact) purporting to reduce or otherwise affect any of such obligations to the intent that the Chargor's obligations under this Deed shall remain in full force and this Deed shall be construed accordingly as if there were no such irregularity, unenforceability, invalidity, law or order;

(iv)   any legal limitation, disability, incapacity or other circumstance relating to the Chargor, any guarantor or any other person or any amendment to or variation of the terms of the Agreement or any other document or security.

(f)   *Immediate Recourse.* The Chargor waives any right it may have of first requiring the Secured Party to proceed against or claim payment from any other person or enforce any guarantee or security before enforcing this Deed.

(g)   *Reinstatement.* Where any discharge (whether in respect of the security constituted by this Deed, any other security or otherwise) is made in whole or in part or any arrangement is made on the faith of any payment, security or other disposition which is avoided or any amount paid pursuant to any such discharge or arrangement must be repaid on bankruptcy, liquidation or otherwise without limitation, the security constituted by this Deed and the liability of the Chargor under this Deed shall continue as if there had been no such discharge or arrangement.

Paragraph 3. Credit Support Obligations

(a)   *Delivery Amount.* Subject to Paragraphs 4 and 5, upon a demand made by the Secured Party on or promptly following a Valuation Date, if the Delivery Amount for that Valuation Date equals or exceeds the Chargor's Minimum Transfer Amount, then the Chargor will transfer to the Secured Party Eligible Credit Support having a Value as of the date of transfer at least equal to the applicable Delivery Amount (rounded pursuant to Paragraph 13). Unless otherwise specified in Paragraph 13, the "Delivery Amount" applicable to the Chargor for any Valuation Date will equal the amount by which:

(i)   the Credit Support Amount

exceeds

(ii)   the Value as of that Valuation Date of all Posted Credit Support held by the Secured Party (as adjusted to include any prior Delivery Amount and to exclude any prior Return Amount, the transfer of which, in either case, has not yet been completed and for which the relevant Settlement Day falls on or after such Valuation Date).

ISDA ®1995

(b)   *Return Amount.* Subject to Paragraphs 4 and 5, upon a demand made by the Chargor on or promptly following a Valuation Date, if the Return Amount for that Valuation Date equals or exceeds the Secured Party's Minimum Transfer Amount, then the Secured Party will transfer to the Chargor Posted Credit Support specified by the Chargor in that demand having a Value as of the date of transfer as close as practicable to the applicable Return Amount (rounded pursuant to Paragraph 13). Unless otherwise specified in Paragraph 13, the "Return Amount" applicable to the Secured Party for any Valuation Date will equal the amount by which:

(i)   the Value as of that Valuation Date of all Posted Credit Support held by the Secured Party (as adjusted to include any prior Delivery Amount and to exclude any prior Return Amount, the transfer of which, in either case, has not yet been completed and for which the relevant Settlement Day falls on or after such Valuation Date)

exceeds

(ii)   the Credit Support Amount.

Paragraph 4. Conditions Precedent, Transfers, Calculations and Substitutions

(a)   *Conditions Precedent.* Each transfer obligation of the Chargor under Paragraphs 3 and 5 and of the Secured Party under Paragraphs 3, 4(d)(ii), 5 and 6(g) is subject to the conditions precedent that:

(i)   no Event of Default, Potential Event of Default or Specified Condition has occurred and is continuing with respect to the other party; and

(ii)   no Early Termination Date for which any unsatisfied payment obligations exist has occurred or been designated as the result of an Event of Default or Specified Condition with respect to the other party.

(b)   *Transfers.* All transfers under this Deed of any Eligible Credit Support, Posted Credit Support, Interest Amount or Distributions, shall be made in accordance with the instructions of the Secured Party, Chargor or Custodian, as applicable, and shall be made:

(i)   in the case of cash, by transfer into one or more bank accounts specified by the recipient;

(ii)   in the case of certificated securities which cannot or which the parties have agreed will not be delivered by book-entry, by delivery in appropriate physical form to the recipient or its account accompanied by any duly executed instruments of transfer, assignments in blank, transfer tax stamps and any other documents necessary to constitute a legally valid transfer to the recipient;

(iii)   in the case of securities which the parties have agreed will be delivered by book-entry, by the giving of written instructions (including, for the avoidance of doubt, instructions given by telex, facsimile transmission or electronic messaging system) to the relevant depository institution or other entity specified by the recipient, together with a written copy of the instructions to the

4   ISDA ®1995

recipient, sufficient, if complied with, to result in a legally effective transfer of the relevant interest to the recipient; and

(iv)   in the case of Other Eligible Support or Other Posted Support, as specified in Paragraph 13(j)(ii).

Subject to Paragraph 5 and unless otherwise specified, if a demand for the transfer of Eligible Credit Support or Posted Credit Support is received by the Notification Time, then the relevant transfer will be made not later than the close of business on the Settlement Day relating to the date such demand is received; if a demand is received after the Notification Time, then the relevant transfer will be made not later than the close of business on the Settlement Day relating to the day after the date such demand is received.

(c)   *Calculations.* All calculations of Value and Exposure for purposes of Paragraphs 3 and 5(a) will be made by the relevant Valuation Agent as of the relevant Valuation Time. The Valuation Agent will notify each party (or the other party, if the relevant Valuation Agent is a party) of its calculations not later than the Notification Time on the Local Business Day following the applicable Valuation Date (or, in the case of Paragraph 5(a), following the date of calculation).

(d)   *Substitutions.*

(i)   Unless otherwise specified in Paragraph 13, the Chargor may on any Local Business Day by notice (a "Substitution Notice") inform the Secured Party that it wishes to transfer to the Secured Party Eligible Credit Support (the "Substitute Credit Support") specified in that Substitution Notice in substitution for certain Eligible Credit Support (the "Original Credit Support") specified in the Substitution Notice comprised in the Chargor's Posted Collateral.

(ii)   If the Secured Party notifies the Chargor that it has consented to the proposed substitution, (A) the Chargor will be obliged to transfer the Substitute Credit Support to the Secured Party on the first Settlement Day following the date on which it receives notice (which may be oral telephonic notice) from the Secured Party of its consent and (B) subject to Paragraph 4(a), the Secured Party will be obliged to transfer to the Chargor the Original Credit Support not later than the Settlement Day following the date on which the Secured Party receives the Substitute Credit Support, unless otherwise specified in Paragraph 13(f) (the "Substitution Date"); *provided* that the Secured Party will only be obliged to transfer Original Credit Support with a Value as of the date of transfer as close as practicable to, but in any event not more than, the Value of the Substitute Credit Support as of that date.

Paragraph 5. Dispute Resolution

(a)   *Disputed Calculations or Valuations.* If a party (a "Disputing Party") reasonably disputes (I) the Valuation Agent's calculation of a Delivery Amount or a Return Amount or (II) the Value of any transfer of Eligible Credit Support or Posted Credit Support, then:

(1)   the Disputing Party will notify the other party and the Valuation Agent (if the Valuation Agent is not the other party) not later than the close of business on the Local Business Day following, in the case of (I) above, the date that the demand is received under Paragraph 3 or, in the case of (II) above, the date of transfer;

(2)   in the case of (I) above, the appropriate party will transfer the undisputed amount to the other party not later than the close of business on the Settlement Day following the date that the demand is received under Paragraph 3;

(3)   the parties will consult with each other in an attempt to resolve the dispute; and

(4)   if they fail to resolve the dispute by the Resolution Time, then:

(i)   in the case of a dispute involving a Delivery Amount or Return Amount, unless otherwise specified in Paragraph 13, the Valuation Agent will recalculate the Exposure and the Value as of the Recalculation Date by:

(A)   utilising any calculations of that part of the Exposure attributable to the Transactions that the parties have agreed are not in dispute;

(B)   calculating that part of the Exposure attributable to the Transactions in dispute by seeking four actual quotations at mid-market from Reference Market-makers for purposes of calculating Market Quotation, and taking the arithmetic mean of those obtained; *provided* that if four quotations are not available for a particular Transaction, then fewer than four quotations may be used for that Transaction, and if no quotations are available for a particular Transaction, then the Valuation Agent's original calculations will be used for that Transaction; and

(C)   utilising the procedures specified in Paragraph 13(g)(ii) for calculating the Value, if disputed, of Posted Credit Support;

(ii)   in the case of a dispute involving the Value of any transfer of Eligible Credit Support or Posted Credit Support, the Valuation Agent will recalculate the Value as of the date of transfer pursuant to Paragraph 13(g)(ii).

Following a recalculation pursuant to this Paragraph, the Valuation Agent will notify each party (or the other party, if the Valuation Agent is a party) as soon as possible but in any event not later than the Notification Time on the Local Business Day following the Resolution Time. The appropriate party will, upon demand following that notice by the Valuation Agent or a resolution pursuant to (3) above and subject to Paragraphs 4(a) and 4(b), make the appropriate transfer.

6   ISDA ®1995

(b) *Not a Relevant Event.* The failure by a party to make a transfer of any amount which is the subject of a dispute to which Paragraph 5(a) applies will not constitute a Relevant Event under Paragraph 7 for as long as the procedures set out in Paragraph 5 are being carried out. For the avoidance of doubt, upon completion of those procedures, Paragraph 7 will apply to any failure by a party to make a transfer required under the final sentence of Paragraph 5(a) on the relevant due date.

Paragraph 6. Holding Posted Collateral

(a) *Care of Posted Collateral.* The Secured Party will exercise reasonable care to assure the safe custody of all Posted Collateral to the extent required by applicable law. Except as specified in the preceding sentence, the Secured Party will have no duty with respect to Posted Collateral, including, without limitation, any duty to collect any Distributions, or enforce or preserve any rights pertaining to the Posted Collateral.

(b) *Eligibility to Hold Posted Collateral; Custodians.*

(i) *General.* Subject to the satisfaction of any conditions specified in Paragraph 13 for holding Posted Collateral, the Secured Party will be entitled to hold Posted Collateral or to appoint an agent (a **"Custodian"**) to hold Posted Collateral for the Secured Party. Upon notice by the Secured Party to the Chargor of the appointment of a Custodian, the Chargor's obligations to make any transfer will be discharged by making the transfer to that Custodian. The holding of Posted Collateral by a Custodian will be deemed to be the holding of that Posted Collateral by the Secured Party for which the Custodian is acting.

(ii) *Failure to Satisfy Conditions.* If the Secured Party or its Custodian fails to satisfy any conditions for holding Posted Collateral, then upon a demand made by the Chargor, the Secured Party will, not later than five Local Business Days after the demand, transfer or cause its Custodian to transfer all Posted Collateral held by it to a Custodian that satisfies those conditions or to the Secured Party if it satisfies those conditions.

(iii) · *Liability.* The Secured Party will be liable for the acts or omissions of its Custodian to the same extent that the Secured Party would be liable under this Deed for its own acts or omissions.

(c) *Segregated Accounts.* The Secured Party shall, and shall cause any Custodian to, open and/or maintain one or more segregated accounts (the "Segregated Accounts"), as appropriate, in which to hold Posted Collateral (other than Posted Collateral in the form of cash) under this Deed. The Secured Party and any Custodian shall each hold, record and/or identify in the relevant Segregated Accounts all Posted Collateral (other than Posted Collateral in the form of cash) held in relation to the Chargor, and, except as provided otherwise herein, such Collateral shall at all times be and remain the property of the Chargor and segregated from the property of the Secured Party or the relevant Custodian, as the case may be, and shall at no time constitute the property of, or be commingled with the property of, the Secured Party or such Custodian.

ISDA ®1995

(d)   *No Use of Collateral.* For the avoidance of doubt, and without limiting the rights of the Secured Party under the other provisions of this Deed, the Secured Party will not have the right to sell, pledge, rehypothecate, assign, invest, use, commingle or otherwise dispose of, or otherwise use in its business any Posted Collateral it holds under this Deed.

(e)   *Rights Accompanying Posted Collateral.*

(i)   *Distributions and Voting Rights.* Unless and until a Relevant Event or a Specified Condition occurs the Chargor shall be entitled:

(A)   to all Distributions; and

(B)   to exercise, or to direct the Secured Party to exercise, any voting rights attached to any of the Posted Collateral (but only in a manner consistent with the terms of this Deed) and, if any expense would be incurred by the Secured Party in doing so, only to the extent that the Chargor paid to the Secured Party in advance of any such exercise an amount sufficient to cover that expense.

(ii)   *Exercise by Secured Party.* At any time after the occurrence of a Relevant Event or Specified Condition and without any further consent or authority on the part of the Chargor the Secured Party may exercise at its discretion (in the name of the Chargor or otherwise) in respect of any of the Posted Collateral any voting rights and any powers or rights which may be exercised by the person or persons in whose name or names the Posted Collateral is registered or who is the holder or bearer of them including (but without limitation) all the powers given to trustees by sections 10(3) and (4) of the Trustee Act 1925 (as amended by section 9 of the Trustee Investments Act 1961) in respect of securities or property subject to a trust. If the Secured Party exercises any such rights or powers, it will give notice of the same to the Chargor as soon as practicable.

(f)   *Calls and Other Obligations*

(i)   *Payment of Calls.* The Chargor will pay all calls or other payments which may become due in respect of any of the Posted Collateral and if it fails to do so the Secured Party may elect to make such payments on behalf of the Chargor. Any sums so paid by the Secured Party shall be repayable by the Chargor to the Secured Party on demand together with interest at the Default Rate from the date of such payment by the Secured Party and pending such repayment shall form part of the Obligations.

(ii)   *Requests for Information.* The Chargor shall promptly copy to the Secured Party and comply with all requests for information which is within its knowledge and which are made under section 212 of the Companies Act 1985 or any similar provision contained in any articles of association or other constitutional document relating to any of the Posted Collateral and if it fails to do so the Secured Party may elect to provide such information as it may have on behalf of the Chargor.

8   ISDA ®1995

(iii)   *Continuing Liability of Chargor*. The Chargor shall remain liable to observe and perform all of the other conditions and obligations assumed by it in respect of any of the Posted Collateral.

(iv)   *No Liability of Secured Party*. The Secured Party shall not be required to perform or fulfil any obligation of the Chargor in respect of the Posted Collateral or to make any payment, or to make any enquiry as to the nature or sufficiency of any payment received by it or the Chargor, or to present or file any claim or take any other action to collect or enforce the payment of any amount to which it may have been or to which it may be entitled under this Deed at any time.

(g)   *Distributions and Interest Amount.*

(i)   *Distributions.* The Secured Party will transfer to the Chargor not later than the Settlement Day following each Distributions Date any Distributions it receives to the extent that a Delivery Amount would not be created or increased by the transfer, as calculated by the Valuation Agent (and the date of calculation will be deemed a Valuation Date for this purpose).

(ii)   *Interest Amount.* Unless otherwise specified in Paragraph 13(i)(iii), with respect to Posted Collateral in the form of cash, the Secured Party will transfer to the Chargor at the times specified in Paragraph 13(i)(ii) the Interest Amount to the extent that a Delivery Amount would not be created or increased by that transfer, as calculated by the Valuation Agent (and the date of calculation will be deemed to be a Valuation Date for this purpose).

Any Distributions or Interest Amount (or portion of either) not transferred pursuant to this Paragraph will constitute Posted Collateral and will be subject to the security interest granted under Paragraph 2(b) or otherwise will be subject to the set-off provided in Paragraph 8(a)(ii).

Paragraph 7. Default

For purposes of this Deed, a *"Relevant Event"* will have occurred with respect to a party if:

(i)   an Event of Default has occurred in respect of that party under the Agreement; or

(ii)   that party fails (or fails to cause its Custodian) to make, when due, any transfer of Eligible Collateral, Posted Collateral, Distributions or Interest Amount, as applicable, required to be made by it and that failure continues for two Local Business Days after notice of that failure is given to that party; or

(iii)   that party fails to perform any Obligation other than those specified in Paragraph 7(ii) and that failure continues for 30 days after notice of that failure is given to that party.

ISDA ®1995

Paragraph 8. Rights of Enforcement

(a)   *Secured Party's Rights.* If at any time (1) a Relevant Event or Specified Condition with respect to the Chargor has occurred and is continuing or (2) an Early Termination Date has occurred or been designated under the Agreement as the result of an Event of Default or Specified Condition with respect to the Chargor, then, unless the Chargor has paid in full all of its Obligations that are then due:

    (i)   the Secured Party shall, without prior notice to the Chargor, be entitled to put into force and to exercise immediately or as and when it may see fit any and every power possessed by the Secured Party by virtue of this Deed or available to a secured creditor (so that section 93 and section 103 of the Law of Property Act 1925 shall not apply to this Deed) and in particular (but without limitation) the Secured Party shall have power in respect of Posted Collateral other than in the form of cash:

        (A)   to sell all or any of the Posted Collateral in any manner permitted by law upon such terms as the Secured Party shall in its absolute discretion determine; and

        (B)   to collect, recover or compromise and to give a good discharge for any moneys payable to the Chargor in respect of any of the Posted Collateral;

    (ii)   the Secured Party may in respect of Posted Collateral in the form of cash immediately or at any subsequent time, without prior notice to the Chargor:

        (A)   apply or appropriate the Posted Collateral in or towards the payment or discharge of any amounts payable by the Chargor with respect to any Obligation in such order as the Secured Party sees fit; or

        (B)   set off all or any part of any amounts payable by the Chargor with respect to any Obligation against any obligation of the Secured Party to repay any amount to the Chargor in respect of the Posted Collateral; or

        (C)   debit any account of the Chargor (whether sole or joint) with the Secured Party at any of its offices anywhere (including an account opened specially for that purpose) with all or any part of any amounts payable by the Chargor with respect to any Obligation from time to time; or

        (D)   combine or consolidate any account in the name of the Chargor (whether sole or joint) in any currency at any of the Secured Party's offices anywhere with the account relating to the Posted Collateral;

    and for the purposes of this Paragraph 8(a)(ii) the Secured Party shall be entitled:

        (X)   to make any currency conversions or effect any transaction in currencies which it thinks fit, and to do so at such times and rates as it thinks proper;

10

(Y)   to effect any transfers between, or entries on, any of the Chargor's accounts with the Secured Party as it thinks proper; and

(iii)   the Secured Party may exercise any other rights and remedies available to the Secured Party under the terms of Other Posted Support, if any.

(b)   *Power of Attorney.* The Chargor, by way of security and solely for the purpose of more fully securing the performance of the Obligations, irrevocably appoints the Secured Party the attorney of the Chargor on its behalf and in the name of the Chargor or the Secured Party (as the attorney may decide) to do all acts, and execute all documents which the Chargor could itself execute, in relation to any of the Posted Collateral or in connection with any of the matters provided for in this Deed, including (but without limitation):

(i)   to execute any transfer, bill of sale or other assurance in respect of the Posted Collateral;

(ii)   to exercise all the rights and powers of the Chargor in respect of the Posted Collateral;

(iii)   to ask, require, demand, receive, compound and give a good discharge for any and all moneys and claims for moneys due and to become due under or arising out of any of the Posted Collateral;

(iv)   to endorse any cheques or other instruments or orders in connection with any of the Posted Collateral; and

(v)   to make any claims or to take any action or to institute any proceedings which the Secured Party considers to be necessary or advisable to protect or enforce the security interest created by this Deed.

(c)   *Protection of Purchaser*

(i)   No purchaser or other person dealing with the Secured Party or with its attorney or agent shall be concerned to enquire (1) whether any power exercised or purported to be exercised by the Secured Party has become exercisable, (2) whether any Obligation remains due, (3) as to the propriety or regularity of any of the actions of the Secured Party or (4) as to the application of any money paid to the Secured Party.

(ii)   In the absence of bad faith on the part of such purchaser or other person, such dealings shall be deemed, so far as regards the safety and protection of such purchaser or other person, to be within the powers conferred by this Deed and to be valid accordingly. The remedy of the Chargor in respect of any impropriety or irregularity whatever in the exercise of such powers shall be in damages only.

(d)   *Deficiencies and Excess Proceeds.* The Secured Party will transfer to the Chargor any proceeds and Posted Credit Support remaining after liquidation, set-off and/or application under Paragraph 8(a) and after satisfaction in full of all amounts payable by the Chargor with respect to any Obligations; the Chargor in all events will remain liable for any amounts remaining unpaid after any liquidation, set-off and/or application under Paragraph 8(a).

(e)   *Final Returns.* When no amounts are or may become payable by the Chargor with respect to any Obligations (except for any potential liability under Section 2(d) of the Agreement), the Secured Party will transfer to the Chargor all Posted Credit Support and the Interest Amount, if any.

Paragraph 9. Representations

Each party represents to the other party (which representations will be deemed to be repeated as of each date on which it, as the Chargor, transfers Eligible Collateral) that:

(i)   it has the power to grant a security interest in any Eligible Collateral it transfers as the Chargor to the Secured Party under this Deed and has taken all necessary actions to authorise the granting of that security interest;

(ii)   it is the beneficial owner of all Eligible Collateral it transfers as the Chargor to the Secured Party under this Deed, free and clear of any security interest, lien, encumbrance or other interest or restriction other than the security interest granted under Paragraph 2 and other than a lien routinely imposed on all securities in a clearing system in which any such Eligible Collateral may be held;

(iii)   upon the transfer of any Eligible Collateral by it as the Chargor to the Secured Party under the terms of this Deed, the Secured Party will have a valid security interest in such Eligible Collateral; and

(iv)   the performance by it as the Chargor of its obligations under this Deed will not result in the creation of any security interest, lien or other interest or encumbrance in or on any Posted Collateral other than the security interest created under this Deed (other than any lien routinely imposed on all securities in a clearing system in which any such Posted Collateral may be held).

Paragraph 10. Expenses

(a)   *General.* Except as otherwise provided in Paragraphs 10(b) and 10(c), each party will pay its own costs and expenses (including any stamp, transfer or similar transaction tax or duty payable on any transfer it is required to make under this Deed) in connection with performing its obligations under this Deed and neither party will be liable for any such costs and expenses incurred by the other party.

(b)   *Posted Credit Support.* The Chargor will promptly pay when due all taxes, assessments or charges of any nature that are imposed with respect to Posted Credit Support held by the Secured Party upon becoming aware of the same.

(c)   *Liquidation/Application of Posted Credit Support.* All reasonable costs and expenses incurred by the Secured Party in connection with the liquidation and/or application of any Posted Credit Support under Paragraph 8 will be payable, on demand, by the Defaulting Party or, if there is no Defaulting Party, equally by the parties.

Paragraph 11. Other Provisions

(a)   *Default Interest.* A Secured Party that fails to make, when due, any transfer of Posted Collateral or the Interest Amount, will be obliged to pay the Chargor (to the extent permitted under applicable law) an amount equal to interest at the Default Rate multiplied by the Value on the relevant Valuation Date of the items of property that were required to be transferred, from (and including) the date that Posted Collateral or Interest Amount was required to be transferred to (but excluding) the date of transfer of that Posted Collateral or Interest Amount. This interest will be calculated on the basis of daily compounding and the actual number of days elapsed.

(b)   *Further Assurances.* Promptly following a demand made by a party, the other party will execute, deliver, file and record any financing statement, specific assignment or other document and take any other action that may be necessary or desirable and reasonably requested by that party to create, preserve, perfect or validate any security interest granted under Paragraph 2, to enable that party to exercise or enforce its rights under this Deed with respect to Posted Credit Support or an Interest Amount or to effect or document a release of a security interest on Posted Collateral or an Interest Amount.

(c)   *Further Protection.* The Chargor will promptly give notice to the Secured Party of, and defend against, any suit, action, proceeding or lien that involves Posted Credit Support transferred by the Chargor or that could adversely affect the security interest granted by it under Paragraph 2.

(d)   *Good Faith and Commercially Reasonable Manner.* Performance of all obligations under this Deed, including, but not limited to, all calculations, valuations and determinations made by either party, will be made in good faith and in a commercially reasonable manner.

(e)   *Demands and Notices.* All demands and notices made by a party under this Deed will be made as specified in Section 12 of the Agreement, except as otherwise provided in Paragraph 13.

(f)   *Specifications of Certain Matters.* Anything referred to in this Deed as being specified in Paragraph 13 also may be specified in one or more Confirmations or other documents and this Deed will be construed accordingly.

(g)   *Governing Law and Jurisdiction.* This Deed will be governed by and construed in accordance with English law. With respect to any suit, action or proceedings relating to this Deed, each party irrevocably submits to the jurisdiction of the English courts.

ISDA ®1995

Paragraph 12. Definitions

As used in this Deed:

"Assigned Rights" means all rights relating to the Posted Collateral which the Chargor may have now or in the future against the Secured Party or any third party, including, without limitation, any right to delivery of a security of the appropriate description which arises in connection with (a) any Posted Collateral being transferred to a clearance system or financial intermediary or (b) any interest in or to any Posted Collateral being acquired while that Posted Collateral is in a clearance system or held through a financial intermediary.

"Base Currency" means the currency specified as such in Paragraph 13(a)(i).

"Base Currency Equivalent" means, with respect to an amount on a Valuation Date, in the case of an amount denominated in the Base Currency, such Base Currency amount and, in the case of an amount in a currency other than the Base Currency (the "Other Currency"), the amount in the Base Currency required to purchase such amount of the Other Currency at the spot exchange rate determined by the Valuation Agent for value on such Valuation Date.

"Chargor" means either party, when (i) that party receives a demand for or is required to transfer Eligible Credit Support under Paragraph 3(a) or (ii) in relation to that party the other party holds any Posted Credit Support.

"Credit Support Amount" means, with respect to a Secured Party on a Valuation Date, (i) the Secured Party's Exposure plus (ii) all Independent Amounts applicable to the Chargor, if any, minus (iii) all Independent Amounts applicable to the Secured Party, if any, minus (iv) the Chargor's Threshold; *provided, however,* that the Credit Support Amount will be deemed to be zero whenever the calculation of Credit Support Amount yields a number less than zero.

"Custodian" has the meaning specified in Paragraphs 6(b)(i) and 13.

"Delivery Amount" has the meaning specified in Paragraph 3(a).

"Disputing Party" has the meaning specified in Paragraph 5.

"Distributions" means, with respect to Posted Collateral other than cash, all principal, interest and other payments and distributions of cash or other property with respect to that Posted Collateral. Distributions will not include any item of property acquired by the Secured Party upon any disposition or liquidation of Posted Collateral.

"Distributions Date" means, with respect to any Eligible Collateral comprised in the Posted Collateral other than cash, each date on which a holder of the Eligible Collateral is entitled to receive Distributions or, if that date is not a Local Business Day, the next following Local Business Day.

ISDA ®1995

"Eligible Collateral" means, with respect to a party, the items, if any, specified as such for that party in Paragraph 13(c)(ii).

"Eligible Credit Support" means Eligible Collateral and Other Eligible Support, including in relation to any securities, if applicable, the proceeds of any redemption in whole or in part of such securities by the relevant issuer.

"Eligible Currency" means each currency specified as such in Paragraph 13(a)(ii), if such currency is freely available.

"Exposure" means with respect to a party on a Valuation Date and subject to Paragraph 5 in the case of a dispute, the amount, if any, that would be payable to that party by the other party (expressed as a positive number) or by that party to the other party (expressed as a negative number) pursuant to Section 6(e)(ii)(1) of the Agreement if all Transactions were being terminated as of the relevant Valuation Time, on the basis that (i) that party is not the Affected Party and (ii) the Base Currency is the Termination Currency; *provided* that Market Quotation will be determined by the Valuation Agent on behalf of that party using its estimates at mid-market of the amounts that would be paid for Replacement Transactions (as that term is defined in the definition of "Market Quotation").

"Independent Amount" means, with respect to a party, the Base Currency Equivalent of the amount specified as such for that party in Paragraph 13(c)(iv)(A); if no amount is specified, zero.

"Interest Amount" means, with respect to an Interest Period, the aggregate sum of the Base Currency Equivalent of the amounts of interest determined for each relevant currency and calculated for each day in that Interest Period on the principal amount of Posted Collateral in the form of cash in such currency held by the Secured Party on that day, determined by the Valuation Agent for each such day as follows:

(x)   the amount of that cash in such currency on that day; multiplied by

(y)   the relevant Interest Rate in effect for that day; divided by

(z)   360 (or, if such currency is pounds sterling, 365).

"Interest Period" means the period from (and including) the last Local Business Day on which an Interest Amount was transferred (or, if no Interest Amount has yet been transferred, the Local Business Day on which Posted Collateral in the form of cash was transferred to or received by the Secured Party) to (but excluding) the Local Business Day on which the current Interest Amount is transferred.

"Interest Rate" means, with respect to an Eligible Currency the rate specified in Paragraph 13(i)(i) for that currency.

"Local Business Day", unless otherwise specified in Paragraph 13(1), means:

(i)   in relation to a transfer of cash or other property (other than securities) under this Deed, a day on which commercial banks are open for business (including dealings in foreign exchange and foreign currency deposits) in the place where the relevant account is located and, if different, in the principal financial centre, if any, of the currency of such payment;

(ii)   in relation to a transfer of securities under this Deed, a day on which the clearance system agreed between the parties for delivery of the securities is open for the acceptance and execution of settlement instructions or, if delivery of the securities is contemplated by other means, a day on which commercial banks are open for business (including dealings in foreign exchange and foreign currency deposits) in the place(s) agreed between the parties for this purpose;

(iii)   in relation to a valuation under this Deed, a day on which commercial banks are open for business (including dealings in foreign exchange and foreign currency deposits) in the place of location of the Valuation Agent and in the place(s) agreed between the parties for this purpose; and

(iv)   in relation to any notice or other communication under this Deed, in the place specified in the address for notice most recently provided by the recipient.

"Minimum Transfer Amount" means, with respect to a party, the amount specified as such for that party in Paragraph 13(c)(iv)(C); if no amount is specified, zero.

"Notification Time" has the meaning specified in Paragraph 13(d)(iv).

"Obligations" means, with respect to a party, all present and future obligations of that party under the Agreement and this Deed and any additional obligations specified for that party in Paragraph 13(b).

"Other Eligible Support" means, with respect to a party, the items, if any, specified as such for that party in Paragraph 13.

"Other Posted Support" means all Other Eligible Support transferred to the Secured Party that remains in effect for the benefit of that Secured Party.

"Posted Collateral" means all Eligible Collateral, other property, Distributions and all proceeds of any such Eligible Collateral, other property or Distributions that have been transferred to or received by the Secured Party under this Deed and not transferred to the Chargor pursuant to Paragraph 3(b), 4(d)(ii) or 6(g)(i) or realised by the Secured Party under Paragraph 8. Any Distributions or Interest Amount (or portion of either) not transferred pursuant to Paragraph 6(g) will constitute Posted Collateral.

"Posted Credit Support" means Posted Collateral and Other Posted Support.

"Recalculation Date" means the Valuation Date that gives rise to the dispute under Paragraph 5; *provided, however,* that if a subsequent Valuation Date occurs under Paragraph 3 prior to the resolution of the dispute, then the "Recalculation Date" means the most recent Valuation Date under Paragraph 3.

"Relevant Event" has the meaning specified in Paragraph 7.

"Resolution Time" has the meaning specified in Paragraph 13(g)(i).

ISDA ®1995

"Secured Party" means either party, when that party (i) makes a demand for or is entitled to receive Eligible Credit Support under Paragraph 3(a) or (ii) holds or is deemed to hold Posted Credit Support.

"Settlement Day" means, in relation to a date, (i) with respect to a transfer of cash or other property (other than securities), the next Local Business Day and (ii) with respect to a transfer of securities, the first Local Business Day after such date on which settlement of a trade in the relevant securities, if effected on such date, would have been settled in accordance with customary practice when settling through the clearance system agreed between the parties for delivery of such securities or, otherwise, on the market in which such securities are principally traded (or, in either case, if there is no such customary practice, on the first Local Business Day after such date on which it is reasonably practicable to deliver such securities).

"Specified Condition" means, with respect to a party, any event specified as such for that party in Paragraph 13(e).

"Substitute Credit Support" has the meaning specified in Paragraph 4(d)(i).

"Substitution Date" has the meaning specified in Paragraph 4(d)(ii).

"Substitution Notice" has the meaning specified in Paragraph 4(d)(i).

"Threshold" means, with respect to a party, the Base Currency Equivalent of the amount specified as such for that party in Paragraph 13(c)(iv)(B); if no amount is specified, zero.

"Valuation Agent" has the meaning specified in Paragraph 13(d)(i).

"Valuation Date" means each date specified in or otherwise determined pursuant to Paragraph 13(d)(ii).

"Valuation Percentage" means, for any item of Eligible Collateral, the percentage specified in Paragraph 13(c)(ii).

"Valuation Time" has the meaning specified in Paragraph 13(d)(iii).

"Value" means for any Valuation Date or other date for which Value is calculated, and subject to Paragraph 5 in the case of a dispute, with respect to:

(i)   Eligible Collateral or Posted Collateral that is:

    (A)   an amount of cash, the Base Currency Equivalent of such amount multiplied by the applicable Valuation Percentage, if any; and

    (B)   a security, the Base Currency Equivalent of the bid price obtained by the Valuation Agent multiplied by the applicable Valuation Percentage, if any;

ISDA ®1995

(ii)   Posted Collateral that consists of items that are not specified as Eligible Collateral, zero; and

(iii)   Other Eligible Support and Other Posted Support, as specified in Paragraph 13(j).

18

Paragraph 13. Elections and Variables

(a)   *Base Currency and Eligible Currency.*

   (i)   "Base Currency" means United States Dollars unless otherwise specified here:....................................

   (ii) "Eligible Currency" means the Base Currency and each other currency specified here:
   ....
   ....

(b)   *Security Interest for "Obligations".* The term *"Obligations"* as used in this Deed includes the following additional obligations:

   With respect to Party A: ....

   With respect to Party B: ....

(c)   *Credit Support Obligations.*

   (i)   *Delivery Amount, Return Amount and Credit Support Amount.*

      (A)   *"Delivery Amount"* has the meaning specified in Paragraph 3(a), unless otherwise specified here: ....

      (B)   *"Return Amount"* has the meaning specified in Paragraph 3(b), unless otherwise specified here: ....

      (C)   *"Credit Support Amount"* has the meaning specified in Paragraph 12, unless otherwise specified here: ....

   (ii) *Eligible Collateral.* The following items will qualify as *"Eligible Collateral"* for the party specified:

		Party A	Party B	Valuation Percentage
(A)	cash in an Eligible Currency	[ ]	[ ]	[ ]%
(B)	negotiable debt obligations issued by the Government of [ ] having an original maturity at issuance of not more than one year	[ ]	[ ]	[ ]%

ISDA ®1995

(C)   negotiable debt obligations issued by the   [ ]   [ ]   [ ]%
Government of [   ] having an
original maturity at issuance of more than
one year but not more than 10 years

(D)   negotiable debt obligations issued by the   [ ]   [ ]   [ ]%
Government of [   ] having an
original maturity at issuance of more than
10 years

(E)   other: ....   [ ]   [ ]   [ ]%

(iii)   *Other Eligible Support.* The following items will qualify as *"Other Eligible Support"* for the party specified:

(A)   ....   [ ]   [ ]

(B)   ....   [ ]   [ ]

(iv)   *Thresholds.*

(A)   *"Independent Amount"* means with respect to Party A: ....
        "Independent Amount" means with respect to Party B: ....

(B)   *"Threshold"* means with respect to Party A: ....
        "Threshold" means with respect to Party B: ....

(C)   *"Minimum Transfer Amount"* means with respect to Party A: ....
        "Minimum Transfer Amount" means with respect to Party B: ....

(D)   **Rounding.** The Delivery Amount and the Return Amount will be rounded [down to the nearest integral multiple of ..../up and down to the nearest integral multiple of ...., respectively[4]].

(d)   *Valuation and Timing.*

(i)   *"Valuation Agent"* means, for purposes of Paragraphs 3 and 5, the party making the demand under Paragraph 3, and, for purposes of Paragraph 6(g), the Secured Party receiving or deemed to receive the Distributions or the Interest Amount, as applicable, unless otherwise specified here: ....

(ii)   *"Valuation Date"* means: ....

---

4   Delete as applicable.

(iii)　*"Valuation Time"* means:

[ ]　the close of business in the place of location of the Valuation Agent on the Valuation Date or date of calculation, as applicable;

[ ]　the close of business on the Local Business Day immediately preceding the Valuation Date or date of calculation, as applicable;

provided that the calculations of Value and Exposure will, as far as practicable, be made as of approximately the same time on the same date.

(iv)　*"Notification Time"* means [10:00 a.m.]/[1:00 p.m.], London time, on a Local Business Day, unless otherwise specified here: ....

(e)　*Conditions Precedent and Secured Party's Rights and Remedies.* The following Termination Event(s) will be a *"Specified Condition"* for the party specified (that party being the Affected Party if the Termination Event occurs with respect to that party):

	Party A	Party B
Illegality	[ ]	[ ]
Tax Event	[ ]	[ ]
Tax Event Upon Merger	[ ]	[ ]
Credit Event Upon Merger	[ ]	[ ]
Additional Termination Event(s):		
....	[ ]	[ ]
....	[ ]	[ ]

(f)　*Substitution.*

"Substitution Date" has the meaning specified in Paragraph 4(d)(ii), unless otherwise specified here: ....

(g)　*Dispute Resolution.*

(i)　*"Resolution Time"* means [1:00 p.m.]/[3:00 p.m.], London time, on the Local Business Day following the date on which the notice is given that gives rise to a dispute under Paragraph 5, unless otherwise specified here: ....

(ii)　*Value.* For the purpose of Paragraphs 5(a)(i)(C) and 5(a)(ii), the Value of the outstanding Posted Credit Support or of any transfer of Eligible Credit Support or Posted Credit Support, as the case may be, will be calculated as follows: ....

ISDA ®1995

(iii)   *Alternative*. The provisions of Paragraph 5 will apply, unless an alternative dispute resolution procedure is specified here: ....

(h)   *Eligibility to Hold Posted Collateral; Custodians.* Party A and its Custodian will be entitled to hold Posted Collateral pursuant to Paragraph 6(b); *provided* that the following conditions applicable to it are satisfied:

(i)   Party A is not a Defaulting Party.

(ii)   Posted Collateral may be held only in the following jurisdictions:
....

(iii)   ....

Initially, the **Custodian** for Party A is ....

Party B and its Custodian will be entitled to hold Posted Collateral pursuant to Paragraph 6(b); *provided* that the following conditions applicable to it are satisfied:

(i)   Party B is not a Defaulting Party.

(ii)   Posted   Collateral   may   be   held   only   in   the   following   jurisdictions:
....

(iii)   ....

Initially, the **Custodian** for Party B is ....

(i)   *Distributions and Interest Amount.*

(i)   *Interest Rate.* The "*Interest Rate*" in relation to each Eligible Currency specified below will be:

Eligible Currency	*Interest Rate*
....	....
....	....
....	....

(ii)   *Transfer of Interest Amount.* The transfer of the Interest Amount will be made on the last Local Business Day of each calendar month and on any Local Business Day that a Return Amount consisting wholly or partly of cash is transferred to the Chargor pursuant to Paragraph 3(b), unless otherwise specified here:...

(iii)   *Alternative to Interest Amount.* The provisions of Paragraph 6(g)(ii) will apply, unless otherwise specified here: ....

(j)   *Other Eligible Support and Other Posted Support.*

    (i)   *"Value"* with respect to Other Eligible Support and Other Posted Support means:
    ....

    (ii)   *Transfer of Other Eligible Support and Other Posted Support.* All transfers under this Deed of Other Eligible Support and Other Posted Support shall be made as follows: ....

(k)   *Addresses for Transfers.*

Party A: ....
....

Party B: ....
....

(l)   *Other Provisions.*

IN WITNESS of which this Deed has been executed as a deed and has been delivered on the date first above written.

PARTY A

EXECUTED as a deed by (Name of Company:)
....   )
acting by (Name of first signatory:)[5] [6].......................................)   .... (Signature)
and (Name of second signatory:)[7]...)   ....(Signature)
[acting under the authority of that company][[8]in the presence of:)

Witness' Signature: ....
Witness' Name: ....
Witness's Address: ....
                            ....]

PARTY B

EXECUTED as a deed by (Name of Company:)
....)
acting by (Name of first signatory:)[5] [6].......................................)   ....(Signature)
and (Name of second signatory:)[7]...)   .... (Signature)
[acting under the authority of that company] [[8]in the presence of:)

Witness' Signature: ....
Witness' Name: ....
Witness's Address: ....
                            ....]

---

5   Where the company is a UK company with a company seal which wishes to execute this Deed under its company seal, the precise manner of execution will depend on the company's articles. Where the company is a foreign company it will be necessary to check that this form of attestation is a valid execution under local law and under that company's constitution.

6   Where the company is a UK company, this signatory must be a Director. Where the company is a foreign company, the signatory must be a person authorised (under local law and under that company's constitution) to sign for that company.

7   Where the company is a UK company, this signatory must be either a Director or the Company Secretary. Where the company is a foreign company, it may be that under local law and under that company's constitution only one signatory is required.

8   Where there is only one signatory, a witness is preferable.

ISDA ®1995

ANNEX 7
ISDA CREDIT SUPPORT ANNEX SUBJECT TO JAPANESE LAW

(Bilateral Form - Loan and Pledge)   (Security Interest Subject to Japanese Law)

ISDA®
International Swaps and Derivatives Association, Inc.

CREDIT SUPPORT ANNEX

between

.... and ....
("Party A")   ("Party B")

made on ....

relating to the

ISDA Master Agreement

dated as of ....between Party A and Part B

This Annex is a Credit Support Document with respect to both parties in relation to the ISDA Master Agreement referred to above (as amended and supplemented from time to time, the "Agreement").

Accordingly, the parties agree as follows:

Paragraph 1.   Interpretation

(a)   *Definitions and Inconsistency.* Capitalized terms not otherwise defined herein or elsewhere in the Agreement have the meanings specified pursuant to Paragraph 12, and all references in this Annex to Paragraphs are to Paragraphs of this Annex. In the event of any inconsistency between this Annex and the provisions of the Schedule to the Agreement, this Annex will prevail, and in the event of any inconsistency between Paragraph 13 and the other provisions of this Annex, Paragraph 13 will prevail.

(b)   *Obligee and Obligor.* All references in this Annex to the "Obligee" will be to either party when acting as a borrower or a secured party and all corresponding references to the "Obligor" will be to the other party when acting as a lender or a pledgor.

Paragraph 2.   Security Interest

(a)   *Loan.* Each party, as the Obligor, hereby lends Lending Collateral to the other party, as the Obligee, as security for its Obligations, and grants to the Obligee the right of Set-off as set forth in Paragraph 8 (a) (iii). On the Early Termination Date of the Agreement, subject to the provisions of Paragraphs 3(b), 4(d) and 8, the Obligee shall return Posted Lending Collateral, free and clear of any lien, charge, mortgage, encumbrance or other security interest to the Obligor; *provided, however*, that where such Posted Lending Collateral is held in the form of securities, the Obligee may repay the Cash equivalent thereof at the option of the Obligee.

(b) *Pledge.* Each party, as the Obligor, hereby grants to the other party, as the Obligee, as security for its Obligations, a first priority continuing security interest (including, without limitation, a statutory pledge (*Shichiken*)) in, and the right of Set-off as set forth in Paragraph 8(a)(iii) against, Posted Pledging Collateral Transferred to the Obligee hereunder, which is given effect to upon the Transfer by the Obligor; *provided* that such security interest shall be a statutory pledge (*Shichiken*), unless otherwise agreed upon between the parties. Upon the Transfer by the Obligee to the Obligor of Posted Pledging Collateral, the security interest granted hereunder in that Posted Pledging Collateral will be released immediately and, to the extent possible, without any further action by either party.

Paragraph 3.   Credit Support Obligations

(a) *Delivery Amount.* Subject to Paragraphs 4 and 5, upon a demand made by the Obligee on or promptly following a Valuation Date, if the Delivery Amount for that Valuation Date equals or exceeds the Obligor's Minimum Transfer Amount, then the Obligor will Transfer to the Obligee Eligible Credit Support having a Value as of the date of Transfer at least equal to the applicable Delivery Amount (rounded pursuant to Paragraph 13). Unless otherwise specified in Paragraph 13, the *"Delivery Amount"* applicable to the Obligor for any Valuation Date will equal the amount by which:

   (i)   the Credit Support Amount

   exceeds

   (ii)   the Value as of that Valuation Date of all Posted Credit Support held by the Obligee.

(b) *Return Amount.* Subject to Paragraphs 4 and 5, upon a demand made by the Obligor on or promptly following a Valuation Date, if the Return Amount for that Valuation Date equals or exceeds the Obligee's Minimum Transfer Amount, then the Obligee will Transfer to the Obligor Posted Credit Support specified by the Obligor in that demand having a Value as of the date of Transfer as close as practicable to the applicable Return Amount (rounded pursuant to Paragraph 13); *provided, however,* that where such Posted Credit Support consists of Posted Lending Collateral in the form of securities, the Obligee may Transfer to the Obligor Equivalent Collateral or repay the Cash equivalent of such Posted Lending Collateral. For this purpose, Transfer of Equivalent Collateral or such Cash equivalent shall be deemed to be a return of Lending Collateral. However, solely for the purpose of this Paragraph 3(b), the Obligee's right to repay such Cash equivalent is subject to the prior consent of the Obligor. Unless otherwise specified in Paragraph 13, the *"Return Amount"* applicable to the Obligee for any Valuation Date will equal the amount by which:

   (i)   the Value as of that Valuation Date of all Posted Credit Support held by the Obligee

   exceeds

   (ii)   the Credit Support Amount.

"Credit Support Amount" means, unless otherwise specified in Paragraph 13, for any Valuation Date (i) the Obligee's Exposure for that Valuation Date plus (ii) the aggregate of all Independent Amounts applicable to the Obligor, if any, minus (iii) all Independent Amounts applicable to the Obligee, if any, minus (iv) the Obligor's Threshold; *provided however*, that the Credit Support Amount will be deemed to be zero whenever the calculation of the Credit Support Amount yields a number less than zero.

Paragraph 4.   Conditions Precedent, Transfer Timing, Calculations and Substitutions

(a)   *Conditions Precedent.* Each Transfer obligation of the Obligor under Paragraphs 3(a) and 5 and of the Obligee under Paragraphs 3(b), 4(d)(ii), 5 and 6(e) is subject to the conditions precedent that:

(i)   no Event of Default, Potential Event of Default or Specified Condition has occurred and is continuing with respect to the other party; and

(ii)   no Early Termination Date for which any unsatisfied payment obligations exist has occurred or been designated as the result of an Event of Default or Specified Condition with respect to the other party.

(b)   *Transfer Timing.* Subject to Paragraphs 4(a) and 5 and unless otherwise specified, if a demand for the Transfer of Eligible Credit Support or Posted Credit Support is made by the Notification Time, then the relevant Transfer will be made not later than the close of business on the third Local Business Day; if a demand is made after the Notification Time, then the relevant Transfer will be made not later than the close of business on the fourth Local Business Day thereafter.

(c)   *Calculations.* All calculations of Value and Exposure for purposes of Paragraphs 3 and 6(e) will be made by the Valuation Agent as of the Valuation Time. The Valuation Agent will notify each party (or the other party, if the Valuation Agent is a party) of its calculations not later than the Notification Time on the Local Business Day following the applicable Valuation Date (or in the case of Paragraph 6(e), following the date of calculation).

(d)   *Substitutions.*

(i)   Unless otherwise specified in Paragraph 13, upon notice to the Obligee specifying the items of Posted Credit Support to be exchanged, the Obligor may, on any Local Business Day, Transfer to the Obligee substitute Eligible Credit Support (the "Substitute Credit Support"); and

(ii)   subject to Paragraph 4(a), the Obligee will Transfer to the Obligor the items of Posted Credit Support specified by the Obligor in its notice not later than the third Local Business Day following the date on which the Obligee receives the Substitute Credit Support, unless otherwise specified in Paragraph 13 (the "Substitution Date"); *provided* that the Obligee will only be obligated to Transfer Posted Credit Support with a Value as of the date of Transfer of that Posted Credit Support equal to the Value as of that date of the Substitute Credit Support.

Paragraph 5.   Dispute Resolution

If a party (a "Disputing Party") disputes (I) the Valuation Agent's calculation of a Delivery Amount or a Return Amount or (II) the Value of any Transfer of Eligible Credit Support or Posted Credit Support, then (1) the Disputing Party will notify the other party and the Valuation Agent (if the Valuation Agent is not the other party) not later than the close of business on the Local Business Day following (X) the date that the demand is made under Paragraph 3 in the case of (I) above or (Y) the date of Transfer in the case of (II) above, (2) subject to Paragraph 4(a), the appropriate party will Transfer the undisputed amount to the other party not later than the close of business on the third Local Business Day following (X) the date that the demand is made under Paragraph 3 in the case of (I) above or (Y) the date of Transfer in the case of (II) above, (3) the parties will consult with each other in an attempt to resolve the dispute and (4) if they fail to resolve the dispute by the Resolution Time, then:

ISDA ® 1995

(i)   In the case of a dispute involving a Delivery Amount or Return Amount, unless otherwise specified in Paragraph 13, the Valuation Agent will recalculate the Exposure and the Value as of the Recalculation Date by:

(A)   utilizing any calculations of Exposure for the Transactions (or Swap Transactions) that the parties have agreed are not in dispute;

(B)   calculating the Exposure for the Transactions (or Swap Transactions) in dispute by seeking four actual quotations at mid-market from Reference Market-makers for purposes of calculating Market Quotation, and taking the arithmetic average of those obtained; *provided* that if four quotations are not available for a particular Transaction (or Swap Transaction), then fewer than four quotations may be used for that Transaction (or Swap Transaction); and if no quotations are available for a particular Transaction (or Swap Transaction), then the Valuation Agent's original calculations will be used for that Transaction (or Swap Transaction); and

(C)   utilizing the procedures specified in Paragraph 13 for calculating the Value, if disputed, of Posted Credit Support.

(ii)   In the case of a dispute involving the Value of any Transfer of Eligible Credit Support or Posted Credit Support, the Valuation Agent will recalculate the Value as of the date of Transfer pursuant to Paragraph 13.

Following a recalculation pursuant to this Paragraph, the Valuation Agent will notify each party (or the other party, if the Valuation Agent is a party) not later than the Notification Time on the Local Business Day following the Resolution Time. The appropriate party will, upon demand following that notice by the Valuation Agent or a resolution pursuant to (3) above and subject to Paragraphs 4(a) and 4(b), not later than three Local Business Days after the demand, make the appropriate Transfer.

Paragraph 6.   Holding and Using Posted Collateral

(a)   *Rights of Obligee to Posted Lending Collateral*. Until the Obligee is required, pursuant to the terms of this Annex, to return the Posted Lending Collateral, the Obligee shall be entitled to have all of the incidents of ownership of the Posted Lending Collateral, including without limitation, the right to sell, transfer, lend or otherwise dispose of, and to register or record the Posted Lending Collateral in the name of the Obligee, a Custodian (as defined below) or a nominee.

For purposes of the obligation to Transfer Eligible Credit Support or Posted Credit Support pursuant to Paragraphs 3 and 5 and any rights or remedies authorized under the Agreement, the Obligee will be deemed to continue to hold all Posted Lending Collateral and, unless the Obligor receives Distributions made thereon with the consent of the Obligee, will be deemed to receive such Distributions, regardless of whether the Obligee has exercised any rights with respect to any Posted Lending Collateral pursuant to Paragraph 6(a).

(b)   *Care of Posted Pledging Collateral*. Without limiting the Obligee's rights under Paragraph 6(d), the Obligee will exercise at least the same degree of care as it would exercise with respect to its own property to assure the safe custody of all Posted Pledging Collateral. Except as specified in the preceding sentence, the Obligee will have no duty with respect to Posted Pledging Collateral, including, without limitation, any duty to collect any Distributions, or enforce or preserve any rights pertaining thereto.

4

(c)   *Eligibility to Hold Posted Collateral; Custodians.*

(i)   *General.* Subject to the satisfaction of any conditions specified in Paragraph 13 for holding Posted Collateral, the Obligee will be entitled to hold Posted Collateral or to appoint an agent (a "Custodian") to hold Posted Collateral for the Obligee. Upon notice by the Obligee to the Obligor of the appointment of a Custodian, the Obligor's obligations to make any Transfer will be discharged by making the Transfer to that Custodian. The holding of Posted Collateral by a Custodian will be deemed to be the holding of that Posted Collateral by the Obligee for which the Custodian is acting.

(ii)   *Failure to Satisfy Conditions.* If the Obligee or its Custodian fails to satisfy any conditions for holding Posted Collateral, then upon a demand made by the Obligor, the Obligee will, not later than seven Local Business Days after the demand, Transfer or cause its Custodian to Transfer all Posted Collateral held by it to a Custodian that satisfies those conditions or to the Obligee if it satisfies those conditions.

(iii)   *Liability.* The Obligee will be liable for the acts or omissions of its Custodian to the same extent that the Obligee would be liable hereunder for its own acts or omissions.

(d)   *Use of Posted Pledging Collateral.* Unless otherwise specified in Paragraph 13 and without limiting the rights and obligations of the parties under Paragraphs 3, 4(d)(ii), 5, 6(e) and 8, if the Obligee is not a Defaulting Party or an Affected Party with respect to a Specified Condition and no Early Termination Date has occurred or been designated as the result of an Event of Default or Specified Condition with respect to the Obligee, then the Obligee shall have the right to:

(i)   re-pledge or re-hypothecate any Posted Pledging Collateral it holds, free from any claim or right of any nature whatsoever of the Obligor, to the extent permitted under applicable law; and

(ii)   register or record any relevant security interest (including the re-pledge or re-hypothecation granted under Paragraph 6(d)(i) above) over any Posted Pledging Collateral in accordance with any applicable law.

For purposes of the obligation to Transfer Eligible Credit Support or Posted Credit Support pursuant to Paragraphs 3 and 5 and any rights or remedies authorized under the Agreement, the Obligee will be deemed to continue to hold all Posted Pledging Collateral and, unless the Obligor has received Distributions made thereon with the consent of the Obligee, will be deemed to receive such Distributions, regardless of whether the Obligee has exercised any rights with respect to any Posted Pledging Collateral pursuant to (i) or (ii) above.

(e)   *Distributions and Interest Amount.*

(i)   *Distributions.* Subject to Paragraph 4(a), if the Obligee receives or is deemed to receive Distributions on a Local Business Day, it will Transfer to the Obligor not later than the third Local Business Day thereafter any Distributions it receives or is deemed to receive to the extent that a Delivery Amount would not be created or increased by that Transfer, as calculated by the Valuation Agent (and the date of calculation will be deemed to be a Valuation Date for this purpose).

(ii)   *Interest Amount.* Unless otherwise specified in Paragraph 13 and subject to Paragraph 4(a), in lieu of any interest, dividends or other amounts paid or deemed to have been paid with respect to Posted Lending Collateral in the form of Cash (all of which may be retained by the

Obligee), the Obligee will Transfer to the Obligor at the times specified in Paragraph 13 the Interest Amount less any applicable withholding tax to the extent that a Delivery Amount would not be created or increased by that Transfer, as calculated by the Valuation Agent (and the date of calculation will be deemed to be a Valuation Date for this purpose). The Interest Amount or portion thereof not Transferred pursuant to this Paragraph will constitute Posted Lending Collateral in the form of Cash and will be subject to the right of Set-off granted under Paragraph 2(a).

Paragraph 7. Events of Default

For purposes of Section 5(a)(iii)(1) of the Agreement, an Event of Default will exist with respect to a party if:

(i)   that party fails (or fails to cause its Custodian) to make, when due, any Transfer of Eligible Collateral, Posted Collateral or the Interest Amount, as applicable, required to be made by it and that failure continues for three Local Business Days after notice of that failure is given to that party;

(ii)   that party fails to comply with any restriction or prohibition specified in this Annex with respect to any of the rights specified in Paragraph 6(d) and that failure continues for three Local Business Days after notice of that failure is given to that party; or

(iii)   that party fails to comply with or perform any agreement or obligation under this Annex other than those specified in Paragraphs 7(i) and 7(ii) and that failure continues for 30 days after notice of that failure is given to that party.

Paragraph 8.   Certain Rights and Remedies

(a)   *Obligee's Rights and Remedies.* If at any time (1) an Event of Default or Specified Condition with respect to the Obligor has occurred and is continuing or (2) an Early Termination Date has occurred or been designated as the result of an Event of Default or Specified Condition with respect to the Obligor, then, unless the Obligor has paid in full all of its Obligations that are then due, the Obligee may exercise one or more of the following rights and remedies:

(i)   all rights and remedies available under applicable law with respect to Posted Collateral held by the Obligee;

(ii)   any other rights and remedies available to the Obligee under the terms of Posted Other Support, if any;

(iii)   the right to (1) Set-off any amounts payable by the Obligor with respect to any Obligations against any Posted Collateral without prior notice or formalities that might otherwise be required, in such order as the Obligee may elect, to the extent permitted under applicable law; *provided, however,* that, where such Posted Collateral consists of Posted Lending Collateral in the form of securities, the Obligee is deemed to opt to repay the Cash equivalent pursuant to Paragraph 2(a) for this purpose, and (2) if necessary in connection with such right to Set-off, convert such Posted Lending Collateral into another currency at the time of effecting such Set-off;

(iv)   the right to liquidate any Posted Pledging Collateral held by the Obligee through one or more public or private sales or other dispositions with such notice, if any, as may be required under applicable law, free from any claim or right of any nature whatsoever of the Obligor,

ISDA ® 1995

including any equity or right of redemption by the Obligor (with the Obligee having the right to purchase any or all of the Posted Pledging Collateral to be sold) and to apply the proceeds (or the Cash equivalent thereof) from the liquidation of the Posted Pledging Collateral to any amounts payable by the Obligor with respect to any Obligations in that order as the Obligee may elect; and

(v)   the right to collect the deposit amount in the case of Posted Pledging Collateral in the form of Cash Deposit and apply the deposit amount to any amounts payable by the Obligor with respect to any Obligations in that order as the Obligee may elect without prior notice or formalities that might otherwise be required.

For the purposes of (a)(iii) above, the Obligee will calculate, valuate or convert currencies at the time of the Transfer or Set-off, as the case may be, in accordance with Paragraph 11(d).

Each party acknowledges and agrees that Posted Collateral in the form of securities may decline speedily in value and is of a type customarily sold on a recognized market, and, accordingly, the Obligor is not entitled to prior notice of any sale of that Posted Collateral by the Obligee, except any notice that is required under applicable law and cannot be waived.

(b)   ***Obligor's Rights and Remedies.*** If at any time an Early Termination Date has occurred or been designated as the result of an Event of Default or Specified Condition with respect to the Obligee, then (except in the case of an Early Termination Date relating to less than all Transactions (or Swap Transactions) where the Obligee has paid in full all of its obligations that are then due under Section 6(e) of the Agreement):

(i)   the Obligor may exercise all rights and remedies available under applicable law with respect to Posted Collateral held by the Obligee;

(ii)   the Obligor may exercise any other rights and remedies available to the Obligor under the terms of Posted Other Support, if any;

(iii)   the Obligee will be obligated immediately to Transfer all Posted Credit Support and the Interest Amount to the Obligor; *provided, however*, that where such Posted Credit Support consists of Posted Lending Collateral in the form of securities, the Obligor may, at the option of the Obligor, demand the Obligee to repay the Cash equivalent of such Posted Lending Collateral notwithstanding Paragraph 2; and

(iv)   to the extent that Posted Collateral or the Interest Amount is not so Transferred pursuant to (iii) above, the Obligor may:

(A)   (1) Set-off any amounts payable by the Obligor with respect to any Obligations against any Posted Lending Collateral without prior notice or formalities that might otherwise be required in that order as the Obligor may elect, to the extent permitted under applicable law, and (2) if necessary in connection with such right to Set-off, convert such Posted Lending Collateral into another currency at the time of effecting such Set-off; and

(B)   to the extent that Set-off is not effected under (b)(iv)(A) above, the Obligor may withhold payment of any remaining amounts payable by the Obligor with respect to any Obligations, up to the Value of any remaining Posted Collateral held by the Obligee until that Posted Collateral is Transferred to the Obligor.

ISDA ® 1995

For the purposes of (b)(iv)(A) above, the Obligor shall calculate, valuate or convert currencies at the time of the Transfer or Set-off, as the case may be, in accordance with Paragraph 11(d).

(c) *Deficiencies and Excess Proceeds.* The Obligee will Transfer to the Obligor any proceeds and Posted Credit Support remaining after liquidation, Set-off and/or application under Paragraphs 8(a) and 8(b) after satisfaction in full of all amounts payable by the Obligor with respect to any Obligations; the Obligor in all events will remain liable for any amounts remaining unpaid after any liquidation, Set-off and/or application under Paragraphs 8(a) and 8(b).

(d) *Final Returns.* When no amounts are or thereafter may become payable by the Obligor with respect to any Obligations (except for any potential liability under Section 2(d) of the Agreement), the Obligee will Transfer to the Obligor all Posted Credit Support and the Interest Amount, if any.

Paragraph 9. Representations

Each party represents to the other party (which representations will be deemed to be repeated as of each date on which it, as the Obligor, Transfers Eligible Collateral) that:

(i) it has the power to grant a security interest in any Eligible Collateral it Transfers as the Obligor and has taken all necessary actions to authorize the granting of that security interest;

(ii) it is the sole owner of or otherwise has the right to Transfer all Eligible Collateral it Transfers to the Obligee hereunder, free and clear of any security interest, lien, encumbrance or other restrictions or in case of re-pledge or re-hypothecation it has the right to Transfer all Eligible Collateral which it Transfers to the Obligee hereunder for such purposes without any restriction, as the case may be, other than the security interest granted under Paragraph 2; and

(iii) upon the Transfer of any Pledging Collateral to the Obligee under the terms of this Annex, the Obligee will have a valid and perfected first priority security interest therein (assuming that any central clearing corporation or any third-party financial intermediary or other entity not within the control of the Obligor involved in the Transfer of that Pledging Collateral gives the notices and takes the action required of it under applicable law for perfection of that interest).

Paragraph 10. Expenses

(a) *General.* Except as otherwise provided in Paragraphs 10(b) and 10(c), each party will pay its own costs and expenses in connection with performing its obligations under this Annex and neither party will be liable for any costs and expenses incurred by the other party in connection herewith.

(b) *Posted Credit Support.* The Obligor will promptly pay when due all taxes, assessments or charges of any nature that are imposed with respect to Posted Credit Support held by the Obligee upon becoming aware of the same, regardless of whether any portion of that Posted Credit Support is subsequently disposed of under Paragraph 6(a) or 6(d), except for transfer, registration, recording or similar taxes that result from the exercise of the rights of the Obligee under Paragraph 6(a) or 6(d).

(c) *Liquidation/Application of Posted Credit Support.* All reasonable costs and expenses incurred by or on behalf of the Obligee or the Obligor in connection with the liquidation and/or application of any Posted Credit Support under Paragraph 8 will be payable, on demand and pursuant to the Expenses Section of the Agreement, by the Defaulting Party or, if there is no Defaulting Party, equally by the parties.

ISDA ® 1995

Paragraph 11. Miscellaneous

(a)   *Default Interest.* An Obligee that fails to make, when due, any Transfer of Posted Collateral or the Interest Amount will be obligated to pay the Obligor (to the extent permitted under applicable law) an amount equal to interest at the Default Rate multiplied by the Value of the items of property that were required to be Transferred, from (and including) the date that Posted Collateral or Interest Amount was required to be Transferred to (but excluding) the date of Transfer of that Posted Collateral or Interest Amount. This interest will be calculated on the basis of daily compounding and the actual number of days elapsed.

(b)   *Further Assurances.* Promptly following a demand made by a party, the other party will execute, deliver, file and record any document and take any other action that may be necessary or desirable and reasonably requested by that party to create, preserve, perfect or validate any security interest, lien or any other rights or privileges granted under Paragraph 2, to enable that party to exercise or enforce its rights under this Annex with respect to Posted Credit Support or an Interest Amount or to effect or document a release of a security interest on Posted Pledging Collateral or an Interest Amount or termination of the loan of the Posted Lending Collateral.

(c)   *Further Protection.* The Obligor will promptly give notice to the Obligee of, and defend against, any suit, action, proceeding or lien that involves Posted Credit Support Transferred by the Obligor or that could adversely affect the security interest, lien or any other rights or privileges granted by it under Paragraph 2, unless that suit, action, proceeding or lien results from the exercise of the Obligee's rights under Paragraphs 6(a) and 6(d).

(d)   *Good Faith and Commercially Reasonable Manner.* Performance of all obligations under this Annex, including, but not limited to, all calculations, valuations, currency conversions and determinations made by either party, will be made in good faith and in a commercially reasonable manner.

(e)   *Demands and Notices.* All demands and notices made by a party under this Annex will be made as specified in the Notices Section of the Agreement, except as otherwise provided in Paragraph 13.

(f)   *Specifications of Certain Matters.* Anything referred to in this Annex as being specified in Paragraph 13 also may be specified in one or more Confirmations or other documents and this Annex will be construed accordingly.

(g)   *Governing Law and Jurisdiction.* This Annex will be governed by and construed in accordance with Japanese law. With respect to any suit, action or proceedings relating to this Annex, each party irrevocably submits to the jurisdiction of the Japanese courts.

Paragraph 12. Definitions

As used in this Annex:-

"Cash" means the lawful currency of Japan.

"Cash Deposit" means a bank deposit including any interest accrued thereon in the account (*"Deposit Account"*) opened and maintained in a commercial bank located in Japan and agreed upon by the parties.

"Credit Support Amount" has the meaning specified in Paragraph 3.

"Custodian" has the meaning specified in Paragraphs 6(c)(i) and 13.

"Delivery Amount" has the meaning specified in Paragraph 3(a).

"Disputing Party" has the meaning specified in Paragraph 5.

"Distributions" means with respect to Posted Collateral in the form of securities, all principal, interest and other payments and distributions of cash or other property with respect thereto less any applicable withholding tax, regardless of whether the Obligee has disposed of that Posted Collateral under Paragraph 6(a) or 6(d).

"Eligible Collateral" means Lending Collateral and Pledging Collateral.

"Eligible Credit Support" means Eligible Collateral and Other Eligible Support.

"Equivalent Collateral" means securities of the same issuer, class, series, maturity, coupon rate and principal amount as Lending Collateral or new or different securities which have been exchanged for, converted into or substituted for Lending Collateral.

"Exposure" means for any Valuation Date or other date for which Exposure is calculated and subject to Paragraph 5 in the case of a dispute, the amount, if any, that would be payable to a party that is the Obligee by the other party (expressed as a positive number) or by a party that is the Obligee to the other party (expressed as a negative number) pursuant to Section 6(e)(ii)(2)(A) of the Agreement as if all Transactions (or Swap Transactions) were being terminated as of the relevant Valuation Time; *provided* that Market Quotation will be determined by the Valuation Agent using its estimates at mid-market of the amounts that would be paid for Replacement Transactions (as that term is defined in the definition of "Market Quotation").

"Independent Amount" means, with respect to a party, the amount specified as such for that party in Paragraph 13; if no amount is specified, zero.

"Interest Amount" means, with respect to an Interest Period, the aggregate sum of the amounts of interest calculated for each day in that Interest Period on the principal amount of Posted Lending Collateral in the form of Cash held by the Obligee on that day, determined by the Obligee for each such day as follows:

(x) the amount of that Cash on that day; multiplied by

(y) the Interest Rate in effect for that day; divided by

(z) 365

10

ISDA ® 1995

"Interest Period" means the period from (and including) the last Local Business Day on which an Interest Amount was Transferred (or, if no Interest Amount has yet been Transferred, the Local Business Day on which Posted Lending Collateral in the form of Cash was Transferred to or received by the Obligee) to (but excluding) the Local Business Day on which the current Interest Amount is to be Transferred.

"Interest Rate" means the rate specified in Paragraph 13.

"Lending Collateral" means, with respect to a party, the items, if any, specified as such for that party in Paragraph 13.

"Local Business Day", unless otherwise specified in Paragraph 13, has the meaning specified in the Definitions Section of the Agreement, except that references to a payment in clause (b) thereof will be deemed to include a Transfer under this Annex.

"Minimum Transfer Amount" means, with respect to a party, the amount specified as such for that party in Paragraph 13; if no amount is specified, zero.

"Notification Time" has the meaning specified in Paragraph 13.

"Obligations" means, with respect to a party, all present and future obligations of that party under the Agreement and any additional obligations specified for that party in Paragraph 13.

"Obligee" means either party, when that party (i) makes a demand for or is entitled to receive Eligible Credit Support under Paragraph 3(a) or (ii) holds or is deemed to hold Posted Credit Support.

"Obligor" means either party, when that party (i) receives a demand for or is required to Transfer Eligible Credit Support under Paragraph 3(a) or (ii) has Transferred Eligible Credit Support under Paragraph 3(a).

"Other Eligible Support" means, with respect to a party, the items, if any, specified as such for that party in Paragraph 13.

"Pledging Collateral" means, with respect to a party, the items, if any, specified as such for that party in Paragraph 13.

"Posted Collateral" means Posted Lending Collateral and Posted Pledging Collateral.

"Posted Credit Support" means Posted Collateral and Posted Other Support.

"Posted Lending Collateral" means all Lending Collateral or Equivalent Collateral, Distributions, and all proceeds thereof that have been Transferred to or received by the Obligee under this Annex and not Transferred to the Obligor pursuant to Paragraph 3(b), 4(d)(ii) or 6(e)(i) or released by the Obligee under Paragraph 8. Any Interest Amount or portion thereof not Transferred pursuant to Paragraph 6(e)(ii) will constitute Posted Lending Collateral in the form of Cash.

"Posted Other Support" means all Other Eligible Support Transferred to the Obligee that remains in effect for the benefit of that Obligee.

"Posted Pledging Collateral" means all Pledging Collateral, Distributions, and all proceeds thereof that have been Transferred to or received by the Obligee under this Annex and not Transferred to the Obligor pursuant to Paragraph 3(b), 4(d)(ii) or 6(e)(i) or released by the Obligee under Paragraph 8.

ISDA ® 1995

"Recalculation Date" means the Valuation Date that gives rise to the dispute under Paragraph 5; *provided, however,* that if a subsequent Valuation Date occurs under Paragraph 3 prior to the resolution of the dispute, then the "Recalculation Date" means the most recent Valuation Date under Paragraph 3.

"Resolution Time" has the meaning specified in Paragraph 13.

"Return Amount" has the meaning specified in Paragraph 3(b).

"Specified Condition" means, with respect to a party, any event specified as such for that party in Paragraph 13.

"Substitute Credit Support" has the meaning specified in Paragraph 4(d)(i).

"Substitution Date" has the meaning specified in Paragraph 4(d)(ii).

"Threshold" means, with respect to a party, the amount specified as such for that party in Paragraph 13; if no amount is specified, zero.

"Transfer" means, with respect to any Eligible Credit Support, Posted Credit Support or Interest Amount, and in accordance with the instructions of the Obligee, Obligor or Custodian, as applicable, as the recipient:

(i) in the case of Cash, payment or delivery by wire transfer into one or more bank accounts specified by the recipient;

(ii) in the case of certificated securities that will not be paid or delivered by book-entry or registration, payment or delivery in appropriate physical form to the recipient or its account accompanied by any duly executed instruments of transfer, assignments in blank, transfer tax stamps, if any, and any other documents necessary to constitute a legally effective loan, transfer or pledge and perfection, as applicable, of the relevant interest to or for the recipient;

(iii) in the case of securities that will be paid or delivered by book-entry, the giving of written or electronic instructions to the relevant depository institution or other entity specified by the recipient, subsequently followed by a written copy thereof to the recipient, sufficient if complied with to result in a legally effective loan, transfer or pledge and perfection, as applicable, of the relevant interest to or for the recipient;

(iv) in the case of securities that will be paid or delivered by registration, the giving of written or electronic demands for the registration to the relevant registrar which is sufficient if complied with to result in a legally effective loan, transfer or pledge and perfection, as applicable, of the relevant interest to or for the recipient;

(v) in the case of Cash Deposit, payment or delivery by wire transfer into the Deposit Account or out of the Deposit Account, as the case may be, together with completion of all requirements necessary to effect a legally effective transfer, or pledge and perfection, as applicable, of the relevant interest to or for the recipient; and

(vi) in the case of Other Eligible Support or Posted Other Support, as specified in Paragraph 13.

"Valuation Agent" has the meaning specified in Paragraph 13.

"Valuation Date" means each date specified in or otherwise determined pursuant to Paragraph 13.

12   ISDA ® 1995

"Valuation Percentage" means, for any item of Eligible Collateral, the percentage specified in Paragraph 13.

"Valuation Time" has the meaning specified in Paragraph 13.

"Value" means for any Valuation Date or other date for which Value is calculated and subject to Paragraph 5 in the case of a dispute, with respect to:

    (i)   Eligible Collateral or Posted Collateral that is:

        (A)   Cash, the amount thereof;

        (B)   JGBs (as defined below) and other securities for which bid and offer quotations are generally available to the Valuation Agent in the over-the-counter market, the bid price quotation obtained by the Valuation Agent multiplied by the applicable Valuation Percentage, if any;

        (C)   a security that is primarily traded on a recognised securities exchange, the closing price on the exchange or, in the absence of such a closing price, the last bid quotation for the securities on the exchange multiplied by the applicable Valuation Percentage, if any; and

        (D)   Cash Deposit, the face amount thereof.

    (ii)   Posted Collateral that consists of items that are not specified as Eligible Collateral, zero; and

    (iii)   Other Eligible Support and Posted Other Support, as specified in Paragraph 13.

Paragraph 13. Elections and Variables

(a)   *Security Interest for "Obligations"*. The term *"Obligations"* as used in this Annex includes the following additional obligations:

With respect to Party A: . . . .

With respect to Party B: . . . .

(b)   *Credit Support Obligations.*

    (i)   **Delivery Amount, Return Amount and Credit Support Amount.**

        (A)   *"Delivery Amount"* has the meaning specified in Paragraph 3(a), unless otherwise specified here: . . . .

        (B)   *"Return Amount"* has the meaning specified in Paragraph 3(b), unless otherwise specified here: . . . .

        (C)   *"Credit Support Amount"* has the meaning specified in Paragraph 3, unless otherwise specified here: . . . .

    (ii)   *Eligible Collateral.* The following items will qualify as *"Eligible Collateral"* for the party specified:

        (A)   Lending Collateral

		Party A	Party B	Valuation Percentage
(1)	negotiable debt obligations issued by the Japanese Government ("JGBs")[1]	[ ]	[ ]	[ ]%
(2)	Cash	[ ]	[ ]	[ ]%
(3)	other:	[ ]	[ ]	[ ]%

        (B)   Pledging Collateral

		Party A	Party B	Valuation Percentage
(1)	JGBs[1]	[ ]	[ ]	[ ]%
(2)	Cash Deposit	[ ]	[ ]	[ ]%
(3)	other:	[ ]	[ ]	[ ]%

---

1 In cases where such JGBs are held in the book-entry system (huriketsu-kokusai), JGBs as "Eligible Collateral" means shares of certificates of JGBs held on a fungible basis.

ISDA ® 1995

(iii) **Other Eligible Support.** The following items will qualify as "**Other Eligible Support**" for the party specified:

		Party A	Party B
(A)	....	[ ]	[ ]
(B)	....	[ ]	[ ]

(iv) **Thresholds.**

(A) "**Independent Amount**" means with respect to Party A: ¥.................
"**Independent Amount**" means with respect to Party B: ¥.................

(B) "**Threshold**" means with respect to Party A: ¥..........................
"**Threshold**" means with respect to Party B: ¥..........................

(C) "**Minimum Transfer Amount**" means with respect to Party A: ¥...........
"**Minimum Transfer Amount**" means with respect to Party B: ¥...........

(D) **Rounding.** The Delivery Amount and the Return Amount will be rounded [down to the nearest integral multiple of ¥......./up and down to the nearest integral multiple of ¥ ...., respectively*].

(c) **Valuation and Timing.**

(i) "**Valuation Agent**" means, for purposes of Paragraphs 3 and 5, the party making the demand under Paragraph 3, for purposes of paragraph 4(d) (ii), the Obligee, and, for purposes of Paragraph 6(e), the Obligee receiving or deemed to receive the Distributions or the Interest Amount, as applicable, unless otherwise specified here: ....

(ii) "**Valuation Date**" means: ....

(iii) "**Valuation Time**" means:

[ ] the close of business in the city of the Valuation Agent on the Valuation Date or date of calculation, as applicable;

[ ] the close of business on the Local Business Day before the Valuation Date or date of calculation, as applicable;

provided that the calculations of Value and Exposure will be made as of approximately the same time on the same date.

(iv) "**Notification Time**" means 11:00 a.m., Tokyo time, on a Local Business Day, unless otherwise specified here: ....

---

* Delete as applicable.

ISDA ® 1995

(d)   **Conditions Precedent and Obligee's Rights and Remedies.** The following Termination Event(s) will be a *"Specified Condition"* for the party specified (that party being the Affected Party if the Termination Event occurs with respect to that party):

	Party A	Party B
Illegality	[ ]	[ ]
Tax Event	[ ]	[ ]
Tax Event Upon Merger	[ ]	[ ]
Credit Event Upon Merger	[ ]	[ ]
Additional Termination Event(s): [2]		
....	[ ]	[ ]
....	[ ]	[ ]

(e)   *Substitution.*

(i)   *"Substitution Date"* has the meaning specified in Paragraph 4(d)(ii), unless otherwise specified here: ....

(ii)   *Consent.* If specified here as applicable, then the Obligor must obtain the Obligee's consent for any substitution pursuant to Paragraph 4(d): [applicable/inapplicable*]

(f)   *Dispute Resolution.*

(i)   *"Resolution Time"* means 11:00 a.m., Tokyo time, on the Local Business Day following the date on which notice of the dispute is given under Paragraph 5, unless otherwise specified here: ....

(ii)   *Value.* For the purpose of Paragraphs 5(i)(C) and 5(ii), the Value of Posted Credit Support will be calculated as follows: ....

(iii)   *Alternative.* The provisions of Paragraph 5 will apply, unless an alternative dispute resolution procedure is specified here: ....

---

[2] If the parties elect to designate an Additional Termination Event as a "Specified Condition", then they should only designate one or more Additional Termination Events that are designated as such in their Schedule.

* Delete as applicable.

ISDA ® 1995

(g)   **Holding and Using Posted Collateral.**

(i)   *Eligibility to Hold Posted Collateral; Custodians.* Party A and its Custodian will be entitled to hold Posted Collateral pursuant to Paragraph 6(c); *provided* that the following conditions applicable to it are satisfied:

   (1)   Party A is not a Defaulting Party.

   (2)   Posted Collateral may be held only in the following jurisdictions:
   . . . .

   (3)   . . . .
   Initially, the **Custodian** for Party A is . . . .

Party B and its Custodian will be entitled to hold Posted Collateral pursuant to Paragraph 6(c); *provided* that the following conditions applicable to it are satisfied:

   (1)   Party B is not a Defaulting Party.

   (2)   Posted Collateral may be held only in the following jurisdictions:
   . . . .

   (3)   . . . .
   Initially, the **Custodian** for Party B is . . . .

(ii)   *Use of Posted Pledging Collateral.* The provisions of Paragraph 6(d) will not apply to the [party/parties*] specified here:

   [ ]   Party A
   [ ]   Party B

and [that party/those parties*] will not be permitted to: . . . .

(h)   *Distributions and Interest Amount.*

(i)   *Interest Rate.* The "*Interest Rate*" will be: . . . .

(ii)   *Transfer of Interest Amount.* The Transfer of the Interest Amount will be made on the last Local Business Day of each calendar month and on any Local Business Day that Posted Lending Collateral in the form of Cash is Transferred to the Obligor pursuant to Paragraph 3(b), unless otherwise specified here: . . . .

(iii)   *Alternative to Interest Amount.* The provisions of Paragraph 6(e)(ii) will apply, unless otherwise specified here: . . . .

---

* Delete as applicable.

    ISDA ® 1995

(i)   *Additional Representation(s).*

[Party A/Party B*] represents to the other party (which representation(s) will be deemed to be repeated as of each date on which it, as the Obligor, Transfers Eligible Collateral) that:

(i)   . . . .

(ii)   . . . .

(j)   *Other Eligible Support and Posted Other Support.*

(i)   *"Value"* with respect to Other Eligible Support and Posted Other Support means:
. . . .

(ii)   *"Transfer"* with respect to Other Eligible Support and Posted Other Support means: . . .
. . . .

(k)   *Demands and Notices.*

All demands, specifications and notices under this Annex will be made pursuant to the Notices Section of the Agreement, unless otherwise specified here:

Party A: . . . .
Party B: . . . .

(l)   *Addresses for Transfers.*

Party A: . . . .
Party B: . . . .

(m)   *Other Provisions.*

(i)   The parties hereto agree that the following is hereby inserted as Additional Events of Default and shall be construed as Section 5(a)(ix) of the Agreement:

"(ix)   *Other financial crisis.* The party:

- (1) has a pre-judgement attachment ("karisashiosae"), post-judgement attachment ("sashiosae") or other court order of enforcement issued in respect of any rights to receive Posted Lending Collateral or the Obligations; or

- (2) transfers, assigns or pledges any rights to receive Posted Lending Collateral or the Obligations to a third party."

(ii)   Section 6(a) of the Agreement is hereby amended by inserting "or specified in Section 5(a)(ix)(1) or (2)" after "or, to the extent analogous thereto, (8)" in line 8 therefor.

---

* Delete as applicable.

ISDA ® 1995

ANNEX 8
BILATERAL AMENDMENT AGREEMENT FOR CERTAIN PROVISIONS IN THE 2001 ISDA MARGIN PROVISIONS

[ISDA Agreements Subject to New York Law Only]

AMENDMENT TO THE CREDIT SUPPORT ANNEX [1]
To the Schedule to the
ISDA MASTER AGREEMENT

dated as of ....

between

.... and ....
("Party A")   ("Party B")

(the "Agreement")

The parties have previously entered into the Agreement, which includes that certain Credit Support Annex (the "Annex"). The parties have now agreed to amend the Annex by this Amendment (this "Amendment").

The International Swaps and Derivatives Association, Inc. ("ISDA") has published a series of modifications to the form of the Credit Support Annex published by ISDA (the "ISDA CSA") that parties may incorporate by reference, singly or in combination, into versions of the ISDA CSA that they have executed. These modifications are set forth in a series of Attachments to the ISDA CSA published on August 1, 2001, which are stated to relate to ISDA Agreements subject to New York law only and are herein referred to as the "Attachments". The purpose of this Amendment is to incorporate the terms of one or more of the Attachments into the Annex.

Accordingly, the parties agree as follows:

1.   **Amendment of the Credit Support Annex**

    (a)   Upon execution of this Amendment by both parties, the Annex shall be and hereby is amended as follows:

        (i)   The Annex is amended in accordance with the amendments set forth in the following Attachments:

            [Transfer Timing Attachment;]
            [Dispute Resolution Attachment;]
            [Dispute Termination Event Attachment;]
            [Substitutions Attachment.]

        (ii)   The following definition of "Credit Support Business Day" is added to the Annex:

"Credit Support Business Day" means:

---

[1] PARTIES SHOULD CONSULT WITH THEIR LEGAL ADVISERS AND ANY OTHER ADVISER THEY DEEM APPROPRIATE PRIOR TO USING THIS FORM OF AMENDMENT. BECAUSE OF THE VARIED DOCUMENTATION STRUCTURES IN THE MARKETPLACE, MODIFICATIONS TO THIS FORM OF AMENDMENT MAY BE NECESSARY OR AN ENTIRELY DIFFERENT FORM OF AMENDMENT MAY BE APPROPRIATE.

(a)   in relation to a Transfer of securities, a "Credit Support Business Day" means a day on which the relevant clearance system agreed by the parties is open for the acceptance and execution of settlement instructions and a day on which the securities intermediary or commercial bank in which the relevant account is located is open or, if delivery of the securities is contemplated by other means, a day on which commercial banks are open for business (including dealings in foreign exchange and foreign currency deposits) in the place(s) agreed between the parties for this purpose;

(b)   in relation to a Transfer of Cash or property other than securities, a "Credit Support Business Day" means a day on which commercial banks, foreign exchange markets and relevant clearance systems settle payments and are open for business (including dealings in foreign exchange and foreign currency deposits) in the place where the relevant account is located and, if different, in the principal financial center (if any) of the currency of any such payment;

(c)   in relation to valuations under this Annex, a "Credit Support Business Day" means a day on which commercial banks are open for business (including dealings in foreign exchange and foreign currency deposits) in the location of the Calling Party and in any other place(s) agreed between the parties for this purpose;

(d)   in relation to any notice or other communication, a "Credit Support Business Day" means a day on which commercial banks are open for business (including dealings in foreign exchange and foreign currency deposits) in the location of the recipient of the notice or communication; and

(e)   in relation to the location of a party, a "Credit Support Business Day" means a day on which commercial banks are open for business (including dealings in foreign exchange and foreign currency deposits) in the place specified as that party's address for notices in Paragraph 13, or if none is specified in this Agreement, such other address as has most recently been notified to the other party in accordance with the Notices section of the Agreement.

All references in the Annex to "Local Business Day" or "Local Business Days" are hereby deleted and replaced with references to "Credit Support Business Day" or "Credit Support Business Days".

(iii)   The following definition of "Notice" is added to the Annex:

"Notice" means an irrevocable notice, which may be written, oral, by telephone, by facsimile transmission, telex, e-mail or message generated by an electronic messaging system or otherwise.

(iv)   The definition of "Interest Amount" in Paragraph 12 shall be amended as follows: insert after "(z) 360" the phrase "(or, if the currency is pounds sterling, 365)."

(v)   The definition of "Valuation Percentage" in Paragraph 12 shall be amended as follows: insert after the phrase "specified in Paragraph 13." the following: ", or if no such percentage is specified, 100%."

(vi)   The definition of "Valuation Time" in Paragraphs 12 and 13(c)(iii) shall be deleted in its entirety and replaced with the following:

"Valuation Time" means 5:00 p.m. in the relevant market on the Credit Support Business Day immediately preceding the relevant Valuation Date.

(b)   As used in the Annex, as amended by this Amendment, the terms "Credit Support Annex", "Annex", "this Annex", "herein", "hereinafter", "hereof", "hereto", and other words of similar import shall mean the Annex, as amended by this Amendment, unless the context otherwise specifically requires, and "Agreement" means as amended by this Amendment.

2. Representations

Each party represents to the other party that all representations contained in the Agreement (including all representations set forth in the Annex) are true and accurate as of the date of this Amendment (with respect to the Agreement and Annex, as amended hereby) and that such representations are deemed to be given or repeated by each party, as the case may be, on the date of this Amendment.

3. Miscellaneous

(a) *Entire Agreement*. This Amendment constitutes the entire agreement and understanding of the parties with respect to its subject matter and supersedes all oral communication and prior writings (except as otherwise provided herein) with respect thereto.

(b) *Amendments*. No amendment, modification or waiver in respect of this Amendment will be effective unless in writing (including a writing evidenced by a facsimile transmission) and executed by each of the parties.

(c) *Counterparts*. This Amendment may be executed and delivered in counterparts (including by facsimile transmission), each of which will be deemed an original.

(d) *Headings*. This headings used in this Amendment are for convenience of reference only and are not to affect the construction of or to be taken into consideration in interpreting this Amendment.

IN WITNESS WHEREOF the parties have executed this Amendment on the respective dates specified below with effect from the date specified on the first page of this Amendment.

....
(Name of Party) (Name of Party)

By: .... By: ....
  Name: Name:
  Title: Title:
  Date: Date:

[ISDA Agreements Subject to English Law Only]

AMENDMENT TO THE
CREDIT SUPPORT ANNEX[1]

To the Schedule to the

ISDA MASTER AGREEMENT

dated as of ....

between

.... and ....
         ("Party A")   ("Party B")

(the "Agreement")

The parties have previously entered into the Agreement, which includes that certain Credit Support Annex (the "Annex"). The parties have now agreed to amend the Annex by this Amendment (this "Amendment").

The International Swaps and Derivatives Association, Inc. ("ISDA") has published a series of modifications to the form of the Credit Support Annex published by ISDA (the "ISDA CSA") that parties may incorporate by reference, singly or in combination, into versions of the ISDA CSA that they have executed. These modifications are set forth in a series of Attachments to the ISDA CSA published on August 1, 2001, which are stated to relate to ISDA Agreements subject to English law only and are herein referred to as the "Attachments". The purpose of this Amendment is to incorporate the terms of one or more of the Attachments into the Annex.

Accordingly, the parties agree as follows:

1.   **Amendment of the Credit Support Annex**

(a)   Upon execution of this Amendment by both parties, the Annex shall be and hereby is amended as follows:

      (i) The Annex is amended in accordance with the amendments set forth in the following Attachments:

            [Transfer Timing Attachment;]
            [Dispute Resolution Attachment;]
            [Dispute Termination Event Attachment;]
            [Exchanges Attachment.]

      (ii)   The definition of "Local Business Day" shall be deleted in its entirety and replaced with the following:

            "Local Business Day" means:

---

[1] **PARTIES SHOULD CONSULT WITH THEIR LEGAL ADVISERS AND ANY OTHER ADVISER THEY DEEM APPROPRIATE PRIOR TO USING THIS FORM OF AMENDMENT. BECAUSE OF THE VARIED DOCUMENTATION STRUCTURES IN THE MARKETPLACE, MODIFICATIONS TO THIS FORM OF AMENDMENT MAY BE NECESSARY OR AN ENTIRELY DIFFERENT FORM OF AMENDMENT MAY BE APPROPRIATE.**

(a) in relation to a transfer of securities, a day on which the relevant clearance system agreed by the parties is open for the acceptance and execution of settlement instructions and a day on which the securities intermediary or commercial bank in which the relevant account is located is open or, if delivery of the securities is contemplated by other means, a day on which commercial banks are open for business (including dealings in foreign exchange and foreign currency deposits) in the place(s) agreed between the parties for this purpose;

(b) in relation to a transfer of cash or property other than securities, a day on which commercial banks, foreign exchange markets and relevant clearance systems settle payments and are open for business (including dealings in foreign exchange and foreign currency deposits) in the place where the relevant account is located and, if different, in the principal financial center (if any) of the currency of any such payment;

(c) in relation to valuations under this Annex, a day on which commercial banks are open for business (including dealings in foreign exchange and foreign currency deposits) in the location of the Calling Party and in any other place(s) agreed between the parties for this purpose;

(d) in relation to any notice or other communication, a day on which commercial banks are open for business (including dealings in foreign exchange and foreign currency deposits) in the location of the recipient of the notice or communication; and

(e) in relation to the location of a party, a day on which commercial banks are open for business (including dealings in foreign exchange and foreign currency deposits) in the place specified as that party's address for notices in Paragraph 11, or if none is specified in this Agreement, such other address as has most recently been notified to the other party in accordance with the Notices Section.

(iii) The following definition of "Notice" is added to the Annex:

"Notice" means an irrevocable notice, which may be written, oral, by telephone, by facsimile transmission, telex, e-mail or message generated by an electronic messaging system or otherwise.

(iv) The definition of "Valuation Percentage" in Paragraph 10 shall be amended as follows: insert after the phrase "Paragraph 11(b)(ii)" the phrase ", or if no such percentage is specified, 100%."

(v) The definition of "Valuation Time" in Paragraphs 10 and 11(c)(iii) shall be deleted in its entirety and replaced with the following:

"Valuation Time" means 5:00 p.m. in the relevant market on the Local Business Day immediately preceding the relevant Valuation Date.

(b) As used in the Annex, as amended by this Amendment, the terms "Credit Support Annex", "Annex", "this Annex", "herein", "hereinafter", "hereof", "hereto", and other words of similar import shall mean the Annex, as amended by this Amendment, unless the context otherwise specifically requires, and "Agreement" means as amended by this Amendment.

2. Representations

Each party represents to the other party that all representations contained in the Agreement (including all representations set forth in the Annex) are true and accurate as of the date of this Amendment (with respect to the Agreement and Annex as amended hereby) and that such representations are deemed to be given or repeated by each party, as the case may be, on the date of this Amendment.

3.   Miscellaneous

(a)   *Entire Agreement*. This Amendment constitutes the entire agreement and understanding of the parties with respect to its subject matter and supersedes all oral communication and prior writings (except as otherwise provided herein) with respect thereto.

(b)   *Amendments*. No amendment, modification or waiver in respect of this Amendment will be effective unless in writing (including a writing evidenced by a facsimile transmission) and executed by each of the parties.

(c)   *Counterparts*. This Amendment may be executed and delivered in counterparts (including by facsimile transmission), each of which will be deemed an original.

(d)   *Headings*. This headings used in this Amendment are for convenience of reference only and are not to affect the construction of or to be taken into consideration in interpreting this Amendment.

IN WITNESS WHEREOF the parties have executed this Amendment on the respective dates specified below with effect from the date specified on the first page of this Amendment.

....
                (Name of Party)   (Name of Party)

By: ....   By: ....
      Name: Name:
      Title: Title:
      Date: Date:

ANNEX 9
2001 ISDA MARGIN PROVISIONS

PART 1

OPERATIONAL PROVISIONS

Section 1.1   Margin Transfer Obligations.

(a)   **Delivery Amount**. Upon a demand made by the Taker on or promptly following a Valuation Date, if the Delivery Amount for that Valuation Date equals or exceeds the Provider's Minimum Transfer Amount, then the Provider will Transfer to the Taker Eligible Margin having a Value as of the date that the Transfer is Initiated at least equal to the applicable Delivery Amount (rounded as specified in the Supplement). The Delivery Amount (adjusted as referred to in the definition of such term) applicable to the Provider for any Valuation Date will equal the amount by which:

(i)   the Margin Required

exceeds

(ii)   the Value as of that Valuation Date of all Margin Received held by the Taker.

(b)   **Return Amount**. Upon a demand made by the Provider on or promptly following a Valuation Date, if the Return Amount for that Valuation Date equals or exceeds the Taker's Minimum Transfer Amount, then the Taker will Transfer to the Provider Equivalent Margin having a Value as of the date that the Transfer is Initiated as close as practicable to the applicable Return Amount (rounded as specified in the Supplement). The Return Amount (adjusted as referred to in the definition of such term) applicable to the Taker for any Valuation Date will equal the amount by which:

(i)   the Value as of that Valuation Date of all Margin Received held by the Taker

exceeds

(ii)   the Margin Required.

In no circumstances shall the Taker be required to Transfer Equivalent Margin with a Value in excess of the Return Amount. The Provider may specify in a demand the Equivalent Margin to be Transferred by the Taker to the extent the Value of such Equivalent Margin is equal to or less than the Return Amount.

(c)   **Lock-up Margin**.

(i)   If Lock-up Margin is specified with respect to a party as Provider, it will not be taken into account in, is separate from, and is in addition to, any calculation of Margin Required with respect to the Provider, but will be Transferred by the Provider to

1

the Taker on the date of the Supplement, or on such date as the parties may agree as specified in the Supplement or otherwise.

(ii)   A Provider may demand the return of Lock-up Margin (if Part 2 applies) or Cash, securities or other property of the same type, nominal value, description and amount as such Lock-up Margin (if Part 3 applies) from Taker in any circumstances specified in the Supplement. Once the specified circumstances are no longer continuing, the Taker may demand delivery of new Lock-up Margin.

(iii)   Notice of a demand will be given by the Taker, and Lock-up Margin will be Transferred by the Provider, as if it were a demand for Transfer of a Delivery Amount. Notice of a demand will be given by the Provider, and Lock-up Margin (if Part 2 applies) or Cash, securities or other property of the same type, nominal value, description and amount as such Lock-up Margin (if Part 3 applies) will be Transferred by the Taker, as if it were a demand for Transfer of a Return Amount.

(d)   **No Offset**.   Except as otherwise provided in these Provisions or in the Supplement, if either party is required to make a Transfer of Lock-up Margin, then that Transfer will be made free of any set-off (as defined in Section 14 of the ISDA Master Agreement), lien or withholding whatsoever, including in respect of any Delivery Amount or Return Amount to be Transferred on the same date or Margin Received held by either party.

Section 1.2   Conditions Precedent. Each Transfer obligation of the Provider and of the Taker under Part 1 of these Provisions is subject to the conditions precedent that:

(a)   no Event of Default (or event which, with the giving of Notice or the lapse of time or both, would constitute an Event of Default) or Specified Condition has occurred and is continuing with respect to the other party; and

(b)   no date on which all outstanding Transactions under the Agreement have been or will be accelerated, terminated, liquidated or cancelled and for which any unsatisfied payment obligations exist has occurred or been designated as the result of an Event of Default or Specified Condition with respect to the other party.

Section 1.3   Transfer Timing.

(a)   Each reference in this Section 1.3 to a time or to a Margin Business Day is a reference to that time or Margin Business Day in the location of the Call Recipient.

(b)   If a Call Recipient receives a demand for the Transfer of Eligible Margin or Equivalent Margin by the Notification Time on a Margin Business Day, then by 5:00 p.m. on that Margin Business Day, the Call Recipient must Initiate the Transfer and provide Notice (such Notice may be in the form of Appendix B) to the Calling Party of:

(i)   the type of Eligible Margin or Equivalent Margin that it will deliver; and

2

(ii)   the Settlement Date for such Eligible Margin or Equivalent Margin.

(c)   If a Call Recipient receives a demand for the Transfer of Eligible Margin or Equivalent Margin after the Notification Time, the demand will be deemed to have been received at the Notification Time on the next Margin Business Day, unless a subsequent demand is received prior to such Notification Time, in which case such subsequent demand will govern.

(d)   Any Transfer contemplated by this Section 1.3 must be completed by 5:00 p.m. in the location of the account of the Calling Party on the Settlement Date.

(e)   If a Transfer of Eligible Margin or Equivalent Margin is not completed in accordance with Section 1.3(d), or the Notice required by Section 1.3(b) is not provided by 5:00 p.m. in the location of the Call Recipient, then:

(i)   Without prejudice to the rights of the Calling Party under sub- Section 1.3(e)(ii) below, the Calling Party may elect to notify the Call Recipient of its failure to Transfer Eligible Margin or Equivalent Margin or its failure to give such Notice (such Notice of failure may be in the form of Appendix C) and request that the Call Recipient remedy such failure by such time and on such day as the Calling Party shall specify in such Notice of failure.

(ii)   The Calling Party may give the Notice provided for under Section 1.4(b)(i), in the event of a failure to Transfer Eligible Margin or Equivalent Margin, or give the Notice provided for under Section 1.4(b)(ii), in the event of a failure to give the Notice required by Section 1.3(b).

Section 1.4   Additional Events of Default.

(a)   Each reference in this Section 1.4 to a Margin Business Day is a reference to that Margin Business Day in the location of the recipient of the related Notice.

(b)   In addition to the Events of Default specified in an Agreement, an Event of Default will exist with respect to a party if:

(i)   that party fails (or fails to cause its Custodian) to make, when due, a Transfer of:

(A)   Lock-up Margin or Cash, securities or other property of the same type, nominal value, description and amount as any Lock-up Margin; or

(B)   Eligible Margin or Equivalent Margin; or

(C)   Equivalent Distributions or any Interest Amount;

and such failure is not remedied on or before the first Margin Business Day after Notice to that party of such failure;

3

(ii)   that party fails to provide the Notice required by Section 1.3(b) below and such failure is not remedied on or before the first Margin Business Day after Notice to that party of such failure; or

(iii)   that party fails (or fails to cause its Custodian) to comply with or perform any agreement or obligation under these Provisions or a Supplement (other than any obligations referenced in sub-Section 1.4(b)(i) and sub-Section 1.4(b)(ii) above and Section 2.3 below) to be complied with or performed by the party in accordance with these Provisions if such failure is not remedied on or before the thirtieth day after Notice to that party of such failure.

(c)   The failure by a party to make a Transfer of any amount which is the subject of a dispute will not be considered a failure to make, when due, a Transfer for purposes of sub-Section 1.4(b)(i) above for so long as such party is performing its obligations in accordance with the dispute resolution procedures set out in Section 1.6 below.

(d)   Any Notice given pursuant to Section 1.4(b) may be in the form of Appendix D.

Section 1.5   Calculations as of Valuation Time. All calculations of Value and Exposure for purposes of Section 1.1 and Section 1.6 will be based on information obtained as of the Valuation Time.

Section 1.6   Procedures for Dispute Resolution.

(a)   **General.**

(i)   Each party agrees to attempt to resolve any dispute as quickly as possible following Notice of the dispute being given or received.

(ii)   If either party fails to comply with any of the requirements for delivery of Notices stated below in this Section 1.6, the failure will not be deemed an Event of Default. However, the party that fails to comply with such requirements for delivery of Notices will, for the purpose of determining the Delivery Amount, the Return Amount or any Value, no longer be able to dispute the information contained in the Notice most recently provided by the other party. Any Delivery Amount, Return Amount or Value will be calculated based on such information and any information previously agreed or notified by the parties.

(b)   **Dispute of Delivery Amount or Return Amount.**

(i)   Each reference in this sub-Section 1.6(b) to a time or to a Margin Business Day is a reference to that time or Margin Business Day in the location of the Call Recipient.

(ii)   If a Call Recipient disputes a demand to Transfer a Delivery Amount or a Return Amount, it must, as Disputing Party, on the same Margin Business Day the demand is received or deemed received, as relevant:

4

(A)   transmit a Notice of dispute (such Notice of dispute may be in the form of Appendix E) for receipt by the Calling Party by 1:00 p.m. that day;

(B)   Initiate Transfer to the Calling Party by 5:00 p.m. in accordance with Section 1.3(b) of Eligible Margin having a Value as of the date Transfer is Initiated equal to the Undisputed Amount, if the Undisputed Amount equals or exceeds the Disputing Party's Minimum Transfer Amount; and

(C)   transmit Portfolio Information for receipt by the Calling Party by 5:00 p.m. that day.

(iii)   The Calling Party must review the Portfolio Information and information held by it regarding the relevant portfolio of Transactions between the parties. The Calling Party will transmit Notice to the Disputing Party by 10:00 a.m. on the next Margin Business Day (the "Second Day") in the location of the Call Recipient of:

(A)   the details of any differences between the Disputing Party's Portfolio Information and information held by the Calling Party regarding the Transactions, including a description of all available evidence (which must be transmitted with such Notice, to the extent practicable), as relevant, of Transactions the Calling Party considers outstanding or a request for evidence of the execution and detailed particulars of relevant Transactions, in the case of differences as to the existence or characteristics of any Transaction; and

(B)   the Calling Party's Valuation Data in the case of a difference as to calculation of the Exposure or the Value of Margin Received.

(iv)   By 1:00 p.m. on the Second Day, the Disputing Party must by Notice to the Calling Party provide any evidence or information requested by the Calling Party, the Disputing Party's relevant Valuation Data and such other information as the Disputing Party considers appropriate.

(v)   In the case of any dispute as to Exposure or Value of Margin Received, if the dispute has not been resolved by 5:00 p.m. on the Second Day, each party must in good faith select one independent reference source and the following procedures shall apply:

(A)   Each independent reference source will be instructed to determine the Exposure associated with any disputed Transaction or the Value of any Margin Received (or determine any constituent element within the calculation of Exposure or Value that has been isolated by the parties as an element in dispute) as of the Valuation Date relating to the relevant demand.

(B)   The independent reference sources will be instructed to report to both parties their determinations by 5:00 p.m. on the Margin Business Day following the Second Day (the "Third Day").

5

(C)   Each independent reference source will be instructed to use the same methods, practices and degree of care that it would use to establish any facts and make any calculations were it required to do so in its own business.

(D)   Each independent reference source must be a leading dealer in the particular type of Transaction in dispute or any entity that provides valuation services with respect to such type of Transaction in the general course of its business and must be independent of each of the parties, which independence will not be deemed diminished solely because the independent reference source is active in the same market in which either of the parties is active or has entered into transactions with either of the parties.

(E)   The parties agree that the arithmetic average of the determinations from each independent reference source will prevail.

(F)   If by 5:00 p.m. on the Third Day:

(1)   the parties are unable to obtain quotes from two independent reference sources; or

(2)   the independent reference sources disagree on any material facts,

the parties may choose (x) to continue the negotiations, (y) to seek such other remedy as each in its discretion determines or (z) if Dispute Termination Event is specified as applicable in the Supplement and the dispute relates to the Exposure associated with specific disputed Transactions, to terminate such disputed Transactions in accordance with the procedures, and in pursuit of such remedies, set forth in the Agreement as they relate to a Dispute Termination Event.

(vi)   In the case of a dispute as to the existence or agreed characteristics of a Transaction, if the dispute has not been resolved by 5:00 p.m. on the Second Day, the parties may choose to continue the negotiations or to seek such other remedy as each in its discretion determines.

(vii)   Following the resolution or deemed resolution of a dispute, the Disputing Party must Transfer Eligible Margin or Equivalent Margin to the Calling Party in satisfaction of the demand for such margin that gave rise to the dispute as if in response to a demand received by the Notification Time on the Margin Business Day following the resolution, subject to Section 1.3 above and without regard to the Minimum Transfer Amount, after taking into account any prior Transfer of any relevant Undisputed Amount and any adjustment agreed between the parties or determined by the independent reference sources in accordance with sub-Section 1.6(b)(v) above (and no further obligations will arise on the part of either party in respect of the dispute).

6

(c)   **Dispute of Value of Transfer**.

(i)   Each reference in this sub-Section to a time or to a Margin Business Day is a reference to that time or Margin Business Day in the location of the Calling Party.

(ii)   If a Calling Party (which term includes a Taker of Substitute Margin for purposes of this sub-Section 1.6(c)) disputes the Value of a Transfer of Eligible Margin, Lock-up Margin (or Cash, securities or other property of the same type, nominal value, description and amount as such Lock-up Margin), Substitute Margin or Equivalent Margin it must, as Disputing Party, on the Margin Business Day following the Margin Business Day Transfer is Initiated, transmit a Notice of dispute (such Notice of dispute may be in the form of Appendix F) for receipt by the other party by 1:00 p.m. on that day.

(iii)   Before 10:00 a.m. on the Margin Business Day immediately following the Margin Business Day on which the Notice of dispute was received, the Call Recipient (which term includes a Provider of Substitute Margin for purposes of this sub-Section 1.6(c)) will recalculate the Value of the relevant margin, using any undisputed values set forth in the Notice of dispute, as of the date the Transfer was Initiated and in accordance with the procedures (if any) in the Supplement.

(iv)   Immediately following a recalculation, the Call Recipient must notify the Disputing Party of the results of the recalculation. The Call Recipient must Initiate Transfer by 5:00 p.m. on the Margin Business Day immediately following the Margin Business Day on which the Notice of dispute was received of any additional Eligible Margin, additional Lock-up Margin (or Cash, securities or other property of the same type, nominal value, description and amount as such Lock-up Margin), additional Substitute Margin or Equivalent Margin required based on such recalculation. The Minimum Transfer Amount shall not apply to margin to be Transferred pursuant to this sub-Section 1.6(c)(iv).

(v)   If:

(A)   the Call Recipient is unable, due to circumstances beyond its control, to recalculate the Value of the relevant margin; or

(B)   the Disputing Party disputes the recalculated Value of the relevant margin,

the parties may choose (x) to continue the negotiations, (y) to seek such other remedy as each in its discretion determines or (z) if Dispute Termination Event is specified as applicable in the Supplement and the dispute relates to the Value associated with the Transfer of Eligible Margin, Lock-up Margin (or Cash, securities or other property of the same type, nominal value, description and amount as such Lock-up Margin), Substitute Margin or Equivalent Margin, to terminate the Agreement in accordance with the procedures, and in pursuit of

7

such remedies, set forth in the Agreement as they relate to a Dispute Termination Event.

Section 1.7   Substitutions.

(a)   **Times.** Each reference in this Section 1.7 to a time or to a Margin Business Day is a reference to that time or Margin Business Day in the location of the Taker.

(b)   **Delivery of Substitution Notice.** Unless otherwise specified in the Supplement, the Provider may deliver a Substitution Notice (such Substitution Notice may be in the form of Appendix G) to the Taker.

(c)   **Timing of Delivery of Substitution Notice.** If the Taker receives a Substitution Notice after 5:00 p.m. or other than on a Margin Business Day, it will be deemed to have been received by the Taker on the next Margin Business Day. References to receipt of a Substitution Notice in this Section 1.7 are references to both actual receipt and deemed receipt, as relevant.

(d)   **Consent to Substitution.** Each substitution pursuant to a Substitution Notice will be subject to Paragraph 8 of the Supplement.

(e)   **Substitute Margin.** The Provider will Initiate Transfer of Substitute Margin having a Value as of the date Transfer is Initiated as close as practicable to, but in any event not less than, the amount specified in the Substitution Notice by 1:00 p.m. on any Margin Business Day on or after the date the Substitution Notice is effective.

(f)   **Timing of Substitutions.**

(i)   If the Taker is able to confirm, to its reasonable satisfaction, that it has received the Substitute Margin by 1:00 p.m. on a Margin Business Day, then the Taker will Initiate Transfer to the Provider of the Equivalent Margin specified in the Substitution Notice by 5:00 p.m. on the same day.

(ii)   If the Taker is able to confirm, to its reasonable satisfaction, that it has received the Substitute Margin after 1:00 p.m. on a Margin Business Day, then the Taker will Initiate Transfer to the Provider of the Equivalent Margin specified in the Substitution Notice by 5:00 p.m. on the next Margin Business Day.

(g)   **Value of Equivalent Margin.** In any substitution pursuant to this Section 1.7, the Taker must Transfer Equivalent Margin with a Value as close as practicable to, but in any event not greater than, the Value of the Substitute Margin as of the date Transfer of the Equivalent Margin is Initiated.

Section 1.8   Distributions and Interest Amounts.

(a)   **Times.** Each reference in this Section 1.8 to a time or to a Margin Business Day is a reference to that time or Margin Business Day in the location of the Taker.

8

(b)   **Distributions**. If, with respect to any Margin Received (and without regard to any use or disposition of Margin Received by the Taker), the Taker is deemed to receive Distributions on a Distributions Date, it will Transfer Equivalent Distributions to the Provider. The Transfer must be Initiated by 5:00 p.m. on the Margin Business Day immediately following the Distributions Date. The Taker is required to Transfer Equivalent Distributions only to the extent that a Delivery Amount would not be created or increased by that Transfer, as calculated by the Taker (and the date of calculation will be deemed to be a Valuation Date for this purpose).

(c)   **Interest Amount**.

(i)   In lieu of any interest or other amounts paid or deemed to have been paid with respect to Margin Received in the form of Cash (all of which may be retained by the Taker), the Taker will Transfer the Interest Amount to the Provider. The Transfer of an Interest Amount will be Initiated no later than two Margin Business Days after the end of the relevant Interest Period. The Interest Amount will be determined by the Taker based on the principal amount of Margin Received in the form of Cash held by the Taker on each day in an Interest Period. The Interest Amount will be computed for each Interest Period on a simple basis, unless otherwise provided for in the Supplement. The Taker is required to Transfer the Interest Amount only to the extent that a Delivery Amount would not be created or increased by that Transfer, as calculated by the Taker (and the date of calculation will be deemed to be a Valuation Date for this purpose).

(ii)   If Eligible Margin in the form of Cash is received after 5:00 p.m. in the location of the Taker, the Taker will have no obligation to pay interest for that day and interest will begin to accrue on the following Margin Business Day, unless that Taker is, in the ordinary course of business, able to invest the Cash so received on an overnight basis.

Section 1.9   Additional Definitions With Respect to Margin Subject to Article 8 of the New York Uniform Commercial Code. In the event that Margin Received or Equivalent Margin is of a type and subject to circumstances to which Article 8 of the New York Uniform Commercial Code would apply, Article 8 of the New York Uniform Commercial Code will apply and the definitions set forth in Annex A to these Provisions will be deemed to be incorporated into these Provisions.

Section 1.10   Miscellaneous.

(a)   **Expenses**. Each party will be liable for and pay its own costs and expenses (including, without limitation, any stamp, transfer or similar transaction tax or duty payable on any Transfer that it is required to make) in connection with performing its obligations in relation to any margin arrangements under these Provisions.

(b)   **Default Interest**. A Taker that fails to make, when due, any Transfer of Equivalent Margin, Substitute Margin, Equivalent Distributions or an Interest Amount will be obligated to compensate the Provider. The Taker must pay the Provider (to the extent permitted

9

under applicable law) interest on the Value of the Cash or items of property that were required to be Transferred, from (and including) the date that the Equivalent Margin, Substitute Margin, Equivalent Distributions or Interest Amount was required to be Transferred to (but excluding) the date of Transfer of that Equivalent Margin, Equivalent Distributions or Interest Amount, at a rate per annum equal to the Default Rate. The Value of these items will be calculated as of the relevant Valuation Date and as if all items are Eligible Margin. Such interest will be calculated on the basis of daily compounding and the actual number of days elapsed.

(c)   **Demands**. All demands referenced in these Provisions may be made or given substantially in the form, if any, attached hereto, and will be effective if delivered in a manner and at the time set forth in the Notices Section, except as otherwise provided in these Provisions or in the Supplement. References in these Provisions to receipt of a demand are references to both actual receipt and deemed receipt, as relevant.

(d)   **Notices**. All Notices referenced in these Provisions may be made or given substantially in the form, if any, attached hereto, and will be effective if delivered in a manner and at the time set forth in the Notices Section, except as otherwise provided in these Provisions or in the Supplement. The place for delivery of any Notice is the place specified as the Calling Party's or Call Recipient's address or contact details for Notices in the Supplement (or if no such details are provided in the Supplement, such details as are provided in the Agreement) or such other address or contact details as has been notified to the other party at least five Margin Business Days (by reference to the location of the party to which the Notice is sent) prior to the relevant demand being made.

(e)   **Specifications of Certain Matters**. Anything referred to in these Provisions as being specified in the Supplement also may be specified in one or more Confirmations or other documents, and these Provisions will be construed accordingly.

(f)   **Good Faith and Commercially Reasonable Manner**. Performance of all obligations under these Provisions, including, but not limited to, all calculations, valuations and determinations made by either party, will be made or conducted in good faith and in a commercially reasonable manner.

10

PART 2

ELECTIVE PROVISIONS – SECURITY INTEREST APPROACH
(NEW YORK LAW)

The parties may elect, by incorporation of this Part 2 into the Supplement, to have the following provisions apply to Transfers of Cash or other property under these Provisions, in which case the provisions of this Part 2 shall be construed in accordance with New York law.

Section 2.1   Security Interest and Set-off. Each party, as the Provider, hereby pledges to the other party, as the Taker, as security for its Obligations, and grants to the Taker a first priority continuing security interest in, lien on and right of set-off in, on or against all Margin Received received by the Taker. Upon the Transfer by the Taker to the Provider of Margin Received, the security interest, lien and right of set-off granted under this Section 2.1 in, on and against that Margin Received will be released immediately and, to the fullest extent possible, without any further action by either party. The Interest Amount or portion thereof not Transferred pursuant to Section 1.8(c) will constitute Margin Received in the form of Cash and will be subject to the security interest, lien and right of set-off granted under this Section 2.1.

Section 2.2   Holding and Using Margin Received.

(a)   **Care of Margin Received.** Without limiting the Taker's rights under Section 2.2(c), the Taker will exercise reasonable care to assure the safe custody of all Margin Received to the extent required by applicable law. In any event, the Taker will be deemed to have exercised reasonable care if it exercises at least the same degree of care as it would exercise with respect to its own property. Except as specified in the preceding sentence, the Taker will have no duty with respect to Margin Received, including, without limitation, any duty to collect any Distributions, or enforce or preserve any rights pertaining thereto.

(b)   **Eligibility to Hold Margin Received; Custodians.**

(i)   Upon Notice by the Taker to the Provider of the appointment of a Custodian, the Provider's obligations to make any Transfer will be discharged by making the Transfer to that Custodian. The holding of Margin Received by a Custodian will be deemed to be the holding of that Margin Received by the Taker for which the Custodian is acting.

(ii)   If the Taker or its Custodian fails to satisfy any conditions specified in the Supplement for holding Margin Received, then upon a demand made by the Provider, the Taker will, not later than five Margin Business Days after the demand, Transfer or cause its Custodian to Transfer all Margin Received held by it to a Custodian that satisfies those conditions or, if no such Custodian is specified, to the Taker.

(iii)   The Taker will be liable for the acts or omissions of its Custodian to the same extent that the Taker would be liable for its own acts or omissions.

11

(c)   **Use of Margin Received**.

(i)   Unless otherwise specified in the Supplement and without limiting the rights and obligations of the parties under Sections 1.1 to 1.8 or Section 2.4, if no Event of Default with respect to the Taker has occurred and is continuing, and if no Specified Condition has occurred with respect to the Taker (or with respect to which Specified Condition the Taker is an Affected Party, in the case of an ISDA Master Agreement), and if no date has occurred or been designated on which all outstanding Transactions have been or will be accelerated, terminated, liquidated or cancelled as a result of an Event of Default or Specified Condition with respect to the Taker (or with respect to which Specified Condition the Taker is an Affected Party, in the case of an ISDA Master Agreement), then the Taker will, notwithstanding Section 9-207 of the New York Uniform Commercial Code, have the right to:

(A)   sell, pledge, rehypothecate, assign, invest, use, commingle or otherwise dispose of, or otherwise use in its business, any Margin Received it holds, free from any claim or right of any nature whatsoever of the Provider, including any equity or right of redemption by the Provider; and

(B)   register any Margin Received in the name of the Taker, its Custodian or a nominee for either.

(ii)   For purposes of the obligation to Transfer Eligible Margin or Equivalent Margin pursuant to Sections 1.1, 1.3, 1.6 and 1.7 and any rights or remedies authorized under these Provisions, the Taker will be deemed to continue to hold all Margin Received and receive Distributions made thereon, regardless of whether the Taker has exercised any rights with respect to any Margin Received pursuant to sub-Section 2.2(c)(i) above.

Section 2.3   Additional Event of Default. An Event of Default will exist with respect to a party (including for purposes of Section 5(a)(iii)(1) of the ISDA Master Agreement) if that party fails to comply with any restriction or prohibition specified in these Provisions with respect to any of the rights specified in Section 2.2(c) and that failure continues for five Margin Business Days after Notice of that failure is given to that party.

Section 2.4   Certain Rights and Remedies.

(a)   **Taker's Rights and Remedies.** If at any time (1) an Event of Default or Specified Condition with respect to the Provider (or with respect to which Specified Condition the Provider is an Affected Party, in the case of an ISDA Master Agreement) has occurred and is continuing or (2) a date on which all outstanding Transactions have been or will be accelerated, terminated, liquidated or cancelled has occurred or been designated as the result of an Event of Default or Specified Condition with respect to the Provider (or with respect to which Specified Condition the Provider is an Affected Party, in the case of an ISDA Master Agreement), then, unless the Provider has paid in full all its Obligations that are then due, the Taker may exercise one or more of the following rights and remedies:

12

(i)   all rights and remedies available to a secured party under applicable law with respect to Margin Received held by the Taker;

(ii)   the right to set-off any amounts payable by the Provider with respect to any Obligations against any Margin Received or the Cash equivalent of any Margin Received held by the Taker (or any obligation of the Taker to Transfer that Margin Received); and

(iii)   the right to liquidate any Margin Received held by the Taker through one or more public or private sales or other dispositions with such prior Notice, if any, as may be required and cannot be waived under applicable law, free from any claim or right of any nature whatsoever of the Provider, including any equity or right of redemption by the Provider (with the Taker having the right to purchase any or all of the Margin Received to be sold) and to apply the proceeds (or the Cash equivalent of the proceeds) from the liquidation of the Margin Received to any amounts payable by the Provider with respect to any Obligations in such order as the Taker may elect.

(b)   **Market Risk**. Each party acknowledges and agrees that Margin Received in the form of securities may decline rapidly in value or is of a type customarily sold on a recognized market and, accordingly, the Provider is not entitled to prior Notice of any sale of that Margin Received by the Taker, except any Notice that is required under applicable law and cannot be waived.

(c)   **Provider's Rights and Remedies**. If at any time a date on which all outstanding Transactions have been or will be accelerated, terminated, liquidated or cancelled has occurred or been designated as the result of an Event of Default or Specified Condition with respect to the Taker (or with respect to which Specified Condition the Taker is an Affected Party, in the case of an ISDA Master Agreement), then, except in the case of a date on which less than all outstanding Transactions have been or will be accelerated, terminated, liquidated or cancelled where the Taker has paid in full all of its Obligations that are then due with respect to payments upon early termination of those Transactions:

(i)   the Provider may exercise all rights and remedies available to a pledgor under applicable law with respect to Margin Received held by the Taker;

(ii)   the Taker will be obligated immediately to Transfer all Margin Received and any Interest Amount to the Provider; and

(iii)   to the extent that Margin Received or the Interest Amount is not so Transferred pursuant to sub-Section 2.4(c)(ii) above, the Provider may:

(A)   set-off any amounts payable by the Provider with respect to any Obligations against any Margin Received or the Cash equivalent of any Margin Received held by the Taker (or any obligation of the Taker to Transfer that Margin Received); and

13

(B)   to the extent that the Provider does not set-off under sub-Section 2.4(c)(iii)(A) above, withhold payment of any remaining amounts payable by the Provider with respect to any Obligations, up to the Value of any remaining Margin Received held by the Taker, until that Margin Received is Transferred to the Provider.

(d)   **Deficiencies and Excess Proceeds**. When no amounts are or thereafter may become payable by the Provider with respect to any Obligations (other than with respect to a contingent tax gross-up or similar ancillary contingent obligation or any contingent obligation under Section 2.6 or Section 1.10(a)), the Taker will Transfer to the Provider any proceeds and Margin Received remaining after liquidation, set-off and/or application under this Section 2.4. The Provider in all events will remain liable for any amounts remaining unpaid after any liquidation, set-off and/or application under this Section 2.4.

(e)   **Final Returns**. When no amounts are or thereafter may become payable by the Provider with respect to any Obligations (other than with respect to a contingent tax gross-up or similar ancillary contingent obligation or any contingent obligation under Section 2.6 and Section 1.10(a)), the Taker will Transfer to the Provider all Margin Received.

Section 2.5   Representations. Each party represents to the other party (which representations will be deemed to be repeated as of each date on which it, as the Provider, Transfers Margin Received) that:

(a)   it has the power to grant a security interest in and lien on any Margin Received it Transfers as the Provider and has taken all necessary actions to authorize the granting of that security interest and lien;

(b)   it is the sole owner of or otherwise has the right to Transfer all Margin Received it Transfers to the Taker pursuant to these Provisions, free and clear of any security interest, lien, encumbrance, claim of a property interest or restriction (including without limitation any restriction or requirement imposed by any securities law or regulation) other than the security interest and lien granted under Section 2.1;

(c)   upon the Transfer of any Margin Received to the Taker under the terms of these Provisions, the Taker will have a valid and perfected first priority security interest in such Margin Received (assuming that any central clearing corporation or any third-party financial intermediary or other entity not within the control of the Provider involved in the Transfer of that Margin Received gives the Notices and takes the action required of it under applicable law for perfection of that interest); and

(d)   the performance by it of its obligations as set out in these Provisions will not result in the creation of any security interest, lien, encumbrance, claim of a property interest or restriction (including without limitation any restriction or requirement imposed by any securities law or regulation) on any Margin Received other than the security interest, lien and right of set-off granted under Section 2.1.

14

Section 2.6 **Distributions**. Without prejudice to Section 2.2(b), on each Distributions Date the Taker will be deemed, for purposes of Section 1.8(b), to have received Distributions in respect of Margin Received.

Section 2.7 **Expenses**.

(a) **Margin Received**. Section 1.10(a) notwithstanding, the Provider will promptly pay when due all taxes, assessments or charges of any nature that are imposed with respect to Margin Received held by the Taker upon becoming aware of them, regardless of whether any portion of that Margin Received is subsequently disposed of under Section 2.2(c), except for those taxes, assessments and charges that result from the exercise of the Taker's rights under Section 2.2(c).

(b) **Liquidation and/or Application of Margin Received**. Section 1.10(a) notwithstanding, all reasonable costs and expenses incurred by or on behalf of the Taker or the Provider in connection with the liquidation and/or application of any Margin Received under Section 2.4 will be payable, on demand and pursuant to the Expenses Section, by the party in respect of which an Event of Default has occurred. If there is no party to which an Event of Default has occurred, each party is liable for its own costs and expenses.

Section 2.8 **Miscellaneous**.

(a) **Further Assurances**. Promptly following a demand made by a party, the other party will execute, deliver, file and record any financing statement, specific assignment or other document and take any other action that may be necessary or desirable and reasonably requested by that party to create, preserve, perfect or validate any security interest, lien or right of set-off created or granted under Section 2.1, to enable that party to exercise or enforce its rights with respect to Margin Received or to effect or document a release of a security interest in or lien on Margin Received.

(b) **Further Protection**. The Provider will promptly give Notice to the Taker of, and defend against, any suit, action, proceeding or lien, encumbrance, claim of a property interest or restriction that involves Margin Received Transferred by the Provider or that could adversely affect the security interest, lien or right of set-off created or granted by it under Section 2.1, unless that suit, action, proceeding or lien, encumbrance, claim of a property interest or restriction results from the exercise of the Taker's rights under Section 2.2(c).

15

PART 3

ELECTIVE PROVISIONS – TITLE TRANSFER APPROACH
(ENGLISH LAW)

The parties may elect, by incorporation of this Part 3 into the Supplement, to have the following provisions apply to Transfers of Cash or other property under these Provisions, in which case the provisions of this Part 3 shall be construed in accordance with English law.

Section 3.1   Transfer of Title and No Security Interest.

(a)   **Transfer of Title.** Each party agrees that all right, title and interest in and to any Lock-up Margin, Eligible Margin, Equivalent Margin, Substitute Margin, Equivalent Distributions or Interest Amount which it Transfers to the other party under these Provisions will vest in the recipient free and clear of any liens, claims, charges or encumbrances or any other interest of the Transferring party or of any third person (other than a lien routinely imposed on all securities in a relevant clearance system). Each Transfer under these Provisions will be made so as to constitute or result in a valid and legally effective transfer of the Transferring party's legal and beneficial title to the recipient.

(b)   **No Security Interest.** The parties do not intend to create in favor of either party any mortgage, charge, lien, pledge, encumbrance or other security interest in any Cash or other property, to which this Part 3 applies, Transferred by one party to the other party under these Provisions.

Section 3.2   Default.

(a)   If at any time a date on which all outstanding Transactions have been or will be accelerated, terminated, liquidated or cancelled has occurred or been designated as a result of an Event of Default or Specified Condition in relation to either party (an "Early Termination Date" in the case of an ISDA Master Agreement):

(i)   in the case of an ISDA Master Agreement for which Market Quotation is the applicable payment measure for purposes of Section 6(e) of the ISDA Master Agreement, an amount equal to the Value of the Margin Received held by the Taker will be an Unpaid Amount due from the Taker to the Provider for purposes of Section 6(e) of the ISDA Master Agreement; and

(ii)   in the case of an ISDA Master Agreement for which Loss is the applicable payment measure for purposes of Section 6(e) of the ISDA Master Agreement, Loss shall include an amount equal to the Value of the Margin Received held by the Taker (expressed as a negative number) for purposes of Section 6(e) of the ISDA Master Agreement.

(iii)   in the case of an Agreement which is not in the form of an ISDA Master Agreement:

16

(A)   if the Provider is the defaulting party or the party impaired by the relevant Specified Condition, then the Taker has the right, without prior notice to the Provider, to set-off any amounts payable by the Provider with respect to any Obligations against an amount equal to the Value of the Margin Received by the Taker; and

(B)   if the Taker is the defaulting party, then the Provider has the right, without prior Notice to the Taker, to set-off the Value of the Margin Received by the Taker against any amounts payable by the Provider with respect to any Obligations.

(b)   For purposes of effecting any set-off permitted by this Section 3.2, the party exercising the right of set-off may convert any obligation to another currency at a market rate determined by that party.

(c)   The Taker will Transfer to the Provider any Equivalent Margin relating to Margin Received remaining after any application of this Section 3.2 after satisfaction in full of all amounts payable by the Provider with respect to any Obligations. The Provider in any event will remain liable for any amounts remaining unpaid by it after any application of this Section 3.2.

Section 3.3   Representation. Each party represents to the other party (which representation will be deemed to be repeated as of each date on which it Transfers Eligible Margin, Equivalent Margin, Substitute Margin or Equivalent Distributions or any other Cash, securities or other property under these Provisions) that it is the sole owner of or otherwise has the right to Transfer all Eligible Margin, Equivalent Margin, Substitute Margin or Equivalent Distributions or any other Cash, securities or other property it Transfers to the other party under these Provisions, free and clear of any security interest, lien, encumbrance or other restriction (other than a lien routinely imposed on all securities in a relevant clearance system).

Section 3.4   Distributions. Without prejudice to Section 3.1, on each Distributions Date the Taker will be deemed, for purposes of Section 1.8(b), to have received Distributions in respect of Margin Received.

17

PART 4

ELECTIVE PROVISIONS[1]

The parties may elect, by incorporation of either Part 2 or Part 3 and the relevant Section of this Part 4 into the Supplement, to have one or more of the following Sections apply to Transfers of Cash or other property under these Provisions, in which case the provisions of this Part 4 shall be construed in accordance with Japanese law.

Section 4.1   Japanese Credit Support Provisions - Loan and Deposit.[1] Provisions for Parties using Japanese Margin.

(a)   **Characterization of the Arrangement.** Solely for the purposes of determining each Party's rights and obligations with respect to the Transfer of Eligible Margin or Equivalent Margin consisting of Japanese Margin, and without prejudice to other provisions of these Provisions or the Agreement, each Party agrees as follows:

(i)   The term "<u>Transfer</u>" under Section 1.1(a) means a loan (for the avoidance of doubt, if these Provisions are governed by Japanese law or if the term *shohi-taishaku* is to be construed under Japanese law) of Japanese Margin held in the form of securities and a deposit (for the avoidance of doubt, if these Provisions are governed by Japanese law or if the term *shohi-kitaku* is to be construed under Japanese law) of Japanese Margin held in the form of Cash.

(ii)   Until the Taker is required, pursuant to the terms of these Provisions, to return the Japanese Margin Received, as long as (A) no Event of Default with respect to the Taker has occurred and is continuing, (B) no Specified Condition has occurred with respect to the Taker and (C) no date has occurred or been designated on which all outstanding Transactions have been or will be accelerated, terminated, liquidated or cancelled as a result of an Event of Default or Specified Condition (with respect to which Specified Condition the Taker is an Affected Party, in the case of an ISDA Master Agreement), the Taker shall be entitled to have all the incidents of ownership of such Japanese Margin, including without limitation, the right to sell, transfer, lend or otherwise dispose of, pledge, assign, invest, use, commingle or otherwise use in its business and register or record in the name of the Taker, its Custodian or nominee for the Japanese Margin Received.

(iii)   Where the Japanese Margin is in the form of securities, the Taker may repay the Japanese Yen Cash equivalent of such Japanese Margin. The Transfer of Equivalent Margin or repayment of the Japanese Yen Cash equivalent shall be deemed to

---

[1] The content of this Part 4 may change from time to time, as published on the ISDA website, www.isda.org, and such content is incorporated into these Provisions automatically, with effect from the date of publication of such content. Margin arrangements incorporating these Provisions that are in existence at the time of publication would not be considered to incorporate such content without further action by the parties. In particular, other jurisdiction-specific modification to this Part 4 may be published from time to time.

[2] Parties should consult their legal advisers in determining whether it is necessary to use either a loan or a deposit in order to assert rights under Japanese Law concerning Close-out Netting of Specified Financial Transactions entered into by Financial Institutions, etc. (Law No. 108 of 1998) in certain Japanese insolvency proceedings.

18

be a return of the Japanese Margin under Section 1.1(b). However, solely for the purpose of Section 1.1(b), and as long as an Early Termination Date has not occurred (in the case of an ISDA Master Agreement) or no date has occurred or been designated on which all outstanding Transactions have been or will be accelerated, terminated, liquidated or cancelled, the Taker's option to repay such Japanese Yen Cash equivalent is subject to the prior written consent of the Provider.

(b)   **Event of Default or Specified Condition**.   If a date has occurred or been designated on which all outstanding Transactions have been or will be accelerated, terminated, liquidated or cancelled (in the case of an ISDA Master Agreement, an Event of Default) as a result of an Event of Default or Specified Condition in relation to a Party (with respect to which Specified Condition, such Party is an Affected Party), the Non-Defaulting Party or the Party which is not the Affected Party, as the case may be, has the right specified below. If such Event of Default is an event to which the Parties specified the Automatic Early Termination provision of Section 6(a) of the ISDA Master Agreement or any provision in an Agreement, other than the ISDA Master Agreement, of like effect, to be applicable, or is one of the Other Japanese Events of Default, then, in any such case, without regard to the intention of either of the Parties, the following shall be deemed to occur automatically as of the time specified in Section 6(a) of the ISDA Master Agreement and, in all other cases, as of the time immediately preceding the occurrence of the relevant event(s):

(i)   Where the Japanese Margin Received is held in the form of securities, the Taker, without any action on the part of either Party, will be deemed to have elected to repay the Japanese Yen Cash equivalent (computed by reference to the actual interest rates, quotations on the relevant exchanges and other indices or market prices) and together with the Japanese Margin Received in the form of Cash, such amounts will be immediately due and payable to the Provider.

(ii)   Any such amounts due under sub-Section (b)(i) above shall be set-off against any Obligations of the Provider, without prior Notice or formalities which might otherwise be required, and if necessary, such amounts are deemed to have been converted into the currency of such Obligations at the relevant rate prevailing on the date when such set-off is effected or deemed to have been exercised.

(iii)   The Taker will Transfer to the Provider an amount, if any, remaining after the application of the foregoing. The Provider in all events will remain liable for any amounts, including, but not limited to, the Obligation under other part(s) of these Provisions to immediately Transfer Margin Received and any Interest Amount under such Part(s) (in the event it is, at such time the Taker of any Margin Received) to the Taker, remaining unpaid or undelivered, if any, after such application. Either or both of such amounts shall be subject to set-off hereunder or the general rights of set-off available to the Parties under the relevant laws. For purposes of effecting any set-off, the amount of an Obligation to Transfer Margin Received shall be equal to the Value of such Margin Received and the party exercising the right of set-off may, together with any other amounts owing to it, convert such amount into another currency at a market rate determined by that party.

19

(iv)   All reasonable costs and expenses incurred by or on behalf of the Non-Defaulting Party in connection with the liquidation and/or application of any Japanese Margin above will be payable on demand by the Defaulting Party and shall be subject to the general rights of set-off available to the Parties under the relevant laws.

(v)   The Provider shall promptly pay when due taxes, assessments or charges of any nature that are imposed on the Taker by any government or other taxing authority with respect to Japanese Margin Received held by the Taker upon becoming aware of the same.

(c)   **Additional Events of Default**. The following shall be Additional Events of Default:

(ix)   **Other Japanese Events of Default**. A Party:

(1) has a pre-judgment attachment (*karisasiosae*), post-judgment attachment (*sashiosae*) or other court order of enforcement issued in respect of any of its rights to receive the Japanese Margin Received or the Obligations; or

(2) Transfers, assigns or pledges any of its rights to receive the Japanese Margin Received or the Obligations to a third Party.

In the case of an ISDA Master Agreement, Section 6(a) of the ISDA Master Agreement is amended by inserting after the words, "or, to the extent analogous thereto, (8)" at the end thereof the words "or specified in Section 5(a)(ix)(1) or (2) of the 2001 ISDA Margin Provisions".

(d)   **Governing Law and Jurisdiction**. The Transaction(s) under this Section 4.1 shall be governed by and construed in accordance with the laws of Japan or, if another governing law is specified as applying for purposes of this Section 4.1, such other governing law. If the laws of Japan apply for purposes of this Part 4, the following shall apply:

Where an election (*sentaku*) to repay in Cash is made or deemed made under Section 4.1(b)(i), the Taker's obligation (such obligation is intended by the Parties to be a *sentaku-saimu* under Japanese laws) to return the Japanese Margin Received will be deemed to be an obligation to return the Japanese Yen Cash equivalent from the time of receipt of the relevant Japanese Margin.[3]

With respect to any suit, action or proceedings relating to Margin Received to which this Part 4 applies and to which Japanese law is applicable, each Party irrevocably submits to the jurisdiction of the Japanese courts in addition to the submission to other courts provided in the Agreement.

---

[3]   Applicable only where the loan is governed by Japanese law. Parties should consult with legal counsel as to whether this provision is valid under other laws.

20

(e) **Definitions.** Part 5 is amended to include the following additional definitions (which will replace any inconsistent definitions of the same terms that may exist in Part 5):

(i) **Equivalent Margin.** "Equivalent Margin" means in relation to Japanese Margin, securities of the same type, nominal value, description and amount and issuer, class, series, maturity, coupon rate and principal amount as that Japanese Margin or new or different securities which have been exchanged for, converted into or substituted for that Japanese Margin.

(ii) **Japanese Margin.** "Japanese Margin" means Eligible Margin consisting of negotiable debt obligations of the Government of Japan and/or Cash denominated in Japanese Yen and such other items specified for a Party as Japanese Margin which is Eligible Margin in the Supplement.

(iii) **Japanese Margin Received.** "Japanese Margin Received" means Margin Received which is Japanese Margin.

21

PART 5

DEFINITIONS

Section 5.1   Additional Margin Amount. "<u>Additional Margin Amount</u>" with respect to a party means the amount (expressed in the Base Currency) specified as such for that party in the Supplement or, if no amount is specified, zero.

Section 5.2   Agreement. "<u>Agreement</u>" means the agreement or agreements specified on the first page of the Supplement. If no agreement is specified, "Agreement" means an agreement in the form of the ISDA Master Agreement and all Transactions will be deemed to be governed by and form part of such an agreement. If more than one agreement is specified in the Supplement, the Exposure of each party will be calculated based on the net aggregate of the Exposures under each separate agreement, and references in the Provisions to the Agreement will include a reference to each such agreement.

Section 5.3   Base Currency. "<u>Base Currency</u>" means the currency freely available and specified as such in the Supplement, or if no currency is specified, the currency (if any) agreed by the parties in the Agreement as the currency in which payment of any amount payable upon the early termination of a Transaction is to be made and otherwise United States Dollars.

Section 5.4   Call Recipient. "<u>Call Recipient</u>" means the party receiving a demand under Section 1.1.

Section 5.5   Calling Party. "<u>Calling Party</u>" means the party making a demand under Section 1.1.

Section 5.6   Cash. "<u>Cash</u>" means an amount of money in one or more of the currencies specified in the Supplement, if such currency is freely available.

Section 5.7   Confirmation. "<u>Confirmation</u>" means such documents or other confirming evidence, if any, which evidences the terms of a Transaction.

Section 5.8   Custodian. "<u>Custodian</u>" means an agent appointed by the Taker to hold Lock-up Margin (if any) or Margin Received for the Taker as specified in the Supplement.

Section 5.9   Default Rate. "<u>Default Rate</u>" means a rate per annum equal to the cost (without proof or evidence of any actual cost) to the relevant payee (as certified by it) if it were to fund or of funding the relevant amount plus 1% per annum.

Section 5.10   Delivery Amount. "<u>Delivery Amount</u>" means, with respect to the Provider and for any Valuation Date, the amount by which the Margin Required exceeds the Value of the Margin Received held by the Taker, as set forth in Section 1.1(a). In performing this calculation, the Value of the Margin Received must be adjusted to include any prior Delivery Amount (or, in the case of any dispute concerning a Delivery Amount, any Undisputed Amount with respect to that Delivery Amount) and to exclude any prior Return Amount (or, in the case of any dispute concerning a Return Amount, any Undisputed Amount with respect to that Return Amount), the

22

Transfer of which, in either case, has not yet been completed and for which the relevant Settlement Date falls on or after the relevant Valuation Date.

Section 5.11 Dispute Termination Event. "Dispute Termination Event" means the following:

(a)   if, under the terms of an Agreement, a process of terminating Transactions under the Agreement on a no-fault basis is provided for, an event triggering such process and for purposes of sub-Section 1.6(b)(v)(F), a termination on a mid-market basis; and

(b)   if the Agreement is an ISDA Master Agreement, an event that will constitute an Additional Termination Event, as described in Section 5(b)(v) of the ISDA Master Agreement, with two Affected Parties.

Section 5.12 Disputing Party. "Disputing Party" means the party referred to as such in Section 1.6.

Section 5.13 Distributions.

(a)   "Distributions" means all payments and distributions of cash or other property to which an owner, holder of record or one similarly entitled to property of the same type, nominal value, description and amount as any Lock-up Margin or Margin Received would be entitled from time to time.

(b)   Distributions do not include:

(i)   any distributions with respect to Lock-up Margin in the form of Cash or Margin Received in the form of Cash; or

(ii)   any item of property acquired by the Taker upon any disposition or liquidation of Lock-up Margin or Margin Received.

Section 5.14 Distributions Date. A "Distributions Date" means each date on which an owner, holder of record or one similarly entitled to Distributions actually would be entitled to receive Distributions or, if that date is not a Margin Business Day with respect to the Taker, the next following Margin Business Day.

Section 5.15 Eligible Margin. "Eligible Margin" means, with respect to a party as Provider, any or all of the items specified as such for that party in the Supplement.

Section 5.16 Equivalent Margin.

(a)   If the parties elect to incorporate Part 2 into the Supplement, "Equivalent Margin" means Margin Received; and

(b)   If the parties elect to incorporate Part 3 into the Supplement, in relation to any Margin Received, "Equivalent Margin" means Cash, securities or other property of the same type, nominal value, description and amount as such Margin Received.

23

Section 5.17 Equivalent Distributions. "Equivalent Distributions" means Cash, securities or other property of the same type, nominal value, description and amount as a relevant Distribution.

Section 5.18 Event of Default. An "Event of Default" means any event or condition described in an Agreement and relating to a party as a result of which all outstanding Transactions under the Agreement may be accelerated, terminated, liquidated or cancelled by the other party or automatically other than any event or condition eligible to be selected as a Specified Condition. With respect to an ISDA Master Agreement, "Event of Default" is as defined in that Agreement (except to the extent modified by these Provisions or the Schedule) and does not include any Termination Event as defined in that Agreement.

Section 5.19 Expenses Section. "Expenses Section" means, with respect to an Agreement, the section, if any, allocating between the parties expenses relating to an Event of Default and any related early termination. With respect to an ISDA Master Agreement, Expenses Section means Section 11 of the ISDA Master Agreement.

Section 5.20 Exposure. "Exposure" means, with respect to a party and a Valuation Date (or other date for which Exposure is calculated), the amount (expressed in the Base Currency), if any, that would be payable pursuant to the Agreement (or where more than one Agreement is specified, the net aggregate amount payable under such Agreements) to that party by the other party (expressed as a positive number) or by that party to the other party (expressed as a negative number) as if all Transactions were being accelerated, terminated, liquidated or cancelled as of the relevant Valuation Time. Any exclusions from the calculation of Exposure described in the Supplement apply solely for purposes of computing Margin Required and do not affect any other provisions of the Agreement.

With respect to an ISDA Master Agreement, "Exposure" means with respect to a party the amount (expressed in the Base Currency), if any, that would be payable pursuant to Section 6(e)(ii)(1) to that party by the other party (expressed as a positive number) or by that party to the other party (expressed as a negative number) as if all Transactions were being terminated as of the relevant Valuation Time, and Exposure shall be determined on the basis of mid-market valuations.

Section 5.21 Initiate. "Initiate" means, with respect to a party, the taking of all necessary steps by that party to achieve a Transfer by the relevant Settlement Date without requiring any further action by that party. "Initiated" will be interpreted accordingly.

Section 5.22 Interest Amount. "Interest Amount" means the amount of interest determined for each relevant currency and calculated for each day in the relevant Interest Period for that currency as follows:

(a) the amount of Cash denominated in the relevant currency on that day, multiplied by

(b) the Interest Rate in effect on that day for such currency, divided by 360 (or, if the currency is pounds sterling, 365).

Section 5.23 Interest Period. "Interest Period" means the period from (and including) the last Margin Business Day on which an Interest Amount was Transferred (or, if no Interest Amount has yet been Transferred, the Margin Business Day on which Margin Received in the form of Cash was Transferred to or received by the Taker) to (but excluding) the days specified in the Supplement as the end dates for the Interest Period. For these purposes, Margin Business Day means a Margin Business Day in the location of the Taker.

Section 5.24 Interest Rate. An "Interest Rate" for Cash denominated in a particular currency means the rate specified for that currency in the Supplement.

Section 5.25 ISDA Master Agreement. "ISDA Master Agreement" means the published form of the 1992 ISDA Master Agreement (Multicurrency – Cross Border) and Schedule; and if an agreement in that form (together with any elections and amendments agreed by the parties) is specified as the Agreement in the Supplement, that agreement.

Section 5.26 Jurisdiction Section. "Jurisdiction Section" means, with respect to an Agreement, the jurisdiction section, if any, of the Agreement. With respect to an ISDA Master Agreement, Jurisdiction Section means Section 13(b) of the ISDA Master Agreement.

Section 5.27 Lock-up Margin. "Lock-up Margin" means the specified type, quantity or amount of Eligible Margin, if any, as set forth for a party in the Supplement.

Section 5.28 Margin Business Day. Unless otherwise specified in these Provisions or in the Supplement, "Margin Business Day" means:

(a) in relation to a Transfer of securities, a day on which the relevant clearance system agreed by the parties is open for the acceptance and execution of settlement instructions and a day on which the securities intermediary or commercial bank in which the relevant account is located is open or, if delivery of the securities is contemplated by other means, a day on which commercial banks are open for business (including dealings in foreign exchange and foreign currency deposits) in the place(s) agreed between the parties for this purpose;

(b) in relation to a Transfer of Cash or property other than securities, a day on which commercial banks, foreign exchange markets and relevant clearance systems settle payments and are open for business (including dealings in foreign exchange and foreign currency deposits) in the place where the relevant account is located and, if different, in the principal financial center (if any) of the currency of any such payment;

(c) in relation to valuations under these Provisions, a day on which commercial banks are open for business (including dealings in foreign exchange and foreign currency deposits) in the location of the Calling Party and in any other place(s) agreed between the parties for this purpose;

(d) in relation to any notice or other communication, a day on which commercial banks are open for business (including dealings in foreign exchange and foreign currency deposits) in the location of the recipient of the notice or communication; and

25

(e)   in relation to the location of a party, a day on which commercial banks are open for business (including dealings in foreign exchange and foreign currency deposits) in the place specified as that party's address for notices in the Supplement, or if none is specified in the Agreement, such other address as has most recently been notified to the other party in accordance with the Notices Section.

Section 5.29   Margin Received. "Margin Received" means all Eligible Margin, other property, Distributions and all proceeds thereof (including, without limitation, Lock-up Margin except for purposes of the calculation of Delivery Amount and Return Amount) that have been received by the Taker under these Provisions and as to which Transfer to the Provider of Equivalent Margin or Equivalent Distributions has not been Initiated pursuant to under Sections 1.1(b), 1.7(f), 1.8 or 3.2 or released by the Taker under Part 2. Any Equivalent Distributions or Interest Amount, or portion thereof, not Transferred pursuant to Section 1.8 will constitute Margin Received.

Section 5.30   Margin Required. "Margin Required" means the sum of the Taker's Exposure and the Additional Margin Amount applicable to the Provider minus the Additional Margin Amount applicable to the Taker minus the Provider's Threshold.

Section 5.31   Minimum Transfer Amount. The "Minimum Transfer Amount" means the amount (expressed in the Base Currency) specified as such for a party in the Supplement or, if no amount is specified, zero. The Minimum Transfer Amount will be zero with respect to any Return Amount demanded by the Provider if there are no Transactions with respect to which the Provider has a current or future payment or delivery obligation outstanding under the Agreement, whether absolute or contingent (other than with respect to a contingent tax gross-up or similar ancillary contingent obligation or any contingent obligation under Section 1.10(a) and Section 2.6 if applicable).

Section 5.32 New York Uniform Commercial Code. The "New York Uniform Commercial Code" means the New York State Consolidated Laws, Chapter 38, as amended.

Section 5.33   Notice. "Notice" means, notwithstanding the Notices Section, an irrevocable notice, which may be written, oral, by telephone, by facsimile transmission, telex, e-mail or message generated by an electronic messaging system or otherwise.

Section 5.34   Notices Section. "Notices Section" means, with respect to an Agreement, the section, if any, governing communications between the parties. With respect to an ISDA Master Agreement, Notices Section means Section 12 of the ISDA Master Agreement.

Section 5.35   Notification Time. "Notification Time" means 10:00 a.m. on a Margin Business Day in the location of the Call Recipient, being the place specified as the Call Recipient's address for Notices in the Supplement, or such other address as has been notified to the Calling Party at least five Margin Business Days prior to the relevant Notice being given.

Section 5.36   Obligations. "Obligations" means all present and future obligations of a party under the Agreement and any additional obligations specified as such for that party in the Supplement.

26

Section 5.37 Portfolio Information. "Portfolio Information" means information in writing regarding all attributes of a Transaction that the Call Recipient considers relevant to establishing the existence, identity or terms of a Transaction. Portfolio Information may include, for example, any one or more of the following: the trade date; the effective date; the maturity date; the Exposure related to such Transaction (as if the date of the Portfolio Information were a Valuation Date and as if such Transaction were the sole Transaction governed by the relevant Agreement); the Transaction type; any strike and/or any underlying; any notional amount; any deal number ascribed to such Transaction by the party providing the information; and any record the party providing the information may have as to the deal number ascribed to such Transaction by the other party. For these purposes, writing includes facsimile transmission, telex, e-mail or messages generated by an electronic messaging system, notwithstanding anything to the contrary in the Notices Section.

Section 5.38 Return Amount. "Return Amount" means, with respect to the Taker and for any Valuation Date, the amount by which the Value of the Margin Received held by the Taker exceeds the Margin Required, as set forth in Section 1.1(b). In performing this calculation, the Value of all Margin Received must be adjusted to include any prior Delivery Amount (or, in the case of any dispute concerning a Delivery Amount, any Undisputed Amount with respect to that Delivery Amount) and to exclude any prior Return Amount (or, in the case of any dispute concerning a Return Amount, any Undisputed Amount with respect to that Return Amount), the Transfer of which, in either case, has been Initiated but has not yet been completed and for which the relevant Settlement Date falls on or after the relevant Valuation Date.

Section 5.39 Settlement Date. "Settlement Date" means:

(a)   with respect to a Transfer of Cash in the form of U.S. Dollars, the same Margin Business Day Transfer is Initiated;

(b)   with respect to a Transfer of Cash other than U.S. Dollars or other property (other than securities), the same Margin Business Day Transfer is Initiated or, if same-day settlement is not customary for such currency or property, the number of Margin Business Days following the Margin Business Day Transfer is Initiated as is customary for payments in the required currency or for Transfers of the required property; and

(c)   with respect to a Transfer of securities Initiated on a certain date, the first Margin Business Day after such date on which settlement of a trade in the relevant securities executed on such date would have been accomplished in accordance with customary practice of the market in which such securities are principally traded or, if the parties have agreed to a clearance system for the settlement of securities, the customary practice of that clearance system. If there is no such customary practice, the "Settlement Date" will be the first Margin Business Day after such certain date on which it is reasonably practicable to settle such securities.

Section 5.40 Specified Condition. A "Specified Condition" means an event or condition specified as such for a party in the Supplement. With respect to an ISDA Master Agreement, "Specified Condition" may include any of Illegality, Tax Event, Tax Event Upon Merger, Credit Event Upon Merger or any Additional Termination Events and any other events, if specified as such for a party, in the Supplement.

27

Section 5.41 Substitute Margin. "Substitute Margin" means the Eligible Margin specified as such in a Substitution Notice.

Section 5.42 Substitution Notice. "Substitution Notice" means a notice which may be in the form of Appendix G informing the Taker that the Provider wishes to Transfer to the Taker specified Substitute Margin in exchange for specified Equivalent Margin.

Section 5.43 Threshold. "Threshold" means, with respect to a party, the amount (expressed in the Base Currency) specified as such for that party in the Supplement or, if no amount is specified, zero.

Section 5.44 Transaction. "Transaction" means any transaction governed by an Agreement or otherwise as specified in the Supplement.

Section 5.45 Transfer. "Transfer" means:

(a) in relation to Cash, payment or delivery by wire transfer into one or more bank accounts, as specified in the Supplement;

(b) in relation to certificated securities that cannot, or which the parties have agreed will not, be paid or delivered by book-entry, payment or delivery in appropriate physical form to the recipient or its account accompanied by any duly executed instruments of transfer, assignments in blank, transfer tax stamps and any other documents necessary to constitute a valid and legally effective transfer to the recipient, as specified in the Supplement; and

(c) in relation to securities that must, or which the parties have agreed will, be paid or delivered by book-entry, Initiating the Transfer by the giving of written instructions (including instructions given by telephone, facsimile transmission, telex, e-mail or message generated by an electronic messaging system or otherwise) to the relevant depository institution or other entity specified by the recipient, together with a written copy thereof to the recipient, sufficient if complied with to result in a valid and legally effective transfer of the relevant interest to the recipient, as specified in the Supplement.

Section 5.46 Undisputed Amount. "Undisputed Amount" means the amount of any demand identified by the Disputing Party as being undisputed if the Disputing Party is the Call Recipient and the amount of Eligible Margin Transferred if the Disputing Party is the Calling Party. The Undisputed Amount is zero when the parties disagree as to which party must Transfer Eligible Margin or Equivalent Margin or disagree as to whether the Minimum Transfer Amount has been exceeded.

Section 5.47 Valuation Data. "Valuation Data" includes all relevant publicly available rates, prices, spreads and statistics (and historical or predictive compilations of the same) and similar materials used in valuing Transactions or Margin Received and such other material as a party may provide to the other party.

Section 5.48 Valuation Date. Unless otherwise specified in the Supplement, "Valuation Date" means each Margin Business Day.

28

Section 5.49 Valuation Percentage. "<u>Valuation Percentage</u>" means, with respect to an item of Eligible Margin, the percentage specified in the Supplement, or if no such percentage is specified, 100%.

Section 5.50 Valuation Time. "<u>Valuation Time</u>" means 5:00 p.m. in the relevant market on the Margin Business Day immediately preceding the relevant Valuation Date.

Section 5.51 Value. Subject to Section 1.6, for any Valuation Date or other date for which Value is calculated, "<u>Value</u>" means:

(a) with respect to Eligible Margin or Margin Received that is an amount of Cash, such amount (expressed in the Base Currency) multiplied by the applicable Valuation Percentage, if any;

(b) with respect to Eligible Margin or Margin Received that is a security, an amount (expressed in the Base Currency) equal to the bid price obtained by the Calling Party multiplied by the nominal amount of such security, plus any income which, as of such date, has accrued but not yet been paid in respect of the security to the extent not included in such price as of such date, multiplied by the applicable Valuation Percentage, if any; and

(c) with respect to Margin Received that consists of items that are not specified as Eligible Margin, an amount equal to zero.

29

NOTE: THIS SUPPLEMENT IS DESIGNED FOR USE WITH THE 2001 ISDA MARGIN PROVISIONS. THIS SUPPLEMENT MUST BE READ IN CONJUNCTION WITH THOSE PROVISIONS.

ISDA

International Swaps and Derivatives Association, Inc.

2001 ISDA MARGIN SUPPLEMENT, dated as of _____

to the following Agreements: dated as of _____

_____ dated as of _____

_____ dated as of _____

_____ dated as of _____

between

_____ and _____
("Party A")   ("Party B")

      This 2001 ISDA Margin Supplement (this "<u>Supplement</u>") supplements, forms part of, and is subject to, the above-referenced Agreements and the 2001 ISDA Margin Provisions (the "<u>Provisions</u>"), as published by the International Swaps and Derivatives Association, Inc. The Provisions are incorporated into this Supplement to the extent set out below. In the event of any inconsistency between this Supplement and the Provisions or the provisions of the above-referenced Agreements, this Supplement will prevail. In the event of any inconsistency between the provisions of any Confirmation and the Provisions (including the Supplement), such Confirmation will prevail for purposes of the relevant Transaction or Transactions.

Supplement

Paragraph 1. Margin Approach. Part [2] [3] [and Section ____ of Part 4] of the Provisions [is] [are] hereby incorporated into this Supplement.][1]

Paragraph 2. Exposure. Transactions or classes of Transactions which are not to be taken into account when calculating Exposure:_____.

Paragraph 3. Base Currency. Base Currency has the following meaning: _____, if such currency is freely available.

---

[1]   In some cases, for legal reasons, parties may wish to apply one margin approach to a particular class of Eligible Margin, and apply another margin approach to another class of Eligible Margin. Accordingly, in lieu of Paragraph 1, parties may wish to include the following sentence: "In respect of any Eligible Margin specified in Paragraph 4 below, the relevant Part of the Provisions corresponding to such Eligible Margin (as detailed in Paragraph 4 below) is hereby incorporated into this Supplement in respect of such Eligible Margin.

30

Paragraph 4. Margin.[2]

Eligible Margin for Party A	Valuation Percentage
(A) Cash (denominated in the currencies specified here)	
(B) Securities (listed by issuer and with any conditions as to remaining maturity)	

Eligible Margin for Party B	Valuation Percentage
(A) Cash (denominated in the currencies specified here)	
(B) Securities (listed by issuer and with any conditions as to remaining maturity)	

Paragraph 5. Structural Parameters[3]

Party A	Fixed amount in Base Currency
Lock-up Margin	
Additional Margin Amount	
Threshold	
Minimum Transfer Amount	

---

[2]   As noted in footnote 1 of the Supplement above, where different Parts apply to different types of Eligible Margin, the parties should specify the Part applicable to each type of Eligible Margin in this Paragraph 4.

[3]   The parties may choose from the parameters offered, deleting those they determine to be inapplicable.

31

Party A may make a demand under Section 1.1(c)(ii) in the following circumstances:

[ ]   if no Transactions are outstanding between the parties and Party A has no payment obligations, absolute or contingent, other than with respect to a tax gross-up or similar ancillary contingent obligation or any contingent obligation under Section 1.10(a) and Section 2.6, if applicable, pursuant to any Agreement.

[ ]   if Party B's Exposure is equal to or less than _____.

Party B	Fixed amount in Base Currency
Lock-up Margin	
Additional Margin Amount	
Threshold	
Minimum Transfer Amount	

Party B may make a demand under Section 1.1(c)(ii) in the following circumstances:

[ ]   if no Transactions are outstanding between the parties and Party B has no payment obligations, absolute or contingent, other than with respect to a tax gross-up or similar ancillary contingent obligation or any contingent obligation under Section 1.10(a) and Section 2.6, if applicable, pursuant to any Agreement.

[ ]   if Party A's Exposure is equal to or less than _____.

Rounding. [The Delivery Amount and the Return Amount will each be rounded down to the nearest integral multiple of .../up and down to the nearest integral multiple of ..., respectively[4]]

Paragraph 6.   Dispute Resolution – Dispute Termination Event.   For purposes of sub-Sections 1.6(b)(v)(F) and 1.6(c)(v), Dispute Termination Event is not applicable between the parties, unless otherwise stated here: _____.

---

[4]   Delete as applicable.

Paragraph 7. Dispute Resolution – Value. For the purpose of sub-Section 1.6(c)(iii), the Value of Eligible Margin or Margin Received will be re-calculated based on the higher of the bid price quoted by the Call Recipient or the offer price quoted by the Calling Party, in each case on the basis of a purchase by the Call Recipient from or a sale by the Calling Party to, independent third party dealers in the relevant security.

Paragraph 8. Consent to Substitution. If specified here as applicable, then the Provider must obtain the Taker's consent for any substitution pursuant to Section 1.7(d): [applicable/inapplicable].[5]

Paragraph 9. Interest Rate, Interest Amount and Interest Period. The Interest Rate in relation to Eligible Margin comprised of Cash in each currency will be:

Cash (specify currency)	Interest Rate

The Interest Amount will be computed for each Interest Period on a simple basis, pursuant to Section 1.8(c), unless otherwise stated here: _____.

The Interest Period end dates will be [the first calendar day of each month] [any date on which a Return Amount consisting wholly or partly of Cash is Transferred to the Provider pursuant to Section 1.1(b)] [specify other Interest Period end dates].

Paragraph 10. Demands and Notices.

Addresses for Demands and Notice:

      Party A: _____.

      Party B: _____.

Paragraph 11. Transfer Information.

      Party A: _____.

      Party B: _____.

Paragraph 12. Conditions Precedent and Rights and Remedies. The following events will be a Specified Condition for the party specified: _____.

---

[5]   The parties should consider selecting "applicable" where substitution without consent could give rise to a registration requirements to perfect properly the security interest in Margin Received (e.g., where a party is the New York branch of an English bank).

33

Paragraph 13. Obligations. The term "Obligations" as used in the Provisions includes the following additional obligations:

       With respect to Party A: _____.

       With respect to Party B: _____.

Security Interest Approach (Part 2) Only:

Paragraph 14. Eligibility to Hold Margin Received; Custodians. Party A and its Custodian will be entitled to hold Margin Received pursuant to Section 2.2(b); *provided* that the following conditions applicable to Party A are satisfied:

    (i)   An Event of Default with respect to Party A has not occurred and is then continuing.

    (ii)   Margin Received may be held only in the following jurisdictions: _____.

       Initially, the Custodian for Party A is _____.

Party B and its Custodian will be entitled to hold Margin Received pursuant to Section 2.2(b); *provided* that the following conditions applicable to Party B are satisfied:

    (i)   An Event of Default with respect to Party B has not occurred and is then continuing.

    (ii)   Margin Received may be held only in the following jurisdictions: _____.

       Initially, the Custodian for Party B is _____.

Paragraph 15. Use of Margin Received. The provisions of Section 2.2(c) will not apply to the [party/parties] specified here:

       [   ] Party A

       [   ] Party B

and [that party/those parties] will not be permitted to:_____.

34

Paragraph 16. Other Provisions. [6]

IN WITNESS WHEREOF the parties have executed this document on the respective dates set forth below with effect from the date of the Supplement referenced on the first page of this document.

_____   _____
        (Name of Party)   (Name of Party)

By: _____   By: _____
    Name: Name:
    Title: Title:
    Date: Date:

---

[6]   Parties should specify any other agreed terms not addressed in the Supplement or Provisions. In particular, parties should note that the following terms will have the meanings given to them in the appropriate Sections of the Provisions unless otherwise specified here: Base Currency, Margin Business Day; Confirmation; Distributions; and Settlement Date. In addition, any other provisions in the 2001 Margin Provisions can be modified by agreement of the parties by including the agreed modification in this Supplement.

DRAFT FORM OF NOTICE OF TRANSFER

ISDA

International Swaps and Derivatives Association, Inc.

NOTICE OF TRANSFER

Date: [   ]

To: [Name and address, telex number, electronic messaging address, e-mail address or facsimile number of [Calling Party]

From: [Call Recipient]

Re: Notice of Transfer

Dear _____:

This Notice is to confirm that the following type(s) of Eligible Margin or Equivalent Margin that the undersigned is delivering to you, the Settlement Date applicable to such Eligible Margin or Equivalent Margin and the fact that the Transfer has been Initiated as required by Section 1.3 of the 2001 ISDA Margin Provisions (the "Provisions") incorporated in the [Agreements] between us. Specifically, [describe type of Eligible Margin or Equivalent Margin and applicable Settlement Date(s)].

_____
(Name of Party)

By:_____
       Name:
       Title:
       Date:

36

DRAFT FORM OF UNDER SECTION 1.3(e)

ISDA

International Swaps and Derivatives Association, Inc.

SECTION 1.3(e) NOTICE

Date: [   ]

To: [Name and address, telex number, electronic messaging address, e-mail address or facsimile number of [Call Recipient] [Taker]]

From: [Party A]

Re: Section 1.3(e)

Dear _____:

This Notice is to inform you that you have failed to

[SPECIFY THE FOLLOWING AS APPROPRIATE:]

[make a Transfer of [Eligible Margin] [Substitute Margin] [Equivalent Margin] [Interest Amount]]

[give Notice of a Transfer of [Eligible Margin] [Substitute Margin] [Equivalent Margin] [Interest Amount] [Equivalent Distributions]]

as required by the 2001 ISDA Margin Provisions (the "Provisions") incorporated in the [Agreements] between us.

You are hereby requested to [make such Transfer] [provide such Notice] by [specify time] on [specify date][1], and in the event you fail to do so, we shall be entitled to exercise such remedies as may be available to us, including, without limitation, under Section 1.4(b) of the Provisions.

_____
(Name of Party)

By:_____
    Name:
    Title:
    Date:

---

[1]   The Calling Party should consider, based on the facts and circumstances at the time, whether a shorter or longer timeframe is appropriate. Where the Notice relates to a failure to give Notice required by Section 1.3(b), the Calling Party may wish to specify a short time period in the event there is concern about whether the failure to give such Notice may relate to a failure by the Call Recipient to Initiate Transfer of Eligible Margin or Equivalent Margin.

37

DRAFT FORM OF NOTICE UNDER SECTION 1.4(b)

ISDA
International Swaps and Derivatives Association, Inc.

SECTION 1.4(b) NOTICE

Date: [   ]

To: [Name and address, telex number, electronic messaging address, e-mail address or facsimile number of [Call Recipient] [Taker]]

From: [Party A]

Re: Section 1.4(b)

Dear _____:

This Notice is to inform you that you have failed to:

[SPECIFY THE FOLLOWING AS APPROPRIATE:]

[make a Transfer of [Eligible Margin] Substitution Margin] [Equivalent Margin] [Interest Amount] [Equivalent Distributions]]

[give Notice of a Transfer of [Eligible Margin] [Substitute Margin] [Equivalent Margin] [Interest Amount] [Equivalent Distributions]]

[comply with [specify relevant agreement or obligation under the Provisions or the Supplement]]

as required by the 2001 ISDA Margin Provisions (the "Provisions") incorporated in the [Agreements] between us. In the event you do not remedy such failure on or before the first Margin Business Day after this Notice, an Event of Default will exist with respect to you for purposes of Section 5(a)(iii)(1) of the ISDA Master Agreement] [_____] will exist with respect to you for the purposes of [the relevant provision in the non-ISDA Master Agreement] dated as of [date] between us, and we will be entitled to exercise such remedies as may be provided for under the Agreement and the Provisions.

_____
(Name of Party)

By:_____
      Name:
      Title:
      Date:

38

DRAFT FORM OF NOTICE OF DISPUTE

ISDA

International Swaps and Derivatives Association, Inc.

NOTICE OF DISPUTE WITH RESPECT TO A DEMAND FOR MARGIN

Date: [   ]

To: [Telex number, electronic messaging address, e-mail address or facsimile number of Calling Party]

From: [Party A]

Re: Demand for Margin

Dear _____:

       This constitutes a Notice of Dispute for the purposes of Section 1.6(b) of the 2001 ISDA Margin Provisions (the "<u>Provisions</u>") incorporated in the Agreement[s] between us. The purpose of this Notice of Dispute is to inform you that we dispute the accuracy of the following demand for margin made by you:

Terms of Demand for Margin	
Time and date when the demand was received in the location of the Disputing Party as specified in the Supplement as its address for Notices:	[ ]
Date of 2001 ISDA Margin Supplement under which the demand for margin was made:	[ ]
Value of margin demanded:	[ ]
Undisputed Amount:	[ ]

Please note that we intend to forward Portfolio Information to you by 5:00 p.m. in the manner agreed by us in Section 1.6(b) of the Provisions referred to above.

39

Please refer to Section 1.6 of the Provisions between us for the timetable and procedures for dispute resolution.

_____
(Name of Party)

By:_____

Name:

Title:

Date:

40

Appendix F

DRAFT FORM OF NOTICE OF DISPUTE

ISDA

International Swaps and Derivatives Association, Inc.

NOTICE OF DISPUTE WITH RESPECT TO THE VALUE OF MARGIN TRANSFERRED

Date: [   ]

To: [Telex number, electronic messaging address, email address or facsimile number of Calling Party]

From: [Party A]

Re: Value of Margin Transferred

Dear _____:

This constitutes a Notice of Dispute under Section 1.6(c) of the 2001 ISDA Margin Provisions (the "Provisions") incorporated in the Agreement[s] between us. The purpose of this Notice of Dispute is to inform you that we wish to dispute the Value of margin (or for which Transfer has been Initiated):

Terms of Demand for Margin		
Time and date when the demand was received in the location of the Disputing Party as specified in the Supplement as its address for Notices:	[	]
Date of 2001 ISDA Margin Supplement under which the demand for margin was made:	[	]
Type of margin Transferred:	[	]
Value of margin required to be Transferred:	[	]
Value of margin Transferred as calculated by us:	[	]

41

Please refer to Section 1.6 of the Provisions between us for the timetable and procedures for dispute resolution.

_____

(Name of Party)

By:_____

Name:
Title:
Date:

42

DRAFT FORM OF SUBSTITUTION NOTICE

ISDA

International Swaps and Derivatives Association, Inc.

SUBSTITUTION NOTICE

Date: [   ]

To: [Name and address, telex number, electronic messaging address, e-mail address or facsimile number of Taker]

From: [Party A]

Re: Substitute Margin

Dear _____ :

This constitutes a Substitution Notice under Section 1.7 of the 2001 ISDA Margin Provisions (the "Provisions") incorporated in the Agreement[s] between us. The purpose of this Substitution Notice is to inform you that we wish to exchange Substitute Margin in accordance with the Section 1.7 of the Provisions. The Substitute Margin specified below will be in exchange for the Equivalent Margin specified below. The Equivalent Margin specified in this Substitution Notice relates to Eligible Margin that was Transferred to you on [date].

Securities[1]	Substitute Margin	Equivalent Margin
Name of issuer of securities:		
Name of the issue of securities:		
CUSIP and/or ISIN number:		
Currency of denomination:		
Cash:		
Currency:		

_____
(Name of Party)

By:_____
    Name:
    Title:
    Date:

---

[1] The characteristics listed are examples of information that would be relevant in connection with Substitution. Parties may wish to include additional items, such as current value, face amount and relevant transfer instructions, for example.

43

Additional Definitions With Respect to Margin Subject to Article 8 of the New York Uniform Commercial Code

(a)   **Entitlement Holder**. "Entitlement Holder" means a party identified in the records of a Securities Intermediary as the party having a Security Entitlement against the Securities Intermediary. If a party acquires a Security Entitlement by virtue of a Transfer pursuant to sub-Section (g)(i)(B) or (C) below, that party is the Entitlement Holder.

(b)   **Entitlement Order**. "Entitlement Order" means a notification communicated to a Securities Intermediary directing Transfer or redemption of a Financial Asset to which the Entitlement Holder has a Security Entitlement.

(c)   **Financial Asset**. "Financial Asset" has the meaning set forth in Section 8-102 of the New York Uniform Commercial Code, as amended from time to time.

(d)   **Securities Account**. "Securities Account" means an account to which a Financial Asset is or may be credited in accordance with an agreement under which the person maintaining the account undertakes to treat the person for whom the account is maintained as entitled to exercise the rights that comprise the Financial Asset.

(e)   **Securities Intermediary**. "Securities Intermediary" means (i) a clearing corporation; or (ii) a person, including a bank or broker, that in the ordinary course of its business maintains Securities Accounts for others and is acting in that capacity.

(f)   **Security Entitlement**. "Security Entitlement" means the rights and property interests of an Entitlement Holder identified as such under Section 8-501 of the New York Uniform Commercial Code, as amended from time to time.

(g)   **Transfer**. Transfer has the meaning specified in Section 5.45, with the addition of the following clauses:

(i)   in the case of a Security Entitlement:

(A)   a Securities Intermediary's indication by book entry that a Financial Asset has been credited to the recipient's Securities Account with the Securities Intermediary; or

(B)   a Securities Intermediary's receipt of a Financial Asset from the recipient or acquisition of a Financial Asset for the recipient and, in either case, acceptance of the Financial Asset for credit to the recipient's account with the Securities Intermediary; or

44

(C)   a Securities Intermediary's incurrence otherwise of an obligation under law, regulation or rule to credit a Financial Asset to the recipient's Securities Account with the Securities Intermediary; or

(D)   the recipient's agreement with a Securities Intermediary, consented to by the other party who is the Entitlement Holder, that the Securities Intermediary will comply with Entitlement Orders originated by the recipient without further consent by the Entitlement Holder; or

(E)   the recipient is the Securities Intermediary for the other party, who is the Entitlement Holder.

(ii)   in the case of a Securities Account, the Transfer of all Security Entitlements contained in the Securities Account.

45

Bibliography and selected readings on collateralisation

Chapters 1–2

International Swaps and Derivatives Association, Inc. (2000): *ISDA Collateral Survey 2000*.
International Swaps and Derivatives Association, Inc. (2001): *ISDA Margin Survey 2001*.

Chapters 1, 3 and 4

International Swaps and Derivatives Association, Inc. (1998): *Guidelines for Collateral Practitioners*.

Chapter 2

David Wechter and Evelyn Dewaele: *Illuminating Collateral* (Futures & Options Weekly – February 2002).

Chapter 3

International Swaps and Derivatives Association, Inc. (1999): *Collateral Arrangements in the European Financial Markets: The Need for National Law Reform*.

Linklaters & Paines (1996): *Collateralising Derivatives Transactions: The English Law ISDA Credit Support Documentation*.

Dr Joanna Benjamin: *Recharacterisation Risk and Conflict of Laws* (Butterworths Journal of International Banking & Financial Law Special Supplement – September 1998),

Paul Avanzanto: *How to use the collateral carousel* (International Financial Law Review – January 1998).

Peter Bienenstock and Gilles Nejman: *Taking Collateral in Euroclear Securities: Title Transfer or Pledge?* (Butterworths Journal of International Banking and Financial Law – December 1998).

Richard Potok: *Legal certainty for securities held as collateral* (International Financial Law Review – December 1999).

Luigi L. De Ghenghi and Bart Servaes: *Collateral held in the Euroclear System: A legal overview* (Butterworths Journal of International Banking and Financial Law – March 1999).

Anthony C. Gooch and Linda B. Klein: *Documentation for Derivatives: Credit Support Supplement* (Euromoney Books 1994).

Dermot Turing: *Risk Management Handbook* (Butterworths 2000).

Chapter 4

Secretariat of the Basel Committee on Banking Supervision: *The New Basel Capital Accord: an explanatory note* (January 2001).

David Wechter: *Collateral: Meeting the Challenges* (Futures & Options Weekly – August 2001).
Simon Lillystone: *Where next in Collateral Management?* (Derivatives Strategy – June 2000).
Simon Lillystone: *Collateral Integration* (Futures & Options Weekly – January 2002).

Chapter 5

International Swaps and Derivatives Association, Inc.: *User's Guide to the ISDA Credit Support Documents under English Law* (1999).

Chapter 6

International Swaps and Derivatives Association, Inc.: *User's Guide to the 1994 ISDA Credit Support Annex* (1994).
Anthony C. Gooch and Linda B. Klein: *Documentation for Derivatives: Credit Support Supplement* (Euromoney Books 1994).
Christian Johnson: *Over-The-Counter Derivative Documentation: A Practical Guide for Executives* (2000), Chapter 4.

Chapter 7

International Swaps and Derivatives Association, Inc.: *User's Guide to the ISDA Credit Support Documents under English Law* (1999).
International Swaps and Derivatives Association, Inc.: *User's Guide to the 1995 ISDA Credit Support Annex (Security Interest Subject to Japanese Law)* (1996).

Chapter 8

International Swaps and Derivatives Association, Inc.: *User's Guide to the 2001 ISDA Margin Provisions* (2001).

Additional selected reading

Articles

Cohn, Joshua D., *The Basics of Collateralization of Derivatives*, 892 PLI/Corp. 101 (1995).
Guest Opinion: Managing Collateral for OTC Derivatives, Standard & Poor's Counterparty Ratings Guide, Second Quarter 1999, at 49.
Hart, David, *Managing the Credit Risk of Capital Market Products*, 77 Journal of Commercial Lending 6, February 1995, at 17.
Levie, Joseph H. and David J. Yeres, *Mark-to-Market Arrangements*, New York Law Journal, Corporate Update: Secured Transactions, 7 April 1994, at 5.
Mayer, Thomas Moers, *Understanding the Business, Bankruptcy and Securities Aspects of Derivatives: Derivatives in Default: Getting Collateral*, 721 PLI/Comm 123 (1995).
Meigs, Frank E., III, *Managing the Credit Risk of Interest Rate Swaps*, 77 Journal of Commercial Lending 8, April 1995, at 11.
Petzel, Todd E., *Managing Collateral On Exchanges and Off: A New Perspective*, The Journal of Derivatives, Spring 1995.
Stoakes, Christopher, *Making Collateral Secure*, Euromoney, March 1996, at 22.
Taylor, Barry W., *Revolving Bilateral Collateral*, 815 PLI/Corp 55, 3–4 June (1993).
Tyson-Quah, Kathleen, *Cross-Border Securities Collateralization Made Easy*, Butterworths Journal of International Banking and Financial Law, April 1996, at 177.